WHY DETROIT MATTERS

Decline, renewal, and hope in a divided city

Edited by Brian Doucet

First published in Great Britain in 2017 by

Policy Press
University of Bristol
1-9 Old Park Hill
Bristol
BS2 8BB
UK
t: +44 (0)117 954 5940
pp-info@bristol.ac.uk
www.policypress.co.uk

North America office:
Policy Press
c/o The University of Chicago Press
1427 East 60th Street
Chicago, IL 60637, USA
t: +1 773 702 7700
f: +1 773-702-9756
sales@press.uchicago.edu
www.press.uchicago.edu

© Policy Press 2017

British Library Cataloguing in Publication Data
A catalogue record for this book is available from the British Library

Library of Congress Cataloging-in-Publication Data
A catalog record for this book has been requested

ISBN 978-1-4473-2787-5 paperback
ISBN 978-1-4473-2786-8 hardcover
ISBN 978-1-4473-2790-5 ePub
ISBN 978-1-4473-2791-2 Mobi
ISBN 978-1-4473-2789-9 ePdf

The right of Brian Doucet to be identified as editor of this work has been asserted by him in accordance with the Copyright, Designs and Patents Act 1988.

Cover design by Hayes Design
Front cover image: Brian Doucet
Printed and bound in the United States of America

Contents

Contents

List of contributors

For more detailed information on each contributor, please refer to the editor's introductions at the start of each chapter.

Joshua Akers is an Assistant Professor of Geography and Urban and Regional Studies at the University of Michigan-Dearborn.

Grace Lee Boggs (1915–2015) was an activist, author, and philosopher based in Detroit.

Lowell Boileau is a Detroit-area-based artist and founder of the DetroitYES website.

Dan Carmody is President of Eastern Market Corporation.

Phil Cooley is a Detroit-based entrepreneur and restaurateur and the owner of Slows Bar-B-Q, Gold Cash Gold, and Ponyride.

Wayne Curtis is a co-founder of Feedom Freedom Growers, a community garden on the East Side of Detroit.

Brian Doucet is a Senior Lecturer at Erasmus University College in Rotterdam, the Netherlands, and from July 2017 an Associate Professor in the School of Planning at the University of Waterloo in Canada.

Nikos Doulos is part of the arts-based collective *Expodium*, located in Utrecht, the Netherlands.

Reynolds Farley is an Emeritus Professor and demographer at the University of Michigan's Population Studies Center.

Richard Feldman is a member of the James and Grace Lee Boggs Center to Nurture Community Leadership.

John Gallagher is a journalist for *The Detroit Free Press*.

George Galster is the Clarence Hilberry Professor of Urban Affairs at the Department of Urban Studies and Planning, Wayne State University.

Tyree Guyton is a painter and sculptor and the artist behind the Heidelberg Project in Detroit.

Sandra Hines is President of the Detroit Coalition Against Police Brutality.

Sharon Howell is a member of the James and Grace Lee Boggs Center to Nurture Community Leadership and a Professor of Communications at Oakland University.

Kimberley Kinder is an Assistant Professor of Urban Planning at the University of Michigan.

Dan Kinkead is an architect and urban designer working in Detroit. He is a principal at the national design firm SmithGroupJJR and visiting architect-in-residence at the Cranbrook Academy of Art.

René Kreichauf is a PhD candidate at the John-F.-Kennedy-Institute for North American Studies at the Freie Universität Berlin, Germany, and at Cosmopolis—Centre for Urban Research at the Vrije Universiteit Brussel, Belgium.

Khalil Ligon is Chief Executive Officer of Vista Vantage Consulting Group, L3C, an urban planning and environmental design firm based in Detroit.

jessica Care moore is a poet, performance artist, playwright, and producer, as well as the Chief Executive Officer of Moore Black Press.

Drew Philp is a freelance writer and journalist from Detroit.

Julia Putnam is a co-founder of the James and Grace Lee Boggs School in Detroit and currently serves as its Principal.

Jason Roche is an Associate Professor of Communications Studies at the University of Detroit Mercy.

Amanda Rosman is a co-founder of the James and Grace Lee Boggs School in Detroit and currently serves as its Executive Director.

Julia Sattler is an Assistant Professor of American Studies at TU Dortmund University, Germany.

Yusef Bunchy Shakur a father, author, neighborhood organizer and educator from Detroit.

Marisol Teachworth is a co-founder of the James and Grace Lee Boggs School in Detroit and currently serves as its Programming Director.

Myrtle Thompson-Curtis is a co-founder of Feedom Freedom Growers, a community garden on the East Side of Detroit.

Jackie Victor is the co-founder of Avalon International Breads in Detroit.

Friso Wiersum is part of the arts-based collective *Expodium*, located in Utrecht, the Netherlands.

Jessica Brooke Williams is a scholar of modern American history and art, with a masters in urban planning. She is a community development practitioner currently focusing on research and evaluation of local, state and national social service programs.

Bart Witte is part of the arts-based collective *Expodium*, located in Utrecht, the Netherlands.

Malik Yakini serves as the executive director of the Detroit Black Community Food Security Network.

List of figures and tables

Figures

Table

Acknowledgments

This edited book has been several years in the making. It stemmed from taking my students from the Netherlands on fieldtrips to Detroit. The aim of these trips was to challenge their ideas of what they thought they knew about Detroit specifically, and about cities more generally. During these visits, we engaged with scholars, journalists, planners, artists and activists who all had important insights and visions into the city. They both inspired and challenged my students. Seeing how the conversations, lectures and tours which featured in these trips made my students think differently about cities was the catalyst for putting together this edited book, which examines the lessons and visions from Detroit and argues that a critical assessment of its decline and renewal is important to understanding the challenges facing cities around the world.

I am grateful for the support, feedback and critical conversations from many people who helped to make this book possible. My Dutch colleagues who traveled with me to Detroit, Martijn Hendrikx and Matthieu Permentier from the Utrecht University and Roy Kemmers from Erasmus University College were extremely helpful in these journeys, as well as in wider discussions about cities and urban change. I also wish to acknowledge the financial support from my two employers during my time in the Netherlands: the Department of Human Geography and Planning at Utrecht University and the Department of Social and Behavioural Sciences at Erasmus University College, in Rotterdam. In addition to visits to Detroit as part of student field trips, their support also enabled me to conduct research visits to the city in conjunction with this project.

While in Detroit, I have received a warm welcome as well as useful information and advice from many people, including George Galster and Robin Boyle from Wayne State University, the volunteers and activists at the Boggs Center and many of the other contributors to this volume who have taught me valuable insights about Detroit as well as taken the time to meet with me and my students to share their passions, experiences, visions and expertise with them. I would also like to thank Jeff Horner and his family and Lowell and Susan Boileau for their hospitality during research visits to the city.

There are several important people to acknowledge for their work in the production of this book itself: Ton Markus for his cartographic assistance, Dianne Proctor Reeder for help editing the chapter with Sandra Hines, and the anonymous reviewers of the initial proposal, individual chapters and completed manuscript. Finally, the excellent staff at Policy Press, including Laura Vickers, for their support, quick communications and professionalism, as well as their enthusiasm for producing an unconventional edited book.

I would like to thank all the contributors who have worked very hard on writing and editing chapters for this book, as well as those who took the time to sit with me for interviews.

Finally, I would like to thank my wife, Helen, for her love, support and patience during the process of putting this book together.

ONE

Introduction:
why Detroit matters

Brian Doucet

Visiting Detroit

For several years, I have taken urban geography students from the Netherlands to Detroit. I never have to work very hard to market the trip. "Detroit"; the very word evokes powerful images and strong meanings, especially to European urbanists. My students come to Detroit wanting to see the ruins; I take them there because I want to challenge them to look beyond them.

The trip is part of a wider course on North American cities. We start in Toronto, my hometown. When the scheduling permits, I like to cross into the US from Canada at Sarnia/Port Huron, 100 km north of Detroit. We drive south along I-94 through the quiet Michigan countryside. However, the rural nature of the interstate does not last long and the freeway is soon bordered by subdivisions, trailer parks, and medium-sized industrial warehouses. Exits become busier and contain more fast-food restaurants, strip malls, and gas stations. When we pass 24 Mile Road, we enter an unbroken zone of development that continues all the way to Downtown Detroit (see Figures 1.1, 1.2, and 1.3).

Most people would continue along I-94 straight into Detroit. However, we head over to Gratiot Avenue in the northeast suburb of Roseville. Continuing our journey south on Gratiot, we drive through ordinary American suburbia (see Figure 1.4). To Americans, this landscape is commonplace and apart from local businesses such as

Coney Island restaurants and the unique "Michigan Left" road system, such a drive could be anywhere in America. To my Dutch students, however, even this mundane landscape is foreign and intriguing.

After a short drive along Gratiot, we cross the famous 8 Mile Road; the first cameras appear trying to grab a quick photo of the street sign. As we enter into the City of Detroit, the students watch as virtually everything they saw in the suburbs literally crumbles before their eyes. The commercial businesses lining both sides of Gratiot disappear into abandonment, burned out buildings, and vacant lots. Down the side streets, many of the houses are abandoned or victims of arson attacks. Vacant lots proliferate. Trash litters the streets. Weeds sprout out from the sidewalks. Even most of the cars have gone elsewhere and traffic on this broad thoroughfare is minimal. This landscape goes on for miles. We pass Coleman Young Airport. Occasionally, we are reminded that we are in the birthplace of mass consumption: a new Tim Hortons and a White Castle burger outlet at French Road. At Harper Avenue, we come across our first major abandoned factories. We drive over the I-94 and through some of Detroit's most blighted neighborhoods (see Figure 1.5; Galster, 2012). Mainstream commercial enterprises have disappeared and liquor stores are one of the few businesses along Gratiot (see Figure 1.6). There are very few people on the streets. Those who are are predominantly black and look poor. Traversing East Grand Boulevard, we catch glimpses of once-elegant mansions lining the city's first ring road, many of them abandoned. Nearby side streets reveal urban prairie (see Figure 1.7). We keep going south along Gratiot; the skyscrapers of Downtown grow larger and larger by the minute (see Figure 1.8).

However, close to Downtown, things start to change. Gratiot literally gets brighter. There are more streetlamps, many with marketing banners hanging from them. The buildings are not only here, but occupied. Cars are parked by the curb and there is more traffic on the road. We have arrived at the edge of Eastern Market. A few minutes later, our coach pulls up to our Downtown hotel. My urban geography students are shocked by this journey. They have never seen a city look like this before. They have never seen such extreme divisions between wealth and poverty, opulence and decay, black and white in such a small geographic area. They have seen photos, read stories, and seen films about Detroit, but they have never been physically confronted with geographies like this before on such a large scale. They do not quite know what to think. This is the introduction I give my students to Detroit.

Figure 1.1 Map of the tri-county Metro Detroit region

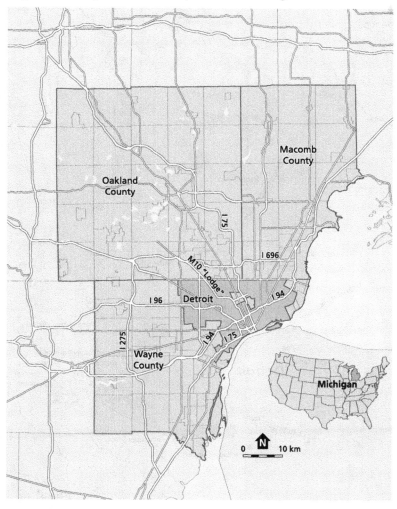

Figure 1.2 Map of Detroit and its northern suburbs

Bloomfield Hills

Troy

Somerset Collection

I 75

Royal Oak

Woodward Ave

Warren

I 696

Roseville

Oak Park

Ferndale

Southfield

Northland Town Center

8 Mile Rd

Eastpointe

Grand River Ave

M10 "Lodge"

Palmer Woods

University of Detroit Mercy

Gratiot Ave

I 94

Highland Park

Hamtramck

Coleman A Young Airport

Brightmoor

I 96

GM "Poletown" Plant

Packard Automotive Plant (abandoned)

Grosse Pointe

D-Town Farms

Detroit

Poletown

Freedom Freedom Growers

Indian Village

Heidelberg Project

Greater Downtown

Belle Isle

Michigan Ave

I 94

Mexicantown - Southwest Detroit

Windsor, ON

Dearborn

Ford River Rouge Complex

Ambassador Bridge

I 75

Detroit

0   5 km

Figure 1.3 Map of central Detroit

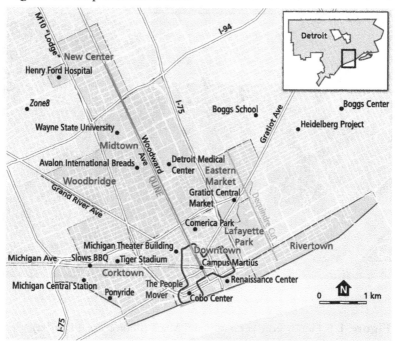

Figure 1.4 Gratiot Avenue in Roseville (Photo, Michael Doucet)

Figure 1.5 Gratiot and Seminole (Photo, Michael Doucet)

Figure 1.6 Liquor store at Gratiot and Mack (Photo, Brian Doucet)

Figure 1.7 Dubois Street north of Gratiot (Photo, Brian Doucet)

Figure 1.8 The skyline of Detroit from Gratiot near Vernor (Photo, Brian Doucet)

Such a journey was inspired by conversations with many Detroiters, including George Galster, who reminded me and my students that in order to understand the City of Detroit, with its approximately 700,000 inhabitants, you need to place it into its wider context of a metropolitan region of more than 4 million people. So, the introduction to the city takes place via its suburbs.

As we continue to get to know the city, the first step is to present them with the city they think they know: the city they have read about in newspapers and seen online. This is the city of ruins, whose population declined by a quarter in the first decade of the 21st century alone. This is the city with around 90,000 vacant and abandoned properties; the city whose poverty rate hovers at just under 40%.

We do not have to look hard to find this city. Less than three minutes' drive from the safe confines of Wayne State University in Midtown and we arrive at an urban prairie where there are virtually no businesses, and each block contains just a handful of houses, many of which are in various states of abandonment and decay. To explain that the near East Side of Detroit was once the city's densest neighborhood (Sugrue, 2013) leaves them stunned. We visit the Packard Plant, a holy grail for urban explorers and photographers. As we walk around outside its rusting and collapsing hulk, cameras and smartphones try to capture every brick, girder, and spot of graffiti. For many students, this is what they came to see.

We drive through Highland Park, which Mark Binelli (2012) described as "Detroit's Detroit," past the birthplace of the assembly line and the Fordist mode of production. Venturing deeper into the city, through neighborhoods such as State Fair, or along streets like Joy Road, we begin to appreciate the overall scale of the city's decline. However, when we visit the Ossian Sweet House (see Galster, 2012) on the city's East Side, or stop and discuss the 1967 riots/rebellions at the corner of 12th and Rosa Parks, the role of race and racism become evident and these ordinary buildings take on new meanings.

Occasionally, there are bright spots. In Indian Village, there is little abandonment (see Figure 1.9). The mansions along Seminole and Iroquois, in particular, initially constructed for the city's first auto barons, are well kept and there are even people (many of whom are white) out jogging or walking their dogs. However, we quickly realize the isolated nature of enclaves such as Indian Village (what the artist Lowell Boileau describes as "islands"; see Chapter Sixteen) as we head two or three blocks east to Crane or Holcomb Streets, where the abandonment is as great as anything else we have seen (see Figure 1.10). Driving back to Downtown along Mack Avenue is one of the grimmest journeys in the city.

While these scenes are dramatic, a tour focused on the city's ruins is insufficient to adequately answer the question of why Detroit is like this (see Apel, 2015). It fails to engage with the city and its residents; it also ignores the fact that while Detroit's population has declined by over 1 million people since its peak, there are still around 680,000 people living there. If Detroit was a city in the Netherlands, it would still be the second-largest after Amsterdam. In the UK, Detroit's population would place it fourth, between Leeds and Glasgow. Detroit would be Germany's fifth-largest city, smaller than Cologne but larger than Frankfurt. While driving around and looking at ruins is important to understanding the scale of the city's decline and the power of the forces that have shaped it, a deeper engagement is required in order to understand the nature of those forces, the experiences of living through such decline, and the solutions being thought of by people who still call Detroit home.

Figure 1.9 Houses in Indian Village, Detroit (Photo, Brian Doucet)

Figure 1.10 Holcomb Street, adjacent to Indian Village (Photo, Brian Doucet)

Therefore, the rest of our visit is spent challenging these initial images of ruin and abandonment and deconstructing the narrative of Detroit as a hopeless and failed city. One of the first contradictions we encounter is the area around our Downtown hotel, where there are an ever-growing number of restaurants, bars, lofts, and offices. The public spaces are cleaner, and there are fewer visible signs of abandonment (see Figure 1.11). Even boarded-up buildings often have hoarding in front of them with statements such as "Opportunity Detroit." There are people on the streets, some black and many white, few signs of poverty, and even the occasional surreal experience, such as listening to piped music playing from loudspeakers above Campus Martius Square. The small pocket of commercial activity along Michigan Avenue in Corktown (see Figure 1.12) sits in stark contrast to the experience of driving along large stretches of Gratiot in northeast Detroit. We see the boundaries first-hand of what has become known as *The 7.2*, the zone of redevelopment, gentrification, and inward investment in Greater Downtown Detroit, encompassing seven neighborhoods: Downtown, Midtown, Corktown, Woodbridge, Eastern Market, Lafayette Park, and Rivertown. It consists of 7.2 square miles, out of a total of 138 for the entire city (see Figure 1.3).[1] While the much-celebrated and dramatic 'comeback' in Greater Downtown is striking, I also pose the question of who profits from this renaissance and who is excluded from it.

Figure 1.11 Campus Martius Square and the Compuware Building, Downtown Detroit (Photo, Brian Doucet)

Figure 1.12 Corktown retail on Michigan Avenue (Photo, Brian Doucet)

However, many of the experiences that help to show Detroit's complexities come not only from what we see, but from who we meet. We learn about the active production of blight from Joshua Akers, from the University of Michigan–Dearborn. We visit *Detroit Future City* and learn about the approaches to planning for decline by focusing on the city's core assets. A discussion with John Gallagher from *The Detroit Free Press* helps to put new practices, such as the spinning off of pieces of Detroit's government (in places like Eastern Market), into a wider context of the city's economic and social trajectories. After seeing Detroit's buildings and lots as "empty" through the windows of our coach, we then meet Tom Derry, the passionate leader of the Navin Field Grounds Crew, a group of volunteers who transformed the old Tiger Stadium site into a park by restoring the old baseball field. Visits to the Heidelberg Project and the Boggs Center challenge us to see hope among the ruins. Before she passed away in 2015, conversations with Grace Lee Boggs always had a profound impact on me and my students. Some were brought to tears when we discussed the link between poverty and poor health, particularly among the city's children. These discussions help us to understand race, resistance, and power in Detroit and how genuine solutions for a fair and just city will require addressing these difficult issues (Doucet, 2015a).

Through the Boggs Center, we meet Wayne and Myrtle Curtis, who started a community garden to help empower local residents and provide a much-needed food source for some of urban America's poorest communities. That they see growing food as an act of revolution stands in stark contrast to our middle-class European practices of urban farming. Malik Yakini talks with us about issues of food justice and food sovereignty while we visit D-Town Farms, the city's largest urban agriculture site. A visit to Eastern Market on a Saturday afternoon shows us a busy, bustling side to Detroit that contradicts the ruination for which the city has become famous. However, such stories of inspiration are then challenged by George Galster's analysis of the structural deficiencies in Greater Detroit; he offers a sobering reality check that makes us question the effectiveness of many of the initiatives we have seen when placed against a wider political-economic backdrop.

One of the most important journeys in our visit to Detroit is leaving the city itself and heading back to the suburbs. A leading right-wing narrative about cities such as Detroit is that through overspending, corruption, or incompetence, they got themselves into their messes and they will have to find a way to sort it out themselves (Perazzo, 2014). Under such a narrative, Detroit becomes a fishbowl, disconnected from those peering in on it, and a "blame the victim" mentality takes hold (cf Apel, 2015). Visiting the suburbs and seeing the vast amounts of wealth that are concentrated there helps to deconstruct such interpretations of the decline of industrial cities. With that in mind, we cross over 8

Mile Road into suburban Oakland County, the wealthiest county in Michigan.

The first stop is not one of prosperity, but of abandonment. Northland Town Center was one of the first shopping malls in America. In the 1950s, it, and the city of Southfield where it is located, represented the pinnacle of white, middle-class suburbanization. However, today, many of these inner-ring suburbs built in the decades after the Second World War have also suffered from economic and population decline. Northland, and other early shopping centers, began to lose out to malls built deeper into the suburbs of Metro Detroit. A visit to Northland in early April 2015 came too late to do any shopping; it had closed down two weeks earlier.

Proceeding further north into the suburbs, we drive through Bloomfield Hills, one of the wealthiest communities in America. In Troy, an upper-middle-class suburb, we see new subdivisions of large, single-family homes, witnessing the physical and spatial manifestation of George Galster's (2012) "housing disassembly line" (see Figure 1.13) before arriving at our destination: the Somerset Collection shopping mall (see Figure 1.14). In many ways, Somerset contributed to the decline of Northland, just as early suburban malls contributed to the decline of Downtown Detroit's retail activities. Somerset is now the premier shopping destination in the Metro area. While Detroit lacks a major department store, Somerset has Nordstrom's, Macy's, Niemen Marcus, and Saks Fifth Avenue. It also has Louis Vuitton, Burberry, Gucci, Ralph Lauren, Tiffany and Co., and Hugo Boss, none of which have branches in Detroit. You cannot understand what has happened to Detroit without leaving the city to visit places like Somerset as capitalism's "creative destruction" is laid bare.

Figure 1.13 Suburban housing in Troy, MI (Photo, Brian Doucet)

Figure 1.14 Somerset Collection, Troy, MI (Photo, Brian Doucet)

These contrasts between poverty and affluence, and black and white, between the city and its suburbs are one of the most surprising elements of the tour and leave the biggest impression on many students. How can a city be so poor yet sit beside people so wealthy? Why don't governments do something about this? Where is the plan to make things better? Coming from the prosperous, egalitarian, and orderly background of the Netherlands brings a touch of naivety to these questions. However, they require us to think not just about why Detroit is the way it is, but about why our own cities are the way they are too. Visiting the city and its suburbs, and understanding the economic, social, political, and racial complexities of the city and region, helps us to understand that there are no easy answers to these questions.

In the end, there is no single narrative, no one lesson, that my students take away from Detroit. I never strive to impart one simple message or try to sum up Detroit from a one-dimensional perspective. They are given the tools to interpret the city and each student comes away with her/his own lessons, insights, memories, and meanings. What they share in common is a greater understanding of the ways in which different forces, playing out at different geographic scales, actively shape cities. They see that if we look beyond the ruins and the one-dimensional images of Detroit, many of the same economic, social, political, and racial/ethnic forces play out in countless other cities around the world, including in our own.

The aim of such a tour is twofold. First, it is to show how different and complex forces such as race, class, politics, economics, and power have shaped Detroit. The second aim is to continually challenge our assumptions about what we think we know about Detroit specifically, and cities more generally (Doucet, 2013). Even things that we have just seen are challenged by what we are confronted with next. This is also the approach to this book. The different chapters, contributions, and conversations each tell *part* of Detroit's story. However, they can only be understood by placing them in the relative context of the other stories, perspectives, and experiences. To do that, this book combines rigorous academic research, strong and well-developed narratives, engaged practitioners, lived experiences, and extraordinary visions. While it is a book on Detroit, it is hoped that the collection of chapters and contributions will allow the reader to critically reflect on the nature of divisions within contemporary cities more generally.

Detroit and the "next Detroit"

In May 2014, I sat reading the Saturday edition of *The Guardian* and was drawn to the headline "The North-East of England: Britain's Detroit?" (Beckett, 2014a). I read through this article with great interest in search of insightful new analysis about the comparisons between these two parts of the world, which, from a structural and economic perspective, have some important similarities.

Sadly, Detroit was scarcely mentioned in Beckett's article. Its primary focus was on politics, the then UK government's cutbacks, economic decline, and the failures of 1990s' and 2000s' regeneration. Its subheading asks the question: "Once a New Labour heartland, Tory cuts have left the North-East teetering on the brink. Can it avoid becoming Britain's Detroit?" Such a title would have led very nicely into an analysis of what political structures and policies have led to the North-East of England, one of Western Europe's poorest regions (Durham and the Tees Valley is the third-poorest region in North-West Europe [*Inequality Briefing*, 2014]), becoming like the largest American city to declare bankruptcy.

Apart from the title and the subtitle, the word "Detroit" is used once more in the article: "'If things carry on as they are now,' says Alex Niven, a left-wing writer from Northumberland, "in five years the situation will get somewhere like Detroit.'" That was it. Detroit, so prominent in the article's title, was scarcely mentioned in the body text of the article.

This article prompted a number of responses, but, again, any real engagement with Detroit, or any real attempt to understand the parallels between the two places, was largely lacking. Local MPs and business leaders criticized *The Guardian* for making the comparison and defended their region against claims that their economy was like the Detroit of the UK (*The Journal*, 2014). Attention was raised to the UK media's bias toward the North-East of England (Pidd, 2014).

The brief, yet intense, media frenzy surrounding this story continued, with hashtags such as #NEandProud trending as a response to Becket's article (BBC, 2014). *Buzzfeed* ran a story titled "*The Guardian* has really annoyed a lot of people in the North East," with a subtitle "National newspaper relies on stereotypes, irks region" (Stokel-Walker, 2014). The crux of their article was that while Beckett painted a picture of a region "teetering on the brink," the people of the North-East vehemently and passionately disagreed.

The main response to come out of this was a concerted effort to show how wonderful and special the North-East of England was. Leading this charge was *The Journal*, a Newcastle-based newspaper, which ran a story with the headline: "100 reasons why it's great up north: how you responded to the *Guardian's* ill-informed rant" (Rowland-Jou, 2014). In it, they posted a number of reader comments. In the 19 comments published in the article (as of February 2016), only one, from Lynn in Gateshead, made any reference to Detroit. She wrote:

> Detroit from the pictures on Google has no resemblance to the North East that I know and love. Newcastle has had its downturns like any city in the UK and we know that, but separating us out to be like the Detroit of the USA is totally wrong. We are proud of our city, Newcastle is a vibrant friendly place bursting with enthusiasm of new entrepreneurs, small business flourishes, we succeed when times are hard, we are made of tough stuff and will defy anyone who tries to knock us down.

The irony is that for anyone familiar with Detroit and Detroiters, many of Lynn's words would ring true there as well (see Care moore, Intermezzo I).

Such was the criticism that Beckett (2014b) went on to write a piece for a local newspaper in the North-East. In it, he explained that "Several of my interviewees, without any prompting from me, compared the situation to Detroit. It was not a comparison that had ever occurred to me before, and I found it disturbing." This is but one example of how Detroit is used as a symbol of fear and urban failure, without any real engagement with the city and its residents. Even in his explanation, what specific elements he found "disturbing" about this comparison remain a mystery.

Through all of this, however, no one bothered to ask Detroiters what they thought of their city being compared to the North-East of England, nor did they ask them about what they thought of their city being used as an example to warn of an entire region's economic decline and political failures. No experts from Detroit were consulted in any of these articles; no ordinary Detroiters were asked to comment on their lives and how good or bad they were. No facts, figures, analysis, or even photos of Detroit were presented to either substantiate or refute the idea that there were parallels between Detroit and the North-East of England, let alone the potential lessons and insights that could be gained from trying to understand the city.

Watching this debate from a distance, I finally decided to pen a response, which was published in *The Guardian* five days after Beckett's original article (Doucet, 2014). *Guardian* editors gave it the title, "What we really find when we compare Detroit and the North-East of England." In it, I highlighted some of the parallels between the two places, such as their painful experiences with deindustrialization and economic restructuring. However, I also pointed out the key differences, population being one of them (Detroit's population is shrinking while the North-East's is growing). However, my main argument focused on the differing roles of central governments and the pooling of tax bases and social services in countries such as the UK standing in stark contrast to the sink-or-swim, fragmented nature of America's urban governance. This means that Detroit's wealthy suburbs, such as Bloomfield Hills or Troy, do not share their resources with the poor city, and that this governance model greatly contributed to Detroit's decline. Two other differences did not make the final cut of this short article, but are important nonetheless: the role of race and the incompatibility of comparing a single city with a large region containing urban, suburban, and rural elements.

Sadly, such simple comparisons are not unique. Many outsiders write about a particular place being "the next Detroit" without ever having set foot in the Motor City. Seattle has been called the next Detroit because of its reliance on one major industry and its rapid growth (Russell, J., 2015). Calgary was described as the next Detroit because its "current growth is built on an industrial base that is at the mercy of fickle consumers, and is increasingly under siege from competitors" (Avari, 2013). Due to its high levels of debt, Oberhausen has been called "Germany's Detroit" (Eddy, 2013; see also Sattler, Chapter Eight). *Bloomberg View* has even questioned whether or not New York will become the next Detroit, stating that: "Over the next few decades, we are going to come face to face with more problems like Detroit's: pensions that must be paid, legally and morally, but cannot be paid while still offering an acceptable level of government services" (McArdle, 2014).

These comparisons are all relatively simplistic and take certain aspects of Detroit out of their wider political, economic, demographic, racial, and social contexts. Calgary may rely on one major industry, but its lack of political fragmentation means that much of its current growth remains as part of the city of Calgary, and not in politically separate suburbs. While cities like New York may have growing concerns regarding pensions in future decades, New York's economy is far more robust, diverse, and connected to major circuits of capital in the global economy (Sassen, 2001), meaning that its ability to pay those pension obligations will be markedly different than Detroit's.

Despite all this attention on Detroit, there is a distinct lack of engagement with its actual history, geography, demography, economy, politics, society, or culture. It is talked *about*, but rarely engaged *with*. Detroit becomes a reference point for extreme urban decline, a cautionary warning or, hoping that readers can tap into some pre-existing images of ruins, arson, and bankruptcy, a sensational, yet simple, way to grab headlines.

Narratives of Detroit: toward a metonym for urban decline and failure

The preceding examples (and many more) illustrate how Detroit is used as a byword for urban failure. They rely on a simplistic and one-dimensional narrative that has been produced over decades of Detroit's decline while, at the same time, reinforcing that narrative by spreading it to new locations and audiences. Until a few years ago, it was rare for a story about Detroit to actively challenge the narrative of decline, so the public's perception of the city (both in America and internationally) has been shaped by this dominant perspective.

Such contemporary portrayals of Detroit are part of a trend that goes back many decades, but this has not been the only dominant depiction of Detroit throughout its history. During the Second World War, the city was heralded as the "Arsenal of Democracy." In the 1950s, the city claimed to be the "most American city" and a 1951 *Time Magazine* article described it as the best representation of modern, 20th-century

America. As late as 1976, blues legend Albert King sung about Detroit as the Promised Land in his song "Cadillac Assembly Line," which describes the journey of an African-American man leaving poverty in the rural South in search of a better life working in an auto factory in Detroit. Whether or not this was still possible in the late 1970s is debatable, but Detroit, and other now-struggling cities in America's industrial heartland, did briefly offer both blacks and whites the possibility to escape poverty and ascend to the middle class.

Despite Detroit's early post-war industrial prowess, this period also marked the beginning of economic decline and racial tensions that would eventually produce the image of a failed, lawless city (Neill, 1995). Its absolute population, racial composition, and economic standing would all undergo radical transformations beginning in the decades after the Second World War. Detroit's population peaked at over 1.85 million in 1950, having grown from less than 300,000 in 1900 (see Figure 1.15). From this peak, Tom Sugrue states that Detroit, and other industrial cities like it, changed from "magnets of opportunity to reservations for the poor" (Sugrue, 1996, p 4). Tom Sugrue accounts for three historical and intersecting forces that caused this decline: economic restructuring, the role of race and racism, and politics. George Galster's (2012) recent work has emphasized the role of suburbanization and political fragmentation across the metropolitan region. In 1950, 57.5% of the region's population lived in the City of Detroit. Since then, the city's population has fallen to 713,777 (in the 2010 census. More recent estimates place the population under 700,000), while the region has grown to over 4 million inhabitants. However, in 2010, only 16.6% of the region's population lived in the city. The city's economic decline will be elaborated upon in Chapters Two and Three.

Racial changes have been equally dramatic: in 1950, the city was around 84% white and only 16% black. By 1970, this had changed to 54% and 44%, respectively. The 2010 statistics were almost the complete reverse of 1950: 11% white and 83% black.

Throughout Detroit's long decline, civic and business leaders have attempted to revive the city and its faltering image, largely through investments in the built environment in the Downtown core. The flagship redevelopment project of the 1970s, the Renaissance Center, was one of many attempts to change the fortunes of Detroit through a mix of public and private interventions. While Detroit's population was declining and white flight to the suburbs was continuing, new projects such as the Joe Louis Arena (which hosted the Republican Convention in 1980) and the Downtown People Mover brought some new investments in Downtown and helped Detroit to shed some of its negative image (see Neill, 1995).

Figure 1.15 City of Detroit and Metro Detroit populations, 1900–2010

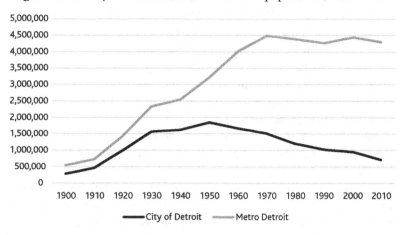

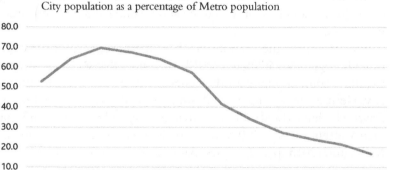

City population as a percentage of Metro population

Yet, most of these initiatives failed to stem the tide of white flight and capital disinvestment from the city. They were criticized on many fronts, not the least of which being that most investment was focused on Downtown and the impoverished neighborhoods received little attention. However, this strategy could not reverse Downtown's decline either; Hudson's, the city's last major department store, closed in 1982, the same year that Ford sold its stake in the Renaissance Center. By the 1990s, the renaissance narrative was even more difficult to sustain, with continued decline and increasing vacancy rates in Downtown. By 1993

(Roush, as quoted in Neill, 1995), an article in *Crain's Detroit Business* depicted "the national image of Detroit as a dangerous wasteland."

As the city's population declined and businesses left the city, Detroit became known as a city of ruins and abandonment, an empty city devoid of people. A 1994 *Detroit News* article predicted that Detroit could become "America's first real ex-city" (as quoted in Neill, 1995, p 155). The focus on ruination, or the derogatory term *ruin porn*, worked to construct simplistic narratives and geographies of picturesque decay and a nostalgia for the past, without any real engagement with or deep understanding of the conditions that led to the production of ruins (see Millington, 2013).

John Patrick Leary (2011) discusses three types of Detroit stories commonly portrayed. The first is as a metonym for the US automobile industry, a point he notes as ironic in that the auto industry has increasingly less to do with the City of Detroit. The second is the *Detroit Lament*, which is a mournful depiction focusing on loss (of people, buildings, way of life). This genre of story, he argues, lends itself most favorably toward ruin photography. The third genre is of *Detroit Utopia* and features stories of the city's possibilities, often focusing on singular examples that tend to be about young and predominantly white residents.

With respect to the ways in which nature is depicted in the city's ruin photography, Millington (2013) concludes that specific, extreme examples come to represent the general images and narratives of the city. He uses the example of Gleamie Dean Beasley, a retired truck driver who hunted and sold raccoons in the city and received significant media attention in 2009 and 2010. Known as the "coon man," Millington (2013, p 292) argues that stories such as his can lead to a:

> quick discursive shift from Beasley as one man to Detroit as a city where many live off raccoon and pheasant meat is the same kind of change that one can see in many stories about Detroit. It does not seem far-fetched to suggest that visitors to Detroit—or, more accurately, people who refuse to visit Detroit—will find their experiences altered by stories like that of the coon man.

As each individual story is published, it becomes easier to understand how Detroit becomes a metonym, in this case, not for the US auto industry, as Leary discussed, but for urban decline and failure more generally.

Dora Apel (2015, p 78) discusses how Detroit has become a "repository for urban nightmares." She highlights a juxtaposition of photos depicting the ruins of the Packard Plant and African-American workers protesting cuts to their pensions as symbolizing both a "warning of the extreme conditions to which many cities are vulnerable, thereby preparing them for their own fiscal austerities, while also presenting Detroit as an isolated example of a racialized city that is responsible for its own disastrous decline" (Apel, 2015, p 79). Consequently, as a symbol of failure, Detroit is often *othered* and depicted as something distinct from the rest of the urban world.

This portrayal as a failed city has piqued the interest of outsiders who come to the Detroit for many different reasons. Scholarly work on the city is increasing and, as mentioned earlier, Detroit attracts more than its share of interest among the media and urban photographers and explorers.

However, there is a distance between the way many outsiders portray the city and its complex economic, social, and racial geographies and histories, an issue poignantly summarized by John Patrick Leary (2011) in his critique of ruin photography. He argues that it:

> aestheticizes poverty without inquiring of its origins, dramatizes spaces but never seeks out the people that inhabit and transform them, and romanticizes isolated acts of resistance without acknowledging the massive political and social forces aligned against the real transformation, and not just stubborn survival, of the city.

In stories such as this, as well as the example from Newcastle, Detroit is the ultimate metonym for urban decline. It is discussed in a one-dimensional way, detached from its complex realities. More "successful" cities such as New York, Amsterdam, or London are almost never boiled down to such simplistic terms. "Detroit" becomes a simple warning; "if we don't do this, we'll end up like Detroit."

Why Detroit matters

Detroit is a divided city. Race, politics, economics, class, and other forces all combine to make the city and the Metro Detroit region one of the most divided and segregated places in America. These divisions play out at a variety of spatial scales. However, in Detroit, they tend to play out in extremes; the wealth gap between the city and the suburbs, the scale of depopulation, abandonment and blight in the city's neighborhoods, and the pace and scope of investment and regeneration currently taking place in the Greater Downtown all contribute to these divisions. These extremes are what draw people to the city—the number and diversity of abandoned buildings draws in urban explorers; the scale of its decline attracts researchers trying to understand the contemporary urban condition; and the cheap rents and a "blank canvass" mentality attracts artists and pioneers (cf Apel, 2015).

However, the economic, social, spatial, and racial trends seen in Detroit are by no means unique. In many ways, the city has always been ahead of the curve: its factories perfected the modern assembly line and gave the world the Fordist mode of production; it was one of the first cities to suburbanize based on the car; and it was one of the first places to feel the full effects of deindustrialization and economic restructuring. Its factories, and the labor struggles that played out in them, gave workers the possibility of climbing to the ranks of the consumer middle class. Detroit's geography was characterized by street after street of "American Dreams": detached houses in quiet neighborhoods with good schools, safe streets and parks for children to play in.

It is not just because the forces shaping Detroit also affect other cities that makes it important to properly understand Detroit. Detroit also matters because of the countless individuals, organizations, and communities who are engaged in practices that seek to challenge or confront divisions within society. It has a long and rich history of social activism based on racial and class struggles (see Boggs and Kurashige, 2011; Galster, 2012). Due to these factors, Detroit is also a place where individuals and groups have taken it upon themselves to develop and implement their own solutions, what Grace Lee Boggs called "finding a way out of no way." So, while there is devastation, abandonment, and decay, there is also no shortage of inspiration and hope. It is the juxtaposition of these contradictions that drew me to Detroit, is what I try to convey to my students, and is what makes the city an important place to understand and engage with.

Today, the city is also a pioneer in post-industrial urbanism and urban decline. This context has given rise to new possibilities, initiatives, and conversations that are rooted in Detroit's extreme, but by no means unique, condition. Andrew Herscher (2012) documented many of these spaces, people, and ideas in his book *The Unreal Estate Guide to Detroit*. He draws on many of the spaces that have grown (literally) out of the ruins and empty spaces of the city, such as the D-Town Farm, the Navin Field Grounds Crew, or Tyree Guyton's Heidelberg Project. Detroit is "a site where new ways of imagining, inhabiting and constructing the contemporary city are being invented, tested and advanced" (Herscher, 2012, p 2). He states that "the challenges of this city have inspired many of its inhabitants to re-think their relationship to the city and to each other" (Herscher, 2012, p 7).

Herscher goes on to ask: "what if Detroit has lost population, jobs, infrastructure, investment and all else that the conventional narratives point to—but, precisely as a result of those losses, has gained opportunities to understand and engage novel urban conditions?" *The Unreal Estate Guide to Detroit* is visually stunning and provides an extensive list of the spaces and groups that fit into the world of unreal estate. Herscher's book reads as a guide to these spaces and there is a certain distance from them. What is missing, however, are the voices, perspectives, and visions of those individuals and groups who are engaged in reshaping the city through its unreal estate spaces. Building on Herscher's theme of possibilities within Detroit's economic, demographic, and social context, many of the contributors to *Why Detroit Matters* are actively engaged in practices rooted in "unreal estate," and this book is a platform for many of their voices to be heard and their visions understood.

Where Herscher documents the ways in which Detroit's abandoned spaces are used by its residents, Dora Apel focuses on how many of these same spaces tap into our wider fears and anxieties about economic and cultural decline. In her book *Beautiful, Terrible Ruins* (Apel, 2015), she describes how Detroit has become the quintessential city of urban abandonment and decay. Detroit, once so successful, has come "to signify modernity in ruins" (Apel, 2015, p 6). This anxiety of decline fuels the appetite for ruin imagery. However, by making this decline aesthetically attractive and beautiful, she argues, we keep that fear at bay, control it, and view it from a safe distance. We can then take pleasure in the ruins while looking at them as separate and disconnected from our own lives. Ruination feeds into two distinct, yet interrelated, narratives of Detroit's decline: the historical inevitability of industrial decline and the poor, racialized city that only has itself to blame (Apel, 2015, p 154). By framing the city from these perspectives, the "real agents of decline—the corporations and the state" (Apel, 2015, p 5)—are able to evade responsibility and Detroit becomes something external to the socio-economic and political contexts of our own lives.

While Apel focuses on wider societal anxieties about decline, George Galster's (2012) *Driving Detroit: The Quest for Respect in the Motor City* examines the way in which economic, political, and racial forces produce extreme anxiety in Metro Detroit, which, in turn, *disrespects* its citizens. Galster is able to place Detroit within its wider regional context in a way few others have been able to do. His diagnostic portrait of the city focuses on three elements. The first is how the region's reliance on the automotive industry (with its fluctuations in demand), combined with oppressive labor policies, produces "the economic engine of anxiety," which leads to a highly insecure population. The second relates to how the extreme regional fragmentation produces property speculation and continued development at the region's fringes, while thousands of homes are abandoned in its core. He calls this the "housing disassembly line" (see Figure 1.12). Finally, he focuses on the dual dialectics of capital and labor and black versus white. As Galster concludes in Chapter Two, the rules of the game are stacked against Detroit, hence his skepticism of the ability of grassroots initiatives to offer genuine solutions to the core political-economic issues affecting the city.

Detroit is a divided city sitting in a divided region in an increasingly divided America. However, these divisions are not static and while some neighborhoods are in the midst of rapid decline, gentrification is spreading in the city's core. The divisions in Detroit are the outcome of decades of conflict and struggle. Today, changes are happening at a very fast pace. As *The 7.2* and a few other spaces in the city witness new investment, many of the spaces depicted in Herscher's *Unreal Estate Guide* have returned to normal circuits of capital investment and those involved have been displaced (for one such account, see Jason Roche, Chapter 7). While the return of mainstream, middle-class spaces of consumption to Greater Downtown Detroit is celebrated in some circles (see Florida, 2012; Tomlinson, 2015), it is only part of the story; Downtown Detroit has seen billions of dollars invested in it while 60,000 properties faced tax foreclosure across the city in 2015 alone (see Bradley, 2015; see also Akers, Chapter Five). Access to basic elements of life such as land and water are now being fought over. The British geographer Tom Slater (2014) recently stated that "Cities are not natural organisms but arenas of political struggles." The outcome of these struggles will determine what type of city Detroit will become.

Approach and aims of the book

While most of the contributors to this book live and work in Detroit, I am an outsider to the city. As I mentioned earlier, outsiders often have a bad name in Detroit. Many outsiders to Detroit come with their own ideas of how to fix the city. They come telling Detroiters what to do, or, as the example from the North-East of England demonstrated, their writing fuels myths and the one-dimensional narrative of decline and failure. Many who actually arrive in Detroit treat the city as their own playground: a blank canvas on which to experiment. My approach is very different. This book will not tell Detroiters what to do; as an outsider to the city, this would be inappropriate, especially given that I was never asked to do so. My approach as an outsider to Detroit has been to listen to the voices and perspectives within the city and to try to bring together a unique combination of contributors to strengthen our overall understanding of Detroit specifically, and divided cities more generally. Being an outsider can have certain advantages in this regard when it comes to seeing the big picture of a place and being able to bring together contributors from a wide variety of backgrounds, experiences, and disciplines, some of whom may be more reluctant to contribute to work organized by someone from a differing, "insider" perspective.

This book is an interdisciplinary collection of different perspectives, strands of research, and voices, which present a complex picture of an extreme, but by no means unique, city. I have sought different approaches and backgrounds, which sometimes contradict each other. However, each one represents a perspective that I believe to be important to our overall understanding of the lessons, insights, practices, and visions from Detroit. Not all voices were sought; many of the city's famous business leaders or property tycoons projecting a capitalist vision for the city devoid of an understanding of the class, racial, or structural forces that shape the city are deliberately absent from this volume. In preparing this volume and its 26 chapters, I explicitly searched for contributions that offer commentary, analysis, and visions on how Detroit's divisions can be genuinely reduced in a meaningful, sustainable, and socially just manner. That requires addressing the root causes of Detroit's condition, rather than simply focusing on its effects. It requires asking difficult questions which confront issues of racial, class, economic and political inequalities. Insights into these forces lead to a powerful deconstruction of the narrative of urban failure and decline.

To do this has required going outside the normal channels for an edited academic book. In order to fully understand the complexities of a city, we need to not only understand the empirical and theoretical work of scholars and researchers, but also contextualize those ideas with actual practices, initiatives, and visions on the ground. So, this book also relies on contributions from planners, activists, community leaders, journalists, educators, artists, and entrepreneurs to give a more holistic picture of why Detroit matters. Each contributor was asked to reflect on two questions when preparing their chapter:

1. What are the major lessons that we can learn from Detroit?
2. What are new visions emerging from Detroit?

The insights, experiences, and perspectives presented in this book will not provide easy answers because the problems and questions are so complex. Instead, they are meant to further our understanding of research, practices, and ideas coming out of the city, and what this means for the challenge of growing inequality and divisions facing all cities.

Outline and structure of the book

The format of this book does not follow a typical academic edited volume. It is divided into three sections. Section One, "Lessons from Detroit," features chapters by scholars and researchers. Section Two, "Practices from Detroit," consists of chapters written by non-academic writers, many of whom are actively involved in shaping new social and spatial practices. Finally, Section Three, "Conversations from Detroit," features interviews with visionary Detroiters, including voices that do not regularly feature prominently in academic publishing (though Herscher [2012] does a good job of describing and contextualizing many of their endeavors). Between each section is a short intermezzo: the poem "You may not know my Detroit" by jessica Care moore and an original essay by Tyree Guyton, creator of the Heidelberg Project, entitled "My Detroit."

In Section One, "Lessons from Detroit," the broad range of scholars present represents both those who have spent a career researching Detroit and urban issues, and young, up-and-coming researchers engaged in innovative and important work.[2] Some chapters provide a holistic contextualization, which helps to understand the broad trends in Detroit, while others focus on one particular aspect of contemporary Detroit. We start with George Galster's long-term account of the city's decline and why its recent bankruptcy does not solve the underlying structural problems facing the city. In Chapter Three, Reynolds Farley takes a more optimistic, if cautious, look at the emergence from bankruptcy and like Galster, looks beyond the city limits to provide a detailed context (including the role of the State of Michigan) of the city's recent economic and social history. In Chapter Four, René Kreichauf focuses on the inequalities of Greater Downtown's recent renaissance. Joshua Akers's work in Chapter Five challenges the assumption that blight simply happens by demonstrating the ways in which it is actively produced and the effects that recent mortgage and tax foreclosures are having on blight and abandonment. In Chapter Six, Kimberley Kinder examines the concept of do-it-yourself urbanism, where, in the absence of a functioning local government, residents struggle with self-provision, including providing basic services and preventing the spread of blight. The concept of bottom-up initiatives is further explored in Chapter Seven when Jason Roche describes the efforts of the Navin Field Grounds Crew, a group of volunteers unconnected to the city or the Detroit Tigers, in turning the abandoned Tiger Stadium site into a park and baseball field. In Chapter Eight, Julia Sattler takes us to Germany's Ruhr Valley to understand how Detroit is used by policymakers and the local arts community to project a contrasting image of Germany's largest deindustrializing region.

Section Two, "Practices from Detroit," begins with John Gallagher's examination of the practice of spinning off pieces of city government into public–private partnerships and non-profits.[3] In Chapter Ten, Dan Kinkead discusses how many of Detroit's perceived liabilities are being reframed as assets for a more sustainable future. Sharon Howell and Richard Feldman discuss the conflicting visions between the city's corporate and activist communities in Chapter Eleven, and focus on resistance movements in three key areas: land, water, and consciousness. In Chapter Twelve, Khalil Ligon, a practicing planner, highlights a rich tapestry of grassroots efforts and initiatives to reconstruct and rebuild the city, and focuses on how they can become part of mainstream planning. In Chapter Thirteen, another planner, Jessica Brooke Williams, looks closely at how the city's official planning documents have historically ignored the arts and culture of Detroit's resident-majority African-American populations, and offers powerful examples of how community arts projects can have meaningful impacts. In Chapter Fourteen, Drew Philp shares his experiences of buying and renovating a home on the East Side of Detroit and discusses the different ways that outsiders can enter into, and engage with, places like Detroit. Finally, the section rounds off with Friso Wiersum, Bart Witte, and Nikos Doulos, the three members of the Utrecht-based arts collective *Expodium*, discussing what they learned from an arts residency they established in Detroit, and how they contributed to existing practices while they were there.

Section Three, "Conversations from Detroit," contains interviews with a diverse group of Detroiters who are all engaged in different initiatives and who have strong visions about the city and their role in it. They were all transcribed and edited down for length.[4] Where possible, the exact words of the respondents were left in place, though, in some cases, these were edited for clarity and/or style in a printed text. Chapter Sixteen is a conversation with Lowell Boileau, artist and founder of DetroitYES. Sandra Hines from the Detroit Coalition Against Police Brutality features in Chapter Seventeen. In Chapter Eighteen, the subject switches to food, first with Malik Yakini and the Detroit Black Community Food Security Network, a major urban agriculture group with the city's largest urban farms. Dan Carmody, President of Eastern Market Corporation, shares his vision for the market and its role in Detroit, as well as reflections on the city's overall food situation, in Chapter Nineteen. Chapter Twenty features a conversation with Jackie Victor, co-founder of the Avalon Bakery, a triple-bottom-line business focused on sustainable practices, which was also a catalyst for much of the transformation of Midtown. In Chapter Twenty-one, another food entrepreneur, Phil Cooley, shares his thoughts on the success of his first major venture, Slows Bar-B-Q, as well as the space he has set up for young entrepreneurs, Ponyride. Chapter Twenty-two rounds off the food discussion with a conversation with Wayne Curtis and Myrtle Thompson-Curtis, founders of Feedom Freedom, which has become an important teaching garden. In Chapter Twenty-three, the role of place-based education is dealt with through a conversation with the three founders of the Boggs School. Yusef Bunchy Shakur shares his transformational story of going from gang member to community organizer in Chapter Twenty-four and explains how racism and white supremacy are still dominant forces in Detroit today. Finally, we round off with a conversation with Grace Lee Boggs, one of the city's most inspirational and influential activists who passed away in 2015 at the age of 100.

Each chapter in this book is prefaced by a brief editor's introduction. The aim of these short texts is to give an overview of the main points and arguments of each chapter, to contextualize each chapter within the book, and to provide a brief introduction to the authors or contributors. They are designed to help the reader navigate through the book and highlight some of the major themes that are recurrent throughout the chapters. The book rounds off with a conclusion that tries to situate the complex messages presented throughout the book against a new one-dimensional narrative of renewal and "renaissance" being produced in Detroit today.

Notes

[1] See: http://detroitsevenpointtwo.com/ and Detroit 7.2 (2015)

[2] All chapters in this section underwent a thorough, double-blinded peer review. In most cases, two external scholars were asked to review and comment on draft versions of each chapter. One reviewer was an expert on Detroit, while the other

was an urban scholar on particular topics central to the chapter being reviewed. These comments were combined with the editor's own comments and incorporated into revised versions of the chapters before submitting the completed manuscript for formal review.

[3] These chapters were reviewed, but as they are written by non-academic writers, they were subject to less rigorous reviews than the chapters in Section One. In general, each chapter was thoroughly reviewed by the editor as well as one other expert on Detroit.

[4] These interviews were all conducted in January 2016 (apart from the interview with Grace Lee Boggs, which was done in April 2014). All interviews were recorded and transcribed in full. Conversations lasted between 45 and 75 minutes, which produced transcripts of between 6000 and 9000 words. These were then edited down to short chapters. During this process, the structure and order of the questions were modified where appropriate. Where possible, original text from the transcripts was left in place, though this often needed to be modified for readability and clarity. Each interviewee was then given the opportunity to carefully read and make any changes to the chapter; in most cases, these changes were minimal, but they help to ensure clarity of argument and style, and, in a few cases, brought in small elements not mentioned in the initial interview.

Section One
Lessons from Detroit

TWO

Detroit's bankruptcy: treating the symptom, not the cause

George Galster

We begin with George Galster's examination of the long-term trends in Detroit, how they led to its bankruptcy, and the role of politics, policy, and structural forces in Southeast Michigan. This chapter also provides a detailed contextualization of Detroit's economic, social, and regional geographies, which will be invaluable for understanding many other chapters throughout this book. For Galster, Detroit's decline is not a recent phenomenon; he argues that the structural forces that led to the city's decline were entrenched as far back as the 1950s, when the city began losing population and jobs. In some cases, he even traces the city's decline to its heyday in the 1920s, when auto companies built multi-storey plants in Detroit that would become obsolete as larger suburban factories built on one-level made these older plants uncompetitive. He also argues that in order to understand the City of Detroit's decline, you need to put it into a wider regional context; while the city's population fell, developers constructed thousands of extra homes surplus to the region's needs on its periphery, a trend that continues to this day. Despite posing some insightful solutions, Galster remains pessimistic as to the long-term political feasibility of genuine structural solutions to the city's problems.

George Galster is the Clarence Hilberry Professor of Urban Affairs at the Department of Urban Studies and Planning, Wayne State University. He earned his PhD in Economics from the Massachusetts Institute of Technology (MIT). He has published over 150 scholarly articles and seven books, and is a leading expert on metropolitan housing markets, racial discrimination and segregation, neighborhood dynamics, residential reinvestment, community lending and insurance patterns, and urban poverty. His latest book, *Driving Detroit: The*

Quest for Respect in the Motor City (Galster, 2012), examines the long-term transformations to Detroit's economic, cultural, commercial, and physical landscapes. He is the fifth consecutive generation of George Galster to live in the City of Detroit.

Introduction

In July 2013, the City of Detroit became the largest municipality by far in US history to declare Chapter 9 bankruptcy (Davey, 2013). Although Detroit's leaders and citizenry are now breathing more easily since the city emerged from the bankruptcy courts relatively unscathed in November 2014, a key question remains to be answered. Will Detroit become a viable financial entity now that it has shed its debt obligations and elected (in November 2013) what, by all accounts, appears to be a fiscally prudent and managerially astute Mayor, Mike Duggan? Unfortunately, I fear that the answer will be "no." Shedding debt through bankruptcy and enhancing efficiencies in city government and service delivery may be necessary conditions for future financial stability, but they are not sufficient. They treat only symptoms; they do not treat the long-term, structural causes of Detroit's financial crisis. These causes are the ongoing fiscal death spiral triggered by net losses of the industrial, commercial, and residential tax base starting in the 1950s, abetted by the retrenchment of state and federal revenue sharing over the last four decades and pervasive racial segregation dynamics.

In this chapter, I first briefly survey the theories that scholars have advanced to explain urban decline so that the case of Detroit can be placed into a broader context. Next, I turn to documenting the structural causes of Detroit's loss of tax base that have played out since the end of the Second World War, emphasizing that these forces were fundamentally beyond the control of the City of Detroit. I then explain how Detroit's attempts to retain solvency by generating more revenue through new forms of taxation and reducing expenditures by reducing public service quality proved self-defeating over the long term by creating a downward fiscal spiral. I argue that this spiral was exaggerated by the destructive segregationist dynamics operating in the region. I show that much of Detroit's fiscal difficulties could have been forestalled had US and Michigan revenue-sharing programs been funded more generously. I speculate about whether the nascent redevelopment actions visible in parts of Detroit are likely to overcome the ongoing structural forces of financial ruin. Finally, I advance a multifaceted strategy for changing these forces threatening the financial stability of Detroit.

The origins of decline: theoretical overview

Shrinking, fiscally distressed cities have been, of course, a long-standing feature of the international urban landscape (Richardson and Nam, 2014). Several, not-mutually exclusive arguments have been advanced by scholars to explain this phenomenon (Sassen, 2000; Mallach, 2012). At its root, a city's decline is seen as emanating from a fundamental restructuring of its current economic (export) base: the industrial sector(s) that primarily sell their products and services to the world outside of the city. When the base's employment and/or earnings provided to the local populace (both directly to those working in the base sector and those who indirectly depend on it through the base multiplier effect) drops for an extended period, impoverishment and, eventually, net out-migration will yield urban decline.

The prosperity-generating capacity of the local economic base can change for reasons both external and internal to the city. Externally, technological progress can render outdated the output, process, or local attributes employed by the economic base. Thus, the advent of land-based oil-drilling techniques eliminated the need for whaling fleets and triggered the decline of places like New Bedford, MA. The birth of railroads broke the monopoly of cities on navigable waterways, spurring, for example, the industrial growth of the food-processing and trans-shipment sectors in places like Chicago. Coal-fired steam engines eroded the comparative advantage of cities located on fast-flowing waterways. The invention of air conditioning and water pumps reduced a constraint on the growth of the tourism industry in the American South and Southwest. Competition can be another powerful external force. If competitors in another region or part of the world produce higher-quality, more innovative, or lower-cost substitutes for the city's predominant goods and services, the city's economic base will wither. This dynamic has been more visibly demonstrated in the product cycles of manufactured goods, wherein a new good typically begins to be produced in the city where it was invented, but inexorably production gravitates to regions where production costs are lower due to cheaper labor (possibly due to different regulatory and union environments), raw materials, and energy. So, the decline of textile production in New England and its migration first to the American South and then overseas provides a clear example of the urban impacts of this competitive pressure, as does the shift of steel production from Pittsburgh to cities in Korea and China.

The internal forces of decline work to erode the competitiveness of a city's existing economic base and deter the development or in-migration of alternative industrial bases. Cities can, for example, simply run out of natural resources that once made them prosperous. Such was the fate of many mining towns in the American West, or port cities whose harbors become unusable due to sedimentation. Cities in the Central Valley of California are now starting to feel such a resource depletion pressure as water for agricultural irrigation becomes increasingly scarce. Urban public policies related to business taxes and regulations, infrastructure, and workforce development can also prove instrumental to decline. Cities with limited, crumbling transportation, energy, and communication infrastructure, draconian tax and regulatory regimes, and poorly educated populations are in an inferior position to compete with other locales in the retention, development, and attraction of economic base industries. Finally, a city's internal social structure may influence its future trajectories. Places that hold on to rigid hierarchies of race and class, are intolerant of new groups or ways of social or economic organization, and are characterized by social strife and lack of cohesion are more likely to see an erosion of their economic fortunes (Florida, 2002).

How does the case of Detroit fit within this theoretical framework of urban decline? Certainly, the dominant economic base for the city for more than a century has been the auto industry (Babson, 1986; Farley et al, 2000). Like most manufacturers of a durable good, the geography of auto production has inexorably shifted from Southeast Michigan, where the domestic industry initially consolidated in the first three decades of the 20th century, to lower-cost regions of the US and then abroad, particularly Mexico, Canada, and, most recently, China (Sugrue, 1996; Silver, 2003). As I will demonstrate in the following, however, it was manufacturing and transportation technological changes that first propelled the post-war auto industry to shift production outside of Detroit into its hinterland, not the quest for lower labor costs. Certainly, competition played a huge role in the saga of the US-bred auto industry as it morphed from supplying virtually all the vehicles to the domestic market after the Second World War to now only about half. Yet, even as its market share has dwindled, the financial impact on the City of Detroit would have been minimal had the Big Three's production remained within the municipal boundary. The role of urban public policy is certainly paramount in the Detroit case. As I explain later, the city's seemingly prudent actions to raise tax rates and institute new taxes proved unwittingly to hasten its decline since it further rendered it an uncompetitive alternative for business and residential location. Finally, the role of social tensions, especially along racial lines, is undoubtedly crucial in abetting Detroit's dynamics of decline and fiscal distress, as I amplify later.

Structural forces eroding Detroit's tax base

Through no fault of its own, Detroit was dealt a staggering, seemingly endless series of one–two–three punches beginning in the 1950s that set in motion the inexorable erosion of its tax base. The first punch came from manufacturers who abandoned older factories in the city in favor of suburban locations (Babson, 1986; Sugrue, 1996, McDonald, 2014). In the 1950s, Detroit's auto companies built 25 new plants in South-East Michigan; none were in the City of Detroit. From 1950 to 1956, 124 other manufacturing firms located in the suburbs; 55 moved out of Detroit to do so. Even greater dispersion followed as firms increasingly switched to trucks as their dominant distribution mode, freed as they were from inner-city congestion by the region's burgeoning network of limited access, high-speed expressways.

Transportation infrastructure alone did not drive manufacturing dispersal, however. Land-extensive production processes were also a prime driver. Within the first decade of mass auto production, industrial engineers discovered that assembly line processes could be much more efficient if raw materials, parts, and semi-finished products were all on the same floor. Moving from multi-storey to single-storey auto plants meant that a given amount of factory floor area would now require more land: a shift from the intensive to the extensive use of land (Galster, 2012).

Unfortunately, by the end of the auto industry's 1920s' heyday, few factories had been built in this new, land-extensive style. Then came the Great Depression, with little motivation to build new facilities. Then came the Second World War, with no opportunity to build new auto plants. Not surprisingly, the pent-up post-war boom in land-extensive auto factory construction occurred at the fringes of metropolitan Detroit, where large tracts of land could be inexpensively assembled. The new suburban factories consumed three times as much land per worker as the older, land-intensive plants. Indeed, to accommodate the City of Detroit's existing manufacturing employees at the density of the newer, land-extensive factories would have absorbed almost half of the city's land area! This new suburban construction put older Detroit plants at a competitive disadvantage. During the 1950s alone,

840 manufacturing plants in the city closed (Hyde, 1980). This loss of city employment has continued unabated.

The magnitude of this dispersal of employment from Detroit to its suburbs is nothing short of staggering (McDonald, 2014). In every 20-year period since the end of the Second World War, the city lost roughly half of its remaining manufacturing jobs, according to periodic manufacturing censuses. This meant that of the 333,000 manufacturing jobs located in the city in 1947, less than 10%—only 23,000—remained by 2007, the peak of the last business cycle. By contrast, the suburbs of metropolitan Detroit had 189,000 manufacturing jobs in 2007.

The second fiscal punch was thrown by the housing development industry, abetted by the federal government, whose guarantees for inexpensive Federal Housing Administration and Veteran's Administration (FHA-VA) mortgages and subsidies for expressway construction spurred massive suburbanization of Detroit's (overwhelmingly white) middle class (Freund, 2007). Since reaching its 1950 census peak of 1.8 million, two thirds of the city's population has systematically been siphoned off by the region's perpetual production of more houses than there were households to occupy them. This process of regional population redistribution has been highly selective in terms of income: suburbanization out of Detroit has overwhelmingly been driven by middle- and upper-income households, those with the financial wherewithal. As a result, the concentration of the poor has intensified in the City of Detroit. According to the 2014 Current Population Survey, Detroit's poverty rate was 38%, the highest among large cities.

During every decade from 1950 to 2010, the tri-county Detroit region's developers built many more dwellings—an average of *over 10,000 per year*—than the net growth in households required (Galster, 2012, ch 9). Developers built this excess supply because they could make a profit; their new suburban subdivisions could typically win the competition for middle- and (increasingly) upper-income occupants when pitted against most of the older housing stock. As the region's number of households grew more slowly than the number of new dwellings produced, some of these new homes were inevitably occupied by residents previously housed in older housing. As they moved out, their dwellings were occupied by other households who perceived the recently available units as preferable to the ones they currently occupied. As this process proceeded, it inevitably resulted in households moving out of the least competitive dwellings in the metropolitan area, with literally no one left to occupy them, at any price. In this fashion, this "chain of moves" linked new construction in the suburbs to the vacating of inferior dwellings located in the most dangerous and deteriorated neighborhoods, which were overwhelmingly located within the City of Detroit. This excess housing supply rendered redundant almost an equivalent number of dwellings, minus those relatively few lost due to highway construction or retail and industrial development. Some of these redundant dwellings were converted to non-residential uses, but the bulk remained vacant, under-maintained, and eventually abandoned by their owners. Typically, after years of increasing deterioration, many of these abandoned dwellings were demolished or left to arson or rot (for how residents live with such structures next to their homes, see Kinder, Chapter Six). The stock of dwellings in Detroit has consequently fallen by an annual average of almost 4000 on net since 1960 (Galster, 2012, ch 9).

This process has systematically stripped value from residential properties in core neighborhoods. From 1970 to 2000, the median value of owner-occupied homes in Detroit, adjusted for inflation, fell by 8%, from $67,000 to $62,000. During the same period, median home values in Detroit's suburbs rose by 50%, from $94,000 to $142,000 (Goodman, 2005). The national mortgage market meltdown in 2007 hastened the downward slide of property values: by 2009, the average price of a home sold in the City of Detroit was less than $13,000.

The third fiscal punch was landed not by manufacturing or housing, but by all other sectors of the economy. Between 1970 and 2000 alone, the number of jobs in Detroit's three-county suburban ring grew 2% per year on average, while jobs in the city declined by 2% annually on average (Farley et al, 2000). This means that, today, over *three quarters* of all the region's jobs in retail and wholesale trade, construction, finance, insurance and real estate, business and repair services, personal services, and professional services—as well as manufacturing—are located beyond the city limits (McDonald, 2014). Even in the transportation, communication, public utilities, and public administration sectors, most employment is now located outside of the city. Of the 20 largest metropolitan areas, Metro Detroit ranks first in its dispersion of jobs away from the core (Galster, 2012). Part of this exodus was driven by the "pull" of the suburbanized manufacturing base and middle- and upper-income households; part was driven by the "push" of declining environmental quality and aggregate disposable incomes in an increasingly impoverished Detroit.

If job counts do not paint a sufficiently vivid portrait of the loss of the non-residential tax base, consider establishments (Galster, 2012). Today, the suburbs have over 400 first-run movie screens, Detroit has 10. The suburbs have 110 bowling alleys, Detroit has two. The suburbs have dozens and dozens of Starbucks, Detroit has seven (though two are inside Downtown casinos). The suburbs have 130 7-Elevens, Detroit has one. The suburbs have 21 major indoor shopping malls, Detroit has none.

In 2009 and again in 2013, the city completed an exhaustive survey of all parcels within its borders (Detroit Residential Parcel Survey, 2009; Detroit Blight Removal Task Force, 2014). The results quantified what is obvious to the casual observer. Over 90,000 of the residential parcels in the city are vacant land. Over 40,000 residential and non-residential structures are blighted and another 38,000 are vacant, abandoned, or otherwise in danger of becoming blighted. Put differently, over a third of Detroit's parcels have been or soon will be wiped out by the excess housing supply built in suburbs.

The consequences of the aforementioned industrial, residential, retail, and commercial relocation and abandonment for the fiscal capacity of the City of Detroit are obvious and severe. The Metropolitan Area Research Corporation estimated that the 2000 property tax base—the assessed value of all residential and non-residential properties—was only $21,546 per resident in Detroit, less than a third of the regional average of $68,286 per resident. The dramatic decline in Detroit's property tax base since 1950 is portrayed in Figure 2.1.

Figure 2.1 Changes in aggregate property tax base in Detroit, 1950–2013, by mayoral administration (Source: *Detroit Free Press*)

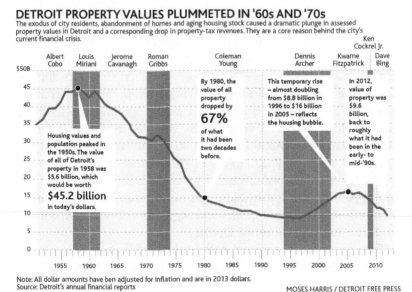

DETROIT PROPERTY VALUES PLUMMETED IN '60s AND '70s
The exodus of city residents, abandonment of homes and aging housing stock caused a dramatic plunge in assessed property values in Detroit and a corresponding drop in property-tax revenues. They are a core reason behind the city's current financial crisis.

Note: All dollar amounts have ben adjusted for inflation and are in 2013 dollars.
Source: Detroit's annual financial reports

MOSES HARRIS / DETROIT FREE PRESS

Fiscal retrenchment by federal and state governments

As if these three fiscal punches thrown again and again by the private sector did not stagger Detroit sufficiently, revenue sharing from both federal and state sources has shrunk dramatically. Since 1974, the federal government has distributed through its Community Development Block Grant (CDBG) program some of its revenues to local governments through a needs-based formula. Sadly, the program has long been woefully underfunded: less than $3 billion for the nation currently, which represented only a sixth of Detroit's accumulated debt at the point at which it declared bankruptcy. Even worse, Washington has been moving in the wrong direction—CDBG has borne an inflation-adjusted reduction of 46% since 2003 (Rohe and Galster, 2014).

Michigan initiated its own revenue-sharing program in 1971, but it, too, has become a trivial source of fiscal support for struggling cities in the state. The inflation-adjusted value of Michigan revenue sharing to Detroit has declined by two thirds since 1998 and now comprises a paltry $75 million (7%) contribution to the city's budget. Michigan enacted several other policies over the years that pushed Detroit toward bankruptcy (McDonald, 2014; Kleine, 2013). It enacted statewide business tax reductions and forced the city to slash its income tax rate in return for a promise to increase state revenue sharing (which was never kept). In 1978, Michigan adopted the Headlee Amendment to its constitution, which forbad local governments' aggregate property tax revenues from growing faster than the national rate of inflation. Of course, it could impose no restraints on how rapidly a jurisdiction's property tax base could decline. This asymmetry proved especially damaging to a place like Detroit since, as in all places with an economic base dominated by durable goods production, its regional business cycle evinced large amplitudes of upswings and downswings. Thus, during the "mini-booms" of the mid-1980s, late 1990s, and mid-2000s, when housing prices in Detroit were rising faster than the rate of inflation, the city was constrained in its ability to "catch up" on property tax revenues that, as we have seen, had been steadily declining.

Detroit's fiscal response and the death spiral

So, what does a fiscally prudent city do in such circumstances of an eroding tax base and revenue sharing? Exactly what Detroit has done

for decades: trim municipal budgets and enhance revenues by raising
tax rates and instituting new taxes.

The city dramatically reduced staff in every department; total
employment has dropped by over 60% since 1960 (see Figure 2.2).
The city also cut municipal bus services, closed parks, health clinics
and recreation centers, deferred maintenance on infrastructure, and
postponed updating technology installations (McDonald, 2014).
Unfortunately, city budgets could not be cut as fast as the population
shrank and the tax base eroded, for two main reasons. First,
infrastructure originally built for a more populous city must still be
maintained, even if it is now underutilized. Second, pensions of earlier,
larger cohorts of city employees must be paid. The growing problem
of pension liabilities is shown in Figure 2.2.

Detroit instituted a series of initiatives to enhance revenues from its
shrinking tax base. The city raised its property tax rate (most notably,
by 30% in 1972) so that it is the highest in the region. Detroit enacted
the region's only income tax for residents and workers employed in
the city in 1962, and raised its rate in 1969 and 1982 (see Figure 2.3).
Despite increasing the rate at which Detroit levied taxes on its properties
and wage-earners, the income earned from these sources continued to

Figure 2.2 Numbers of active and retired Detroit city employees,
1960–2013, by mayoral administration (Source *Detroit Free Press*)

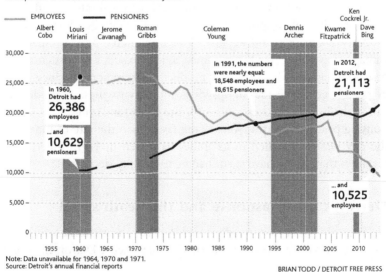

DETROIT NOW HAS TWICE AS MANY PENSIONERS AS EMPLOYEES
Fifty years ago, active city employees outnumbered municiap retirees by more than 2-1. But with workforce downsizing,
the city now has more retiress thana ctive workers. Unlike many other municipal systems, Detroit's active workers are
not required to contribute to the General Retirement System.

Note: Data unavailable for 1964, 1970 and 1971.
Source: Detroit's annual financial reports

BRIAN TODD / DETROIT FREE PRESS

drop, as made clear in Figure 2.3. Property tax revenues exhibited a 79% decline from their peak in 1958 and income tax revenues exhibited a decline of 76% from their peak in 1972. This frustrating response to higher tax rates led to the search for other revenue sources, such as a utility tax in 1970 and (after three casino licenses were granted to Detroit) a wagering tax in 1999. As Figure 2.3 makes clear, none of these attempts proved successful in reversing the trend of falling revenues for the city (for more budgetary details, see McDonald, 2014).

The results of cutting city services and raising tax rates are twofold. First, Detroit put itself at a competitive disadvantage, as households in equivalent circumstances must pay three times more in taxes to live in Detroit than in the average Michigan city; the comparative figure for businesses is twice as much tax in Detroit. As an illustration, a Detroit residential property-owner pays $2,800 more in property taxes annually for each $100,000 in assessed value compared to the regional median (see also Akers, Chapter Five). Second, Detroit created an exceptionally burdensome and unfair tax regime. A Detroiter earning $50,000 can expect to pay 11% of that income in city and state taxes each year, a rate ranking eighth among 50 major cities nationwide. Tragically, the burden is disproportionately heavier for Detroiters earning just above

Figure 2.3 Aggregate tax revenues in Detroit, 1950–2013, by source and mayoral administration (Source: *Detroit Free Press*)

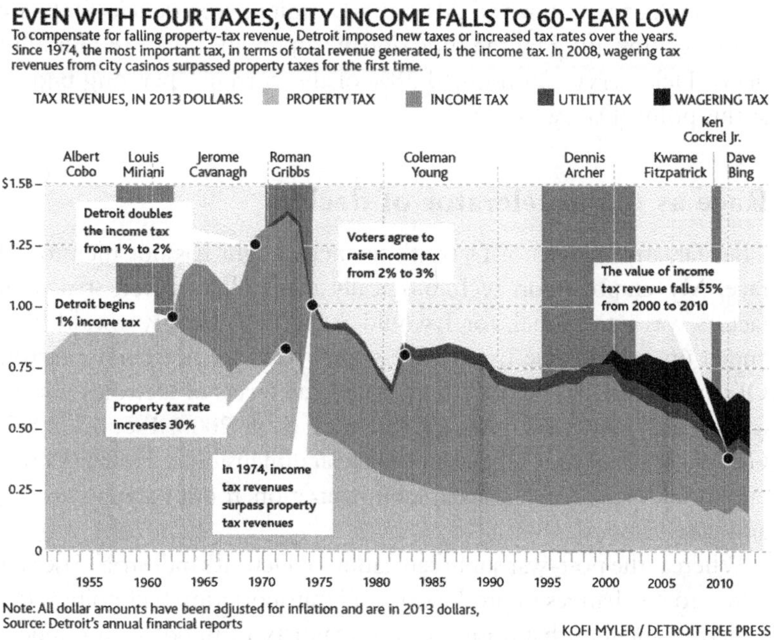

EVEN WITH FOUR TAXES, CITY INCOME FALLS TO 60-YEAR LOW
To compensate for falling property-tax revenue, Detroit imposed new taxes or increased tax rates over the years. Since 1974, the most important tax, in terms of total revenue generated, is the income tax. In 2008, wagering tax revenues from city casinos surpassed property taxes for the first time.

TAX REVENUES, IN 2013 DOLLARS: PROPERTY TAX   INCOME TAX   UTILITY TAX   WAGERING TAX

Note: All dollar amounts have been adjusted for inflation and are in 2013 dollars,
Source: Detroit's annual financial reports

KOFI MYLER / DETROIT FREE PRESS

the poverty line of $25,000. They pay almost 14% of their income in city and state taxes, the second-highest in the nation, primarily due to the regressive nature of the city's steep property taxes and utility taxes (Galster, 2012).

Thus, such acts of austerity, though sensible, inadvertently produced a fiscal death spiral for Detroit. The reduced quality of public services and higher rates of taxation made the city an increasingly uncompetitive location in the eyes of current and prospective households and businesses. Their resultant geographic choices further contracted the city's property, income, and utility tax bases, forcing still more cuts in services and increases in taxes—and so on.

Perversely, the ever-tightening financial constraints on Detroit have occurred coincident with *growing* demands to increase city spending. More firefighters are needed to deal with arson, more health and social services are needed for an ever-poorer population, more abandoned buildings need to be demolished, and more clouded titles need to be cleared so that the land can eventually be transferred to the city and repurposed. The extent of this capacity–needs mismatch was made clear in a 2007 US Department of Housing and Urban Development-commissioned study, which found that Detroit had the lowest "fiscal capacity"—the ability to raise revenues for city services—but the greatest community needs among the nation's 50 largest cities. It is hardly surprising that caught between falling revenues and limits on how much expenditures could be cut, Detroit has run deficits for many years, accumulating by the time of bankruptcy in 2013 $18 billion in debts. Debt service consumed 38% of the current operating budget at this point (Davey, 2013).

Race as the accelerator of decline

Thus far, my analysis of Detroit's financial plight has not mentioned race. My emphasis on technologically and policy-driven structural factors was intentional, for I would argue that the city would have ended up in the same fiscal distress even had race not been a factor. Of course, race has played a huge role in all facets of Detroit's history (cf Sugrue, 1996; Thomas, 1997; Farley et al, 2000; Freund, 2007; Galster, 2012). Three aspects of the racial dimension of Detroit's fiscal saga should be noted: racialized suburbanization, routine activity spaces, and state politics.

Whereas the post-war suburbanization of Detroit's industrial base was spawned by changes in production and transportation technology, the concomitant suburbanization of the majority of middle- and upper-class white Detroiters was abetted by discriminatory federal mortgage policies. The attractive financial terms of mortgages available through the FHA-VA were *de facto* available only to white homebuyers, since the FHA-VA underwriting practices forbad such lending in racially diverse communities (Freund, 2007). Although this blatantly discriminatory policy applied nationwide, its impacts were especially dramatic in metropolitan Detroit, as the racialized suburbanization trends after 1950 make clear in Figure 2.4. Of course, the data shown in Figure 2.4 were produced jointly not only by the aforementioned racially selective "pull factors," but also by "push factors" involving fearful and often bigoted white people fleeing Detroit neighborhoods when their actual or prospective share of black people become uncomfortable. Thus, both policy and prejudice sped up the process of white suburbanization and thus hastened the erosion of Detroit's tax base.

The racialized changes in activity spaces are a more difficult aspect to quantify, but it takes little time living in the region before one observes the startling homogeneity of most public places in which people congregate. This is hardly surprising given the stark patterns of segregation in metropolitan Detroit: three quarters of the region's black population live within the City of Detroit whereas only 4% of the region's white population does (Galster, 2012). This segregation of residences naturally yields the segregation of routine activity spaces

Figure 2.4 Population changes in Detroit and its suburbs since 1900, by race

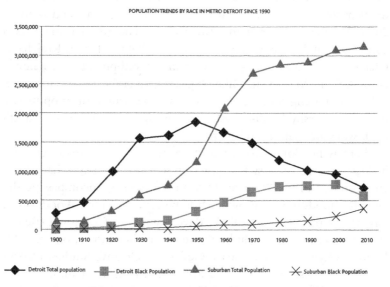

since such spaces are heavily linked by proximity to home. However, in Detroit, propinquity is abetted by more pernicious sentiments. Opinion polls have revealed that many black people feel that they are unwelcome—indeed, would feel threatened—living, shopping, or even travelling in some suburban places, and many white people feel similarly about the city (Farley et al, 2000; Galster, 2012). Since the aggregate disposable income of suburban white people is relatively large compared to that of Detroit residents', the literal economic boycott of the city by many exacerbates the decline of its retail, commercial, and entertainment tax bases.

Finally, the fear, mistrust, and geographic balkanization of the region undoubtedly contribute to the divisive politics at the state level. State representatives from predominantly white-occupied districts typically perceive few common interests with those representing the predominantly black-occupied City of Detroit (Rich, 1989; see also Shakur, Chapter Twenty-four). Instead, both white and black politicians in the region have grown adept at "playing the race card" as part of their game of identity politics (Galster, 2012). This has often resulted in unproductive rhetorical and policy responses to Detroit's fiscal crisis. The most insidious example has been the tendency among many in the legislature to misdiagnose Detroit's woes as a product of inept, cowardly, and/or corrupt Detroit (read: black) elected officials.

Will Detroit's revitalization relieve its fiscal plight?

Plenty of (virtual) ink has been used recently in the international media to rhapsodize about the "Detroit renaissance" (eg Katz and Bradley, 2013). Billions of dollars in investments in the core (think Dan Gilbert's and Mike Ilitch's enterprises; see Farley, Chapter Three; Kreichauf, Chapter Four), glitzy housing and retail redevelopments, and a newly elected, "can-do" Mayor, Mike Duggan, give visible reasons for hope. While containing some seeds of veracity, this drumbeat of optimistic reports can easily be distorted, however, into a belief that Detroit's fiscal woes are maladies of the past.

There is no doubt that there have been some dramatic changes in Detroit over the last five years or so. These changes have been concentrated in the "Greater Downtown" sector, encompassing the neighborhoods of Downtown, Midtown, New Center, Woodbridge, Eastern Market, Lafayette Park, Rivertown, and Corktown (Bell et al, 2015). This sector includes the major anchor institutions of DTE Energy, Wayne State University, College of Creative Studies, Detroit Institute of Arts, Henry Ford Hospital, and Detroit Medical Center.

It is located between Interstate 94 and the Detroit River, centered on Woodward Avenue (Michigan Route 1) and about two miles wide (see Figure 2.5).

Figure 2.5 Population changes in Detroit census tracts, 2000–10

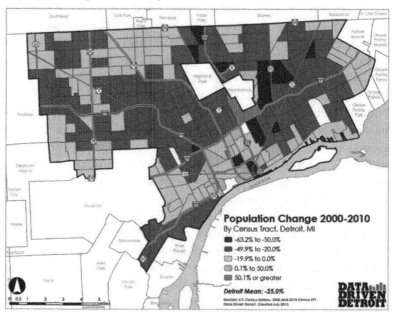

Indeed, these areas have exhibited several indicators suggesting a reversal of the phenomenon of population loss with residential and non-residential decay and abandonment (Bell et al, 2015; Doucet and Smit, 2016). Several pockets within the area saw substantial population gains from 2000 to 2010 (though others lost population) (see Figure 2.5). The area saw 1258 new housing units added and 1754 housing units rehabilitated between 2010 and 2014. Furthermore, since 2013, 77 restaurants have opened (see Cooley, Chapter Twenty-one).

While the reality of this revitalization cannot be denied, its significance can easily be exaggerated. Even if all of Greater Downtown were filled with people, jobs, and high-valued properties at much higher densities than currently, the area would comprise only 7.2 square miles of the city's 139 square miles. The fiscal fate of Detroit clearly rests on what transpires in the 94% of its area that is outside of Greater Downtown. In this vast area, there are three distinct types of places where the situation varies from optimistic to grim.

The first type of place is composed of traditionally strong neighborhoods with high-quality, historical architecture and strong social capital, such as Boston-Edison, Indian Village, Palmer Woods, Rosedale Park, Sherwood Forest, and the University District. These have generally retained their high socio-economic status even during the worst days of Detroit and have witnessed a rebound in property values and reinvestment over the last two years. The second type of place is the immigrant gateways, most notably, South-West Detroit (Mexican-origin immigrants) and Central Detroit bordering on the City of Hamtramck (South Asian-origin immigrants). These areas have been increasing in population (see Figure 2.5) and retail investments, but represent only a modest boost to the city's tax base because the in-movers are generally of modest means. The third type of Detroit place is the residual neighborhoods characterized by generic, obsolete housing stocks, vacant buildings and land, high concentrations of African-Americans in poverty, and high crime rates. They have experienced a continuation of the net population loss and concomitant deterioration and abandonment of residential and retail properties. It is this last group of neighborhoods evincing no change in the long-term disinvestment patterns that still predominates in Detroit (see Figure 2.5).

Metaphorically, Detroit is like a bathtub for "water" comprising people and investment. Undoubtedly, the spigot is now open and water is flowing into the tub (primarily into the Greater Downtown area, but also in the immigrant ports of entry). Unfortunately, the tub's drain is also wide open, and the water level is still going down (though perhaps more slowly). Census and American Community Survey estimates indicate that Detroit's population dropped 25% from 2000 to 2010, and continued to drop another 7% from 2010 to 2013 (United States Census Bureau, 2015). The fundamental forces pulling and pushing the tax base out of Detroit are fundamentally unchanged, despite the vaunted revitalization of Greater Downtown, the exit from bankruptcy, and the new political regime.

Proposals for structural changes

What is required to break out of the fiscal death spiral in which Detroit still finds itself is addressing the underlying structural forces that produced this problem in the first place and are still alive and well today. It is a crisis that emergency financial managers and bankruptcy declarations cannot allay but temporarily.

Any serious solution must address the structural roots of fiscal crisis: (1) manufacturing, residential, commercial, and retail interests that find it more advantageous to build on vacant land at the suburban fringe than on previously used sites in the core; (2) stark fiscal disparities across localities that serve to reinforce household and retail demands for suburban locations; and (3) the resulting concentrations of poverty in the City of Detroit that also serve to reinforce household and retail demands for suburban locations. Ferreting out and eradicating these roots obviously requires a coordinated, region-wide solution. This must originate at the state and/or federal levels of government, since the prospects for comprehensive voluntary cooperation among the vast number of local governments in South-East Michigan (221 to be exact) are nil.

Such a state–federal initiative must embody three core components:

- a regional growth boundary delineating the existing urbanized footprint, outside of which building permits would not be issued and infrastructure would not be extended for a defined long-term period;
- a regional tax-base sharing and/or seriously funded intergovernmental revenue-sharing scheme; and
- a "fair-share" assisted housing scheme, whereby both place-based and tenant-based housing subsidies would be directed away from the City of Detroit and into suburban areas.

These three components would work synergistically were they all to be enacted. A growth boundary would force residential and non-residential development into the existing footprint of the metropolitan area, eventually even repurposing vacant acreage in the City of Detroit. This would help erase blight, rebuild the city's tax base, and improve job and retail accessibility to the city's needy residents. Fiscal equalization strategies would stop the downward spiral of the city's "falling tax base–raise tax rates–drive out more tax base" regime. Resulting improvement in city services and employment opportunities would help stanch the outflow of population. Improving access to affordable housing throughout the suburbs (not merely reconstituting poverty pockets there) would improve the opportunities for low-income families to gain employment and raise children in safer, healthier environments with superior educational options. Over the long term, this would reduce the financial burdens on Detroit. It would also encourage more redevelopment of the city and remove a prime motivator for middle-class flight and avoidance.

Having advanced this plan, I am under no illusions that it would be politically easy to implement. As noted earlier, the staggering city–suburb racial divide and the long-standing practice of racialized identity politics makes the prospects for a politically potent regional coalition rather dim. Moreover, the current Republican governor and legislature would undoubtedly greet my proposal with derision since it clearly involves enhanced government activism in counterpoint to the current *laissez-faire* rules of the game. Nevertheless, the potential for collective movement on these issues is growing due to several factors. First, more established, inner-ring suburbs are experiencing many of the same forces of fiscal distress that have previously been focused on Detroit. Second, the City of Detroit is beginning to diversify ethnically and racially (as explained earlier), which, when coupled with a well-regarded white mayor, may make stereotyping more difficult among some state legislators. Third, concerns over the environment and the growing expense of maintaining and repairing transportation infrastructure mitigate against a perpetuation of a metropolitan development process that essentially abandons the core while despoiling farmland at the fringe.

Conclusion

A historical and structural understanding of Detroit's financial plight requires one to dismiss facile, myopic bromides like emergency financial managers and bankruptcy declarations. The city's bankruptcy has been produced by an over half-century-long process of private, state, and federal actions that have systematically stripped the city of revenues and forced it into an inescapable fiscal death spiral. Since 1950, Detroit's Democratic and Republican administrations and all its African-American and white mayors have been relatively powerless to stem these structural forces. Despite the heralded revitalization of parts of the city, the same structural forces remain at work today.

My analysis also requires one to recognize that, while extreme, the process creating Detroit's fiscal crisis is not unique. It is at work in many older American cities; think Baltimore, Buffalo, Chicago, Cincinnati, Cleveland, Pittsburgh, and St. Louis. Cities cannot solve this situation by themselves; actions coordinated at the regional level—which can only be mandated by states—will be required.

THREE

Detroit in bankruptcy: what are the lessons to be learned?

Reynolds Farley

Reynolds Farley, another long-standing scholar on Detroit, takes a more optimistic view of Detroit's current situation. In this chapter, he argues that Detroit's emergence from bankruptcy leaves the city in a far stronger position than it has been for some time. As in Galster's chapter, Farley provides insightful analysis of, and context for the city's decline, with this chapter focusing more on recent events, rather than Galster's long-term perspective. It also outlines some of the background and legality of a municipal bankruptcy. Farley argues that municipalities have a brighter future after emerging from bankruptcy. He highlights some of the spin-offs of government departments such as Eastern Market and Belle Isle, a point further elaborated upon by John Gallagher (Chapter Nine) and Dan Carmody (Chapter Nineteen). However, such optimism is also challenged through conversations with Sandra Hines (Chapter Seventeen) and Yusef Bunchy Shakur (Chapter Twenty-four), highlighting the often contentious nature of governance change in the City of Detroit.

However, Farley is also critical of the way in which local governments are financed, particularly in the State of Michigan, which he argues has augmented Detroit's financial predicament. In America, cities are creatures of the state and Farley contends that the century-old Michigan Home Rule Law is no longer fit for purpose. The chapter also takes us through Detroit's history of racial segregation and how Detroit's recent population exodus means that many middle-class African-Americans now live in the suburbs. Farley ends by questioning the planning logic of continued population and economic growth, arguing that new approaches are necessary to deal with decline. He asks whether the federal government needs to become active in supporting cities through revenue sharing once again.

Reynolds Farley is an Emeritus Professor and demographer at the University of Michigan's Population Studies Center. His extensive research focuses on racial and urban issues. He is an author of *Detroit Divided* (with Sheldon Danziger and Harry J. Holzer, Russell Sage Foundation, 2000) and maintains the website www.Detroit1701.org. His current work examines the residential consequences of the revitalization of Rust Belt cities.

Introduction

Detroit's city government ran out of funds to pay its bills in early 2013. Emergency Manager Kevyn Orr, with the approval of Michigan Governor Snyder, sought and received bankruptcy protection from the federal court. Detroit became the largest city ever to enter bankruptcy. There are four lessons that should be learned from the city's bankruptcy:

1. Local governments may have brighter futures after bankruptcy than before.
2. The organization and financing of local governments in the US must change when there are massive demographic shifts and fundamental economic changes.
3. The consequences of this nation's history of racial inequality and the recent diminution of economic opportunities for those lacking either highly valued skills or an advanced education must be addressed.
4. Urban planning and local governance must realistically deal with the likelihood of slow economic growth and population decline.

The first section of this chapter explains why the City of Detroit entered bankruptcy. A second section describes how the bankruptcy process was accomplished, since this strongly influenced the future of the city. Then, there is a discussion of the four lessons to be learned from Detroit's bankruptcy.

Detroit: Why did the city enter bankruptcy in 2013?

City governments in the US are primarily supported by taxes imposed upon residents, property-owners, and those who operate businesses in the municipality. A few federal programs provide substantial capital funds for transportation and public housing in cities but federal tax revenues seldom directly fund the operation of local governments. Furthermore, unlike some other countries, there are no federal programs to assist cities that have dramatically lost population and jobs. Cities are legal entities created—often more than a century ago—by the state in which they are located. For the most part, taxes collected by the state government are not used to directly support a city's government. Thus, the taxes that the local government collects from property-owners, businesses, and residents determine what funds will be available to provide services. Cities thrive or fail because of the tax revenue they generate from their residents and the businesses that operate there.

Very few cities in the US have gone bankrupt. The advantage of bankruptcy for a failing city is that only federal courts have the unambiguous power to abrogate contracts, including the great debts that cities owe to lenders such as the major banks and to their retired employees. Quite a few major cities including New York in the 1970s experienced severe financial problems. Typically, the states in which they were located tried to provide enough support to avoid a federal court bankruptcy. States are strongly motivated to do that since if a bankruptcy court frees a city from paying back the money it has borrowed, the state and other local governments in that state will likely have to pay much higher rates to borrow money.

Bankruptcy court hearings and the detailed reports of Emergency Manager Kevyn Orr revealed the fundamental reason for Detroit's financial crisis: the collapse of its tax base after the Second World War (see also Galster, Chapter One). This may be easily summarized[1]:

- from 1950 to 2015, the population fell by 63%;
- from 1950 to 2015, the number of occupied homes and apartments fell by 50%;
- from 1947 to 2012, the number of manufacturing firms in the city fell by 88%;
- from 1947 to 2012, the number of manufacturing workers employed in the city fell by 95%;
- from 1947 to 2012, the number of retail stores fell by 89%;
- from 1947 to 2012, the number of wholesale businesses fell by 81%; and
- from 1950 to 2015, the number of Detroit residents holding a job declined by 73%.

The recession that began in 2008 explains the timing. Between 2007 and 2013, per capita income in Detroit dropped by 13% in constant dollars, the number of employed residents fell by 18%, the assessed value of residential property by 47%, while the poverty rate of residents increased from 34% to 41%. By 2011, property taxes were being paid on only 53% of taxable properties in the city (Citizens Research Council of Michigan, 2013). In addition, the census 2010 count and a major change by the state legislature in how Michigan's sales taxes receipts were distributed to local governments reduced Detroit's revenue flow from the state by 7% of the city's general fund budget (Oosting, 2014). The disappearance of the tax base is the key reason for the bankruptcy of Detroit but there were other contributing factors.

The city's insolvency was hastened by the decisions of elected city officials and by their corruption and erroneous decisions. Recognizing the decline in tax revenues after the 1950s, they initiated new taxes and raised traditional ones, making Detroit a much less attractive place to live or do business. Facing a financial crisis in the 1960s, Detroit became the first Michigan municipality to impose an income tax. That tax was eventually raised to 3% of income. Detroit is the only Michigan city with a 5% tax on all utility bills and is the only city in the state with a 2% corporate income tax. Property tax rates in Detroit were raised to the maximum level permitted by state law and numerous other levies were imposed so that Detroit continues to have the highest property and income tax rates in the state. Furthermore, it is the only Michigan city to obtain a large fraction of its general funds revenue from casino gambling.

Given the financial crisis, city leaders greatly reduced municipal services (Kinder, 2016). The term "Rust Belt" refers to that area toward the center of the US where many cities flourished in the manufacturing era, that is, from the late 19th century to the mid-20th century, as the economic base of the country shifted from agriculture to industrial production. Similar to other Rust Belt local governments, Detroit officials were unable to offer municipal workers large wage increases. In lieu of raises, the city promised extensive retirement and fringe benefits, promises that could not be kept as the tax base shrank. As tax revenues plummeted, the city borrowed tremendous sums to maintain minimal services using traditional and innovative financial instruments. Once again, it turned out that the city lacked the resources to pay those obligations.

Detroit gained a reputation for administering its basic functions poorly, perhaps because of the lack of money. The city's water and sewerage system—a system that served all of Southeast Michigan—was superintended by federal judges from 1977 through 2013. Due to civil rights violations, the Department of Justice monitored the police department for 14 years after 2000. The federal government took control of the city's Housing Commission in 2005 due to financial mismanagement. The state of Michigan took over the city school system in 1999, returned it to local control in 2005 and then took it over again in 2008. Appointees of the governor of Michigan, not an elected board, continue to make all decisions regarding the city's public schools, although this may change in 2017.

Numerous elected and appointed officials were sentenced to jail. Phillip Hart, Chief of Police when Coleman Young served as mayor in the 1970s and 1980s, was convicted of stealing city funds and sentenced to 10 years. Kwame Kilpatrick, mayor from 2003 to 2008, briefly benefited from a "Pay to Play" scheme. After six years of litigation, 34 were convicted and Mayor Kilpatrick is now serving a 28-year sentence in federal prison (Schaffer, 2013). Monica Conyers, President Pro-Tem of Detroit's Common Council in 2008 and 2009, was sentenced to 37 months for her role in steering municipal contracts to friends (White, 2010). Officials administering the city's pension system were convicted of looting funds (Snell, 2014), and city building inspectors were recently convicted of accepting bribes (Yearout, 2014).

Detroit's bankruptcy is not the result of the venal behavior of its officials. Given the collapse of the city's tax base, perhaps no mayor could have produced the miracle needed to prevent bankruptcy. Nevertheless, Detroit officials contributed to the image that the city could not manage its own finances or competently administer the services that it was obligated to provide.

Detroit: the bankruptcy proceedings and the resolution

Michigan's legislature enacted an Emergency Financial Manager law in 1988 to mitigate the financial problems of cities whose tax revenues were so minimal that they could not pay their bills. Should a city approach insolvency, the state treasurer was to alert the governor. If the governor agreed, the treasurer was to work out a consent agreement in which the local government would promise to balance its accounts, primarily by reducing wages, firing workers, and deferring the payment of debts. If little progress were made to solve the crisis, the state treasurer again alerted the governor, who had the authority to appoint an Emergency Manager. This person would have almost total control of a local government. He or she could abrogate labor contracts, reduce employment, cut wages, sell municipal assets, and eliminate expenditures but was obligated to pay bond-holders. He or she could recommend but not impose new taxes and would serve until the financial crisis were solved, even if that were many years.

In 2012, the state treasurer notified Governor Snyder that Detroit was on the edge of insolvency. The city entered into a consent agreement. City employees were laid off, wages were cut by 10%, and the already-minimal level of city services was reduced even more. In early 2013, the treasurer reported that Detroit was not making sufficient progress in slashing spending. Governor Snyder concurred and, in March 2013, appointed Kevyn Orr to run the City of Detroit. He is an African-American bankruptcy lawyer who played important roles in the federal government's support of the bankrupt Chrysler Corporation and its sale to Fiat. He holds two degrees from the University of Michigan and attended law school there, with Governor Snyder as a classmate. Given the history of racial conflict in Detroit, it would have been provocative had the governor turned over control of Detroit to a white man or woman.

Orr examined Detroit's finances and concluded that the only feasible solution required reducing payments to all who were owed monies. Governor Snyder agreed and Orr requested bankruptcy from the federal court so that Detroit could be freed from its legal obligations, including those to bond-holders and pensioners. State of Michigan courts and local officials did not have the authority to free a city from paying those who loaned it money, but the federal courts could do that, as well as free a city from paying pensions to retirees. Federal bankruptcy Judge Stephens Rhodes held hearings. Orr stressed the city's lack of resources, its indebtedness, and its inability to pay for usual city services. Creditors—particularly bond-holders and pensioners—argued that Orr overestimated debts and greatly underestimated assets that might be sold, especially paintings in the Detroit Institute of Arts. This is the nation's sixth-largest gallery with a magnificent collection of European art and the world-famous Diego Rivera murals. After evaluating these arguments, Judge Rhodes approved bankruptcy in the summer of 2013.[2]

Federal Chapter 9 bankruptcy is designed for local governments and assumes that cities will continue to function during and after their insolvency. The process calls for the bankrupt municipality to negotiate with debtors to reach settlements. If agreements are not reached, the bankruptcy judge "crams down" a settlement, typically by paying off the city's debts at a very low rate. However, assets and revenue streams are to be maintained so that the city can provide minimal services during bankruptcy and improve services thereafter. Bankruptcy Judge Rhodes appointed Gerald Rosen, senior federal judge for the Eastern District of Michigan, as the lead negotiator.

When Kevyn Orr requested bankruptcy, many assumed that Detroit had numerous valuable assets that could be sold to pay bond-holders, pensioners, and other debts: a water and sewerage system that served almost all of Southeast Michigan, a system for distributing electricity, more than 100 parks, a share of the tunnel that linked Detroit to Canada, many revenue-generating parking lots, and three museums, in addition to the Detroit Institute of Arts and a large zoo. It soon became clear that the only assets that could be sold quickly for cash were the masterpieces in the Detroit Institute of Arts. That organization faced a financial crisis in 1919. At that time, Detroit was prosperous, so the trustees of the gallery gave their holdings to the city in return for a generous annual stipend, and in the 1920s, the city not only supported the construction of their magnificent gallery, but paid for the purchase of classic European art (Peck, 1991, ch 3).

The most vocal parties in the bankruptcy negotiations were spokespersons for bond-holders and for the two funds that provided pensions for municipal employees: 9000 currently employed workers and more than 20,000 retired. Retirees asserted that Michigan's constitution required that pensions must be paid even if a city were bankrupt but Emergency Manager Orr challenged their view, pointed out that federal bankruptcy law trumped state law, and suggested that it might be necessary to cut pensions by 30% or more.

At this point, the lead negotiator, Judge Rosen, orchestrated a "Grand Bargain" to simultaneously protect pensions and save the art. Using his influence, he arranged an agreement whereby prosperous foundations linked to Detroit–Ford, Kellogg, Kresge, Mott, and Skillman—provided $366 million, the state of Michigan provided $350 million, while the Detroit Institute of Arts agreed to raise $100 million over 20 years. These monies were placed into the pension trust funds, while the art and the Gallery were transferred to a private non-profit organization. The pensions of uniformed officers will be paid at 100%, while other city workers will be paid at 95%, although adjustments for inflation have been reduced or eliminated. Emergency Manager Orr's final Plan of Adjustment called for reducing the city's debt from $19 billion to $7 billion while reserving $1.7 billion for investments in the city over the next decade.

As the bankruptcy trial proceeded, lawyers for the firms that insured bonds feared that they might get as little as six cents on the dollar. They negotiated with Kevyn Orr, who agreed to permit bond insurance firms to operate for profit-but not own-revenue-generating city assets, including a share of the international tunnel and Downtown parking structures. In addition, those insurers were able to purchase, at a discount, valuable city-owned parcels, including choice ones near the riverfront that may be developed for commercial and residential use. Presumably, these insurers will recoup their losses by investing in real estate in Downtown Detroit, investments that will eventually increase the city's tax base. Judge Rhodes accepted the settlements negotiated by Kevyn Orr, and in December 2014, Detroit's city government exited from bankruptcy. Kevyn Orr concluded his service as Emergency Manager and elected officials—Mayor Duggan and the Common Council—resumed administering the city. Detroit will differ from other Michigan cities since a state-appointed Financial Review Commission will monitor and control the city's spending and borrowing (Bomey, 2015).

What may we learn from the bankruptcy of Detroit?

Local governments may have much brighter futures after bankruptcy than before

Fewer than a dozen US cities entered bankruptcy since the end of the Second World War. Most of them were much smaller than Detroit, so it is difficult to generalize about the consequences of bankruptcy. There are many reasons to believe that the bankruptcy in Detroit was a success and the city's government will be more financially stable and secure than it was before the financial crisis. A base has been established for progress in Detroit. The city's indebtedness was drastically reduced and Detroit may once again borrow the funds it needs to operate. Perhaps more important is the restructuring of the city's government that took place: a process that led to a cut of about 20% of the city's workers. However, the bankruptcy process approved by Federal Judge Rhodes reserved $1.7 billion to be spent over a decade to improve the city's fire and police departments, to raise the wages of uniformed officers, and to implement modern information technology that will make the city's bureaucracy operate efficiently. Some of those funds and additional federal funds will be used to demolish or deconstruct many of the 85,000 vacant and abandoned structures that line the streets (Detroit Blight Removal Task Force, 2014).

The city transferred control of many of its major assets that it could support when it was a prosperous place of almost 2 million residents but can no longer afford. This greatly reduces the need to make capital appropriations. Belle Isle was rented to the state of Michigan for 30 years and the state—not the city—will renovate this potentially beautiful park. The Detroit Institute of Arts is no longer a city responsibility, but rather run by a private non-profit organization. The city's water and sewerage system is now run by a coalition of city and suburban governments. The Detroit Farmer's Market and the major convention center, Cobo Hall, are two of many valuable city assets that were transferred to management by private–public consortia, with the capital investments no longer made by city taxpayers.

When Detroit exited bankruptcy in 2014, several favorable developments encouraged revitalization, developments that did not occur in other financially challenged cities. The Detroit area retains its status as the most important site for the world's vehicle industry. The home office of General Motors is in the city while the headquarters of Ford and the North American home of Fiat-Chrysler are just outside the city. Those firms have invested billions in modernizing manufacturing plants in Detroit and the suburbs. The three major vehicle firms' 2015 contract with the United Auto Workers includes commitments to invest $20 billion in new facilities in the US over the next four years, with a substantial share in the Greater Detroit area. Vehicle production is steadily increasing in metropolitan Detroit but this does not promise substantial increases in blue-collar employment since labor productivity in the industry has been steadily increasing at 4% per year for the last quarter-century (United States Bureau of Labor Statistics, 2015). Perhaps of more consequence, the vehicle industry invests extensively in research as vehicles increasingly resemble sophisticated computers attached to an engine and wheels. A civil or mechanical engineering degree was once the requirement for the modal white-collar job in the auto industry. Soon, it may be a degree in information technology. The recent prosperity of the auto industry is an economic stimulus to the city and the suburbs.

Detroit currently benefits from major capital investments in Downtown and Midtown being made by two large firms with strong ties to the city. Dan Gilbert, chief executive of the Quicken Loans financial services, not only moved his employees from the suburban ring to Downtown Detroit, but also purchased or obtained options on 80 Downtown buildings, with the aim of creating a center for information technology and computing, especially as it relates to the vehicle industry. Many once-abandoned office buildings, hotels, and retail stores in Downtown Detroit have been renovated for business activity, so employment is increasing. The Ilitch family, owners of the

Little Caesar's pizza empire, the Detroit Red Wings hockey team, and the Detroit Tigers baseball team, invested extensively in a successful effort to make Downtown Detroit a regional center for entertainment, recreation, and dining. They are now constructing a massive innovative sports arena that will be the centerpiece of a new urban village with shops, stores, and residences near Downtown Detroit. Some of the new residential units will be reserved for moderate- and low-income families. Wayne State University continues to expand in Midtown as it constructs new buildings, particularly for biomedical research. Two large medical complexes adjoin Midtown Detroit: Detroit Medical Center and the Henry Ford Hospital system.

In the US, there is a tradition of very rich individuals and families establishing foundations that then disperse substantial funds for generations. Typically, they have donated monies to the arts, for music, for medical research, and for advanced education. Seldom have these foundations devoted their great resources to supporting traditional governmental functions. During and after bankruptcy, Detroit experienced something unusual. The deep pockets of local foundations and wealthy entrepreneurs began to fund those capital investments that were once made by local governments. Then they became involved in economic development, education reform, and quality-of-life issues. Detroit may be the first large city to greatly benefit from investments now being made by many foundations and individuals. The Skillman Foundation is devoting $100 million over 10 years to improving the health and educational achievement of youth in six Detroit neighborhoods. Ten major foundations combined their resources to establish a New Economic Initiative for Southeast Michigan. This is now an active organization promoting new businesses, with the specific aims of creating 1000 new businesses, 20,000 new jobs, and $1 billion investment in the short-run future. In addition, that organization realizes that many Detroit residents are poorly trained for the sophisticated jobs becoming available. Therefore, one of their key goals is to provide local residents with the skills they need to thrive in the new labor force. A variety of for-profit and non-profit organizations are now encouraging entrepreneurship in Detroit, including the promotion of businesses that may be initiated by persons lacking capital or an advanced degree.

The organization and financing of local governments in the US must change when there are massive demographic shifts and far-reaching, long-enduring economic changes. A governmental structure effective in one era may be useless if there are great shifts in technology and the economy

In 1909, Michigan adopted a system of local government that may have been appropriate for the pre-automobile era when people lived, worked, shopped, and sent their children to schools in their own municipality. Presumably, those residents, their employers, and retail businesses where people shopped, paid local taxes to support the local government. As the population of the municipality grew and economic activity increased, local governments saw their tax revenues increase, so they could provide more and better services. The Michigan Home Rule Law made it easy for townships, villages, and other population clusters to form their own highly independent governments. It gave them great power to tax, assume debts, and manage their own responsibilities, such as zoning, policing, fire protection, and economic development. It provided localities with no incentives to cooperate with neighboring governments. The state established few rules about what minimum level of services had to be provided, set almost no limits on what a local government might spend, and allowed them to borrow as they wished. With few exceptions, the Home Rule Law made annexations and mergers difficult, so the boundaries of cities established in the pre-auto age continue to define Michigan's cities.

The Michigan Home Rule system is not suitable for the modern era. Automobiles, expressways, and suburbanization radically changed local government. Figure 3.1 presents data about the three-county Detroit metropolis: Macomb, Oakland, and Wayne counties. It reports the percentage of the total metropolitan population living in the suburban ring rather than in the City of Detroit. When the state legislature established the system of local governance in 1909, less than one quarter of the metropolitan population resided in the suburbs. After two decades of road building—in 1940—the suburban population was substantial, but two thirds of metropolitan residents resided in the City of Detroit. By 1955, the suburban population was as large as the city's. The federal government's programs to encourage suburban home building and their program to build expressways quickly and dramatically changed the distribution of population. By 2014, more than four of five metropolitan residents lived in the suburbs, not the City of Detroit.

Figure 3.1 Percentage of the Metropolitan Detroit population living outside the City of Detroit, 1900–2014

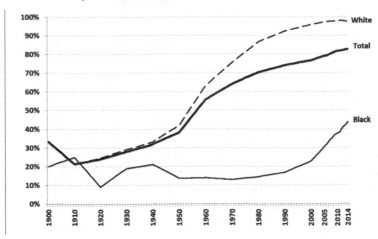

Local governance became a metropolitan issue in the years after the Second World War. Thanks to the Home Rule Law, by 1960, Detroit was surrounded by 124 suburban governments. There is also the Detroit city public school district and 93 separate and distinct suburban school districts. No longer are municipalities local places where people live, work, shop, worship, and raise their children. Individuals travel throughout the metropolitan region with little attention to corporate limits of individual cities or suburbs. A public transportation system, you might think, would be designed to serve city and suburban residents. Parks in one part of the metropolis might capitalize upon environmental features and attract visitors from a wide area. Economic development, land use, and protecting the environment are certainly dealt with best at the metropolitan or regional level, but that seldom happens in Michigan. School districts would be more efficient and less costly if they served more than one small suburb where the district enrollment might be less than 1000. Michigan's Home Rule Law precludes regional solutions to regional problems.

As George Galster (2012; see also Chapter Two) emphasizes, great competition emerged in metropolitan Detroit after the Second World War: the suburbs against the city and individual suburbs against each other. When it came to offering incentives to residential developers or providing sites for new factories, warehouses, or shopping centers, Detroit did not fare well in competition with its suburbs. By 1950, almost all land in the city was occupied but the suburbs had vast stretches of unoccupied land that could be offered to developers.

After the Second World War, urban officials and planners across the nation understood the growth of the suburbs and the rapidly diminishing resources of older cities, especially those where 19th- and early 20th-century factories were closing. In numerous states, legislatures allowed cities to annex outlying land so that their tax base could increase. Detroit annexed no land since 1926. Thus, the city missed out on the tremendous population and economic growth that occurred in Southeast Michigan from the 1940s through the 1970s.

Figure 3.2 presents information about the land area of the 25 largest cities in the US in 2010. It shows the city's land area in 2010 as a percentage of its land area in 1950. Detroit, the fourth-largest city in 1950, fell to rank 21 in population size in 2015, now surpassed by eight Southern, seven Western, and three Midwestern cities. A major reason is that Detroit did not annex outlying land. Jacksonville, at present, is 25 times bigger than it was in 1950; Nashville is 22 times bigger in land area; and San Jose is 10 times bigger. If the City of Detroit had annexed as much outlying area as Columbus, Ohio, or Indianapolis, Indiana, its population would be approaching 2 million rather than the 677,000 estimated for 2015—and the city would not be bankrupt. Similarly, if the state government had realized in the 1950s that economic development, transportation, environmental protection, education, and parks were regional issues and established administrative authorities whose scope spanned metropolitan Detroit, the city would not have entered bankruptcy.

The century-old Michigan Home Rule Law created a situation in which cities that are growing—both economically and in population—are likely to have a tax base sufficient to pay the costs of local governments. However, Michigan cities that have been losing population and employment throughout the post-Second World War era—Detroit, Flint, Pontiac, Benton Harbor, and many smaller sites— have seen their tax base plummet while their obligations to provide services declined more modestly. It is time to retire the Home Rule Law in Michigan. The state should consider a statewide property tax keyed to the actual value of property. The funds might then be allocated to municipalities on the basis of their population size, as well as any other special needs that a place might have. In 1993, a school district in rural Michigan ran out of funds and closed its schools. Within two years, the state fundamentally changed the way public schools are supported. The state sales tax and the tax on tobacco were raised and a sales tax on property was introduced while taxes on residential properties were reduced. Thus, the costs of educating students were shifted from local property taxes to revenues collected across the entire state. These funds

Figure 3.2 Land area of 25 largest cities in 2010 as a percentage of their land area in 1950

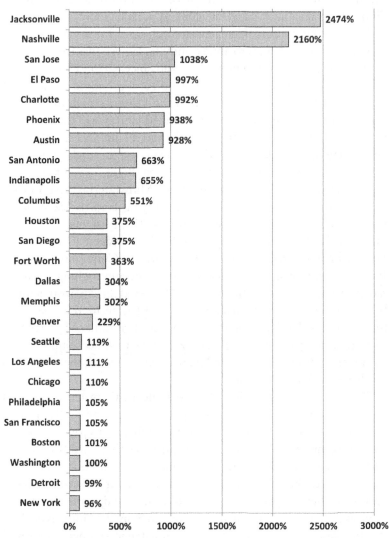

are then distributed to school districts primarily on the basis of their enrollments. This has done a great deal to equalize educational funding across Michigan's school districts. A similar change could be made so that the residents of Detroit could expect a response from their police, fire department, or emergency medical teams as quickly as a resident in the most prosperous suburb.

There are other models to avoid Detroit's bankruptcy that the state could have—but did not—adopt. Minneapolis and St. Paul are older cities that did not annex after the Second World War, so their populations declined while their suburbs flourished. In 1971, the state of Minnesota adopted a fiscal disparities policy for the seven-county Minneapolis metropolitan area in which a share of the increase in a municipality's tax revenues from new commercial and industrial properties goes into a pool of monies (Orfield and Luce, 2011). These monies are then distributed to all local municipalities on the basis of their tax base and population size. Governments that benefit from new shopping centers, office parks, and factories share their rising revenues with neighboring municipalities that may be losing their tax base. This minimizes competition among local governments and encourages collaboration for economic development. The story we tell about Detroit would be very different had a metropolitan fiscal-sharing program been adopted 50 years ago.

Those who develop urban policy and write laws must consider how the consequences of the nation's history of racial inequality interact with current changes in the labor market to greatly disadvantage African-Americans in Detroit and Rust Belt metropolises

No metropolis has been as riven by race as Detroit. It is the only city where federal troops were dispatched to the streets four times to stop black people and white people from killing each other: twice in the 19th century (Katzman, 1975) and twice in the 20th. The black population of Detroit was miniscule until the First World War, when German submarines terminated the flow of European immigrants but the need for workers grew as auto-makers switched to producing armaments. The American South became the source of labor and, for the first time, thousands of African-Americans migrated to Detroit. Jim Crow had not been the rule in Detroit. Before the First World War, the small black population was not racially segregated and a few highly educated black professionals served integrated clienteles. As early as 1890, a black man was elected to represent Detroit in the Michigan state legislature. However, strict segregation became the norm after the First World War as Jim Crow policies quickly developed and were rigorously enforced (Katzman, 1975; Boyle, 2004). Residential segregation – and the school segregation that followed – were major issues. In Detroit, intimidation, real-estate marketing practices, and restrictive covenants restricted black people to specific neighborhoods: one on the East Side and another on the West Side.

The Second World War heightened racial conflicts (see Jenkins, 1991), but after the war, no city experienced as much and as prolonged racial conflict as did Detroit. Many white people feared that the arrival of black people in their neighborhoods would decimate the value of their homes, increase crime, destroy the quality of schools, and put their wives and daughters at risk of violence. As Thomas Sugrue (1996) reports, white people sought to preserve the racial homogeneity of their neighborhoods by using a variety of strategies to guarantee that no black people resided there. However, the full employment and high wages of the Second World War meant that many African-Americans had the resources to secure much more attractive housing than in the neighborhoods where they were confined. Detroit became a center for block-busting: real-estate brokers frightening white people to sell their properties for low prices and then marketing the same property to African-Americans for a higher price. Many white people grew tired of their struggle to maintain their neighborhood's racial homogeneity and came to understand that federal housing policies provided them with an appealing opportunity: higher-quality homes in the suburbs where real-estate practices and other techniques ensured that all their neighbors would be white (Jackson, 1985).

The white population of Detroit fell by 360,000 in the 1950s, by 340,000 in the 1960s, and by 425,000 in the 1970s. More than one and a half million white people lived in Detroit in 1950; the Census Bureau estimates that in 2014, only 70,000 white people resided in the city. Figure 3.1 shows that by 2014, only 2% of metropolitan white people lived in the city.

Suburban politicians made every attempt to prohibit black people from settling in their communities. Orville Hubbard served as mayor of Dearborn, one of the most prosperous and largest suburbs, from 1942 to 1978. He stridently opposed the entry of black people, and by the 1960s, became a well-known national symbol of suburban hostility to African-Americans (Good, 1989). L. Brooks Patterson, who became Oakland's County Prosecutor in 1976 and has served as the county's chief executive since 1992, forcefully argued that the interests of the white suburban ring not only differed from, but often conflicted sharply with, those of the black-dominated city (Williams, 2014). The soul music radio stations of the 1960s played the tune, "Chocolate City, Vanilla Suburbs," one that celebrated black people taking control of the nation's biggest cities thanks to the exodus of white people. No location illustrated that divide more clearly than Detroit. By 2000, African-Americans made up 83% of the population of the city, while the suburban ring was 86% white. The city–suburban divide was a black–white divide.

For decades, Detroit activists played key roles in the struggle for equal opportunities. Those efforts were successful with the passage of the Civil Rights Act in 1964, the Voting Rights Act in 1965, and the Open Housing Law in 1968. The racial attitudes of white people shifted as younger individuals with more egalitarian views and more extensive educations became adults. Federal courts overturned state, local, and employer policies that unfairly protected the advantages of white people. Although affirmative action become unpopular and is now an all but illegal strategy, a norm of diversity is now widely accepted, meaning that most employers stress that they hire and promote minorities and women into their most visible jobs.

Optimists expected that following the Civil Rights Revolution of the 1960s, there would be steady declines in the residential segregation that created the American apartheid system—a system that attained its apogee in Detroit (Massey and Denton, 1993). They expected that schools would be increasingly integrated and that black people would attain much higher levels of education. This, foreseeably, would lead to more social integration and an increase in interracial marriage. Removing racial discrimination in employment would, presumably, be followed by much greater success for black people in the labor market and, eventually, to a reduction in the huge gap that separated black people from white people in terms of earnings, income, and assets. It did not work out this way in metropolitan Detroit.

The attitudes of white people about the key issue that separated the races changed as the Open Housing Law helped overturn real-estate practices that separated black people and white people in metropolitan Detroit (Farley, 2011). No longer are the suburbs closed to black people. Between 2000 and 2014, the city's black population dropped by 242,000, while the suburban ring gained 183,000 African-Americans. Detroit is now losing black residents almost as rapidly as it lost white people in the past. This black flight has not created homogeneous ghettos in the suburbs. Rather, black people are now widely distributed throughout the suburbs, with substantial numbers residing in suburbs with histories of hostility to black people (Darden and Thomas, 2013, Table 52). Both prosperous and lower-income suburbs of Detroit that had virtually no black residents in 1970 are now home to much more than token numbers of African-Americans. This integration occurred without violence or protests. The norm of having the right to live in a home if you can afford it regardless of your race is now widely accepted. Perhaps due to this residential integration, social integration is also occurring as Detroit-area black and white people increasingly intermarry. In 1970, only 2% of younger black married men had white wives. In 2014, it was 8%. Due to interracial marriage, a mixed-race population is growing and 1 in 40 Detroit-area children under 10 are now listed by their parents as both black and white by race (United States Census Bureau, 2015).

The election of Michael Duggan as mayor in 2013 is another indicator of how racial attitudes changed in a generation. Duggan grew up in the City of Detroit and, following the demographic trends of his era, moved to the suburbs, where he prospered as a health system administrator and county official. He returned to Detroit in 2012 and then handily defeated Benny Napoleon, the African-American county sheriff, to win the mayor's job. An electorate that was 82% African-American chose the first white mayor in 40 years; an outcome that was unimaginable during the decades when bitter racial conflict and city–suburban hostility infused every issue.

Despite declines in residential segregation, more interracial marriage, and the removal of barriers that kept black people in low-level jobs, the economic status of most black people deteriorated since the Civil Right Revolution, both in absolute levels and relative to white people. The restructuring of employment in manufacturing—many fewer blue-collar jobs and modest to substantial declines in wages for the skilled and unskilled—had a great impact. The median income of white households in metropolitan Detroit—in constant 2014 dollars—fell by $10,000 between 1970 and 2014. However, the median income of black households declined $18,000, leading to a larger racial gap.[3] On a per capita basis, adult black men in metropolitan Detroit had incomes $27,000 smaller than white men in 1970; by 2014, that gap had grown to $33,000. In 1970, black women were more likely to be employed and had, on average, higher incomes than white women; however, by 2014, that was reversed. In metropolitan Detroit in 1970, 81% of black men aged 25 to 64 were employed; in 2014, just 58% had a job. As William Wilson (1996) perceptively observed, jobs disappeared for those living in the segregated neighborhoods of Rust Belt cities. Black–white gaps in homeownership and the value of owned homes increased, suggesting that black people fell further behind white people in asset holdings (Farley, 2015, Table 1). None of those who advocated for the successful Civil Rights Revolution in the 1960s imagined a circumstance in which racial discrimination would decline, a norm of diversity would become popular, but the economic status of the typical black person would drop sharply. That happened in metropolitan Detroit and the Rust Belt.

What explains why black people, as a group, are falling further behind white people? It cannot be an increase in blatant racial discrimination or a hardening of racial attitudes. The disappearance of the highly paid, blue-collar jobs is the most important explanation. In 1970, 102,000 black men in the Detroit area worked in manufacturing, transportation, utilities, and construction—the industries where workers were union members and wages were high. The multibillion-dollar investments now being made by Ford, General Motors, and Fiat/Chrysler in Detroit-area factories mean that more cars will be produced there, but there may be few new jobs. By 2014, only 53,000 black men worked in manufacturing, transportation, utilities, and construction. The average earnings of those men—in constant 2014 dollars—were $48,400 in 1970, but fell to $44,000 in 2014. The key jobs that once sustained a large and financially secure black middle class in Detroit greatly diminished in number. They are unlikely to return.

How is this linked to the current problems of Detroit and the city's future? The exodus of white people from the city occurred on a selective basis: the most prosperous moved out first, followed later by those with middle and lower incomes. The same selectivity characterizes black suburbanization. Figure 3.3 categorizes white and black households in metropolitan Detroit into six income groups, ranging from impoverished to those households with incomes five or more times the poverty line, that is, in excess of $139,000 for a family of four in 2014 dollars (classified as "comfortable" in the figure). The figure displays the percentage of Detroit-area households in each economic category living in the suburban ring rather than in the City of Detroit in both 1980 and 2014, that is, all white and black Detroit-area households were classified by economic status and whether they lived in the City of Detroit or the suburbs. Figure 3.3 shows the percentage in the suburbs rather than the city. For example, in 1980, only 18.5% of black people in the metropolitan region considered economically "comfortable" lived in the suburbs; by 2014, 65.5% of economically "comfortable" black people lived in the suburbs, suggesting a substantial suburbanization of middle- and upper-income African-American households.

By 1980, virtually all financially successful white households had moved into overwhelmingly white and racially segregated suburbs. However, among white people below the poverty line, more than one quarter were still city residents. A generation later – in 2014 – almost all white households lived in the suburban ring regardless of their finances. The American apartheid system in 1980 closed the suburbs to African-Americans, so black people lived in the city regardless of their economic status. However, that changed, and by 2014, the majority of black households with middle-class incomes or better had homes in the suburbs. As Erbe (1975) pointed out, during the era of strict residential segregation, prosperous black families could not move far away from poorer black families. However, this changed as the Fair Housing Law became effective. The out-migration of black people from Detroit seems likely to continue as they seek to reside in suburbs that are perceived to be safer, have better schools, have lower tax rates, and offer better services than Detroit.

Figure 3.3 Percentage of Metro Detroit's white and black populations living in the suburbs rather than in the City of Detroit, broken down by economic status, 1980 and 2014

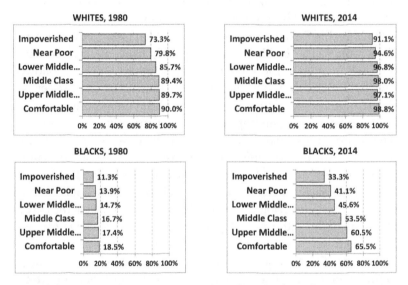

Impoverished: Incomes below the poverty line. Near Poor: Incomes 100% to 199% of poverty line. Lower Middle Class: Incomes 200% to 299% of poverty line; Middle Class: Incomes 300% to 399% of poverty line; Upper Middle Class: Incomes 400% to 499% of poverty line; Comfortable: At least five times the poverty line.

Source: U. S., Bureau of the Census; Public Use Microdata files from Census 1980 and the *2014 American Community Survey*.

Urban planning and local governance must realistically deal with the likelihood of population decline and modest economic growth
The colonies and then the US grew more rapidly in population and economic output than European nations since the late 18th century. Most governmental officials and urban planners assume that there will be steady population and economic growth into the future. Population growth in a state or metropolis is a widely accepted sign of prosperity, while population decline is often interpreted as an indicator of fundamental problems, such as incompetent governance

and confiscatory tax rates. Almost all urban and governmental planning is accomplished with the assumption that more residents will eventually come to whatever area is under consideration and their incomes will steadily rise. It is unrealistic to assume that such growth will occur in the future, and even if there is national economic and population growth, there will be major regions of the country where jobs disappear and the population moves away. There are few locations in which governmental services spending decrease in tandem with population declines. Detroit has to maintain much the same infrastructure—streets, parks, and fire and police services—as it had when there were 2 million residents, not the current population of under 700,000.

One year after the end of bankruptcy, there are signs of progress in Detroit. As a result of the current economic revitalization, an increasing number of jobs and residents are locating in Downtown, Midtown, along the east waterfront, and in a few adjoining areas (see Galster, Chapter One). Progress is most apparent in those prospering sites. It may be that current efforts only benefit those who live in a few areas or have the talents to work in highly skilled occupations (Doucet, 2015b), but progress is being made in many sections of the city. Abandoned homes are being demolished in several neighborhoods (see Akers, Chapter Five), and the Detroit Land Bank now has a more effective program for selling foreclosed homes to those who will repair and live in them, not to speculators. Through a new funding procedure, street lights have been repaired in most neighborhoods. During the summer of 2015, most of the city's 140 parks were at least minimally maintained and, thanks to a federal grant, 80 new buses were added, improving the reliability of a bus system that serves a city where one in four households have no access to a vehicle. However, given current trends in the labor market and the specific problems of many of Detroit's neighborhoods, that is, an undesirable stock of aged and dilapidated housing and a population that lacks educational credentials, the city's future is uncertain.

A concluding comment about the federal government and cities approaching bankruptcy

In the 1970s, the federal government attempted to address issues of local government funding such as those confronting Detroit and many other cities that lost their tax base. By the 1960s, economic planners realized that while the national economy was growing rapidly, there were substantial declines in employment in many locations, driving local governments into crisis. Manufacturing employment was plummeting in older cities, while in rural areas, farm jobs were disappearing. Walter Heller, who served as a chief economic advisor to President Kennedy, knew that with strong national economic growth and rising incomes, federal tax revenues were increasing rapidly while tax revenues were declining sharply in many local areas. He proposed that 1–2% of the federal government's income tax revenue be shared with local governments (Wallin, 1998). The idea gained widespread bipartisan support, and then New York City and many other Northeastern towns faced great difficulties as they lost population and jobs at a great rate. At that time, the Northeast and Rust Belt had considerably greater representation in Congress than at present. By the early 1970s, the Republican governors of New York and Maryland successfully encouraged President Nixon to endorse an extensive program of sharing federal revenues. As a prominent part of his re-election campaign in 1972, Nixon signed legislation that shared federal income tax collections with states and 39,000 local governments. One third of the monies went to states that could spend them as they wished; the other two thirds of revenue-sharing monies went to local governments down to the lowest level. They were dispersed on the basis of population size, local tax bases, and local income levels. Thus, a city with a limited tax base and low-income residents received more than did a similar sized city with a strong tax base and a prosperous population. Revenue sharing proved to be popular and was a key support for local governments in the fiscal crisis that raged at the end of the 1970s. Revenue sharing continued in the 1970s but with the elections of Margaret Thatcher in 1979 and Ronald Reagan in 1980, political ideologies shifted. Due to demographic changes, rapidly growing areas in the South and West—where fewer cities confronted a financial crisis—gained more power in Congress. By 1986, Congress and President Reagan ended the federal revenue-sharing program, increasing the financial pressures on Rust Belt cities.

The financial problems of cities were also addressed by a measure that President Ford and Congress enacted in 1974: the Community Development Block Grant (CDBG) program. This was designed to send federal dollars to cities to reduce poverty, stabilize troubled neighborhoods, remove urban blight, and promote economic development at the local level. These are the programs that would have benefitted Detroit. Those who favored a smaller federal government supported CDBGs since non-profit welfare and community development organizations in challenged cities could obtain funds to promote local economic activities, shelter the homeless, or provide meals to the impoverished. A variety of community development organizations benefited from these funds and continue to operate in Detroit. The CDBG program was a popular one since organizations in most congressional districts were funded. In 1978, Congress reauthorized the program to provide monies to many growing cities and rural areas. Over the years, Congress has greatly expanded what might be supported by this program but, as Galster points out in Chapter One of this volume and elsewhere (Rohe and Galster, 2014), the overall funding for the program declined quickly, so the CDBG program does little to mitigate the fundamental problems of cities that lose their tax base. It is time to once again consider whether revenue sharing or a new federal program should be implemented.

Notes

[1] Unless otherwise noted, demographic data were obtained from the Public Use Microdata Files from the American Community Survey, the decennial censuses, and the Current Population Survey available from the University of Minnesota Population Center (Ruggles et al, 2015). Additional tabulations of these public-use data generated by the Census Bureau were obtained from Social Explorer (www.socialexplorer.com).

[2] The opinions of Judge Rhodes of the bankruptcy court and relevant information about the financial status of the City of Detroit are available at: http://www.mieb.uscourts.gov/apps/courtOpinions/searchRes.cfm

[3] In constant 2014 dollar amounts, the median household incomes of white people were $70,800 in 1970 and $60,900 in 2014. For black people, they were $48,500 in 1970 and $30,900 in 2014. In 1970, black median household income was 69% that of white people; in 2014, it was 51% that of white people (Farley, 2015, Table 10).

FOUR

Between economic revival and social disruption: the redevelopment of Greater Downtown and the emergence of new socio-spatial inequalities

René Kreichauf

The next two chapters examine forces central to the production of inequality in contemporary Detroit. We start with the work of René Kreichauf, who, as part of the research project "Smart Decline? Shrinking Cities in the USA" (Technical University Berlin, 2009/10) and the ongoing project "Crisis Cities and the Development of New Socio-Spatial Inequalities," started in 2014, investigates the effects of the revitalization taking place in Greater Downtown Detroit. The approach of these two projects has been to focus on the impact of growth-centered urban regeneration strategies and urban austerity politics on socio-spatial disparities in declining cities. Their empirical research uses both quantitative data analysis and qualitative interviews and observations, the latter being drawn upon for this chapter. Interviews with stakeholders and local residents leads to an empirically rich case study which argues that Detroit's much-celebrated recovery is deeply unequal and is taking place along racial, class, and spatial lines. Theoretically, Kreichauf uses a neo-Marxist perspective on the causes of urban decline and the policy and political reactions to it. One of this chapter's strengths is its ability to explain these theories for readers who may be unfamiliar with them, while also contextualizing Detroit within neo-Marxist theories for readers who already have a strong theoretical background. Kreichauf sees the concept of a declining city not as a new permanent urban development type, but rather as a consequence of the system of capitalism, which cities such as Detroit are inherently connected to.

In the conclusion, he also highlights the concern that while Detroit's renaissance is celebrated in some circles, there is a danger that this could be seen as a "successful" economic model for other shrinking cities to follow, furthering social and spatial inequalities within cities. Kreichauf reminds us to critically question these assertions in light of the extreme divisions being produced in Detroit today. Using Chrysler's celebrity-filled Super Bowl commercials, he cautions against simplistic narratives of either "decline" or "renewal."

René Kreichauf is a PhD candidate at the John F. Kennedy Institute for North American Studies at the Freie Universität Berlin, Germany, and at Cosmopolis— Centre for Urban Research at the Vrije Universiteit Brussel, Belgium, with a background in urban planning and sociology. He is a graduate of the international Master's Program in Urban Studies (run jointly through the Vrije Universiteit Brussel, Université Libre de Bruxelles, Universität Wien, Københavns Universitet, Universidad Autónoma de Madrid, and Universidad Complutense de Madrid. In 2011, Kreichauf lived and worked in Chicago and Detroit investigating social polarization processes and urban shrinkage. His research and publication activities focus on urban transformation trends, social inequality, urban minorities, and migration.

Introduction

Since 2010, Chrysler's Super Bowl commercials have featured famous artists repeatedly proclaiming the rebirth of Detroit. In the inaugural advertisement, rapper Eminem drives through the Motor City, declaring that Detroit "has been to hell and back," again producing automobiles not only for America, but also for the whole world. In the 2012 version, actor Clint Eastwood argues that "the world will hear the roar of Detroit's engines," implying the hope that Detroit will help to reclaim the USA's global economic hegemony. After the crisis in 2008, the two themes of promoting the return of America's (and Detroit's) economic power and the fear of losing that power through competition from European and Asian economies are strongly rooted in these commercials. In 2014, Bob Dylan calls Americans to "let Germany brew your beer" and to "let Asia assemble your phone," but Detroit "will build your car."

Detroit is *the* symbol of urban decline and the demise of an economic era (Gallagher, 2010a). Until recently, media coverage and academic debates focused on the city's long history of decline and its economic, political, and social consequences. Detroit has been described and stigmatized as an "urban wasteland" (Holton, 2013), "Ghost Town" (Koremans, 2013), and "deserted city" (Harvey, 2009). However, from around 2012, media stories and scholarly research interests have begun to change. The aggravation of Detroit's situation due to the global economic and the American housing crisis in 2008, as well as filing for bankruptcy in 2013, have encouraged an atmosphere of a fresh start (see Farley, Chapter Three). Today, it is not only white, male, middle-aged millionaires such as the ones participating in Chrysler commercials who are celebrating this change, media reports about "Detroit's rebirth" (Martelle, 2014), the "Comeback of Detroit" (Tomlinson, 2015), or a "Brooklynization[1] of Detroit" (Flanagin, 2015) are becoming more numerous and starting to change the general narrative about the city. Simultaneously, there is a rise of critical newspaper articles and scholars asking *whether* and *where* there really is regrowth taking place and finally *who* are the ones profiting and suffering from it (see also Howell and Feldman, Chapter Eleven; Putnam et al, Chapter Twenty-three; Victor, Chapter Twenty).

This chapter analyzes Detroit's approaches to redeveloping its Downtown and Midtown (see Figure 1.2) and the consequences for the urban society. To do so, it briefly presents neo-Marxist perspectives on the study on the causes of, and policy reactions toward, urban decline. Applying this theoretical fundament, it unfolds the relations between economic revival and social disruption by focusing on three analytical angles: first, Detroit's recent regeneration attempts and urban policies; second, the (re-)rise of private capital and actors; and, third, findings on the socio-spatial polarization process between core urban areas and more peripheral neighborhoods. Overall, it argues that Detroit's regeneration is strongly growth-oriented; the focus of investment by private actors in Downtown and Midtown dramatically impacts the development of socio-spatial disparities across the city. Detroit's deeply one-sided redevelopment fails to tackle the city's core problems of disinvestments, social-spatial and racial inequalities, and poverty (see Galster, Chapter Two). Its economic revival is only directed to specific areas and population groups of the city. It strategically excludes the city's traditional and industrial workforce, its African-American majority population (see Williams, Chapter Thirteen), and low-income households, and thus not only reinforces existing socio-spatial inequalities, but causes new ones between central areas and the urban peripheries.

Methodologically, this chapter concentrates on the investigation of socio-spatial patterns, demographic changes of neighborhoods, and the residents' perception of the urban development process by applying the following approaches and empirical methods:

1. Expert and key stakeholder interviews with:
   - administrative bodies (representatives of the City of Detroit Planning & Development Department);
   - private investors (representatives of Bedrock Real Estate Services, neighborhood-based private planning agencies, and a real-estate company); and
   - researchers (Alex B. Hill, John Gallagher, Tam E. Perry, David Fasenfest) and activists (representatives of Mt Elliott Makerspace, Cass Community, Eviction Defense).
2. Interviews with Downtown and Midtown residents (23) and shop-owners (9) experiencing or fearing displacement.
3. Participatory observations of the usage of public spaces in Downtown and Midtown Detroit.
4. Analysis of socio-economic data on the city and neighborhood level.
5. The study of political decision-making processes, planning documents, and urban development concepts (particularly focusing on Detroit Future City Strategic Framework).

Understanding urban decline

Urban decline appears to be a complex and multidimensional process, which is examined with the application of different angles. Haase et al (2014) define five main theoretical explanations and research fields on urban development and decline, which I complement by applying a sixth and a seventh cause and research body:

1. stage or life-cycle theories of urban development, as well as neighborhood life-cycle theories, as most prominently proposed by Berry (1977), Hoover and Vernon (1962), and Van den Berg et al (1982), arguing that urban decline is an inherent part of urban development;
2. research on suburbanization as a cause of the population decline of the core city;
3. literature on the accumulation of capital and its spatial-temporal circulation in urbanization under capitalism (ie Harvey, 1989a);

4. theories on territorial divisions of labor (ie Massey, 1995 [1984]);
5. demographic changes (aging, etc);
6. racism, race, and ethnicity (ie Sugrue, 1996; Wilson, 1996); and
7. research on specific urban forms and their relationship to decline, such as one-company towns, cities dominated by a single industry (ie the automobile industry), and processes of lock-in in urban development (ie Sugrue, 2005; Heßler and Riederer, 2014).

These causes and research fields are strongly linked to each other, but the differentiation shows that urban shrinkage has a variety of forms depending upon national, regional, and local contexts, and that it depends on the perspective and ideology on how to analyze and explain it. Following a Marxist perspective on the primacy of the economy, political adaptions, and sociocultural consequences, classical urban scholars focus on the globalization of the economy, global financial flows, and the internationalization of production processes leading to the shrinking of numerous (industrial) cities such as Detroit.

Applying his idea of the *spatial fix*, Harvey (1989a) explains the uneven development of cities as a consequence of the internal contradictions and crisis-prone nature of capitalism and capitalistic socialization (crisis of the over-accumulation of capital). Castells' (1991) concept of the *space of flows* describes that technological innovations have enabled businesses to become more footloose. His abstraction illustrates that spaces, locations, and users are organized by, and around, flows (ie of capital, technology, and communication), which create a network (ie transport and communication networks) between nodes. These nodes are physical spaces (ie cities) that have a specific function for the space of flows. A disruption of the network could lead to the exclusion of a city from the space of flows, resulting in its economic downfall (Castells, 1991). Soja (1992) argues that the mobility and volatility of capital and foreign investment, for which cities in a post-Fordist economic system are intensely competing, are unprecedented in their speed and scope. In the era of flexible accumulation, international outsourcing, and lean production, footloose enterprises have abandoned obsolete industrial plants and infrastructure, and deserted many urban places, giving way to the post-industrial city, whose economic basis is increasingly oriented toward services. Smith (2002) further underlines that urban decline is not only a result of the manifestation of contemporary capitalism's creative destruction of the built environment, but also a form of neoliberal urbanism.

The spatial distribution of "productive capital" (Paland, 2005) and the concentration of political, economic, and cultural power in some cities have caused the decline of other cities that have not been able to position themselves in the global competition for capital. As a result of deindustrialization and the emergence of flexible post-Fordist economic models and neoliberal political approaches, former industrial and Fordist-shaped cities and regions have experienced an economic and urban downturn, whereas new economic centers or even inner-city neighborhoods have gained in political and economic importance (Hall, 1988).

Due to the international division of labor and restructuring of the economy, including a massive relocation of manufacturing jobs from so-called developed to developing countries, cities create decline in the restructuring process, resulting in being cut off from international engines of growth (Massey, 1995 [1984]). Simultaneously, these cities are experiencing an outflow of capital and human resources (Martinez-Fernandez and Wu, 2007). Moreover, innovation and knowledge economies are local development engines, whose futures are more than ever influenced by the strategies of international corporations. Sassen (2001) sees in these trends the emergence of a small number of "global cities," which gather high-level financial and service activities, as well as information and communication networks, whereas others have experienced decline "depending on the restructuring of global networks in specific industries" like automobiles and banking (Martinez-Fernandez et al, 2012, p 220). In this context, Bernt and Rink (2010, p 678) refer to declining cities as "backyards of globalization," which have been abandoned by global capital. Brenner (2004) finally argues that the uneven urban development in capitalism illustrates social and economic inequality in spatial dimensions. Urban decline can thus be understood as the result of these global transformation processes and of the uneven spatial development of immobile capital that is inherent to capitalism.

Detroit, in particular, symbolizes two other valid causes and research bodies: its reliance on a single-industry economy and its ongoing history of racial inequalities and racism. Sugrue (2005) argues that Detroit's economic structure has been primarily based on the auto industry, creating a link to urban development and structure, as well as to social mobility, that led not only to the rise of Detroit, but also to its decline. Sugrue (1996) highlights race and racial struggles as other factors, especially in the North American context. His main argument is that there is a direct relation between urban decline/deindustrialization and racial violence/discrimination, causing the structural poverty of predominantly African-Americans.

Managing decline to generate growth

In the discourse on city shrinkage, scholars call for a paradigm shift from traditional theories and approaches of urban growth, to other ways of planning urban life that would focus on the quality of space, slower but smarter growth, as well as a governed urban retreat (Weidner, 2004). There is an agreement that urban decline has to be accepted and that—mostly on the local scale—new planning approaches have to be defined. Within this framework, there are three approaches and ideologies relating to different ways of understanding and tackling this phenomenon:

1. *Urban decline is seen as a chance.* Cities shall take advantage of the shrinking process by focusing on the individual city's resources and characteristics, aiming to eventually return to a growth path or stop the declining process (see, eg, Lampen and Owzar, 2008).
2. *Neoliberalism and market fundamentalism.* According to this research based on political economy (Harvey, 2005; Hackworth, 2007, 2014a), urban decline is an outcome of market forces and therefore a city would shrink until it reaches a new equilibrium of supply and demand but—driven by market interests and neoliberal policies—aiming to grow (see Glaeser, 1998; Glaeser and Gyourko, 2005): *market-only or market-first planning approaches* (Hackworth, 2014a).
3. *Managed decline.* There is the perspective of perceiving current economic growth as unsustainable everywhere. Decline should be managed by finding alternative development paths neglecting growth.

Recent studies on declining cities provide empirical evidence that after a long phase of shrinkage, some cities experience a stabilization or even a regrowth (see, eg, Turok and Mykhnenko, 2006; Power et al, 2010; Brake and Herfert, 2012). Nevertheless, Martinez-Fernandez et al (2012) establishes that when it comes to the analysis of the impact of different planning and policy strategies in shrinking cities, the evidence is scarce. Some studies highlight that policies are characterized by (1) a restructuring of institutional resources and the strengthening of private interests (Bernt et al, 2012), as well as (2) an increase of socio-spatial disparities due to one-sided growth attempts.

For example, Haus and Heinlt (2004) illustrate that neoliberalism as an answer to transforming economic structures results in the centralization of decision-making processes and selective growth policies by the private sector. Roberts and Sykes (2000) demonstrate that regeneration strategies in declining cities often refer to policy approaches that are defined by regrowth attempts, area-based approaches, public–private partnerships, a prioritization of flagship projects, and higher-income residents in the urban redevelopment process. Flagship urban redevelopment projects, a common strategy in the neoliberal era, further these divides by focusing on selected (often "core") parts of the city, as well as affluent residents, investors, and tourists (Ganser and Piro, 2012; Doucet, 2013). This can result in the intensification of disparities between urban areas and residents, disintegration, and a concurrency of growth and decline.

Peck (2015, p 20) goes on to delineate how neoliberalism has tightened its grip on cities since the Great Recession, with *austerity urbanism* being "the coldest logic of neoliberal rule." His concept explains that public sector functions are often reduced and/or privatized to improve the conditions for investments of the private sector (see also discussions about Eastern Market by Gallagher, Chapter Nine, and Carmody, Chapter Nineteen) at the costs of marginalized groups (cutting social services and the wages of public sector workers, slashing school budgets, and eliminating affordable housing units). According to the logics of austerity urbanism, Peck (2015) states that most cities finally succumb to the (austerity) pressures created by state or federal governments, which transfer budget cuts to the local level of cities, leaving cities and towns in a position of fending for themselves.

Respecting that urban decline is mainly a result of the transformation of national and local production and distribution systems within the context of globalization, the management and organization of decline is restricted at the local level by mechanisms of the political-economic system. As a consequence, shrinking cities are tempted to develop strategies to generate economic activity due to the nature and primacy of the capitalist system. Marxist scholars like Cox (1993) and Harvey (1989a) highlight that due to the dominance of the capitalist system, local politics are structurally obligated to pursue growth. Hackworth (2014a, p 7) summarizes that "within that system, capital regularly flees certain places to pursue higher profit elsewhere. City efforts deemed too regulatory or non-growth-oriented are punished with capital flight." The acceptance of the shrinkage and the implementation of policy responses such as *regeneration*, *redevelopment*, and *renewal* may therefore be a strategic alibi employed by cities, urban policies, and private actors, behind which hides a long-term (and often aggressive) economic growth orientation.

Detroit's one-sided revival and its socio-spatial consequences

Due to its bankruptcy, Detroit was under the receivership of Governor Michigan Rick Snyder and his "emergency manager" Kevyn Orr until December 2014, resulting in a major restructuring of the local budget, privatization processes, and the strict implementation of seizures and evictions. At the same time, Detroit's recent crises and insolvency have inspired speculation about returning to a new economic power.

Urban regeneration attempts

Detroit Future City, a strategic framework plan published in 2013, was written in reaction to Detroit's urban decline and proposed short-term and long-term projects and perspectives. Even though it is not a city document and has not been developed by the city's urban planning department, but by an association of different stakeholders, foundations, planning agencies, and private developers, it has become the city's major guideline for developing Detroit. A city representative explains the influence of the Detroit Future City in an interview: "We [the City of Detroit] plan on integrating things into the city's master plan that came out of the Detroit Future City and we apply the plan for decision-making processes." On the one hand, the Detroit Future City framework refers to transforming declining neighborhoods that are affected by high vacancy rates into farms, forests, or other landforms. On the other hand, it aims to conduct a regrowth of economic activity and population by promoting prosperous neighborhoods, so-called "employment districts," which are understood as dense areas of investments. Downtown and Midtown are two of the primary employment districts where, according to the plan, strategies of economic and population growth and public and private investments are mainly directed toward. The Detroit Future City plan thus aims to further strengthen Greater Downtown due to its concentration of private and public capital. Simultaneously, its strategy is to cut investments and services in less-populated and statistically poorer neighborhoods, with residents ultimately in danger of displacement, such as the neighborhood described by Drew Philp (Chapter Fourteen) or Malik Yakini (Chapter Eighteen).

There is strong evidence for both the introduction of private-led and growth-oriented regeneration policies and the manifestation of racist and unequal housing practices. The plan is dominated by approaches to generate economic activity in Downtown and Midtown in the fields of "digital and economic growth," flagship infrastructure projects such as the development of the M-1 light rail line along Woodward, the establishment of both public–private partnerships, and the adaption of the public sector to private interests. It greatly honors investors pursuing growth strategies such as Quicken Loans founder Dan Gilbert. It was elaborated and funded by organizations focusing on economic growth, including the Detroit Economic Growth Corporation, multimillion-dollar foundations such as Kresge, and private developers. The composition of relevant actors also explains the main perspective of the plan: it sees the organization of decline, together with investments in Greater Downtown and the dismantling of buildings in "Innovation Productive and Innovation Ecological land-use typologies" as a starting point for the long-term goal of recapturing economic activity and the increase of a specific (wealthy) population group as new residents.

In fact, Clement's (2013, p 107) study of the plan proves, in contrast to Schindler (2014), that it is a crisis-driven neoliberal plan for spatial injustice, affecting "impoverished, undereducated, and public transportation-reliant citizens" due to the cut of city services and the planned introduction of large-scale farming. He argues that the plan asserts a top-down restructuring to further dispossess the residents from control over their immediate urban space. His analysis demonstrates that the plan is an instrument that intensifies Detroit's long history in choosing investment in Downtown, Midtown, and other central parts over investment in neighborhoods. Also, Salazar (2014) critiques the strategy of the plan to transform areas of high vacancies into areas of innovation and ecology. He states that this results in the city cutting services, razing houses, and letting roads fall apart, forcing people to leave these low-occupancy areas and to finally let businesses turn it into profit. He predicts that the plan will result in the "land of Detroit, whether individually or publicly held, ending up in a much smaller, wealthier, predominantly white, group of hands."

Detroit as an epicenter of private capital

The aggravation of Detroit's crises, together with the sale of public properties, has stimulated land speculation, change of ownership structures, and investment in the "employment districts," especially in Downtown and Midtown. Also, a representative of Detroit's urban planning department assumes in an interview that the crisis and bankruptcy have stimulated investors to buy properties in Detroit, "seeing the crises as opportunities to come in and buy property that they would have not bought before that happened" (see also Akers,

Chapter Five). This development is primarily driven by only a handful of private actors and it is strongly promoted by tax reliefs and the endowment of public properties (Azikiwe, 2015; Hill, 2014).

In 2010, Dan Gilbert moved his family of companies to Detroit's central business district "in an effort to help lead the transformation of a great American city" (Quicken Loans, 2015). His company, Bedrock Real Estate Services, is a firm specializing in purchasing, leasing, financing, developing, and managing commercial space based in Downtown Detroit, investing $1.7 billion to purchase and renovate more than 75 commercial properties accounting for approximately 12 million square feet in the city's urban core (Quicken Loans, 2015). Under the banner of Opportunity Detroit, it has attracted a broad range of digital and creative entrepreneurs and start-ups (Eisinger, 2015), and it has developed luxury housing in former abandoned buildings and skyscrapers along Woodward Ave. Gilbert's dramatic impact on Downtown's revitalization has resulted in the privatization and "festivalization" (Häußermann and Siebel, 2013) of public spaces (by surveillance cameras, piped music, and private security services, as well as concert and sport events on central squares such as Campus Martius, which are organized by Bedrock). Between 2010 and 2015, Gilbert's group realized new offices and housing, open air markets, extensive street-level retail, street benches, restaurants and bars, a beach at Campus Martius park (where there is no water), food trucks, a dog park, a children's playground, and other green space. Gilbert also succeeded in creating a heroic picture of himself; a representative from Bedrock Real Estate stated in an interview that: "He is not in it for the money, but for the greater good and for Detroit". The role of Gilbert in Downtown represents a *single-interest-led urban regeneration*: Gilbert does not only "own Downtown" (Field, 2013), he designs it according to his visions. The City of Detroit, as the interviewed representative depicts, "helps if he needs help. If we have vacant property, we try to sell it to him according to certain requirements that we ask him to fulfill."

Dan Gilbert's revitalization attempts are not the only, but certainly the most prominent, examples of investors abusing Detroit's situation for their own profit-making. A city representative from the urban planning department also describes in an interview that:

> "in the passing years, there have been a lot of private actors buying buildings and sitting on these buildings, holding up for five, ten, fifteen years for investment, which is the reason why so many buildings were and still are vacant causing blight."

John Mogk, Wayne State University law professor, states that these business models "hold the city hostage" (Mogk, quoted in MacDonald, 2011), preventing progressive urban development strategies and establishing power to plan Detroit.

In an interview, a representative of the urban planning department concedes that Downtown's regeneration lacks democratic decision-making processes and participation. The public sector would have strong limits to influence the development. Hackworth (2014a, p 24) even sees in Detroit's urban policy a *market-only principle* that gives investors, "who have little intent of returning property to tax-paying status," an almost unrestricted access to property: "The pathways for less-than-honorable investors are relatively unimpeded." The "rebirth of the city" (Martelle, 2014) serves predominantly as an advertisement of private actors for Detroit, denying the reality that social problems continue to be a major concern. Due to the restructuring of planning authorities and public assets, privatization, and the growth of private developers, Detroit increasingly depends on the private sector and its interests. While public and democratically legitimated authorities are practically paralyzed due to budget cuts and the clearance and selling off of public services and spaces, increasingly, only a few private investors influence Detroit's urban development. This process, as the case of *Gilbertville*[2] already predicts, results in *de-democratization*—the decline of the democratically legitimized scope of actions of the public sector and citizens—as well as in an *urban incapacitation* of the urban society being put in chains by private development interests.

Referring to the consequences of the urban crises and Detroit's bankruptcy, Peck (2015) explains that economic and political elites contrive to reassert their power over the political arena through privatization and austerity, resulting in weakening the poor, minorities, migrants, and those depending on services in the city:

> They outsource, marketize, and privatize governmental services and social support, thus further incapacitating the state and the public sphere. Furthermore, they concentrate both costs and burdens on those at the bottom of the social hierarchy, compounding economic marginalization with state abandonment. (Peck, 2015, p 22)

Socio-spatial polarization between Detroit's core and peripheral areas

Detroit's bankruptcy has also involved major restructuring of the local budget for services provided by the city. Electricity, gas, and water distribution have been in the process of privatization or being transferred to the responsibility of the state; city employees have been dismissed and wages and pensions have been reduced. In the spring of 2014, the restructuring and privatization of water distribution raised media coverage. Due to the impending sale of Detroit's water department, 30% of the employees were fired and 3000 households that are in default of payment were cut off from service (Kishore, 2014). This sanction primarily affects socially weak residents and has been critiqued by the United Nations as a violation of human rights (Ahmed, 2015; see also Howell and Feldman, Chapter Eleven). Furthermore, it illustrates socio-spatial inequalities in Detroit: low-income neighborhoods in decline are most affected, whereas Downtown and Midtown are not. As Kishore (2014) summarizes:

> This is the real face of the Detroit bankruptcy. While the media and the political establishment proclaim the "revival" of Detroit, what is taking place is the wholesale theft of public resources and the pensions and benefits of city workers and their families.

In an investigation of Detroit's bankruptcy, sociologist Desan (2014, p 126) comes to the conclusion that the bankruptcy is pushing social inequalities in Detroit:

> Many Detroiters are being made to pay for a crisis they did not create. The cycle of austerity into which the city is being dragged may balance the budget in the short term, but it will do little to make Detroit a better place for its people.

Researchers and the media increasingly raise the issue that the revitalization of Greater Downtown exists simultaneously with the neglect of peripheral neighborhoods. Corrigan (2015) underlines that "the wave of gentrification sweeping the downtown Detroit area is part of the bankruptcy restructuring of the former Motor City." Detroit's long-term crisis and bankruptcy have resulted in the intensification of socio-spatial polarization processes. The privatization of public infrastructures, collective dismissals, and cuts in payments have dramatically affected economically weak households. Altogether, there are three trends indicating the development of socio-spatial disparities in Detroit. However, at the moment, there is a lack of empirical data comprehensively proving these trends.

White regeneration

Hill (2014) reports that mainly white actors are organizing and leading the revitalization of the Greater Downtown areas. Investigating organizations, foundations, start-up companies, urban planning actors, and the distribution of fellowships and jobs related to urban revitalization, he found that in a city that is 82% African-American, almost 70% of all regeneration activities are conducted by white people. In an interview, Alex Hill explains that investments are particularly concentrated in Downtown and Midtown—neighborhoods with the lowest share of people living in poverty. This results in the manifestation of "old" segregation patterns and the displacement of African-Americans in neighborhoods of investment. Detroit's recovery is thus deeply unequal and taking place along racial, class, and spatial lines. The media often perceive the redevelopment of particularly Downtown's historic buildings and landmarks to offices and apartment housing as positive for the City of Detroit. However, investigations show that a real-estate company selling and renting apartments on Woodward Ave in Downtown targets exclusively "homogeneous, and not mixed residents," ensuring a "stable relation between the neighbors." Asked about the composition of residents in the visited apartment buildings, the interviewed representative confirmed that the majority is white, often single or couples without children, often working in Detroit's rising tech and creative industries.

Displacement

Elliott (2011) and Perry (cited in Kleyman, 2015) further show that the gentrification of Downtown and Midtown is strongly linked to the displacement of population groups in these areas. They generally critique the narrative that sees Detroit and its core as empty space, thus justifying the speed of regeneration and the neglect of minority groups in the regeneration process. Elliott (2011) argues that "In talking about Detroit as unsettled frontier, we have effectively removed anyone living in marginalized, underfunded, or neglected neighborhoods from the conversation." Tam E. Perry investigates the displacement of elderly and poor population groups in Midtown and Downtown. She gives evidence that the gentrification of these neighborhoods results in the forced relocation of elderly and poor African-Americans. In an interview, she says that she sees a major cause for this development in the sale of Department for Housing and Urban Development (HUD)-housing[3] projects in Downtown and Midtown to private developers. Perry has identified at least a dozen federally subsidized buildings in Detroit's now-thriving Midtown and Downtown areas that might be converted to market-rate apartments in the coming decade, displacing more than 2000 people. A representative from Detroit's urban planning department also points to the problem of displacement, especially of elderly and deprived residents, applying the example of the Griswold Apartments. The interviewee outlines that the conversion of a low-income senior housing center in Downtown's Capitol Park district into market-rate units caused "the feeling of senior citizens to be priced out of Downtown." The Wayne State University sociologist Dr David Fasenfest, however, states in an interview that Detroit's central areas experienced a dramatic change in the demographic structure and forms of *cultural gentrification*, which is starting to cause the displacement of socially weak households. He assumes that the issue of displacement will play a significant role in the future since the housing situation in these areas is intensifying.

My research on businesses in Downtown and the residents' perceptions of the Downtown and Midtown revitalization exemplify that traditional businesses and residents fear or experience displacement. In an interview, a shop-owner, who had opened his clothing store at East Grand River Avenue/Center Street 20 years ago, reports that the white regeneration has resulted in a change of ownership in his building and an increase of rents. He explains that mostly black customers shop at his store, but that this group is decreasing, whereas new stores in the same street, which have opened in the past five years, attract predominantly white people. Nathan Ketcham, a white Downtown resident living on East Jefferson Avenue, states that he would avoid the Downtown area since it has developed to a "Disneyland for white suburbanites and Millennials who enjoy bad public concerts and Starbucks coffee." He is not afraid of a direct displacement, but highly criticizes forms of cultural gentrification that result in particular groups not feeling welcome to visit and live in Downtown anymore. Furthermore, participatory observations conducted in 2011 and 2014/15 illustrate that the places and patterns of homeless people have changed dramatically in the intervening years. In 2011, "everyday spaces" have been concentrated along Woodward, Michigan Avenue, and East Jefferson, whereas the 2014/15 data show that these spaces have been pushed to the area around the Rosa Parks Transit Center and out of the freeway belt surrounding Downtown. In Midtown, there is a further increase of concentration along 2nd Street, 3rd Street, and the southern sections of Cass Avenue, whereas the visibility of homeless people has declined in Midtown's central areas (Woodward and the northern sections of Cass Avenue). Construction works along Woodward due to the development of the M-1 light rail project and *defensive urbanism*,[4] along with the production of privately secured areas in Downtown and Midtown, have changed the pattern of spaces for homelessness.

Further decline of peripheral areas

The housing crisis since 2008 and the insolvency of the city have triggered a phase of seizures and evictions. The foreclosure of homes takes place after three years of not paying taxes. Sheehan (2015) reports that "Between 2011 and 2014 the county repossessed 28,000 properties—homes to some 75,000 people—effectively creating an eviction conveyor belt that escorted Detroit's mostly black residents out of the city." Salazar (2014) and Sheehan (2015) exemplify the correlation between Downtown's and Midtown's revitalization, the objectives of the Detroit Future City plan, and the deprivation of poor and majority black neighborhoods. On the one hand, Sheehan (2015) states that the plan, the bankruptcy, and the dominance of private investors have resulted in foreclosures and evictions in areas that are—by the Detroit Future City plan—future farms and lands of ecology, whereas, on the other hand, "economic titans ... are pumping money into downtown Detroit ... and leaving struggling neighborhoods to crumble." During an interview, a city representative critiques the disinvestment in outer areas of the city, but submits that "there are only a few [urban development] projects; the redevelopment is currently centered on Downtown ... but it should be the focus in the future." Occupied homes have been sold in online auctions, making former owners into tenants charged with paying rents that they often cannot afford, resulting in an eviction conveyor belt that destabilizes communities. The concentration of foreclosures and auction sales in Detroit is mostly in peripheral areas of the city. Hackworth (2014a) states that "the older, blacker Detroit starkly contrasts with a whiter, wealthier new Detroit that's been wooed in by tax breaks and living incentives—which gives these evictions a heavily racial subtext." Harris calls the Detroit auction, foreclosure, and eviction process a massive form of "racial dispossession" (Harris, quoted in Hackworth, 2014a). After properties have been sold at auctions, they are often directly demolished by the Blight Removal Task Force,[5] which aims to position the land on the property market and to open up new economic utilization of the land. Dan Gilbert is one of its three chairs. He argues:

> When all the utilities are there and the land is close to free ... it becomes very cheap for a builder-developer to develop a residential unit. And they are going to develop them ... in mass as soon as we get the structures down and maybe we don't have to worry about raising peas or corn or whatever it is you do in the farm. (Gilbert, quoted in Jamiel, 2013)

Thus, there appears to be a causality chain between neighborhoods of disinvestment, foreclosures and evictions, further disinvestment, blight removal (legitimized and stimulated by the Detroit Future City plan as the city's semi-official development concept), and speculations by new landowners and investors. The areas outside of Greater Downtown, in particular, neighborhoods in the outer eastern and western parts of the city, are significantly affected by water cut-offs, foreclosures, and poverty. However, in Downtown and Midtown, these trends are barely visible.

Conclusion: Detroit as a trendsetter for urban development in capitalism?

The development of a declining city depends on its size and location, the way it is integrated (or not) into (international) economic structures, and the interests and objectives of economic and political actors in implementing growth-focused regeneration policies. It has to be acknowledged that the process is a consequence of the transformation of national and local production and distribution processes in the context of post-Fordist trends, globalization, and the emergence of a concurrency of "winners" and "losers" in the global economic system. Consequently, in the long run, even declining cities aim to generate (economic) growth to further compete in the global economy. Both urban decline and urban policies addressing growth are inherent characteristics of the capitalist economic system; socio-spatial disparities are substantial and unavoidable outcomes of it (Brenner, 2004), not only in Detroit. Due to the difficult economic and financial situation, urban development policies for declining cities are dramatically oriented toward economic growth in order to stabilize both the physical urban fabric and the local municipal budget. As a result, shrinking cities are characterized by regeneration policies that are led by austerity approaches and a few private developers, resulting in the further social polarization of the urban society, the incapacity of the city's administration, and the incapacitation of local residents because of the lack of democratic decision-making processes and the economic and financial dependency of the city on supra-local and private capital.

The case of Detroit exemplifies an urban regeneration process that is one-sided, led by austerity urbanism, and features the unequal spatial distribution of investment. This focuses on central areas and is led by a handful of private investors (*single-interest-led urban regeneration*). They see Detroit's crisis as an opportunity that allows them to reorganize institutional resources and to pick up assets at bargain prices (compare this with Grace Lee Boggs' view on how grassroots leaders respond to crisis in Chapter Twenty-five). The concentration of investment in these central areas, combined with the city's low land costs, land speculation, and privatization of public services and properties, have resulted in the intensification of social-spatial disparities between Downtown's and Midtown's new urban elites and Detroit's deprived population. Eisinger (2015) makes clear that these current investments do nothing to address the city's core problems of disinvestment and abandonment propelled by corporate decisions framed and aided by government policies, from housing and free trade, with an overlay of persistent racism. In this context, Doucet and Smit (2016, p 1) argue "that rather than passively reflecting the socio-spatial divides, these private initiatives in Greater Downtown Detroit actively contribute to the production of socio-spatial inequalities across the city," making Detroit an extreme example of fragmented and polarized urbanism.

Kühn (2005, p 31) reports that there is a lack of interdisciplinary and sophisticated theorizing that is able to explain the complexity of the structural stabilization, the political-strategic strengthening, and the regrowth of cities. However, maybe the declining city is not a new permanent urban development type after all, for example, as Häußermann and Siebel (1988, p 84) outline, but it is a *burning lens of trends in the capitalistic city*. Processes such as regeneration, gentrification, neoliberal urban policy, and the emergence of flagship projects can be found in both growing and declining cities. However, the big difference is that methods, dimensions, and composition of actors vary; in shrinking cities, such processes are intensified due to the weaker position of local governments (in Detroit's case, augmented by bankruptcy) relative to cities more centrally connected to primary circuits of capital. In the Detroit context, there is, for example, the question of whether you can call the interrelated processes of foreclosure, eviction, blight removal, and transfer of masses of land to a small ruling class gentrification. Detroit's establishment of the triangle austerity urbanism, single-interest-led urban regeneration and colonialization of land (Safransky, 2014) may develop into a business model for declining cities, which could potentially replicated this strategy; Salazar (2014) predicts "a modern plantation system for the American city, one that could be easily exported to any municipality also facing high levels of vacancy."

In the 2014 Chrysler commercial, Bob Dylan emotionally expressed that "what Detroit created was the first, and became an inspiration to the rest of the world." Respecting the concentration and intensification of general trends in urban development and the development of new profit-making approaches in land consumption, Detroit may (again) be the pioneer and daunting trendsetter for the city in capitalism, this time in the 21st century. This can also mean that the aggravation of socio-spatial disparities in the context of market-driven urban redevelopment can support new discourses on social justice and a social and smart urban development. Detroit could be the hotbed for this discussion and the development of progressive politics, as well as resistance approaches. Contributions in this volume, such as Kinder (Chapter Six), Howell and Feldman (Chapter Eleven), Shakur (Chapter Twenty-four), and Boggs (Chapter Twenty-five) already represent strategies and groups taking radical steps against austerity politics and the gentrification of Greater Downtown. These anti-privatization initiatives, local campaigns to defend public services, and anti-eviction movements, together with local journalists' and academics' increasing critique of Detroit's current development, show signs of progressive forms of counter-politics. Cities such as Detroit exemplify the social and spatial consequences of neoliberal redevelopment, with growing inequality and polarization. However, they also have the opportunity to develop as beachheads and staging grounds for alternative visions, protest, and fightbacks against neoliberalism and urban revanchism.

Notes

[1]   The term "Brooklynization" represents a model or image which illustrates that an area is being gentrified like the New York City borough.

[2]   Since Dan Gilbert moved his family of companies to Downtown Detroit in 2010, "Gilbertville" has developed as a term that describes Gilbert's drive to buy huge amounts of properties and thus design Downtown (Counts, 2014).

[3]   HUD-housing describes housing projects owned by the federal state for people in need (nursing homes, care homes for the homeless, etc). HUD refers to the US Department for Housing and Urban Development, whose programs aim to

support and strengthen the development of sustainable, affordable, and inclusive neighbourhoods in American cities.

[4] Defensive urbanism—also known as defensive or disciplinary architecture—is a form of urban design implemented in public spaces to prevent particular people from using spaces in ways not intended. It has developed into a popular term when referring to architecture that discriminates against the homeless, that is, due to spikes, video surveillance, and park seats instead of benches (Giermann, 2015).

[5] The Blight Removal Task Force is a public–private partnership aiming to 'to remove every "blighted" residential structure, commercial structure and public building, and clear every blighted vacant lot in the City of Detroit as quickly as possible' (see: http://www.timetoendblight.com/ [accessed September 1, 2015]).

FIVE

A new urban medicine show: on the limits of blight remediation

Joshua Akers

In this chapter, Joshua Akers examines the contemporary practice of blight removal, which he situates in a long line of policies that employ demolition and displacement in urban space. Akers focuses specifically on the role of the private sector in both the production of blight and in blight remediation. Central to his work is the idea that blight is an active, rather than a passive, process and that the emphasis on the removal of blight ignores the actors, policies, and structures that produce blighted and abandoned structures in the first place. As with René Kreichauf's chapter, Akers' work is rooted in a structural, political-economy perspective. He also argues that interventions in blight removal ultimately work toward further inequalities in Detroit and do not contribute to long-term improvements for the city's poorest and most marginal groups (who are often the ones living next door to blight).

Empirically, Akers focuses on the way in which mortgage and tax foreclosures are part of the active production of blight. He specifically examines the role of speculation and a handful of property speculators in the tax-foreclosure auction process, developing four typologies of speculation on Detroit's foreclosed properties. He questions official reports that tens of thousands of solid homes and buildings somehow "morphed" into ugly blight, and articulates the counter-narrative that blight is rooted in how social relations (economic, racial, political) manifest themselves in property and the built environment. Enacting the analogy of an American medicine show, Akers argues that blight removal treats the symptoms, rather than addressing its root causes.

Joshua Akers is an Assistant Professor of Geography and Urban and Regional Studies at the University of Michigan-Dearborn. His work is focused on the market-based production of decline and crisis dependency in neoliberalism. Recent work has focused on responses to crisis in Detroit and New Orleans.

Introduction

> Blight is cancer. Blight sucks the soul out of anyone who gets near it, let alone those who are unfortunate enough to live with it all around them. (Detroit Blight Removal Task Force, 2014, intro)

US cities are again plagued with metaphorical disease. After absorbing mass housing foreclosures, weathering an economic crisis, and withering under urban austerity, a broad coalition of policymakers, foundations, and financiers have dusted off an old urban playbook, cribbing notes on how to remake the inner city through demolition. Flashy tech tools, gobs of data, nifty online maps, and slick design booklets give form and shape to this resurgent threat of urban blight. The fierce urgency of these demolition programs is belied by how these conditions have persisted in disinvested, neglected, and marginalized communities in cities across the US through economic booms and the active erasure of neighborhoods in the name of "progress" over the past century. Contemporary blight remediation is a new urban medicine show, a spectacle built on false promises and negligible outcomes. It is an extension of long-running US urban policies that deploy instruments of displacement and demolition in the spatial reordering of urban economies and racial boundaries.

Past policies such as slum clearance and urban renewal drew heavily on metaphors of disease and primarily benefited wealthy elites. Yet, these programs were overseen by government agencies that held the possibility of constructive public investment. However anemic this conception of the public was in practice, it is now replaced by a deep and destructive cynicism. Contemporary blight remediation is thoroughly dominated by the private sector and its non-profit and foundation proxies. It is a set of policies with limited public benefit and fully dependent on public dollars to dismantle and erase the evidence of the most recent economic crisis and years of willful neglect in US cities. This chapter offers a critical analysis of the interrelated practice of blight discourse and real-estate speculation. The focus on this relationship demonstrates that the primary issue in current urban policy is the paucity of imagination in addressing underlying issues that make daily life a struggle for survival, particularly in post-great migration cities. The invocation of metaphors of disease serves to naturalize these conditions rather than address the ways in which they are historically constructed and perpetuated through investment practices and policies.

Over the past few years, blight remediation programs have been rolled out with various scopes, from places in chronic decline, such as Detroit, St. Louis, Cleveland, and Gary, to more stable or growing areas, such as Indianapolis, Columbus, Jacksonville, and Sacramento. Cities of all sizes with differing economic conditions and growth outlooks are "fighting blight," declaring "war on blight," or attacking the "cancer of blight" (Editorial, 2013; Chieppo, 2014; Coggans, 2014). Although most cities carry some inventory of vacant and abandoned housing, the fallout of the mortgage crisis generated tens of thousands of unoccupied properties caught in foreclosure loops of claims and counterclaims, constricted credit, and anemic demand (Immergluck, 2011). In Detroit, where vacancy and abandonment remain a multi-decade epidemic, the estimated cost of demolishing all vacant and abandoned structures in the city is nearly $2 billion (Detroit Blight Removal Task Force, 2014). A 2014 report by the Detroit Blight Removal Task Force estimated that residential demolitions alone would cost nearly $850 million, with the majority of that money expected as federal funds (Detroit Blight Removal Task Force, 2014). The Detroit Blight Removal Task Force was a corporate- and foundation-funded initiative to map and survey property conditions in the city, develop tools to measure and evaluate blight, and identify sources of funding for demolition. Mortgage magnate Dan Gilbert, founder of Quicken Loans, was the main funder and co-chaired the Task Force. The primary strategy is mass demolition. The primary purpose is the protection of property values.

In general, blight policies rely on federal funding and local coordination to execute a strategy of demolition, and use punitive measures and tools, such as code enforcement, to insulate islands of investment in the urban core. Although blight is on the agenda of many cities, the focus here is on the case of Detroit, where a confluence of chronic decline and mortgage malfeasance resulted in a particularly volatile real-estate market. The response to the growing inventory of vacant properties has been the allocation of federal funds, first through the three phases of the Neighborhood Stabilization Program (NSP) and then through the Troubled Asset Relief Program (TARP), directly targeted at demolition. Alabama, Illinois, Indiana, Michigan, Ohio, and South Carolina are all coordinating the use of TARP funds for demolition. A 2015 audit of the TARP Blight Elimination Program found that the money was distributed to local officials with few controls and a directive to spend all of the money by the end of 2017 (Romero, 2015).

Contemporary blight remediation addresses various conditions. First, it attempts to address persistent and emergent urban conditions in the US. It addresses the material outcomes of chronic decline in many US cities, particularly in the Rust Belt and the Midwest. Cities such as Baltimore, Buffalo, Chicago, Detroit, Milwaukee, and St. Louis continue to struggle with large portfolios of vacant and abandoned properties. Second, it is a response to the material remains of the foreclosure crisis, which left public agencies and cities throughout the US dealing with properties in various stages of foreclosure, vacancy, and abandonment. Local government approaches to vacancy and abandonment are varied and multifaceted. Cities such as Baltimore and Memphis sought to hold banks responsible for the effects of the mortgage crisis; some are trying to use eminent domain to seize foreclosed properties, while other local governments forge ahead with aggressive demolition plans (Relman et al, 2013). The expansion of land banks, side-lot sales, property transfers to community development organizations, and greening programs have all increased during the foreclosure crisis (HUD, 2014). These programs transfer publicly held land to private developers, non-profits, or residents. Although activists, community organizations, and some policymakers have sought to situate this issue within the crisis from which it emerged, these efforts have remained outside dominant policy frameworks that seek to redress an amorphous category of blight as a public responsibility.

A focus on the *production* of blight, rather than on blight *remediation*, is necessary to mitigate the extreme socio-economic costs generated by these conditions. This chapter situates the approach of the Detroit Blight Removal Task Force within a history of urban reconfigurations such as slum clearance and urban renewal by examining the role of rhetoric, technology, and quantification in each of these programs. Unlike previous programs, current approaches eschew the twinned justifications of housing and economic development that animated past practices. Instead, demolition is the means and the end. What underlies contemporary practice is the economic crisis of the past decade and particularly its manifestation in mortgage markets. These crises animate the discourse of blight in the political and public imaginations. It is no coincidence that the most damaging effects are situated in black neighborhoods and impoverished sections of cities (Darden and

Wyly, 2010). Blight remediation is an intrinsically racialized practice (Thomas, 1997; Pedroni, 2011; Darden and Thomas, 2013). Housing abandonment and disinvestment are driven in large part by racial division in US cities, and policy responses facilitate displacement, dispersion, and replacement (Smith, 1996; Sugrue, 1996; Weber, 2002; Self, 2003). What varies is the velocity of destruction, not the target of planning and development. Black and poor areas of US cities are made and remade as policymakers and corporate elites pursue the "highest and best use" or seek to protect investments. Despite the ahistorical and depoliticized rhetoric of contemporary approaches, the target remains the same.

The chapter concludes with an examination of the contours of the mortgage crisis in Detroit and the speculative and predatory real-estate sub-markets that have emerged in the aftermath. The activities of lenders and financial institutions have generated both blight and real-estate sub-markets in which speculators and predatory investors churn properties from individuals and families who lost their homes to an array of buyers, as well as credit to wholesalers operating online boiler-room operations and international firms selling rental investments to pensioners in Europe and the UK (Akers, 2013). The argument *engages* Galster's (2012) regional analysis of a housing disassembly line and *pushes it* by animating the activities of speculators excavating profits from the margins of housing obsolescence (see also Galster, Chapter Two). The need for blight remediation remains, but the focus on the condition of physical structures and their demolition does little to alleviate the factors that continue to generate unevenness in the city. Compared with traditional approaches, a focus on the production of blight and its makers offers greater potential to address the dire conditions than many urban residents across the US endure on a daily basis.

Situating blight

The current spate of blight remediation policies draw heavily on the logic of urban redevelopment exercised in previous decades. The rhetoric of disease, the deployment of new technologies, and the abstraction of social relations through quantification construct specific areas or conditions in the city as spaces in need of intervention. In the 20th century, much of this intervention was justified primarily through a language of economic development, though housing policy was important in softening brute economic force. This section ties the current moment to past practices of slum clearance and urban renewal. It argues that the race- and class-targeting practices of past programs remain firmly entrenched in contemporary policies. What has changed is the withdrawal of social services. The contemporary imagining of the city is a thoroughly unpeopled one—one of dilapidated structures and property values that must be disciplined and then transformed by the logic of finance and technology.

The fear of blight as contagious disease threatening US cities and their continued existence has been invoked in times of crisis over the past century. It is an agenda that addresses a material product of economic crisis. Blight remediation programs, past and present, are driven by elite partnerships, a heavy reliance on technology and quantification, and the rhetoric of disease.[1] Slum clearance and urban renewal were well-funded machinations of a *blight–industrial complex* (policy advocates, philanthropy, corporate elites, real-estate developers, financiers, and politicians) that sought to remake the city for economic gain while rescaling patterns of residential segregation (Hanlon, 2011). Contemporary approaches draw heavily on the quantitative tools, developing technologies, and rhetorical invocations of disease to demonstrate the severity of the issue and the necessity of particular types of intervention. Earlier practices drew on emerging media technologies (photography), computing, and planning and design to frame and illustrate the menace of blight (Chronopoulos, 2014). These tools of expertise are framed as operating like a medical protocol allowing for the identification and location of a deadly pathogen or metastasizing tumor. The rhetorical construction of urban blight influenced not only public opinion, but also legal definitions of government power and its role in economic development (Pritchett, 2003).

In the 1930s, as the Great Depression deepened, the focus of scholars and policymakers shifted from intervention in the slum to identifying its precursors. In her writing at the time, Mabel Walker, a research and executive secretary for the General Welfare Tax League, settled on the following definition as the "nearest satisfactory approach" to the "insidious malady that attacks urban residential districts": "We may define the term 'blight area,' therefore, as any area in which economic development has been considerably retarded, as compared with the development in the larger area, of which the area under consideration is a part" (Walker, 1971, p 8).

In other words, blight is a condition where it is not profitable to make or maintain improvements. For Walker, one of the primary issues in blight remediation was that an owner's price and the amount that could be paid for rational and probable development were incompatible. In the programs that emerged in the following decades, the issue of price was resolved through eminent domain and a legal reconfiguration of the concept of fair market value. However, the inability to mitigate price anomalies persists in spaces of decline, reflective of failing property markets rather than individual demands. This market failure is addressed through massive reconfigurations of the urban landscape; people are shifted and dispersed as land is allocated and developed for other purposes while risk and inequality are shifted elsewhere.

Early slum clearance and urban renewal programs hinged on the objectives of economic development and housing provision. Pritchett (2003) argues that the centrality of public housing in early clearance programs changed definitions of public use and individual property rights, opening avenues for more aggressive demolition programs focused on bolstering economic development projects. For Pritchett, the language of urban blight was a rhetorical tool that increased governments' powers to take property from one owner and pass it to another. A highly contested activity in the early 1900s, the use of eminent domain became increasingly common and more difficult to challenge in subsequent decades. As the power of eminent domain expanded, so did the scope of demolition and development projects. Blight became an essential marker in these projects, and the ways in which it was measured and quantified became increasingly important. In the era of slum clearance, progressive reformers relied on the circulation of photographs and tabloid media to generate public support. The crisis of the urban poor was depicted as a public health crisis and a metaphorical threat to the health of cities and the nation (Craddock, 2000). Slum clearance was a moral imperative that relied heavily on emerging scientific understandings of disease and contagion to justify demolition and displacement. By the 1930s, this movement helped produce a social science and federal policy apparatus that identified "urban blight" as a precursor to the slum. The targeting of blighted areas became a priority, and the emphasis switched from a need for public housing and public health to the economic demands of the city (Walker, 1971). The understanding of how urban real estate and urban blight functioned drew heavily on the Chicago School, from its centrality thesis to its bodily metaphors of the city and the idea of natural transition in housing areas. The racialization of space through redlining, housing covenants, and white violence were subsumed in models of circulatory systems, metabolisms, and the plexus of various activities. From the 1930s to the present, the rhetorical construction of blight—with a focus on physical condition, property values, and business types measured against potential economic gains—has disproportionately affected marginalized communities. Rather than tackle the systemic production of poverty and structural racism, the evaluation of these places as blighted and their destruction are justified through expertise exercising an economic or market rationale. This is not to say that areas suffering from predatory lenders, unscrupulous landlords, disinvestment, and socio-economic isolation should be ignored by policymakers. However, the primary issue remains policymakers' inability to address the conditions that make daily life simply about survival for too many. These issues include inadequate housing, a collapsing education system, limited and marginal employment, and ineffective mass transit responded to with housing demolition, punitive code enforcement, the mass privatization of schools and public resources, water shut-offs, and displacement. These are ongoing programs that disperse people and disrupt lives in the hope of economic gain.

In the post-war years, efforts to quantify the potential revenue generated by mass demolition and construction projects took precedence while the full costs of displacement were neither measured nor accounted for (Berman, 1988; Weber, 2002). The deployment of aerial photography, institutional films, and brochures with futuristic project renderings became an essential tool in the promotion of blight remediation and demolition (Chronopoulos, 2014). These brochures juxtaposed the conditions of the present, quantifying the cost to the city of older infrastructure and poorer residents, with renderings of modern corporate office towers, stadia, residential towers, and their potential economic benefits (Authority, 1946). The targeted areas were marked on aerial photographs with thick red boundaries, illustrating the need for containment and treatment. In the decades following the Second World War, blight was seen as a menace and threat contributing to a rhetoric of a deepening urban crisis (Beauregard, 2003). New tools and techniques were developed to target this metastasizing condition. Politicians and corporate elites often engaged in property shopping, seeking the most advantageous sites for development. This practice was masked as objective analysis by quantifying the subjective evaluations of blight with increasingly abstract forms of measurement.

The construction of blight both as an object of study and as a rhetorical device in policymaking played a key role in reshaping US cities, targeting areas to be uprooted while determining who would reap the spoils of redevelopment. As Pritchett (2003) and Gordon (2003) detail in their historical examination of blight, the rhetoric of disease and the practice of remediation fundamentally altered the balance of power in urban development, reopening the city to subsidized and low-risk investment. Hanlon (2011) takes this analysis further, arguing that slum clearance and urban renewal became a means to demolish black neighborhoods that were out of place in emerging social orders. Drawing on Goldberg (1993) and Sibley (1995), Hanlon argues that the removal of neighborhoods in slum clearance and targeted urban renewal programs is complicit in the rescaling of residential segregation in the US. This builds on Goldberg's (1993) argument that patterns of spatial confinement and separation are reproduced in responses to threats to the established social order. This occurs through a new conceptualization of order that maintains social hierarchies seen in the patterns of urban redevelopment and suburbanization.

Urban renewal marked a particularly aggressive period of publicly financed demolition. Yet, the urban neighborhoods that were most affected by the federal subsidy of suburbanization, broader economic transitions, and industrial relocation were largely untouched by modernist planning programs (Ryan, 2012). The fate of these neighborhoods and the policy interventions within them occurred in a more ad hoc fashion as local governments sought to stabilize neighborhoods and protect property values through clearing vacant and abandoned housing (Hackworth, 2015). In cities such as Detroit, where urban renewal served as the primary economic development tool, the ripping out of neighborhoods, mass displacement, and grand modernist projects were no match for the federal subsidies pouring into suburban development. Driven by interstate and highway expansion, research dollars advancing building technology, generous tax policies, and underwriting mortgages, the boom in single-family home construction quickly pushed the oldest housing stock of many industrial cities past its expiration date (Checkoway, 1980; Galster, 2012; Ryan, 2012). This expiration date was hastened in industrial cities like Detroit by the type of development that occurred in the pre-war years, namely, cheaply constructed and densely clustered working-class homes (Freund, 2007; Ryan, 2012).

Although urban renewal left many deteriorating neighborhoods untouched, changing federal policies opening new markets for finance capital drastically transformed these spaces in the years that followed, with an uncanny echo in the present. The Fair Housing Act 1968, intended to extend credit and homeownership to those living in previously redlined areas of US inner cities, produced massive fraud and predatory practices that left behind hundreds of thousands of vacant and abandoned homes in cities across the US (Boyer, 1973; Downie, 1974; Madway and Pearlman, 1974). Predatory speculators, mortgage brokers, and appraisers colluded to generate loans backed by the Federal Housing Administration (FHA) for low-income residents who lacked the means to make mortgage payments or repairs. When these loans failed, which occurred early and often, residents abandoned homes, mortgage lenders were paid in full by the federal government, and the Department of Housing and Urban Development (HUD) took possession of the house. In Detroit, between 20,000 and 40,000 houses were vacant and government-owned by 1974. HUD officials claimed the lower number while investigative journalists arrived at the higher number by combining the federal demolitions with standing structures.[2] What became known as the HUD-FHA scandal illustrates the variety of actors and practices at work in the production of blight. Fraud and predation were the primary tools used to extract profit from poor and marginalized residents and to raid the FHA insurance fund while transferring the costs of these outcomes on to the public. Responsibility for mitigating the rapid production of vacancy and abandonment was then passed on to local governments with fewer resources.

Despite historical and contemporary claims of blight as a contagion and threat to the entire city, blight remediation remains aimed at narrow targets, from particular neighborhoods in slum clearance and urban renewal to individual structures in ad hoc approaches and contemporary programs. The broad rhetorical sweep lent legitimacy to the programs of slum clearance and urban renewal that focused primarily on economic development and racial reorderings of the city (Gordon, 2003; Pritchett, 2003; Hanlon, 2011). Within a broader framework, rather than using blight remediation as a means to create islands of economic development, current practices service emerging islands of highly subsidized development in urban cores across the US by shifting the costs of blight remediation to the federal level and focusing local development subsidies and service delivery on more stable and wealthier enclaves in the city. Demolition both creates a buffer and erases the visible inequities of the city. The shift to targeted trickle-down service models over the past decade is deployed with increasingly regularity and efficiency in central cities where legacy costs, concentrated poverty, and intense marginalization have persisted and deepened over the past five decades (Akers, 2015).

Blight production

A balanced approach is key to rebuilding and reviving our neighborhoods. It is imperative that all blight be removed to create the right environment and market conditions for successful rehabilitation of other homes and even new construction. (Detroit Blight Removal Task Force, 2014, p 8)

Mass abandonment is one legacy of chronic urban decline, but the rapid increase in vacant and unoccupied structures in the wake of the mortgage collapse in seemingly stable neighborhoods drew the attention of policymakers, politicians, and scholars. Urban blight or blight remediation became the rhetorical container for a suite of practices to mitigate the physical wreckage of the crisis. Since 2009, private corporations and philanthropic organizations have focused on mapping, surveying, and cataloguing Detroit's property conditions. Detroit is not the only city undergoing intense surveillance, but it is the site of sustained multimillion-dollar efforts. The atrophy of municipal government and its incapacity to gather, collect, and analyze data has been replaced by a stream of corporate and philanthropic grants and programs attempting to make property markets legible in the City of Detroit. The Detroit Blight Removal Task Force led a massive effort to survey and map the condition of every property in the city and was funded by Gilbert's Quicken Loans and Rock Ventures and the Kresge and Mott Foundations. This project followed Kresge's 50-year planning framework, known as Detroit Future City, which revealed the scope of public land holdings and the incapacity of municipal government to manage short- and long-term planning projects.

The Detroit Blight Removal Task Force and the firms it contracted with characterize conditions in Detroit as the result of an "information crisis" (Detroit Blight Removal Task Force, 2014, p 72). For the Task Force, this "lack of visibility" hinders the city's ability to "prioritize actions and solutions." The report recommends user-generated mapping, data dashboards, and a mobile app to resolve this crisis. The authors claim that this will allow local officials to make better decisions and empower residents by making the information public. However, there are real difficulties in coordinating information across municipal bureaucracies, and information asymmetries make coordination between agencies and the public difficult. An important aspect of the Task Force's work and recommendations is what is made visible and whom it benefits. These new visualizations and data tools are focused on property conditions; they form a data set that captures broader socio-economic conditions such as poverty and deprivation. However, rather than generating interventions in housing or improved services, these tools are characterized as identifying "market obstacles." The argument for improved public access through online data portals and smartphone apps does not account for the estimated 40% of households in the city without Internet access (Callahan, 2014). The public served in this case is a very narrow section of city residents and a broad swath of real-estate investors and financial interests.

The outcomes of this project and similar programs, such as Detroit Future City, produce a very particular view of the city, one in which the city's operating logic is based primarily on economic activity, specifically standard real-estate markets. The assumption underlying these projects is that markets in cities such as Detroit (as well as Cleveland, Milwaukee, and St. Louis) reflect institutional issues, such as high taxes and limited municipal services, and aesthetic obstacles categorized as blight. This section puts forth the counter-narrative that these conditions are produced *through* the market, as evidenced by the chronic housing crisis in Detroit and the recent mortgage meltdown—a process that produced widespread vacancy and abandonment while generating new speculative and predatory markets that fuel the proliferation of vacant and abandoned structures.

In the introduction to the Detroit Blight Removal Task Force report, the chairs claim that "ruin porn" did not emerge accidentally; rather, "it emerged because it is rooted in the truth that tens of thousands of well-built homes, commercial buildings and clean vacant lots have morphed into an unprecedented amount of ugly blight" (Detroit Blight Removal Task Force, 2014).[3] This observation raises the question of exactly how these structures "morphed" into blight, a question that remains unanswered in the 354-page report. A focus on the production of blight leads to avenues of intervention beyond brute demolition and punitive code enforcement, which is the targeting of specific neighborhoods for violation of city codes with fines and the threat of expropriation if repairs are not carried out. Blight is an issue rooted in how social relations manifest in property. An analysis of blight is necessarily incomplete without examining the interplay of government policies targeting real-estate markets, changes in financial regulation and practices, and the way property is held and exchanged in cities. A focus on the production of blight requires a multi-scalar analysis that bridges the hyper-local with regional activities, state and federal policy, and global financial markets. Galster's (2012) "housing disassembly line" situates the production of blight at the regional scale through analysis of a suite of practices and policies. In essence, he argues, the continued subsidization of an overproduction of housing on the urban periphery generates a surplus of housing units, accelerating vacancy and abandonment in the urban core. In Detroit, this has translated to an excess of 10,000 units per year since 1950 (Galster, 2012). This intervention calls into question contemporary practices of blight remediation by tying blight to an active process, yet it leaves ongoing practices within urban centers unexamined. There is, indeed, an overproduction of housing within the region, but near the end and beginning of the disassembly line, there remains an active contingent of vultures and predators milking, flipping, and exploiting the housing shortage in cities such as Detroit. The housing shortage in the City of Detroit may be attributed to three factors: the first is Galster's demonstration of oversupply in the suburbs; the second is the inhospitable conditions of vacant and abandoned housing in the city— many structures are simply uninhabitable as they are stripped of wiring, plumbing, and windows; and the third is the entrenched structural racism of Southeast Michigan and the intense poverty within the city limits of Detroit that limit the opportunity and ability of residents to access housing in more established suburbs and the suburban fringe.

Mortgage and tax foreclosures

The production of blight in Detroit is illustrated through two types of foreclosure: mortgage foreclosure and tax foreclosure. The mortgage crisis and its aftermath offer an understanding of both the overheated conditions of real-estate finance in the early 2000s and how financial industries actively target the city and its residents. Mortgage foreclosures in Detroit illustrate the depressed conditions of Southeast Michigan but also the industry's relentless pursuit of mortgages to package and sell to the market. Tax foreclosures demonstrate the dire economic conditions within the city and the active practices of speculation and market manipulation at work.

In 2005, Detroit had the highest rate of subprime lending in the country, with 68% of all home loans issued. Between 2004 and 2008, over $4 billion in subprime loans were written on Detroit properties. Since 2005, over 65,000 homes have been foreclosed on in Detroit, 56% of which are blighted or abandoned, and 35% of those are slated for demolition, at a cost of nearly $200 million (MacDonald and Kurth, 2015a). By 2014, Detroit's mortgage market had cooled considerably. Cash sales accounted for the majority of housing purchases in the city. There were 4000 homes sold in 2014, and only 160 were purchased using a mortgage.

For the Detroit Blight Removal Task Force co-chair and Quicken Loans founder Dan Gilbert, there is not enough evidence that mortgage foreclosures resulted in blight. "Existing blight causes other blight. Poor city services, all of it together," he told *The Detroit News* (MacDonald and Kurth, 2015a). Over the past decade, Quicken Loans was the fifth-largest originator of loans in Detroit that ended in foreclosure. Over half of those loans that entered foreclosure are now characterized as blighted by the Task Force (MacDonald and Kurth, 2015b). Beyond the data provided by Gilbert's Task Force, scholars have documented the link between the recent wave of mortgage foreclosures and blight (Immergluck, 2011; Deutsch, 2012; Aguirre and Reese, 2014). This relationship between the excesses of financial services and housing conditions is long established (Boyer, 1973; Downie, 1974; Metzger, 2000; Gottdiener, 2010). The most compelling historical analogue is the massive wave of mortgage foreclosures of the late 1960s and early 1970s. As in earlier crises, the current moment has disproportionate effects on people of color and the poor (Darden and Wyly, 2010; Wyly et al, 2012).

There is an expanding scholarship unpacking the multiplicity of actors and policies that generated the mortgage crisis, from transitions in federal policies to the urban outcomes of demand for derivatives (Mallach, 2008; Gotham, 2009; Immergluck, 2009). A curious facet in the Detroit case is that the founder of a mortgage company is now pushing for federal money to tear down the abandoned shells that he once profited from by writing mortgages. As part of the Detroit Blight Removal Task Force, Gilbert's antics in a White House meeting with Senior Advisor Valerie Jarrett and former HUD Secretary Shaun Donovan included slamming his fist on the table, raising his voice, and demanding the White House figure out how to pay for blight remediation (Halperin, 2015). The wreckage of the subprime crisis has left cities throughout the US dealing with widespread vacancy and abandonment. However, connecting the increasing cost of a growing public land portfolio to the actions of private industry has not been part of the blight remediation agenda. Rather than address this issue as a market failure with a chain of responsibility, the rapid expansion of blight is characterized as a disease and threat for which the cost of treatment should fall on the general public. It is an externalization of the cost of creating liquidity out of spatial fixity.

Beyond the financial practices that generated incredible swaths of vacancy and abandonment, tax-foreclosure auctions remain a mechanism through which the costs of the mortgage collapse and economic crisis are externalized. In just over a decade, nearly one third of all Detroit properties have appeared in the Wayne County Tax Auction. The property auction serves as a proxy for tracking the depth of failure in the Detroit real-estate market. It offers an annual snapshot of speculative practices, investor abandonment, and the economic conditions faced by residents (Akers, 2013). The 2015 property auction had 28,545 properties, with over 10,000 of those being occupied (Kurth and MacDonald, 2015). The initial foreclosure proceedings filed by the county included over 75,000 properties, many of which were removed after owners agreed to payment plans or disputed the county's tax assessment (Kurth and MacDonald, 2015).

Properties enter the auction primarily due to the non-payment of taxes for three years.[4] The county then offers these properties in an online auction, with starting bids covering taxes owed plus fees. If the property does not sell, it is offered again in a second auction where the starting bid is $500. Nearly 90% of all properties that sell at auction are sold in the second round. As the number of properties in the auction has increased and bidding activity has moved mainly to the low-bid second auction, the gap between taxes owed and bids paid has jumped to over $250 million. The majority of properties do not sell in the auction and become public liabilities. The government loses all claims to past taxes and takes on the cost of maintenance, upkeep, and demolition. The speculative market has undergone remarkable consolidation. Between 2002 and 2010, nearly half of all auction sales involved purchasers acquiring 20 or more properties. These purchasers accounted for less than 4% of auction participants in this period. Three quarters of all sales involved buyers acquiring more than five properties. Individual purchases of sole properties —the explicit rationale for the institution of the auction system by the state of Michigan in 1999— accounted for one tenth of all auction transactions during this period (Wojtowicz, 2011).

An analysis of auction data from 2002 to 2012 reveals four types of speculation active in Detroit (Akers, 2013). These speculative types are categorized by the outcome or intent of the practice and include various subtypes within each category. Table 5.1 offers a summary of each type. Although each of these types is quite active, the remainder of this section focuses on auction participants seeking to build real-estate sub-markets from the foreclosure fallout.

The role of speculators in the Detroit real-estate market has a long history. Freund (2007) and Sugrue (1996) have documented the role of speculators in blockbusting by moving black families into white neighborhoods to cause panic and generate quick sales to speculators throughout the Detroit metropolitan region. Speculators would then mark up the property for sale to other black families seeking housing. Boyer (1973) reported on the fallout of the HUD-FHA mortgage scandal in the late 1960s and early 1970s, when mortgage lenders, speculators, and slumlords colluded to sell crumbling overpriced properties to black families on government-backed loans. More recently, speculators are utilizing access to tax-foreclosed properties and flipping them site unseen to investors around the world or local buyers with limited credit options, particularly those who have lost their homes in foreclosures (Goldstein and Stevenson, 2016; Kruth, 2016).[5]

Table 5.1: Speculative typologies

Type	Practice
Speculation	Outright betting on a short-term rise in property values resulting from either demand or ignorance.
Protectionism	A collection of property-owners who bought into the city early in the period of decline and are seeking to hold their property with limited cost until growth returns or the government pays them more than the property is worth. This group includes business-owners using failing property markets to expand their holdings around key infrastructure projects and to gain legal standing in challenging projects that might infringe upon their businesses.
Legalized extortion	(1) The manipulation of the public financing system or the market for advantage by purchasing property within or adjacent to proposed government-led redevelopment projects. These actions push up the cost of the project and create lucrative gains for investors and speculators. (2) The use or manipulation of wrinkles in the property-recording system to purchase a portion of another person's property and demand payment. (3) The use of cheap properties for mortgage fraud. (4) Any act of creating gains by using property and its privileges as a lever against individuals or government.
Tax-washing	The practice of an owner dodging tax bills by allowing a property to move through the tax reversion system and then repurchasing it in the second auction. This practice carries some risk as valuable properties may sell at auction for more than the current tax bill, but these properties are increasingly purchased for the minimum bid in the second auction, allowing owners to avoid thousands of dollars in unpaid taxes.

Public officials are reticent to acknowledged speculation and its affects. In interviews with officials from the City of Detroit, Wayne County, and state of Michigan, there was little consensus or willingness to venture beyond the abstract acknowledgment that speculation existed and was an issue for government intervention and planning (Interview, 2011c, 2011d, 2011e; Anderson, 2012; Sabree, 2012). Outside of large-volume auction buyers, the most common definition became one of "I know it when I see it" (Interview, 2011b). For some officials, the line between investor and speculator was 20 properties, while others drew distinctions between speculation and investment within an individual's property portfolio. As for property-owners, developers, and realtors, the distinction was even less clear. As one property-owner put it when asked if he was a speculator: "No one wants to be called a speculator, and even those that are don't see themselves that way" (Interview, 2011a).

Even volume purchasers refuse the label of "speculator," preferring the term "investor." Michael Kelly and Manuel "Matty" Moroun, two of the largest property-holders in the City of Detroit, claim that their actions are a benefit to the city. They are self-declared investors. Kelly told the *Detroit News* in 2011: "People went out West speculating for gold. That's what it is. You need speculators. It's called investors" (MacDonald, 2011). Moroun told the *Detroit Free-Press* in 2010 that his vast holdings reflected his interest in the city's future:

> For me to own land in Detroit, it was a badge of honor, and it was support for the city. Our fortunes are linked to the city. If the city doesn't have any prosperity, we don't have any value in the land, right? (Gallagher, 2010b)

However, such behaviors are more speculation than investment as they rely on someone else betting on Detroit's future, whether it is government or private development. The holding of property without improvement, the boarding-up of houses left to rot, the quick flip, and the extortion of occupants and business-owners through title errors are all means of the largest "investors" in Detroit. The auction accelerated these predatory practices and increased property holdings for minimum cost.

The derivatives market for home mortgages is often cited as a primary culprit in the collapse of the housing market and the fallout from mass foreclosures fed a national property auction market that grew by 12.5% between 2006 and 2007, to $16 billion in annual sales (Elphinstone, 2007). The type and frequency of auctions are increasing. Wayne County now utilizes an online auction company. In-person auctions continue in small suburban hotel conference centers, often offering bank foreclosures in cities across the country (Gregory, 2007). Some of the most active auction buyers are small firms that specialize in purchasing tax-foreclosed properties in depressed markets and then selling the houses to individuals or other investors. These speculators deploy a web of opaque limited-liability companies that allow for various investors to participate, spread liability, and make tracking actual ownership exceedingly difficult as properties are transferred between various corporations where a rotating cast of investors serve as representatives often from multiple companies. The marketing techniques range from advertisements in investor magazines and online investor sites, to yellow or white plastic signs posted in traffic medians and easements promising a house for little money down with low monthly payments, to Craigslist ads and Facebook pages promising no credit checks.

These speculators often operate in property markets from a distance. Three of the largest out-of-state investors in Detroit are Thor Real Estate of Sherman Oaks, California, Detroit Progress LLC, based in Palm Beach, Florida, and LandConnection.com, a California-based real-estate company. These companies primarily market to investors.[6] Each is active in the Wayne County tax auction and has varying investment strategies. All are running wholesale businesses that focus on other investors while marketing some properties to individual buyers. Although there are differences in their business models, the activities of Detroit Progress captures a variety of approaches deployed in Detroit and cities across the US.

Detroit Progress LLC, based in Palm Beach, Florida, positions itself as a distribution point for both large and small investors:

> An amazing opportunity has been created by the sub-prime mortgage meltdown; will you profit from it? Detroit has seen record numbers of foreclosures with one of the highest rates in the country. This window of opportunity provides a surplus of housing made available to you through DetroitProgress.com. Join us by investing and improving one of the United States most historic and treasured cities. (Detroit Progress LLC, 2012)

The company, run by Edward Azar, sells Detroit houses on its website under the slogan "Rebuilding Detroit One Home at a Time." Azar purchased 249 properties in 2010 for over $325,000 (Wojtowicz, 2011). Some of these properties are offered on the Detroit Progress website for between $1500 and $8500. Over the past two years, the company has expanded its staff in Detroit and extended its marketing from individual home sales to investors and speculators. Detroit Progress posts videos on its website in which it interviews "home-buyers" about their experience with Detroit Progress, focusing on the ease of buying from the company compared with similar operations active in the city. These videos target individual buyers, but the website also promotes the company's services to speculative investors. The company claims to have developed a special relationship with banks that allows it to purchase foreclosed properties prior to being auctioned or publicly listed, though many of the properties featured on the website are county auction purchases in which the company does not have a privileged buying position. The company claims this relationship "effectively puts DetroitProgress.com at the front of the distribution channels of foreclosed housing" (Detroit Progress LLC, 2012). Detroit Progress is moving property titles as a wholesaler to wholesalers. The company offers properties purchased at auction for markups of 15 to 20 times the initial acquisition price at auction. Rather than investing in neighborhoods and housing, these companies are operating as title wholesalers, flipping and trading titles among investors while selling off the occasional property to individuals seeking affordable housing at inflated prices with heavy interest.

The speculators at work in the tax auction saw the aftermath of the financial crisis as an opportunity to cash in on the damaged credit and broken dreams of thousands of people and to appeal to investors and speculators. This developing property sub-market does little to stem growing vacancy and abandonment. Wayne County has foreclosed on 78% of the property it has sold at auction since 2011 by using a "reverter clause" it places in the deed. The property reverts to the county if no improvements are made or taxes are unpaid. This is the pinnacle of speculative investment, in which short-term bets on the ability to move the property quickly to desperate or uninformed buyers resulted in little more than another year of dilapidation. The result is a perpetual cycle of bidding, private holding, deterioration, and return to public inventory for eventual demolition.

Freddie Mac spokesman Brad German offered a succinct summary of the position of speculators and mortgage brokers: "There is no post-sale responsibility" (MacDonald and Kurth, 2015b). This is a common refrain of blight producers, from the new wave of home sellers and speculators scavenging profits from the wreckage of the crisis to large-scale brokers such as Quicken Loans, Ameriquest, Washington Mutual, New Century, and Countrywide, whose loans resulted in the vast majority of foreclosures in Detroit. More simply, responsibility ends once the risk is sold to someone else. This is the same closed loop in the rhetoric of blight remediation: properties morph, things change, but those active in producing these conditions remain obscured. It is these same actors who are quick to point to government as the manufacturer of disaster and demand that the public pay.

Conclusion

The conditions that are captured in the definition of urban blight have debilitating effects on people and communities. Scholars working in public health have repeatedly documented the negative health outcomes of these conditions, such as high infant mortality rates, impaired psychological well-being, high frequency of chronic diseases, and lowered life expectancy for those living in neighborhoods with widespread vacancy and abandonment (Semenza and March, 2008; Dwyer, 2011). These findings illustrate how the material environment created in the production of blight, coupled with entrenched poverty that is spatially isolated and highly racialized, has profound consequences for those living in these areas (Saegert et al, 2011).

On its face, contemporary blight remediation might appear to address the dire conditions of everyday life for those living in these places. Mass demolition clears vacant and abandoned structures from the landscape. It removes or displaces dangerous activities and targets for arson. Yet, it does little to address the underlying paucity of opportunity in these areas or the systems that allow for the continued reproduction of blight. The deeply troubled historical practices of urban regeneration, from slum clearance and urban renewal to urban triage and ad hoc demolition, are intimately connected to the current proposals for blight remediation, replete with the targeting of the most marginalized communities. The presumption of market obstacles fails to account for the fact that markets *produced* these conditions; blight did not emerge in markets' absence. The long history of blight remediation and the practice of demolition in US cities demonstrate how capital externalizes the cost of destruction and captures subsidy for creation while unmaking and remaking the boundaries of segregation and spatial confinement. These past practices coupled reconfigurations of urban space with housing programs and economic development schemes, but the primary end of contemporary blight remediation policies is the demolition of derelict buildings and abandoned houses. Current policies are uncoupled from immediate economic development and completely disconnected from the reality of the housing crisis facing residents in shrinking cities such as Detroit.

The re-emergence of blight as a focus of urban policy is driven by the intense production of vacancy and abandonment by the mortgage crisis. For cities such as Detroit, where the legacies of earlier economic crises remain visible on the urban landscape, blight has been imbued with incredible power. The chairs of the Detroit Blight Removal Task Force argue that:

> Blight is a cancer. Blight sucks the soul out of anyone who gets near it, let alone those who are unfortunate enough to live with it all around them. Blight is radioactive. It is

contagious. Blight serves as a venue that attracts criminals and crime. It is a magnet for arsonists. Blight is a dangerous place for firefighters and other emergency workers to perform their duties. Blight is also a symbol. It is a symbol of all that is wrong and all that has gone wrong. (Detroit Blight Removal Task Force, 2014, intro)

However, for all of the work that blight allegedly does, there is little by way of explanation of how it comes into being, how it affects people's lives, and what happens once the "cancer" is removed.

By placing blight in the broader context of its production, or, more particularly, the production of decline, the focus shifts to how the material condition of property captures the socio-economic frameworks through which the city is mediated and profit is extracted. Decline is an active and evolving process in which speculative practices are enabled by regulatory frameworks and market-centric policies. The mortgage crisis produced vacant and abandoned housing, destroyed life savings, and displaced thousands; it also generated sub-markets of speculators preying on need and perpetuating the cycle of blight. Current policies of remediation and clearance are inadequate and punitive in addressing the consequences of these crises and practices. Rather than a new urban renewal, the contemporary urban condition in US cities demands reparations and reconstruction.

Notes

[1] Emerging technologies have played an intimate role in the construction and identification of blight from the use of photography in slum clearance, mainframe computing in urban renewal and web and smart phone applications in contemporary practices.

[2] The demolition of a home allowed HUD to avoid reporting the property as housing.

[3] This quote is from the opening letter of this report (unnumbered page). The term "ruin porn" is a description of a genre of photography focusing on abandoned buildings in US cities. Professor and cultural critic John Patrick Leary says that the moralistic connotations of the term, of an interest in abandoned spaces as dirty, are misplaced, but argues that "the one place I do think it is appropriate though is in just how formulaic the ruin photographs became. In a pornography movie you know what you're going to get. You don't go there to be challenged artistically and that became the routine of these ruin photographs. They didn't really challenge perceptions they tended to satisfy the expectations one had coming in" (Leary, 2015).

[4] The payment on a mortgage generally covers property taxes. When this is not the case, mortgage-holders can redeem the property prior to auction. In this scenario, the property is redeemed and then the mortgage-holder begins foreclosure proceedings against the owner. Increasingly, these properties reappear in the auction

after the owner is evicted and the mortgage-holder abandons the property, neither boarding it nor paying taxes.

5   Many local buyers are aware of some of the risks of purchasing property in this manner, but they are making decisions based on the limited options available to them, particularly a tight rental market and limited or no access to typical mortgage instruments.

6   LandConnection.com offers properties over the Internet to investors. It lists properties throughout the West and Southwest, Michigan, and Mexico. In 2010, Danielle Ahmadieh purchased 198 properties in the Wayne County land auction. According to the company's website, LandConnection.com began operations in 2000 and offers a "varied selection of land at favorable prices." The company claims that many of its buyers are repeat customers. There is limited information available about the company, and inquiries did not generate a response.

SIX

Reshaping the gray spaces: resident self-provisioning and urban form in Detroit

Kimberley Kinder

After several chapters focusing on the context and structural forces shaping Detroit, we now shift toward understanding how residents live under such conditions. In Chapter Five, Joshua Akers critiqued current strategies of blight remediation. In this chapter, Kimberley Kinder examines strategies local residents employ to manage the disinvestment seen in their neighborhoods, including blight. Her chapter focuses on the concept of "do-it-yourself [DIY] urbanism." Rather than celebrating this process, as others have done, Kinder situates the struggle of self-provisioning in wider national and global trends of economic restructuring and neoliberal policymaking. In contrast to Akers, Kinder demonstrates that purchasing foreclosed properties at auction is one of the DIY strategies used to help prevent further neighborhood decline.

Using examples from her vast empirical research, Kinder illustrates three ways in which DIY urbanism transforms the urban environment: rearranging people in space, renegotiating access to resources, and reshaping ethical norms. This last point is important because many DIY practices are illegal (such as entering into an abandoned home to remove items that might make it conducive for drug dealing). To deal with this, residents adopt a position of ethical relativism, which she defines as "conforming to locally negotiated rules of action that technically violated municipal law while nonetheless maintaining social legitimacy."

DIY urbanism and self-provisioning are common practice for many Detroiters and a recurring theme throughout this book. The community garden of Wayne Curtis and Myrtle Thompson-Curtis (Chapter Twenty-two) or the work of the Detroit Black Community Food Security Network (Chapter Eighteen) provide fresh and healthy food to neighborhoods no longer served by grocers from mainstream capitalism; the Boggs School (Chapter Twenty-three) offers quality, place-based education in the absence of a strong local school district. Such initiatives fit within Grace Lee Boggs' (Chapter Twenty-five) vision of revolution and share the idea that citizens and communities need to take power over their situation because the formal systems of government, services, and investment either do not exist or do not cater to their needs (for perspectives of how racism contributes to this, see the conversations with Malik Yakini, Chapter Eighteen, and Yusef Bunchy Shakur, Chapter Twenty-four). Kinder's chapter also reminds us that it is not just community leaders or activists who engage in DIY urbanism; ordinary residents are often central to these transformations.

Kimberley Kinder is an Assistant Professor of Urban Planning at the University of Michigan. She is the author of the recently released book, *DIY Detroit: Making Do in a City Without Services* (Kinder, 2016). Her first book, *The Politics of Urban Water: Changing Waterscapes in Amsterdam* (University of Georgia Press) was published in 2015.

Introduction

The post–1970s political economic era decisively reshaped cities around the globe. By choice or by force, entrepreneurialism, austerity, and financialization have become key buzzwords defining contemporary urban growth and governance. Alongside the consolidation of flexible business models and market–based urban administration, a parallel and equally distinctive trend has been the coercive entrepreneurialization of residents' everyday lives, a trend most forcefully imposed on low-income communities of color. This chapter explores resident self-provisioning in this involuntary context and its effect on urban form.

In 2014, the City of Detroit attracted international attention when its Water and Sewerage Department began terminating service to thousands of residents whose utility bills were past due. Concerned activists quickly mobilized to form the Detroit Water Brigade. This volunteer-led alliance launched public relations campaigns pressuring the city to reverse its termination policies. Although those campaigns had limited effect, the group had greater success in raising donations of cash and bottled water to provide emergency relief for affected households—predominantly low-income African-Americans (Barrabi,

2014; Detroit Water Brigade, 2015; Russell, K., 2015). The city's termination policy reflected the utility company's newly financialized operating protocols. This policy decision to prioritize money over human life reflected the general failure of austerity politics—both within and beyond Detroit—to provide for basic humanitarian needs (Peck, 2014). In response, the Detroit Water Brigade mobilized "people as infrastructure" (Simone, 2004) by using activists—rather than pipes—as the primary means of distributing critical resources to vulnerable households.

The pressure for Detroit residents to engage in self-provisioning on many fronts—not just in water delivery—is deeply rooted in national and global trends of industrial restructuring and neoliberal policymaking. In the post-Second World War era, the economic transition from large-scale, integrated, industrial production to decentralized, flexible production involving rapid innovation and built-in obsolescence proved profitable for corporations but created new conditions of vulnerability for urban governments and residents. As companies became more mobile, municipal officials felt pressure to compete for investment through pro-business development subsidies and tax incentives (Harvey, 1989b, 1990; Graham and Marvin, 2001), policy shifts that reduced funding for inner-city social welfare programs. New corporate hiring practices also fueled the growth in day laboring and subcontracting, creating a landscape of workers with reduced job security and limited employment benefits (Ross, 2003; Doussard, 2013).

The emergence of financialized urban administration and beyond-the-state governing in recent decades intensified this precariousness. These practices reworked the political identities of urban residents, transforming them from citizens entitled to basic services into consumers shopping for services in a competitive marketplace. In low-income communities of color where residents—for reasons of race and class—had limited access to market choices, residents felt increasing pressure to either self-provision the basic services once associated with urban administration—such as land management, utility provisioning, and public safety—or to forgo those services altogether (Dolhinow, 2010; Mukhija and Loukaitou-Sideris, 2014).

This chapter explores resident self-provisioning in this context of vulnerability. Other scholars explore the creative and romantic side of this new urban paradigm, for instance, through narratives of pop-up beer gardens, impromptu city beaches, and provisional artist enclaves (Stevens, 2011; Herscher, 2012). Those lines of inquiry are important, but the residents enjoying those creative innovations are also the lucky elites within the larger political-economic sphere. The number of people selling food from pushcarts, subletting auxiliary housing units, and adopting abandoned land is rising, and those practices do not come with employee-sponsored health insurance or retirement accounts. Instead, these practices reflect the precarious living conditions that flexible, entrepreneurial, and financialized government administration paradigms have produced for marginalized social groups in cities across the country (Doussard, 2013; Mukhija and Loukaitou-Sideris, 2014).

This vulnerability creates pressure for residents to self-provision alternatives to precarious life. In these endeavors, the normal struggles of everyday living are transforming the logic of cities in places where the normalizing structures of urban administration have collapsed. One of those cities is Detroit, a place routinely mobilized as a prime example of municipal failure in media, policy, and academic circles (see Doucet, Chapter One; see also Hackworth, 2014b). Detroit is also the city where I conducted mixed-method qualitative research in 2012 and 2013 while writing a book on do-it-yourself (DIY) urbanism (Kinder, 2016). For that project, I completed 82 semi-structured interviews, 80 participant observations, 71 door-to-door surveys, and 275 vacant property surveys in four predominantly residential neighborhoods. At the time, after six decades of racialized economic disinvestment and on the heels of the Great Recession, Detroit residents were living through an especially acute moment of crisis. For example, in 2012: the city had 80,000 vacant buildings; over half the municipal streetlights were inoperable; one third of roads were in poor condition; the violent crime rate was among the highest in the nation; and the poverty rate was 36% and rising. Then, the following year in 2013, the city was legally declared bankrupt (Detroit Works Long Term Planning Steering Team, 2012; Bomey et al, 2013).[1]

Alongside these fiscal, social, and infrastructural troubles, in the early 2010s, Detroit was also gaining a reputation for being a DIY city, a place where residents swept public streets, built neighborhood playgrounds, planted community gardens, and organized security patrols (Kellogg, 2010; Laitner, 2012; Christoff, 2013; Williams, 2013). My discussions with residents focused on the strategies they developed at the household scale to manage the disinvestment around them. My larger findings indicated that, given the weaknesses of the private market and municipal government, resident activism was crucial on a case-by-case basis in helping residents stabilize their blocks and improve their living conditions (Kinder, 2016). In this chapter, I reflect back on that research by highlighting a collection of DIY practices that were transforming the urban environment in three important ways:

rearranging people in space, renegotiating access to external resources, and transforming the ethical norms surrounding everyday life.

For residents taking action, their interventions into property management and social control were about improving the safety, stability, and quality of life on their blocks. The strategies that residents used varied widely and included things like recruiting new neighbors, defending vacant housing, repurposing abandoned lots, self-provisioning shared services, patrolling neighborhood streets, and organizing research initiatives. Some residents hoped that these interventions would stimulate market reinvestment as well, but residents without such aspirations also participated with the hope of mitigating the negative effects of disinvestment. These practices were especially effective in neighborhoods where residents combined informal DIY activism with formal civic engagement. Even without significant formal collaboration, however, household scales of action were often strong enough—at least temporarily—to re-pattern the micro-texture of everyday life in many Detroit neighborhoods.

The paragraphs that follow are divided into three sections analyzing the effect that resident self-provisioning had on the city. The first section summarizes in broad brushstrokes the economic constraints surrounding real-estate investment in Detroit and explains how resident interventions in real estate reorganized people in space. The second section reflects on the changing role of the municipal government, and explains the strategies of self-representation that residents developed to renegotiate their access to government and non-profit resources. The third section considers the effect that the atmosphere of coerced entrepreneurialism had on residents' judgments about the ethics of their actions. The chapter concludes with a brief review of the changing role that residents played in urban governance, as well as with a few thoughts about the policy frameworks that could improve the outcomes associated with self-provisioning practices.

Rearranging people in space

Resident self-provisioning in Detroit reorganized people in space. The Great Recession amplified the city's long history of market disinvestment. The tangible correlate of disinvestment congealed in the form of vacant housing, which to residents, looked like holes in the property market. These holes then became points of intervention for concerned neighbors, who used their personal resources and connections to fill those holes by reshuffling people in space.

Detroit's high vacancy rates reflected the city's long history of industrial outmigration and white flight (Sugrue, 1996; Hackworth, 2007; Galster, 2012; see also Galster, Chapter Two). This disinvestment occurred in fits and starts, and the Great Recession was merely the most recent in a long series of economic troubles. Census data revealed that 51 out of 54 Detroit neighborhoods lost population between 2000 and 2010 (SEMCOG, 2011). Property values also declined citywide, although estimates varied widely. Conservative estimates based on changes in the taxable value of property indicated a drop of 15.8% between 2008 and 2012 (Turbeville, 2013), but since most properties inherited their assessed values from pre-recession years, this measure likely understated the extent of losses. By contrast, more sensationalist reports from the real-estate industry indicated that median housing values in Detroit reached a peak of somewhere between $83,400 and $97,800 by 2006, and then fell to around $11,500 to $16,400 by about 2010 (Detroit Board of Realtors, 2009; Detroit Home Prices and Values, 2014). Those numbers likely overstate the magnitude of decline partly because they do not reflect the subsequent rise in sales prices as the recession ended. Despite these numerical vagaries, those numbers nonetheless functioned as important indicators that residents used to frame their concerns about neighborhood depreciation.

Cycles of investment, disinvestment, and reinvestment in real estate are common, partly because it is sometimes profitable to invest in infrastructure and other times profitable to disinvest in that same infrastructure as circumstances change. Disinvestment can become profitable for many reasons. One reason involves "parasitic urbanism," a term used to describe urban growth in one region that is predicated on the decline of other regions (Beauregard, 2006). For example, in Detroit, auto-industry moguls who built factories in the region during the first half of the 20th century then amassed even greater wealth during the second half of the century by disinvesting in those factories and funneling the capital into larger, modernized, non-unionized factories in the sunbelt and overseas instead. "Rent-gap" theories (Smith, 1996) offer additional insights into the logic of disinvestment, for instance, by explaining that older housing units often lose value over time simply because developers build newer units with added amenities, trendier floor plans, and safer construction methods located in more desirable neighborhoods elsewhere (Smith, 1996, pp 58–64). These insights help explain why the growing supply of new housing in the Detroit suburbs, for instance, would reduce consumer demand— and market rates—for older housing in the central city. Falling rates of return encourage landlords to disinvest—for instance, by delaying maintenance or avoiding upgrading—which protects profit margins in the short run even as infrastructure decays (Smith, 1996, pp 64–5; see also Galster, Chapter Two).

This depreciation of the built environment can facilitate redevelopment if some profitable new use for the depreciated property can be devised (Smith, 1996; Lees et al, 2007). However, in many of Detroit's vast residential neighborhoods, vacant or underutilized land abounds, and market demand for those properties is extremely low. As a result, even when real-estate developers and community development organizations acquire depreciated property free of charge, those entities still have limited market capacity to organize neighborhood redevelopment. In a few fortunate cases, urban boosters have touted the economic revival of small sections of Downtown and Midtown Detroit (see Kreichauf, Chapter Four). In general, however, countless public, private, and non-profit-led efforts to redevelop the city's sprawling residential neighborhoods have proven unsuccessful from a market perspective (Orr and Stoker, 1994; Thomas and Blake, 1996; Ryan, 2012). Recognizing this profoundly limited market potential, by the early 2010s, the municipality was routinely demolishing thousands of buildings annually with no expectation for their eventual redevelopment (Wilgoren, 2002; Dolan, 2011).

These trends may give the misimpression that the story of Detroit is wholly one of decay, but this conclusion is far from the truth. Instead, at the peak of the Great Recession, locally embedded business leaders, philanthropic organizations, community organizations, and residents were actively intervening in urban affairs to stem the challenges associated with disinvestment. From residents' perspectives, the interviewees I spoke with about vacant and abandoned property voiced particular concerns about lost equity, social stigmatization, emotional strain, and anti-social behavior.[2] As the Great Recession intensified and vacancy mounted, many residents searched for opportunities to intervene in real-estate markets, most notably, by rearranging the patterns of disinvestment materializing around them.

Patrice[3] was one such resident. Patrice was a recently retired African-American woman who lived in a neighborhood of predominantly African-American professionals and homeowners. The vacancy rate in Patrice's neighborhood quadrupled during the Great Recession, and in 2012, the local government auctioned nearly 180 tax-foreclosed homes in her area. Patrice had several nieces and nephews who were renting housing in other areas of Detroit, and they were complaining to her about the growing problems they faced in their neighborhoods as well. Their landlords were becoming increasingly unresponsive and their neighborhood conditions were deteriorating, all while sturdy, high-quality, single-family homes around Patrice stood empty.

Concerned both about her relatives' well-being and about the future stability of her own street, Patrice decided to buy some of the tax-foreclosed properties at auction.[4] Reflecting on the experience, Patrice told me that she got a little carried away during the online event. She bought seven single-family homes for around $15,000 or $20,000 each. She then telephoned all of her nieces and nephews in Detroit to tell them how nice her neighborhood was and to convince them to move into the new homes and buy them back from her over time. Using this strategy, Patrice filled the vacancies closest to her home, creating a local kinship cluster geographically centered around her house.

About half of the residents I interviewed reported engaging in similar strategies to plug holes in the local real-estate market. Some people spread out, for instance, by taking control of adjoining duplexes or adopting vacant lots just to fill the space. Some residents bought vacant buildings on their blocks and rented or resold them at a loss, just to get them occupied. Many residents who could not afford those financial losses recruited friends and family to buy, rent, or squat in nearby vacancies instead. A few especially proactive and well-connected residents also organized their own informal boosterism campaigns, using mural tours, home tours, and garden tours to attract the attention of likeminded residents and build a real-estate buzz for their area.[5]

These accounts were not stories of an invisible hand guiding the marketplace, nor were they stories about fictitious markets reducing property to its mere exchange value. Instead, these were stories about informal resident realtors searching for alternatives to disinvestment. In theory, these actions could spark something akin to resident- or activist-led re-urbanization (Mele, 2000; Lees et al, 2007), though I did not observe those trends in 2012 and 2013. This limited market response, however, does not mean that resident realtors had no effect on the urban landscape. On the contrary, through their interventions, these residents created geographic clusters of residents sharing common bloodlines or common interests. Vacancy still grew on an aggregate level, but residents intervened to reorganize its lumpy distribution, which created new logics for how people grouped together in space.

Negotiating accessing to external resources

Alongside this reshuffling of people, residents involved in self-provisioning also used public displays of entrepreneurialism to negotiate access to external resources. Public displays of entrepreneurialism were important because city officials in Detroit (and nationwide) had moved away from models of universal service delivery and toward discretionary spending models where resources were allocated based on market potential, not citizen entitlement or social need. With limited political capacity to resist these trends, many residents co-opted neoliberal rhetoric by characterizing themselves as sweat equity investors with legitimate claims to government funds. Public displays of volunteerism should be interpreted within the larger history of shifting modes of municipal governing.

The common ideal-type of a centralized municipality providing universal services emerged in the context of late-19th-century industrial growth (Einhorn, 2001). Cities during this period developed specialized economies, for example, with auto factories clustering in Detroit, slaughterhouses in Chicago, and steel mills in Pittsburgh. Despite this product specialization, industrial cities nonetheless contained a rich mix of functions, including corporate headquarters, professional service firms, industrial factories, and local labor forces. This co-location, combined with the post-Second World War economic boom and financial support from state and federal governments, created sufficient municipal revenue to support moderate wealth redistribution and centralized service provisioning for the benefit of working- and middle-class white people.

This managerial governing model became increasingly untenable during the post-Fordist era of industrial transformation. As the 20th century progressed, US firms faced greater competition from overseas competitors. Concurrently, innovations in production, transportation, and telecommunication technologies made it possible for companies to vertically and horizontally disintegrate their manufacturing processes. These changes transformed the inter-urban division of labor. Instead of specializing by industry, post-Fordist cities specialized according to their relative position within global production networks, for instance, with corporate headquarters relocating to London, factories moving to Shenzhen, and new consumer centers emerging in middle-tier cities like Atlanta, Phoenix, and Denver. Within these reconfigured global inter-urban networks, a handful of global cities consolidated their hold on wealth and influence while the majority of industrial centers in the US Midwest experienced significant disinvestment (Harvey, 1989b; Sassen 2001; Beauregard, 2006; Brenner and Keil, 2011).

Within this context of growing inter-urban inequality, municipal officials began competing aggressively to attract new investment that they hoped would elevate their city's relative position within the global urban hierarchy. These officials moved away from general service provisioning and became more entrepreneurial in their funding decisions, for instance, by providing business incentives and constructing specialized infrastructure in specially targeted innovation districts and tourism zones (Castells, 1996; Harvey, 1989b, 1990; Graham and Marvin, 2001). These trends manifest in Detroit in the 1970s through the 1990s in the form of municipal support for bricks-and-mortar projects, such as the construction of iconic Downtown office towers and convention facilities (Thomas, 1997), as well as policy reforms intended to create a pro-business economic climate for speculative investment (Hackworth, 2007, pp 37–8).

By the century's end in cities nationwide, an intensification of these practices emerged as neoliberal policy advocates pressured municipal officials to privatize and financialize municipal administration, for instance, by selling public assets, subcontracting municipal services, charging market-based user fees, and replacing municipal bureaucracies with public–private partnerships (Peck, 2014). In Detroit in the early 2010s, these trends manifest in the partial privatizations of municipal lighting, water, and waste management authorities (Helms and Guillen, 2013; Cwiek, 2014b; Nichols, 2014; see also Galster, Chapter Two). They also surfaced in public debates over whether to lease or liquidate municipal assets, such as the artistic masterpieces housed in the Detroit Institute of Arts or the historic Downtown park Belle Isle (Gibbs, 2013; Kennedy, 2014). These practices reflected the national shift to "beyond-the-state" municipal governing (Swyngedouw, 2005), a situation that creates not only the opportunity, but also the necessity, for civil society actors to step in and provide services that municipal governments "offload" but that profit-oriented economic actors do not pick up (Herbert, 2005).

Although critics have clearly shown that these political-economic transformations produce landscapes of hyper-inequality and resident precariousness (Castells, 1996; Harvey, 1989b; Graham and Marvin, 2001; Peck, 2014), an awareness of risk does not imply the capacity to resist those trends, at least in the short run.[6] For some Detroit residents, a more productive—if also limited—mode of action involved efforts to redefine the types of practices that counted as investments in urban development. Their interventions did not refute the neoliberal logic of entrepreneurial and financialized governance, but they nonetheless made room in the conversation for discussions about sweat equity investment and informal social capital.

Camille, a middle-aged African-American woman, was one such resident who used public displays of entrepreneurialism to renegotiate her access to government resources. Camille lived in a neighborhood infamous for vacancy, crime, and blight that was nonetheless also an area where informal resident realtors were revitalizing the neighborhood by recruiting new residents committed to community gardens and grassroots activism. Inspired by the changes occurring around her, Camille decided to adopt several abandoned lots on her street and transform them into a child-oriented garden where the neighborhood kids could play. Camille organized neighborhood "fish fries" to "hustle" for the money she needed to buy fresh soil and plants, and she found a suburban, faith-based volunteer group to help with the planting. However, to get the land ready for planting before the volunteers arrived, Camille had to remove the extensive piles of illegally dumped trash that had accumulated on the lots over many years of neglect.

A bulk trash day was approaching. On bulk trash days, which occurred three or four times each year, city contractors drove special vehicles through the neighborhoods to collect oversized waste.[7] As the collection date approached, Camille and her neighbor spent two labor-intensive days hauling the heavy, bulky, and sometimes toxic trash spread across five vacant lots to the sidewalk, where they stacked it in consolidated piles for easy municipal collection. However, on the date of collection, the city contractors drove by without taking the trash because, according to municipal policy guidelines, contractors were only supposed to remove up to one cubic yard of non-building material from the fronts of occupied homes, making Camille's trash pile ineligible on three counts.

Distraught, Camille took action. She telephoned several local television stations and gave on-the-air interviews, where she asserted that city officials had a responsibility not to provide trash services in general, but just to pitch in and use their discretionary resources to help residents like her who were working on their own to reduce blight. The mayor's office responded, and the trash was removed. Importantly, if Camille had simply complained about neighborhood trash in general, the mayor's office would not have responded. For instance, the piles of illegally dumped waste accumulating on other nearby streets were not removed. However, by showing TV cameras physical evidence of her own entrepreneurial labor, Camille portrayed herself as a city investor, albeit an informal one, with a legitimate claim to municipal funds.

Other residents also engaged in public displays of volunteerism to renegotiate their access to public and non-profit resources. For example, some residents led philanthropic donors on show-and-tell tours of the vacant lots they adopted, the gardens they planted, and the murals they painted to demonstrate their merit as potential grant recipients. Other residents organized volunteer security events so that police officers would get to know them personally, come to see them as valuable contributors to neighborhood safety, and give their 911 calls added priority. Residents also created their own neighborhood maps and surveys so that when government money for demolition became available on short notice, residents could use the documentation to convince city officials to spend scarce funds on their streets instead of spending it a few blocks away.

These accounts are not narratives of citizen entitlement to universal services. On the contrary, invocations of residents' rights to basic services were notably lacking in these examples. Activists in other contexts did frame their demands for basic services as a fundamental human right, for example, during the public outcry over the municipal decision to terminate water and sanitation services to low-income households. However, these citizenship-based demands failed to reverse government practices (Cwiek, 2014a; NAACP, 2014a). Instead, experiences like Camille's were stories of residents using public displays of volunteerism, rather than need, as leverage to get access to external resources. Their successes revealed how important such performances have become for residents seeking assistance and demanding accountability from municipal governments, government contractors, or their non-profit partners.[8]

Constructing contingent moral geographies

Within this weak-government context, the pressure for residents to self-provision solutions to neighborhood challenges fueled an ethos of ethical relativism. In the previous era of strong, centralized managerial governing, municipalities institutionalized urban norms by codifying legal landscapes, disciplining nonconformity, and using citywide policies to promote shared expectations. In the context of a hollowed-out metropolitan government, however, self-provisioning became an important mechanism for renegotiating the contextualized moral topographies of local cityscapes.

The city is a legal concept, as much as a physical and economic space, and the transformation of governing practices often comes with debates not only about the moral obligations that municipal governments owe residents, but also about the ethics and virtues that governing officials wish to instill in the urban citizenry (Osborne and Rose, 1999; Valverde, 2011). Histories of urban politics show that the legal protocols of urban morality have assumed many forms in different times and places. In early modern mercantile towns in what is now the UK, for instance, the ruling elite formed political alliances with rural peasants and leaders of neighboring city-states by rewarding people for their support or terrorizing them for their defiance, which created expectations of social obligations among the various parties (Frug, 2001). Jumping forward to the early industrial cities in the 19th-century US, the legal purpose of the municipal government had changed. At that time, city governments were expected to give people the services they paid for, no more and no less. This system of special assessment taxes guaranteed inequality since wealthier groups could afford to buy more services than poorer residents. The system was nonetheless popular because it protected residents against wealth redistribution, which, in the preceding aristocratic era, usually meant redistributing wealth upward to support the rich (Einhorn, 2001).

The growth of industrialization in the late 19th and early 20th centuries generated new instabilities that changed the legal practices and presumed moral obligations of city government yet again. The unparalleled pace of urbanization generated epidemics that jeopardized factory productivity, boom-and-bust property markets that eviscerated the fortunes of large-scale real-estate speculators, and fires that destroyed large sections of urban infrastructure within a matter of hours. These economic threats incited a new chapter of urban governing where the municipality was tasked with ensuring the universal delivery of basic services to all residents and with coordinating economic development for the interests of the city as a whole (Weiss, 1987; Hoyt, 2003). Although the utopian ideals of universal services and a unified public good were never fully realized, for the growing white middle class, this era of governing instilled deep-rooted expectations that local governments ought to have a moral responsibility to improve the human condition through infrastructure development, social services, and the even-handed enforcement of law.

One important question, beyond simply recognizing that these dreams were always utopian, involves asking how the changing practices of urban governance in the era of beyond-the-state entrepreneurialism—including the growing pressure for residents to self-provision—have reworked the moral landscape of the city. The contraction of municipal governments and the curtailment of civic services in cities like Detroit meant that residents in this racialized, deindustrialized, neoliberalized, financialized city had few reasons to comply with government-prescribed problem-solving protocols. Interviewees who engaged in self-provisioning did not abandon their ethical ideals, but the changing character of the city nonetheless fostered a new set of moral geographies and ethical fault lines in practices of DIY urban administration.

Connie, a white middle-aged woman living in a predominantly low-income, Latino neighborhood, provided a case in point. One day in the early 2010s, neighborhood gang members took over a vacant house on her street and began using it as a weekend drug house. Connie was concerned that the drug activity would lead to violence on her block, and she wanted to prevent it from happening. One option would have been for Connie to follow formal municipal protocols developed in the Fordist era of centralized municipal administration prescribing how residents should respond in these sorts of situations. For instance, she could have contacted municipal officials for help and collaborated with police officers to document illegal activity. However, as Connie knew from local media stories and personal experience, it often took several years before the written record of drug activity was sufficiently detailed to justify arrests. Even then, she feared that corrupt officials would dismiss the charges or angry gang members would retaliate against her. Moreover, Connie considered this state-sanctioned option unethical because many of Connie's neighbors were wary of police officers who, while patrolling the neighborhood to control illegal activity, might also arrest or deport friends and family members or write tickets to homeowners for property violations that they could not afford to correct.

Instead, Connie opted for a self-provisioned solution designed to yield immediate results and protect her neighbors from incurring additional risk. On a weekday morning, after the drug dealers had left for the week, Connie went door to door on her street asking her neighbors for help. In her words, Connie "shamed" the men on her block, saying that they had a moral obligation to protect their children from gangs and drugs. She also cheerfully offered to pick up a couple of cases of beer and host a barbeque for anyone who wanted to join her in some community service that day. Her neighbors responded. They met at the house where they used sledgehammers to destroy the walls and stairs, hoping to make the house so uninhabitable that the drug dealers would not want to be there. Then, they removed the porch steps and interior closet doors and used the wood to barricade the doors and windows to prevent people from entering the space. When the gang members returned a few days later, a small standoff ensued involving shouts and posturing, but with the house in shambles and without anyone specific to blame, they eventually left and did not return.

This story raises ethical questions because entrepreneurial residents sometimes used problem-solving strategies that were technically illegal—like trespass and vandalism—but not stigmatized, or even really criminalized, in certain contexts. For residents in precarious circumstances, some types of risky, destructive, or illegal behavior appeared socially legitimate to neighbors who were making trade-offs between different types of risk. For those residents, the dream of using formal methods to solve problems in fully knowable environments was both impossible to sustain and came with significant risks for the people who clung to those protocols. Connie did not abandon her optimism or her moral value system. Instead, she and her neighbors adopted a stance of ethical relativism, conforming to locally negotiated rules of action that technically violated municipal law while nonetheless maintaining social legitimacy.

Other residents adopted similar stances of embedded ethics in their self-provisioning work. For example, many residents said that they favored owner-occupancy and opposed squatting in principal, but if owner-occupancy was impossible and vacancy left their blocks vulnerable to scrapping or drug dealing, those same residents were often willing to recruit illegal squatters for vacant homes as a deterrent against other types of anti-social behavior. Similarly, many residents forcefully condemned scrappers who, in their eyes, destroyed their neighborhoods, but if a house was not going to be reoccupied anyway, then those same residents felt justified salvaging the material themselves and using it to rebuild neighborhood homes, businesses, and community amenities.

All of these actions were technically illegal, but they were also community-sanctioned in certain circumstances. Saying that residents adopted a stance of ethical relativism is different from saying that an imagined "culture of poverty" explains "deviant" behavior as an understandable response by marginalized groups to systemic abuse and exploitation.[9] The residents I interviewed were aware of this "culture of poverty" discourse and often applied it to people they knew, such as the gang members in Connie's neighborhood involved in the drug trade. Residents used different narrative tropes, however, when evaluating the legitimacy of their own actions. Instead of seeing their actions as understandable but "deviant," residents like Connie interpreted their actions as moral and heroic, the actions of upstanding citizens defending the laws that they felt were important for the protection of their neighborhoods. The line between sympathetic and dangerous was blurry, but from a local perspective, one set of actors appeared socially legitimate, and the urban landscape that residents self-constructed reflected those locally negotiated social norms.

Conclusion: outside the mainstream of entrepreneurial governance

The standard trope of neoliberal urban renewal focuses on public–private partnerships, entrepreneurial governance, austerity policymaking, and financialized city management. These trends were evident in Detroit neighborhoods like the Downtown and Midtown redevelopment districts, where venture capital firms, philanthropic foundations, and municipal officials were funneling resources into discrete, profitable neighborhoods. This same urban governing logic generated new disconnects between those privileged areas and the sprawling residential neighborhoods of chronic underinvestment and government neglect. Residents responded to disinvestment in many ways. While some people moved away or withdrew from public life, others developed DIY strategies to mitigate the effects of disinvestment on their street. These DIY practices reworked the logic of the city by reorganizing people in space, mediating residents' access to external resources, and transforming the ethical parameters of problem solving and urban activism.

Resident-led interventions offered many benefits: they slowed neighborhood decay; promoted feelings of safety; and brought much-needed resources to communities. However, self-provisioning also had many limitations: it was fragmented; there were few mechanisms to coordinate among competing interests; and not everyone had equal capacity of participate. Additionally, self-provisioning alone appeared too weak and reactionary to reverse the regional and international structural forces propelling aggregate disinvestment in cities like Detroit. Despite these important caveats, understanding self-provisioning remains crucial because the pressure to self-provision has become a central trait of neoliberal urbanism nationwide and because the strategies that residents use to enact self-provisioning is changing the way cities get structured internally.

From a social justice perspective, the challenge is not necessarily to eliminate self-provisioning, especially when politically viable alternatives are not available. Instead, the challenge might be to help these practices become more stable and equitable, for instance, by giving residents greater legal rights over the properties they adopt, by providing more reliable mini-grants to residents addressing local problems, or by using community organizations to coordinate goals and working methods. These strategies could potentially help residents use entrepreneurial decisions about where to live, how to get money, and how to rewrite laws to generate more lasting grassroots reforms.

Acknowledgment

This article is based on research and analysis developed in my book *DIY Detroit: Making Do in a City Without Services* (Kinder, 2016), copyright by the Regents of the University of Minnesota.

Notes

[1]   For more on Detroit's bankruptcy, see Galster (Chapter Two).

[2]   The relationship between vacancy and anti-social behavior is not clear-cut. For more on these topics, see Mallach (2012) and Raleigh and Galster (2014).

[3]   To protect resident anonymity, all names in this chapter have been changed.

[4]   For more information on this auction, see Akers (Chapter Five).

[5]   The informal resident realtors I spoke with were working to reinforce and stabilize neighborhood property values and improve the local quality of life. Plenty of other people were simultaneously exploiting the weak markets and weak municipal capacity by scrapping vacant structures or co-opting them for anti-social purposes (for instance, see Kinder, 2014). Those practices also influenced settlement patterns but those dynamics are only reflected in this chapter to the extent that they spurred the residents I interviewed to take defensive action to prevent those unwanted activities.

[6]   For competing views on this debate, see Harvey (1989b) and Savitch et al (2002).

[7]   Municipal trash collection was privatized a few years later, but that change had not yet happened at the time that this event occurred.

[8]   The transition toward financialized city governing models following the Great Recession and the Detroit bankruptcy proceedings will likely influence the efficacy of these methods in the future.

[9]   For a critical analysis of this discourse, see Anderson (2000) and Gowan (2010).

SEVEN

Preserving Detroit by preserving its baseball history

Jason Roche

More than one third of the land in Detroit is vacant. For some people, driving past the corner of Michigan and Trumbull, just west of Downtown, means passing by one of countless abandoned lots. However, to millions of others, this particular space is special. As Jason Roche argues, many consider it to be sacred ground. For more than 100 years, Michigan and Trumbull was home to professional baseball in Detroit. It was the home of the Detroit Tigers from 1912 until September 1999. After that, Tiger Stadium lay empty for 10 years until it was finally demolished in 2009. Remarkably, the dirt in the infield—and even anchor for home plate—remained in place (the Tigers moved the actual home plate to their new Downtown home at Comerica Park).

A year later, a small group of baseball enthusiasts—many of whom had worked tirelessly over the previous decades to try to preserve Tiger Stadium—started removing debris and cutting the weeds that had grown over the grass to more than two meters in height. They considered the site to be special and wanted to make the field playable once again. The site is owned by the City of Detroit and the group, named the Navin Field Grounds Crew (after the initial name of the stadium), initially got into trouble with the police for trespassing. Although the threat of arrest subsided, as Downtown Detroit's "renaissance" has grown, so too has the interest in redeveloping this site, which is very close to downtown. While a big box retail development envisioned by many municipal leaders never materialized, the land is now in the hands of the Detroit Police Athletic League (PAL) and a developer, who will turn it into a mixed-use development (including the new headquarters for the PAL), with an artificial turf field for youth sports.

The story of the Navin Field Grounds Crew highlights several important threads of this book; as Kimberley Kinder also showed in Chapter Six, it focuses on the grassroots initiatives of "do-it-yourself urbanism," and Roche vividly details the efforts of the Grounds Crew to restore and maintain a site that they have no formal ownership of, nor legal claim to. Equally important, it also brings to light the existing and growing conflicts about urban space in Detroit. It makes for an insightful case study as to how grassroots initiatives fill the voids left by capital flight and the inability of the city to provide services and amenities to its inhabitants (it is one of Herscher's [2012] examples of "unreal estate"). It also demonstrates how quickly those groups can disappear and be sidelined when business, civic, or municipal entities covet a site in the city. Roche's chapter also illustrates how baseball in Detroit is intertwined with wider historical patterns of race, economic growth and decline, and place attachment.

Jason Roche is an Associate Professor of Communications Studies at the University of Detroit Mercy. He is the director of the documentary *Stealing Home*, which tells the story of the Navin Field Grounds Crew. He moved to Michigan in 2009, shortly after the ballpark had been demolished, and never saw a game at Tiger Stadium. When he learned that these devoted fans were willing to risk arrest and give up their weekends to preserve their field of dreams, he dedicated his professional life to telling their story.

The Navin Field Grounds Crew

"It's 45 degrees outside, the Tigers game is cancelled because of the rain. It's a great day to pick up trash outside the old ball park," says Tom Derry as he bends over to pick up litter with his good friend Dave Mesrey on a blustery Sunday in Detroit in May 2011. A mail carrier by day, Derry is perhaps spurred on by the unofficial motto of the US Postal Service: "neither snow, nor rain, nor heat, nor gloom of night stays these couriers from the swift completion of their appointed rounds." Indeed, no inclement weather has been able to stop Tom Derry, Dave Mesrey, and their associates from their self-appointed rounds. On hot summer days when Detroit's temperature peaks in the high 90s, on cold, snowy days in February when the roads are slippery, and in temperate or rainy conditions in between, Tom Derry and a small group of his comrades can be found donating their time and labor to preserving a small but important piece of Detroit. They spend their Sunday mornings and afternoons picking up trash, cutting weeds, mowing grass, shoveling dirt, and lovingly maintaining the 9.5-acre site they call Detroit's Field of Dreams.

One of the most remarkable stories coming out of Detroit in recent years is the story of the Navin Field Grounds Crew, a dedicated group of local citizens who have spent countless hours of labor and thousands of dollars of their own money to clean up and maintain the abandoned lot at the most famous street corner in all of Michigan. The corner of Michigan Avenue and Trumbull Avenue was, for more than a century, the site of Detroit's historic Tiger Stadium (previously known as Briggs Stadium and Navin Field), a beloved structure, a landmark, and a gathering place for generations of Michiganders. What makes the story even more remarkable than dozens of volunteers performing six years of physically demanding landscaping work is the fact that they have carried out their labors under the threat of arrest. Detroit police have repeatedly kicked them off the field and threatened to arrest them for trespassing. However, they remain undeterred.

What is it that could inspire such devotion despite the risk of arrest and the lack of any tangible reward? One answer is a profound and unfailing love of the place. Such sentiments are felt not only by the Navin Field Grounds Crew, but also by many Detroiters and Michiganders.

In 1989, long-time sports writer Joe Falls (1989, p 6) wrote that Tiger Stadium "has become an enduring part of Detroit." At that time, Tiger Stadium was still the home of the Tigers, Detroit's American League baseball team, but a large number of fans and sportswriters from Detroit and elsewhere were struggling to save the ballpark. Despite a well-organized, concerted effort, their attempt to save the stadium came up short. The Tigers opened a new stadium, Comerica Park, in Downtown Detroit in 2000. Their historic home was abandoned, like many old buildings in Detroit.

Today, Tiger Stadium is gone, but the memories remain, and love for the site also remains in the hearts of the generations of fans who attended games there. The baseball field also remains, surrounded by grass, weeds, and more than a few partially buried chunks of concrete and rebar where the stadium stood. Also present is the 125-foot (38-meter) flagpole with a massive American flag standing in center field, the largest obstacle in the field of play in major league baseball history. To an outside observer, it appears to be a large city block surrounded by a chain link fence. If not for the labor of love by Tom Derry and the two dozen or so regular members of the Navin Field Grounds Crew, the most famous street corner in Michigan would likely resemble just another neglected, blight-filled lot in a city so full of blight in such breathtaking proportions that tourists and filmmakers frequently visit just to observe and document the "ruin porn."

The story of the Navin Field Grounds Crew is the story of how Detroit's baseball history and the memories associated with a beloved civic space brought together a small, diverse group of people whose determination has brought positive change and has inspired many others to get involved. It is the story of ordinary community members taking an active role in determining the future of community space. The story includes many of the important elements that make up Detroit—determination, hope, history, racial tension, love of the city, love of the team, political wrangling, new models replacing the old, abandoned property, and even crime (if the misdemeanor of trespassing can be considered a crime for the purposes of this story).

Although set in Detroit, the story also contains many of the important elements common to humanity—preservation of memory, family, and a sense of connection, even a spiritual connection, to place—that make it resonate universally. In his award-winning and influential book *The Origins of the Urban Crisis: Race and Inequality in Postwar Detroit*, historian Thomas J. Sugrue (1996) offers Detroit as a symbol and model for the ills that have plagued America's cities since the second half of the 20th century. In a 2014 interview with the *Detroit Free Press* newspaper, Professor Sugrue expressed pessimism that Detroit will overcome the segregation and economic depression that have dragged it down over the last half-century. However, in the same interview, Sugrue said that the people of Detroit are more optimistic, as evidenced by the actions by ordinary citizens: "There's a real optimism among Detroiters about the possibility of changing the city for the better" (quoted in Gallagher, 2014).

Detroit is a city with many problems. However, it is a vibrant, edgy town, a city of opportunity, where people are doing some amazing things. Sometimes they do not wait for permission. Artist Tyree Guyton got tired of looking at deterioration in the neighborhood where he grew up. In 1986, he started decorating abandoned houses with paint and discarded junk items. Today, the Heidelberg Project covers two city blocks (see Intermezzo II). The city did not like it at first, but now it is a world-renowned work of art that draws tourists from all over. Graffiti artist and community activist Erik Howard started The Alley Project in Southwest Detroit without permission. Since 2011, it has transformed an alley and surrounding vacant lots into an inspirational gallery of graffiti art with an emphasis on youth arts education. Sometimes, it takes a grassroots effort to bring life back to a community. That is exactly what the Grounds Crew is trying to do.

That energy, indomitable spirit, and perseverance have been displayed by the Navin Field Grounds Crew since 2010, when Derry and his "merry band of trespassers" decided to take their lawn equipment and restore the field they love. During these past six seasons, the people of Detroit have embraced what they are doing, but city leaders have not. The City of Detroit, which owns the property, and the Detroit Economic Growth Corporation, the quasi-governmental agency that oversees the property, both view the site as a real-estate asset. They would prefer to sell the land to developers who would put the site back on the tax rolls and provide economic development and jobs. They fear that any baseball-related activity could drive away potential investors. Therefore, this case study not only highlights the inspiring bottom-up initiatives found in Detroit, but also demonstrates how urban space is a source of conflict between grassroots initiatives and the city's corporate and municipal leaders (see also Howell and Feldman, Chapter Eleven).

This chapter draws on interviews, analysis, and observations as part of the making of the documentary film *Stealing Home*. Work on this film was done between 2011 and 2013 and the film was premiered on October 25, 2013. It was entered into film festivals in 2014 and was broadcast in June 2015. The excerpts from interviews featured in this chapter were conducted as part of this project or were subsequent interviews to elaborate on work for this chapter. Interviews included not only members of the Grounds Crew, but also with experts on Detroit's baseball history, as well as others who reflected on the role that such sites play in society.

The Tigers and Detroit: an intertwined history

The nearly universal love for Tiger Stadium among Michiganders and Detroiters stems from the many memories of many generations of baseball fans who attended games there for more than a century. This story begins with the long history of baseball at the corner of Michigan Avenue and Trumbull Avenue. The next several paragraphs will attempt to briefly summarize 104 years of baseball at the corner, and how the city has changed over the decades.

At the turn of the 20th century, baseball's popularity was growing. Bennett Park, the first professional stadium at the corner, was built in 1896, holding between 5000 and 8000 spectators (Bak, 1998; Cantor, 2007). Attendance that season was 122,148 (Bak, 1998).

With future Hall-of-Famer Ty Cobb on the roster, the Tigers won the American League pennant in 1907, 1908, and 1909. However, they lost the World Series in each of those seasons. Fans turned out in droves. In fact, so many fans came to the corner that after the 1911 season, team-owner Frank Navin tore down the wooden structure of Bennett Park and constructed a new concrete and steel stadium that held 23,000 fans, changing the name to Navin Field. Navin Field would be expanded several times over the next 25 years, eventually reaching a capacity of 36,000 (Pastier et al, 2007).

In the early 1900s, thousands of immigrants came to Detroit to find work for five dollars a day in one of Henry Ford's factories or for other automakers. If the US was a melting pot of cultures, baseball was the stick that stirred the pot. In an interview, author Tom Stanton describes how the Tigers helped his grandfather, who had ventured to the US from Poland, make a new home in the new world:

> "He didn't know anything about baseball. But he knew that if he were going to assimilate, he would have to learn about the sport. So he started going to games at what was then Navin Field. He saw Ty Cobb play, and saw some of the greats that would come later on."

As he learned to converse about baseball, he learned the informal language of his new country. Baseball at the corner grew to be an important part of his life and his family. The story is by no means unique. For many, love for the stadium is inherently linked to the deep connections of family and friends that grew over generations, says Stanton.

When the stock market crashed in 1929 and the Great Depression shut down many factories, Detroiters were pulled together through their love of the Tigers. In 1934, Navin Field hosted its first World Series games. The Tigers lost to the St. Louis Cardinals in 1934. The following year would be especially sweet as Detroit earned the nickname "The City of Champions." Detroit native Joe Louis won the heavyweight boxing title; the Lions won the National Football League Championship; and the Red Wings won the National Hockey League championship. However, baseball was still the most popular sport (Sumner, 2015). In 1935, the Tigers won the American League pennant, then beat the Chicago Cubs to win the World Series, four games to two. Exuberant fans raced onto Navin Field, throwing their hats in the air and mobbing their hometown heroes. The Tigers would again bring hope to Detroit, winning the American League pennant in 1940. Alas, they would lose the World Series at the hands of the Cincinnati Reds, but enthusiasm for the team remained high.

The war years presented additional challenges for Detroit. The industrial might of America's automobile manufacturing capital turned to war. Automobile factories were converted to produce tanks, jeeps, and airplanes in support of the war effort. The Motor City was given a new moniker: the Arsenal of Democracy.

Many of baseball's best athletes joined the fight against the Axis powers. Tigers slugger Hank Greenberg served 47 months in the Army Air Corps, the most time served in the military by any major league player (Sumner, 2015). Greenberg was a hero to Detroit baseball fans and a shining light to the Jewish people in Detroit and in America who were facing bigotry and hostility not just from the genocidal Nazis in Europe, but also at home, where anti-Semitic rhetoric was commonplace, perpetuated by Father Charles Coughlin, a Catholic priest and host of a popular political radio show, and by Detroit's leading industrialist Henry Ford, among others (PBS, 2013).

When Greenberg returned to the Tigers in July 1945, fans and sportswriters wondered whether his military service had slowed his reflexes. He responded to doubters in his first game back, hitting a home run. The Tigers went on to win the pennant, aided by Greenberg's clutch grand slam against the St. Louis Browns. Greenberg would hit two more home runs against the Chicago Cubs in the World Series as the Tigers won their second title, prompting another raucous celebration for the people of Detroit just six weeks after the nation celebrated its victory over Japan.

As the economy soared in the 1950s, the Motor City roared back to life and automobiles once again rolled off the assembly lines. However, as the US started building highways to accommodate the dramatic increase in drivers, suburban sprawl started redefining cities. Detroit's population, which peaked at approximately 1.85 million in 1950, started to drop. In addition to the convenient commutes offered by highways, white flight—white residents fleeing the more racially diverse city to the more homogeneous suburbs—was another factor in Detroit's population decline. This was exacerbated in July 1967 when five days of violent unrest (described alternatively as a riot or a rebellion, depending on the perspective) erupted in Detroit. By 1970, Detroit's population had dwindled to just over 1.5 million. By 1980, it was just over 1.2 million. Today, the city's population is estimated at approximately 689,000.

Racial prejudice would also affect the Tigers. Jackie Robinson broke the color barrier in 1947, becoming the first African-American major-leaguer. Baseball as a whole quickly integrated as other teams added stars from the Negro leagues to their rosters. However, the Tigers did not have an African-American on their roster until 1958, a significant point of contention among Detroit's large African-American community. Some preachers, union representatives, and other civil rights leaders formed the Boycott Briggs Stadium Committee (Bak, 1998). Many black Detroiters felt unwelcome at the stadium, a fact that, even four decades later, would impede efforts to save Tiger Stadium.

In 1961, new team-owner John Fetzer renamed the building Tiger Stadium. Although they did not win a world series from 1945 until 1968, the team generated excitement, contending for a pennant in several years. In 1953, outfielder Al Kaline joined the squad. He would end up playing for 22 seasons, earning the nickname "Mr. Tiger." In 1963, Willie Horton joined the team. The youngest of 21 children, Horton had grown up in Northwest Detroit. He would become the first African-American star of the Tigers. In addition to his exploits on the field, Horton is also renowned for his efforts to restore peace during the rioting in 1967. While large parts of the city were burning, Willie Horton ventured into the volatile 12th Street neighborhood in his Tigers uniform, urging people to stay calm, but to no avail (Cantor, 2007).

The Tigers nearly won the American League pennant in 1967, losing the final game of the season to the California Angels and missing the playoffs by one game. In 1968, the highly motivated Tigers succeeded in winning the pennant, helping bring some healing to the deeply divided city and region.[1]

The Tigers faced the National League champion St. Louis Cardinals in the World Series. Down three games to one in the best-of-seven series, the Tigers were facing elimination. However, the heroic play of left-fielder Willie Horton and pitcher Mickey Lolich helped the team win three games in a row and win the World Series. Black and white Detroiters came together to celebrate with a victory parade through Downtown.

In the 1980s, crime increased. Some people called Detroit "the Murder City" instead of the Motor City. Detroit's white and middle-class black population plummeted, and auto manufacturing slumped. However, the 1984 Tigers inspired the city by doing the unthinkable. Led by manager Sparky Anderson and such stars as Alan Trammel, Lou Whittaker, and Kirk Gibson, they shocked the major leagues with an astonishing start to the season, winning 35 out of their first 40 games, a feat unmatched before or after. They would win the American League East, the American League pennant, and the World Series at the corner. The Tigers captured baseball's crown in convincing fashion, beating the San Diego Padres four games to one.

Detroit rejoiced. However, outside Tiger Stadium, pandemonium erupted as the celebration turned violent. Fans, most of them white, overturned and burned at least two cars, including a police car. According to University of Detroit Mercy professor emeritus and historian John Staudenmaier, the 34 arrests were slightly fewer than the number of rowdy fans arrested after the San Francisco 49ers won the National Football League's Super Bowl in 1985. However, because of racial bias in the media and the general public, Detroit's reputation was further tarnished in the national media, which viewed Detroit's celebrations as "rioting" and San Francisco's celebrations as "an explosion of joyful excitement."

After the mayhem, the city celebrated properly. For Navin Field Grounds Crew member Joe Michnuk, a clubhouse security guard for the Tigers at the time, it was a dream come true: "I was the luckiest guy in Detroit," he recalls. Tigers manager Sparky Anderson invited Michnuk to ride with him in a convertible in the Tigers victory parade through the streets of Detroit: "I kept telling him to pinch me because I must be dreaming," Michnuk recalls.

It was about this time that team-owners started making rumblings about the need for a new stadium. The stadium had been built in 1912 as Navin Field, expanded and renamed Briggs Stadium in 1938, and updated several times before 1984. Tigers' owner Tom Monaghan, founder of Domino's Pizza, believed a new stadium would be better suited to making money and helping the team remain competitive in the world of baseball free agency, when players' salaries were rising exponentially.

However, fans fiercely resisted efforts to exit their beloved baseball home. The stadium contained so much important baseball history that they felt it must be preserved. The Tiger Stadium Fan Club was formed, actively seeking to save the ballpark and prevent public financing of a new one. On April 20, 1988, exactly 76 years after the opening of Navin Field, more than 1000 fans joined hands and encircled the building, baseball's first-ever "stadium hug."

However, Monaghan, and later his successor Mike Ilitch, the founder of Little Caesar's Pizza, who bought the team in 1992, wanted a new stadium that would generate more revenue—a stadium with luxury suites, restaurants, and team-owned parking lots. Through most of the 1990s, a public relations and legal battle was waged between the team and the Tiger Stadium Fan Club. The Fan Club achieved notable successes. In 1991, the stadium was listed on the National Trust for Historic Preservations' annual list of most important endangered historic places and listed on the National Register of

Historic Places (Bak, 1998). In 1992, Detroit residents passed a ballot referendum stating that "no public tax subsidies shall be used for any stadium construction."[2] However, in 1995, the city council repealed this referendum, clearing the way for a new stadium to be built near Detroit's Downtown.

The public relations efforts on behalf of the new stadium deal were illustrative of Detroit's deep racial divide. Politicians in favor of the deal, including then Mayor Dennis Archer, publicly argued that opponents of the new stadium were "outsiders," a not-so-thinly veiled reference to white former Detroiters who had fled to the suburbs. The Tiger Stadium Fan Club included many members, both black and white, who lived within the city limits, as well as many suburbanites. However, the message appealed strongly to Detroit's mostly black voting base. In March 1996, after a $600,000 public relations and advertising blitz by the Tigers (Bak, 1998), voters overwhelmingly approved the deal for a new stadium.

The 1999 season marked the Tigers' final season at the corner of Michigan and Trumbull. Newspaper publisher and author Tom Stanton sold his newspapers and devoted his summer to attending every home game at Tiger Stadium, the basis for his award-winning book *The Final Season* (Stanton, 2001). In the final game, on September 27, 1999, fans waved banners with messages that read "Goodbye, old friend," "Detroit's home of baseball," and "today there is crying in baseball."

Adam Milliken, a lifelong Detroiter and member of the Navin Field Grounds Crew, recalls sitting in the upper-deck bleachers at the final game:

> "I had my camera with me, and I put it down. And I'm just bawlin' like a little kid. And I'm just filming this and I see all these men crying. So I just put my camera down and I let it film me crying too…. I've looked at that tape, but I've never looked at the tape of the final game. I cannot watch it. It breaks my heart."

The Tigers moved to the new stadium to open the 2000 baseball season, named Comerica Park after its corporate sponsor Comerica Bank. It features a beautiful view of a vibrant Downtown that is enjoying a new renaissance. The concourses are filled with restaurants, souvenir shops, and rides and games for children. There are also monuments to the great teams and men of the Tigers' past. However, to Tiger Stadium fans, something is still missing: "These seats don't compare," pined Tom Derry at a game in Comerica Park in 2011, "They're much further away. They are much higher in the air and much further away from the action."

Despite promises that a new stadium would help make the team more competitive, the Tigers' first few seasons at Comerica Park did not produce any championships. The Tigers endured their worst season ever in 2003, winning only 43 games and losing 119, one of the worst seasons by any team in the history of modern baseball. Just three years after that abysmal season, the Tigers won the American League pennant. They lost to the St. Louis Cardinals in the World Series, but the team brought hope back to the city.

The years 2007 through 2010 were especially tough for the Motor City. The nation was in the depths of the Great Recession. Two of Detroit's "Big Three" automakers declared bankruptcy in 2009. The future of the automotive industry, Detroit's bread and butter for nearly a century, was seriously in doubt. Chrysler and General Motors survived by accepting government bailouts. In a show of community spirit, the Tigers provided free advertising space in Comerica Park for long-time Tigers advertiser Chevrolet, a General Motors brand. The Tigers narrowly missed making the playoffs in 2009, losing 6–5 to the Minnesota Twins in a 12-inning tie-breaker game.

Fans move to preserve Tiger Stadium's ball field

Tiger Stadium, still owned by the city, sat empty and forlorn for nearly a decade. However, fans had still not given up on preserving it. Thanks to the efforts of US Senator Carl Levin, a non-profit group called the Old Tiger Stadium Conservancy was awarded a $3.5 million earmark from the federal government to try to preserve the site. However, the Detroit Economic Growth Corporation rejected all proposals to save the stadium. In 2008, the city began demolition. Despite attempts to preserve a portion of the stadium and turn it into a museum, demolition was completed in September 2009.

The idea for the Navin Field Grounds Crew came about in 2010, one year after Tiger Stadium was demolished. Long-time Tigers broadcaster Ernie Harwell passed away in early May. The Tigers hosted a public tribute at Comerica Park, where his body lay in state. Tom Derry joined thousands of other fans in paying tribute to the beloved announcer, whose colorful descriptions of baseball games had earned him a spot in the National Baseball Hall of Fame. That night, watching the news on television, Derry saw a report about some fans paying their respects by playing catch at the old field. He decided to do the same.

145

The following Sunday, Mother's Day of 2010, he took his girlfriend Sarah Aittama and her son Erik, 11, to the field. When he saw the field, his heart sank. Tall weeds had taken over the base paths, the infield, and the pitcher's mound: "You could barely recognize the field," he recalled. He could not stand the thought of this important gathering place becoming just another abandoned lot in Detroit. "Heck, I've got a riding mower," he thought to himself; "I knew I could cut the grass and thought maybe some of my friends would help."

Still stinging from the loss of Ernie Harwell, Tom's conscience would not let him walk away from this beloved site that held so many memories, not just for Tom, but for countless other fans. He was not sure how to go about it or who to call for permission. However, when he returned home, he phoned his friend Frank Rashid, a professor at Marygrove College in Detroit and a founding member of the Tiger Stadium Fan Club. Rashid wished him luck and said he would support Tom in his efforts, but did not expect a great deal of success.

Tom called a few of his friends to help him get started. Dave Mesrey organized an event and invited many others to help to clean up the site. The following Wednesday, Tom, Dave, and about two dozen others showed up: "We were just literally digging weeds out by hand, with shovels, turning over the dirt," Derry recalls. The event was captured by a television news crew. Derry, a resident of the suburb of Redford, Michigan, less than two miles (1.6 km) west of the city limits, declined to be interviewed, fearing that he would be labeled an outsider. Another volunteer, Detroit resident John Prusak, was interviewed instead.

The volunteers were not expecting opposition from the city. However, that evening, an official from the Detroit Economic Growth Corporation saw them working and stopped to chide them. As Derry recalls, "He asked Frank Rashid, 'Why didn't you ask for permission?' But Frank said, 'Where would that get us?' He knew it was better to ask for forgiveness than to ask for permission." After making it clear that these amateur groundskeepers were not welcome there, the official left. However, a short time later, a police car drove up. The officer asked if anyone had called in a complaint. The volunteers told him that they had not, so the officer left them alone. However, that was not the last they would hear from police. As there was so much work to do, Tom and Dave and the crew decided to make clean-up a weekly task. Several times, the police chased them off and threatened them with trespassing. Tom noted:

"They told us to get off the field and if we ever came back, we'd be arrested. So we decided to start showing up on

Sundays instead, flying under the radar. City offices are closed on Sundays and we're less likely to be bothered.... That first year was rough physically but worse mentally, being threatened with arrest for trespassing. How would it affect my job? Would they confiscate my mower? I don't have a lot of money to buy a new one. It was very tough."

Undeterred, they rolled up their sleeves and kept busy at the corner. In addition to Dave Mesrey and Tom Derry, a significant group of regular workers added their labor. Tom's boyhood friend "Baseline" Bob Blanchard, Tom's girlfriend Sarah Aittama, her son Erik, Corktown resident John Prusak, freelance photographer Sean Connelly, Doug Puz, professor Frank Rashid, and his son Joe were among those who showed up at the beginning of 2010. As word spread, more people would join, including Joe Michnuk, a native Detroiter who had worked as a clubhouse security guard for the Tigers in the 1980s.

Using a few riding mowers and a few push mowers, they made slow progress. They focused on the ball field itself. When they did, tall weeds sprung up around the perimeter of the field where the stadium itself once stood. In some cases, the weeds had grown over eight feet (2.6 meters) tall (see Figure 7.1). In most places, they were more than five feet (1.6 meters) tall. The weeds proved to be a formidable foe. A dozen volunteers with consumer-grade equipment did not make much of a difference to the overall appearance of the site. With more than nine acres to cover, they quickly realized that this would not work. For nine Sundays in 2010, Tom Derry rented a Brush Hog, a motor-propelled push mower capable of cutting down brush up to six feet (two meters) tall and saplings with a diameter of up to two inches.[3] Rental fees were about $100 per day. Derry paid the costs out of his own funds, deciding that even on his modest postal worker's salary and six-day work week, he would devote his Sundays—his only day off—and a significant amount of cash to his cause (see Figure 7.2). He was not going to let more than a century of Detroit's history fall prey to neglect and turn into yet another blighted property. Other supporters chipped in money and equipment from their own pockets as well.

By 2011, Derry had come up with a name for the volunteers—the Navin Field Grounds Crew. As the baseball season started, Dave Mesrey, Joe Rashid, and some other community members had secured a meeting with the Detroit Planning and Development Department, where they would ask for the city's permission to maintain the field. A representative from the Detroit Economic Growth Corporation attended, as did a representative from the mayor's office. A representative

Figure 7.1 Navin Field Grounds Crew member Dave Mesrey in tall weeds in 2010 (Photo, Shawn P. Connelly)

Figure 7.2 Tom Derry on a riding mover (Photo, Jason Roche)

from Senator Carl Levin's office reminded city officials that the senator had worked very hard to secure the $3.5 million earmark for preserving the site, adding that it would be even harder for the senator to secure federal money for other Detroit projects if the city failed to use the earmark. The implied threat did not sway the officials; nor did earnest pleas from community members. However, city officials agreed to meet again in two weeks, possibly with a favorable decision. The second meeting was postponed twice, then abandoned.

However, the volunteers kept coming back. As they continued their labor of love, more people joined them. Jerry Bagierek, a retired school principal, began making the drive every week from the western part of Michigan, about three hours away. Bart Wilhelm makes frequent drives from Traverse City, about four hours from Detroit.

As their work continued, more and more visitors came to see the field. From all over Michigan and from many other states, people came to share memories of their favorite games at the corner. Couples reminisced about how they met their spouses at the ballpark. Fathers brought their sons to run the bases and reminisce. Grandchildren batted balls and played catch while their elders told them stories about Al Kaline, Willie Horton, Alan Trammell, Lou Whittaker, and Ernie Harwell. After an article in *ESPN: The Magazine* and a report on National Public Radio, people came from as far away as Idaho, California, and Florida. People even came to the field from Canada, England, Norway, the Netherlands, and Australia.

Personal connections to baseball stadiums: Tiger Stadium as sacred ground

Since its release in 1989, the movie *Field of Dreams* has become a cultural meme in America. According to the American Film Institute, the classic line "If you build it, he will come" is the 39th most famous movie quote on the list of the top 100 quotes in American movie history. In the movie, author Terrence Man assures trepid farmer Ray Kinsella that people will come to see his baseball field in a cornfield in Iowa.

The movie was filmed on a farm in the tiny town of Dyersville, Iowa, population 4115. The farmhouse and the actual baseball field still exist, surrounded by acres of corn. In an interview, Karla Thompson, executive director of the Dyersville Chamber of Commerce, explained that about 65,000 tourists visit the site every season.

It is as if the scripted lines from the movie were prophetic. People drive to this tiny Iowa town just to see the field and reminisce, even though the movie was purely fiction. The same thing is happening in Detroit, though the memories are not fictional. People come back to walk in the steps of baseball greats from the past, and to share stories about their connection to the corner. However, city leaders do not embrace the baseball tourism, even though thousands of visitors have come to see the field over the past six seasons. (No formal quantification exists, but this is a conservative estimate based on more than 100 visitors per day on weekends in the summer and dozens per weekend day in the spring and fall.) Yet, even without promotion and without support from the city, visitors still come. It is as if people are drawn by an irresistible force to reconnect with their roots.

There is something that draws people home. It is the reason we donate to our alma mater. It is the reason we will drive 20 minutes out of our way to drive past the house where we grew up, or knock on a stranger's door and say "My family used to live in this house, do you mind if I stop in and have a look around?" The familiar spaces we love create a sense of permanence. "We need to be able to identify with certain places and feel at home in those places. It's like we think those places know something about us. But really it's us knowing something about those places," says architect and professor Claudia Bernasconi. Cities and landmark buildings are vital for helping us make those connections; they offer a tangible expression of the concept of permanence, Bernasconi adds. We find a sense of permanence, possibly touching our spiritual longing for immortality, as we connect with long-standing, culturally important places. We recognize the past that has come before us; the apparent stability and longevity of the place allow us to envision a future that will remain after we are gone. Preservation of our favorite places and of our memory, collectively and individually, is a vital part of what makes us human: "You cannot keep down this urge in people to preserve the very place that they love," says mythologist Phil Cousineau, a filmmaker and author who has travelled the globe exploring dozens of cultures.

For many fans, the site of the old Tiger Stadium is not merely historical; they connect with the place on a spiritual level. It is sacred ground. Some even perform sacred rites at the site. Since the stadium was demolished in 2009, dozens of people have come to sprinkle the ashes of deceased loved ones on the field. Catherine Collins, a member of the Tiger Stadium Fan Club, insisted to her children that some of her ashes be sprinkled just beyond second base in the outfield. In a special ceremony in 2010, her family obliged her. Other sacred activities at the field include marriage ceremonies. Numerous couples have exchanged wedding vows on the field, including Tom Derry and long-time sweetheart Sarah Aittama, who were married at home plate on August 3, 2014.

Can consecrated activities make a baseball field sacred ground? From some perspectives, even clergy members say "yes." Jesuit priest and University of Detroit Mercy Professor of Catholic Studies Simon J. Hendry says that it could be true from a certain Catholic perspective:

> "There's a sense of memory that's involved in baseball. And everybody I know has memories that are tied to religion and

to Tiger Stadium. Now all of those things take place in a ballpark. The ballpark is where the community experiences what Neil Durkheim would call 'collective effervescence,' which is kind of the roots of ritual. So all these things that put you in touch with different dimensions take place in a ballpark. In that sense I think it's a sacred space."

Rabbi Jason Miller, a Detroit native and long-time Tigers fan, provides a similar perspective from a Jewish point of view:

"Baseball stadiums have the essence of holiness, of sacredness, perhaps even godliness, because of our experiences there. It's not the same as the holy ground that we read about in the Bible, in the Torah, when Moses encounters God at the burning bush. These are places in which our American pastime takes place, and so we ascribe a certain sense of holiness to these places."

Dr Achmat Salie, Imam and Professor of Religious Studies, says that Islamic tradition would allow for such an interpretation as well: "There's a saying of the prophet … that the whole earth is a cathedral. So, that is the perspective that any place could be sacred."

Perhaps even some Detroit police officers have recognized the importance of the site and the benefits of the Ground Crew's labors. Instead of an overgrown city block where anyone could commit crimes and remain hidden from view, police can see across the field and know if anyone is there. On April 28, 2012, the Grounds Crew hosted a 100th anniversary party for Navin Field. Dozens of people gathered to work, play ball, and roast hot dogs. A police van pulled up along the fence on Michigan Avenue and several officers dressed in black riot gear exited. The trespassers watched in dismay as the officers approached. The lead officer approached Joe Michnuk, who was standing next to a push mower eating a hot dog. "Are you the guys who mow the lawn here and rake the field?" the officer asked. "Yes, officer, I am," replied Joe. "Well thank you," replied the officer, handing Joe a business card; "If anyone ever gives you any trouble, just call me at this number." The gathered crowd rejoiced and the festivities continued. Police have not evicted the groundskeepers since April 2011.

To many, Grounds Crew members are seen as folk heroes fighting against city hall. Beginning in 2012, the Navin Field Grounds Crew has been invited to march in the annual St. Patrick's Day Parade, which passes directly past the ball field on Michigan Avenue. Restaurateur

Ron Cooley, the president of the Corktown Business Association, has frequently lauded the efforts of the Grounds Crew to make the Corktown neighborhood attractive to visitors. Before the 2012 baseball season, Michigan State Representative Rashida Tlaib, whose district includes Corktown, issued an official commendation to the Navin Field Grounds Crew from the state legislature of Michigan.

The story of the Navin Field Grounds Crew continues to be told. These devoted volunteers have been profiled on National Public Radio, *ESPN: The Magazine*, Grantland, *Rolling Stone*, the *New York Times*, *Preservation* magazine, NBCSports.com, the Mitch Albom Show, and numerous radio, television, newspaper, and Internet stories in Michigan and the Metro Detroit area.

Their labor of love has been strenuous; every week, with one riding mower and one or two push mowers, they cut more than nine acres of grass, they rake the infield, and they pick up bags of trash that have blown onto the field. Since starting in 2010, the Navin Field Grounds Crew has made the field playable and respectable (see Figure 7.3); they have installed a mesh net backstop behind home plate; they have brought in benches and picnic tables, which many people enjoy; and they have even constructed a Little League field on the northwest corner of the site where the left-field stands once stood. Their only reward has been seeing the joy on the faces of the visitors who come to play ball and enjoy the park.

Figure 7.3 Vintage baseball being played at Navin Field in the summer of 2014 (Photo, Brian Doucet)

Many visitors who initially came out of curiosity have become regular members of the Grounds Crew, volunteering their time and talents on weekends. Fans at Comerica Park routinely greet people who wear Navin Field Grounds Crew T-shirts, thanking them for their efforts. Grounds Crew members have also found grateful fans in other major league ballparks around the country; people have heard of their labor and laud it. The field itself is frequently used by Detroit's Cass Tech High School baseball team, which holds practices at the corner, by vintage baseball teams who wear period costumes and play by 1860s' rules, and by unorganized groups who play pick-up games of softball or baseball. There is even a group that plays kickball on Sunday evenings, with some regular players driving from as far away as Pontiac, Michigan, about 30 miles (50 km) away.

Navin Field and conflicting visions for Detroit

In 2009, when the stadium was demolished, the Detroit Economic Growth Corporation declared that the site is "reserved for a comprehensive development that will bring substantial investment and new economic activity." However, in late 2014, the Corporation approved a proposal that would redevelop the site with retail space, housing, sports, and history. The baseball component of the project was proposed by the Detroit Police Athletic League (PAL), a non-profit agency that supports athletic leagues for Detroit youths. The plan includes a small stadium with an interactive history area and a conference center. While the projects would provide temporary construction jobs, they would not provide a significant number of new permanent jobs to employ Detroiters.

The PAL proposal would maintain the historic dimensions of the old Tiger Stadium. However, to the chagrin of the Navin Field Grounds Crew, it would replace the natural grass with artificial turf. PAL argues that this would allow more games to be played and would require less maintenance than natural grass. The PAL proposal would also allow youth soccer, football, and lacrosse games at the corner. Members of the Grounds Crew contend that artificial turf would be a sacrilege, dishonoring the memories of countless ballplayers and fans who love the site. Grounds crew members and their supporters are lobbying hard and circulating online petitions to save the grass. Detroit native and senior writer for *ESPN: The Magazine* David Fleming says that the future of the corner holds the key to the future of the city:

"That spot is either where Detroit dies or where it is reborn. And if it is reborn it is because of people like the people who have saved that field, who have said 'I don't care what the law says, I don't care what the leaders say. I know right from wrong and I am going to go down there and cut a hole in the fence and fix up this field.'"

Detroit's city seal is engraved with the motto that, when translated from Latin, says: "We hope for better things; From the ashes it will rise." Written after a terrible fire in 1805, the city has risen from the ashes and been burned again. However, members of the Grounds Crew embody the hope and determination necessary to revitalize the city they love. They show up once, twice, or more times per week to clean up trash, mow the grass, and make the field a playable, welcoming site. Their devotion and faithful service demonstrate the importance of preserving memory and preserving place. They are some of the brightest testaments to the energy and determination of Detroiters to restore the city by taking pride in its history and taking an active role in its future. They have exhibited the spirit of determination, of perseverance, and of grit that represent Detroit. They have shown their community and the world that their city is worth fighting for—that Detroit matters.

In the Tigers' first-ever game at Navin Field, on opening day of the baseball season in 1912, the legendary Ty Cobb won the game for the home team by stealing home. Despite the long odds and opposition from the city, members of the Grounds Crew are working to steal back this baseball home for the people of Detroit, and in the process, to preserve the city's history.

Epilogue

The era of the Navin Field Grounds Crew's labor of love at the corner came to an end in the summer of 2016. The Grounds Crew held a farewell baseball game in the cold rain on April 9. Groundbreaking for PAL's new site, officially named "Willie Horton's Field of Dreams," after Tigers great Willie Horton, came on April 13. Bulldozers dug up a patch of the outfield and dignitaries with golden shovels posed for pictures to ceremonially break ground. Former US Senator Carl Levin, who had secured $3.8 million in federal funds to preserve the historic site in 2009—money that would now go to PAL's project—praised the efforts of the Grounds Crew and lauded the new PAL field.

Some members of the Grounds Crew abandoned the site. However, Tom Derry and some other members continued to pick up trash and mow the grass because work had still not begun. The Grounds Crew had another farewell event on June 5. However, in late June, the excavation began in earnest. By mid-July, the entire historic baseball field had been bulldozed to make way for the new athletic field. The timetable for completion of the project remains uncertain. PAL continues to raise funds and is seeking a corporate sponsor to pay for naming rights for the stadium.

Members of the Grounds Crew are profoundly disappointed at the latest developments, but remain proud of their legacy. Without their work for more than six years, the field would likely have been turned into warehouse space or something other than a youth sports site. However, their six years at the corner have forged friendships and community that will last forever. "As much as I love this site, I love the people I've met even more," Tom Derry has repeatedly said. Other volunteers share the sentiment. Their work has certainly helped spark interest in Detroit's revitalization, helped bring people to the Corktown neighborhood, and helped rekindle passion for historic preservation.

These friends continue to meet and continue to celebrate baseball. Inspired by Byron Hatch, a Flint, Michigan, truck driver who brought a birthday cake to the corner on August 14, 2011, Dave Mesrey has begun organizing an annual birthday bash for Mark "the Bird" Fidrych, the Tigers' star pitcher from 1976. Tom Derry organizes an annual Babe Ruth Birthday Party event in February. Both events are held at Nemo's, the sports bar one block east of the corner. Grounds Crew members have also discussed the possibility of taking on another preservation project, but have not decided which one. One idea is Hamtramck Stadium, a historic baseball field where the Detroit Stars (a team from the Negro leagues) played.

The field is gone, but the memories and the friendships remain. This chapter of the history of the corner demonstrates the continuing commitment of community members to their city—it shows that Detroit matters.

Notes

1. Armen Keteyian's (2002) documentary *A city on fire: The story of the '68 Detroit Tigers* offers great insight into the role of the team in bringing stability and the power of sports to unite a community.
2. See: http://crcmich.org/PUBLICAT/1990s/1996/memo1040.pdf
3. See: http://www6.homedepot.com/tool-truck-rental/Brush_Hog/BC2600HM/

EIGHT

This is (not) Detroit: projecting the future of Germany's Ruhr region

Julia Sattler

As was discussed in Chapter One of this book, Detroit has become a metonym for urban failure, and many places around the world use "Detroit" as a warning to further a particular message or agenda. The city is talked about, but rarely actively engaged with. In this chapter, Julia Sattler examines the ways in which Detroit is used and interpreted in Germany's Ruhr Region. She starts by deconstructing the popular idea presented in the German media that a Detroit-style bankruptcy is possible in poorer municipalities within the Ruhr. The chapter then examines the similarities and differences between these two areas, particularly in their economic trajectories and current state of deindustrialization and political fragmentation. Sattler focuses on the different trajectories that have been taken, specifically examining how each place deals with the legacy of industrial decline. The Ruhr has been an innovator in using its industrial heritage as a tool for economic growth; Sattler critically examines major events such as the 2010 European Capital of Culture which was held in the Ruhr.

Empirically, the chapter focuses on two specific projects that make direct reference to Detroit. The first is *Learning from Detroit*, a manifesto focusing on the "right to the city" in a deindustrializing context. The second is the *Das Detroit Projekt*, a publicly financed art project that emerged in response to the closure of General Motors' Opel factory in Bochum, a city in the eastern part of the Ruhr Region. It paints a decidedly negative picture of Detroit. With its slogan "This is not Detroit," it focuses quite literally on not learning from the city.

Sattler argues that both projects provide only superficial references and no real engagement with Detroit. She is highly critical of the ways in which *Das Detroit Projekt* deliberately accentuates the differences so that Detroit is, in her words, portrayed as the "absolutely horrific version of what could happen in Bochum," and that the Ruhr's strategies for reinvention (including high-end flagships and cultural events) are painted in a much more positive light by comparison. This is an important example of the actual practices of using Detroit as a warning, which, in this case, also serves to justify and legitimize major redevelopment projects and top-down cultural initiatives.

Julia Sattler is an Assistant Professor of American Studies at TU Dortmund University, in Germany. She is the editor of *Urban Transformations in the United States: Spaces, Communities, Representations* (Transcript, 2016). She has worked on multiple urban redevelopment projects in the Ruhr. In 2012, she curated a photographic exhibit on abandoned industrial spaces. In 2013, she was a visiting scholar at the University of Michigan's Taubman College of Architecture and Urban Planning.

Introduction

Detroit's bankruptcy did not only cause a stir in the US; it also led to significant attention about its situation in the rest of the world. This is specifically true for places where, for one reason or another, the story of Detroit resonates: be it due to a legacy of deindustrialization and urban shrinkage, or due to financial concerns that have already led to or threaten to lead to the reduction of public services. The interest in the city can also be attributed to the presence of Detroit-based automakers in other places, leading public officials, as well as local citizens to the question of whether or not Detroit's bankruptcy might affect them and their communities. The summer of 2013 made clear that *Detroit matters* beyond Michigan, beyond the US.

One area outside the US that was particularly concerned with Detroit's financial situation and with how the bankruptcy was handled by the city and its people was Germany's Ruhr region. This region, located in Western Germany, is oftentimes dubbed the German "Rust Belt" or "coal pit," due to its long-term legacy of coal mining and heavy industry. Using the example of the Ruhr region, this chapter discusses how regions, cities, and projects apply "Detroit"[1] as both a model and image in processes of structural transformation. It also focuses on how "Detroit" is abused as a term in these contexts.

This chapter centers on two examples from the Ruhr that use "Detroit" in different ways in order to advance certain goals and not others: the publicly financed *Detroit Projekt* by Urban Arts Ruhr, an art project that emerged in the context of the closing of an auto plant in the Ruhr; and the citizen initiative *Learning from Detroit*, criticizing contemporary redevelopment strategies in the region. My analysis in this chapter is largely based on a close reading and analysis of websites and other documents available on the Internet, such as newspaper articles reporting about these projects. Both projects discussed here are rather visible in the ongoing discussion about the Ruhr's future development and, due to their different approaches to both the Ruhr and to "Detroit," point to the different ends to which "Detroit" is currently referenced in the Ruhr, and possibly also beyond that.

The Ruhr is both similar enough to Detroit for the city's challenges and opportunities to resonate and be picked up on by the media and by citizen initiatives, and yet different enough to make clear that solutions to Detroit's and other communities' problems by and large have to be made on the local level. The reference to "Detroit" in the Ruhr is, in some cases, more accurate than in others, of course, and while this chapter can only provide a limited scope, its ultimate goal is to show how Detroit can be and is made relevant to other parts of the world.

The Ruhr region: Germany's Detroit?

In December 2013, the Ruhr region and, more specifically, the city of Oberhausen, a medium-sized city located in the Western corridor of the region, made it into the *New York Times* (Eddy, 2013). This led local newspapers around the Ruhr to report about the *New York Times* article in turn, almost taking pride in the city merely being mentioned in such an international and visible context. The reason why the city of Oberhausen made it into the *New York Times* in the first place, however, has very little to do with pride. Melissa Eddy's article characterizes Oberhausen as a "polished but ailing city," asking an important question right at the start: "What is it like to be 'Germany's Detroit'?" Oberhausen, formerly a coal and steel town, had been given this questionable title—"Germany's Detroit" (eg Mallien, 2013)—earlier in 2013 due to its high communal debt, the highest in Germany at that time: about $11,450 per capita. Oberhausen, a city of roughly 209,000 inhabitants in 2013,[2] is one of several cities in the Ruhr region having to deal with a comparatively high levels of debt per capita.

Within Germany, no other region has such an accumulation of impoverished and indebted communities as the Ruhr region. One main reason for this noteworthy situation is the overall high unemployment levels of roughly around 11%,[3] leading to both rising social costs for Ruhr cities and shrinking tax bases. This also means that fewer investments can be made into the Ruhr region's infrastructure, making it less attractive to investors in the long run. The German federal government's Poverty Report (Armuts- und Reichtumsbericht der Bundesregierung) of 2011 called the region "Germany's Poorhouse" (Öchsner, 2013, author's translation) and the situation has not necessarily improved in recent years.[4]

The challenges confronting the Ruhr are the long-term results of systematic deindustrialization—often given the more friendly sounding term "structural change" in Germany—and structural disinvestment. Unless one wanted to point to large-scale developments that affect all Western industrialized cities, such as globalization, this specific situation certainly has nothing to do with Detroit, or with Detroit's declaration of bankruptcy and its larger effects.

The mere fact that the Ruhr Valley and Detroit are struggling financially, though, has strengthened the existing narratives linking the two places in the German media. This link has a long history and relates back to the shared fate of deindustrialization and economic transformation. It also became manifest, for example, in the "Shrinking Cities"[5] project initiated by the German Federal Cultural Foundation (Kulturstiftung des Bundes). The "Shrinking Cities" project ran between 2002 and 2008, and opened an extensive dialogue about post-industrial regions in transformation. Detroit and the Ruhr Valley were two of the major examples used in this project.

According to recent media reports, the Ruhr has turned into, or will turn into "Germany's Detroit," with all the complex implications of such an idea: "Detroit is bankrupt—will the Ruhr go bankrupt, too?" (Institut der deutschen Wirtschaft Köln, 2013, author's translation) was only one of the headlines emerging shortly after the news from Detroit had come in. Upon closer examination, the idea of a "German Detroit" in terms of municipal finances is inaccurate; German law does not permit cities to go bankrupt in the way that American law made it possible for Detroit to declare its bankruptcy in the first place (cf Deuber, 2013). The insolvency of a commune in Germany is simply not legally possible. In case a city is unable to pay off its debts, the German state, and by implication the taxpayers, will step in. As a consequence of Germany's shared tax base, "municipalities in great fiscal distress do not experience the kinds of interest rate spreads or disparities experienced in this country [the US]" (Schafroth, 2014). However, based on the number of newspaper articles that have made these comparisons, it is safe to assume that this important legal difference is relatively unknown among the German population.

In Germany, a quite strong and well-established system of state support ensures that its deindustrializing and financially strapped cities receive funding from the state should they become dependent on such support. This is not to say that this is a desirable situation for a city; emergency government funding means that a city, in effect, loses its financial independence and, in turn, has to cut back its public facilities, including library services and the opening hours of city offices (cf *Pleite-Ruhrstädte*, 2012). It is an undesirable situation that city governments want to avoid for as long as possible. While, in practice, household consolidation in Germany is thus not entirely different from the Chapter 9 bankruptcy plan that was installed in Detroit (see Farley, Chapter Three), due to the shared fiscal responsibility, poor communities are not overly dependent on raising property taxes (cf Schafroth, 2014).

The Ruhr and Detroit: similarities and differences

While the story of Detroit—its growth, its power, and its dramatic economic and demographic decline—is much better known internationally than the story of the Ruhr, it cannot be denied that a reading of both in tandem makes evident a number of important similarities. There is not only their 21st century financial struggles; there are similar trajectories in their rather late process of industrialization—the Ruhr, much like Detroit, grew rapidly between the late 19th and early 20th centuries. The region also shares with Detroit the intense focus on one major industry that essentially created the region we speak of today. The Ruhr was not more than an agglomeration of small villages until the mid-19th century. The region rapidly industrialized and urbanized and consequently contributed heavily to the rise of the German economy in the 20th century. This also includes the post-war "economic miracle" (Wirtschaftswunder). The region was shaped intensely by different streams of migration, first from other places in Germany and Central and Eastern Europe, then, after the Second World War, from Southern and Southeastern Europe—for example, Turkey, Greece, Spain, and Italy—creating a complex cultural mosaic that shapes the Ruhr to this day (cf Hanhörster, 2011).

Rapid urbanization and the ever-growing needs of the coal, steel, and iron industries in the Ruhr have contributed to the formation of a rather unique urban landscape shaped by intense contradictions, a landscape uniting urban and rural, industrial and pastoral features (cf El Khafif and Roost, 2011). It is rather scattered in itself, and this landscape has been described more recently as having a unique urbanity—*Ruhrbanität (Ruhr-banity)*.[6] The Ruhr is an intensely fractured region; its internal order is not easily recognizable as many different physical, cultural, and administrative layers overlap (cf Davy, 2004, p 25). United by the legacy of industrial prosperity and demise, these 53 separate municipalities depend on each other, and have begun to learn what it means to work together across administrative and spatial boundaries that are a result of the industrial past (Davy, 2004). These often contradictory urban features make it hard to grasp the Ruhr as a coherent region rather than a patchwork of different pieces that have been made to fit and were tied together by sheer need (eg El Khafif and Roost, 2011). Finally, just like Detroit's ultimate decline began in the 1950s, the Ruhr has gone through an equally long process of deindustrialization and decline—the first coal mine closed in 1957, the last one will be closing in 2018. While these parallels do not mean that the Ruhr—a polycentric city-region—and Detroit—the center of its own metropolitan context—are exactly alike, I am of the opinion that they still encourage a dialogue into how places deal with economic transformations and the role of culture in shaping new directions for these areas.

Long-term economic transformation in the Ruhr

Almost ironically, one attempt at diversifying the Ruhr's industrial base created a genetic connection between this region in the West of Germany and the "Motor City": the arrival in 1960 of General Motors (GM) to Bochum, a medium-sized city situated between Essen and Dortmund. This was supposed to ease the long-term effects of deindustrialization and to create new jobs via the transition from a "coal pit" into a "Motown." However, this proved to be short-lived; December 2014 saw the closing of the Bochum auto production plant because it no longer met GM's expectations. This was just one of many such plant closures that the Ruhr has experienced since the onset of deindustrialization. This plant closure also affects companies producing materials for the auto industry and possibly amounts to the loss of around 10,000 jobs (cf Wyputta, 2014).

There is not yet a coherent vision with regard to how the newly available land in Bochum will be used in the future. It remains rather difficult to convince large-scale production companies to invest in the Ruhr, and the location itself might not lend itself ideally to small-scale redevelopment. For now, the Bochum GM plant is being torn down, a development that has been commented on by the German *Handelsblatt* (2015, author's translation) as the emergence of "The New Detroit in the Ruhr" in a short article complete with photographs of the abandoned plant devoid of any human life and the ongoing destruction of it.

In effect, the photographs used in this very article are reminiscent of Detroit's representation in numerous coffee-table books that have earned the supposed "ruins of Detroit" worldwide fame (Marchant and Meffre, 2010; Moore, 2010). The closing of the Bochum auto plant is an instance where, in a very concrete and simple sense, *Detroit matters* in the Ruhr and in public discussions about its future because decisions taken in Detroit—such as the decision to close the Bochum auto plant—have a significant effect on the social and economic structure of the region.

Dealing with industrial legacies

One example of where differences become specifically evident across a number of disciplines is the way in which the Ruhr and Detroit deal with their industrial legacies in the post-industrial age. This heritage, which visually and narratively defines the Ruhr, is not as important in the City of Detroit. These differences are certainly not only locally determined; they also relate to how Germany, with its very strong system of state support and its strong focus toward the past, and the US, with its more liberal government and its inherently progressive orientation toward the future, more generally deal with the challenges of deindustrialization. In the US, "the first priority in the cleaning of industrial sites typically is to find a new economic use" (Kotval and Mullin, 2011, p 203), meaning that there is a stronger focus on new investment, or even letting land lie bare: in contrast to Germany, "America is a land rich country" (Kotval and Mullin, 2011, p 203). Brownfield remediation is not only an expensive process for which there is hardly any central funding available in comparison to Europe, but the reuse of such sites combining preservation and openness for play—as is central to the Ruhr—is also a question of liability and of what Kotval and Mullin (2011, p 201) refer to as "America's almost excessive zeal in terms of safety and insurance," turning conversions of this kind into a rather difficult undertaking.

Some of these issues also become apparent when looking at Detroit's industrial landscape. As Brent D. Ryan and Daniel Campo (2013) show in their article on "Autopia's end: the decline and fall of Detroit's automotive manufacturing landscape," in the context of Detroit's crisis of the manufacturing industries, the factory spaces, as physical sites, were by and large absent from public discourse. While, in the 20th century, the auto industry's impact on the city was visible in its urban landscape, "[i]n the twenty-first century, this traditional relationship between Detroit, automobile production, and the industrial landscape is significantly changed" (Ryan and Campo, 2013, p 95). By and large, and despite their architectural significance, many of these formerly industrial sites have either been erased and/or replaced by office parks or parking lots, or lie abandoned.

One of Detroit's most iconic industrial sites, the Packard Plant, has, much to the dismay of many Detroiters, gained worldwide fame due to its dramatic visual qualities even despite—or more likely because of—its current state of ruination and instability. Overall, Detroit's industrial landscape, or rather what remains of it, does not apparently define (neither in the positive nor in the limiting, negative sense) the city's possible futures. Nevertheless, a re-conception and long-term preservation of structures like Packard, for example, for non-profit cultural use, might still, as Ryan and Campo (2013, p 124) argue, open up new possibilities for the city.

Compared to Detroit, the Ruhr has chosen quite a different route when dealing with its industrial heritage. This also attests to the way in which its different financial and political structures are intensely shaped by social democracy. Throughout the 1980s and 1990s, the Ruhr put forward a massive publicly funded heritage concept that might, indeed, be so locally specific that it cannot be copied anywhere else (cf Kunzmann, 2011, p 179). At the same time, it is considered a model of the revitalization of an industrial landscape (Kunzmann, 2011, p 177). In fact, it is argued by some (eg Kunzmann, 2011) that this very concept, implemented in the framework of the *Internationale Bauausstellung Emscher Park* (International Architecture Exhibition, IBA Emscher Park, 1989–99), has created the contemporary Ruhr in the first place. During the IBA Emscher Park, a social and spatial restructuring took place in the region (cf Brownley Raines, 2011, p 184). The overall concept of the project aimed at the preservation, conservation, and regeneration of the industrial landscape instead of its large-scale demolition (cf Brownley Raines, 2011, pp 195ff). This project has led to the creation of a rather unique post-industrial landscape characterized by industrial markers that have been re-inscribed as sites of cultural activity. These former factory halls are now museums and theaters, surrounded by landscape parks shaping the identity of the Ruhr in important ways (see Figure 8.1). While it is not entirely clear whether the density of such redeveloped and re-designated sites has possibly led to an identification of the Ruhr with the past rather than the future, the IBA's legacy is—at least culturally speaking—a success that is celebrated and used as a useful model for urban restructuring (cf Kunzmann, 2011, p 171):

> The changes in the Ruhr District are reflected also and in particular in the change in cultural ways of seeing, which in turn are responsible for the creation of a specific aesthetic and a new awareness of landscape. This aspect finds expression in particular in the artistic staging of landscapes, in the context of industrial landscapes and their transformation processes. (Reicher et al, 2011, p 19)

In addition to this aesthetic contribution, the IBA has also established cooperative structures between the different cities and patterns of regional thinking, led to strengthening administrative links within the region, and helped initiate a debate about urban planning in and

Figure 8.1 Landschaftspark in Duisburg, a former coking plant turned into a landscape park (Photo, Julia Sattler)

the urban qualities of the Ruhr (cf Reicher et al, 2011, pp 18–19). It created something for the citizens to identify with, and it has added to the improvement of the overall quality of life in the Ruhr by building a dense landscape of parks that can be accessed freely.

Its economic contribution, however, is not quite as significant. While the project also had a focus on work and establishing job perspectives, it could not make up for the overall job losses during deindustrialization. The IBA coincided with the Ruhr's economic restructuring that also went along with the development of technology centers and similar kinds of structures, which, in the long run, certainly contributed more to the long-term development of jobs than the IBA (cf Hospers, 2004, p 155). This lack of the IBA's economic success is often not directly addressed (cf Kunzmann, 2011, p 179), quite possibly because as a project, it had so many other dimensions across which it achieved or even transcended its goals.

Despite these large-scale investments in its redevelopment and despite other efforts to economically restructure the Ruhr region, such as the focus on environmentally friendly technologies and research-based initiatives (cf Hospers, 2004, pp 154ff), the Ruhr of the early 21st century is still plagued by social as well as economic pressures. This is also still the case even though the German economy is relatively strong. Even at a time when new companies come to the region or established companies expand, there are still too few jobs for the current population of the region (cf Hollmann, 2011, p 93). Although the transformation process can, of course, be told in terms of a success story, the Ruhr has not become a place of the "rich and famous" and also, by and large, does not cater to such a population (cf Basten and Utku, 2011, p 179). Rather, an increasing inner fragmentation has led to a situation where discourses about the region being "left behind" (Kohlstadt, 2013, author's translation) and the emergence of so-called "no-go areas" have emerged alongside new luxury housing (see Figures 8.2 and 8.3).

Just like the IBA could not turn around these economic pressures, neither did its follow-up project, the European Capital of Culture, which took place in the Ruhr in 2010 (RUHR.2010) and that worked with the slogan "Change Through Culture—Culture Through Change." RUHR.2010 relied on volunteer work for many of its projects and otherwise employed people on a short-term basis, such as in the areas of ticketing or tourist assistance (cf Hollmann, 2011, p 41). Since its economic agenda was only vaguely formulated, it is rather difficult to evaluate whether the project achieved these goals. While it is almost impossible to prove a connection between the European

Figure 8.2 Dortmund, Germany: new luxury housing on the Phoenix Sea, a man-made lake on the site of a former steel factory (Photo, Julia Sattler)

Figure 8.3 Working-class housing, partially abandoned, near the Phoenix Sea, Dortmund (Photo, Brian Doucet)

Capital of Culture and investments made in the Ruhr during 2010 or around that time, one area of the economy that has likely profited from the extensive promotional work in the context of 2010 is the creative economy (cf Hollmann, 2011, p 117). At the same time, this sector has also remained behind expectations, and in 2015, only employs roughly 2% of employees in the Ruhr—less than in many other regions in Germany (cf Deppe, 2015).

While RUHR.2010 continued working with the cultural agenda that was established during the IBA, it also aimed at putting the Ruhr on the "map" globally, proclaiming that it was about to rise to a different league: to be read in line with Paris, London, or other places of importance. In many ways, it was a huge regional marketing project that tried to reinvent the Ruhr as a "metropolis," and as a formerly industrial landscape that in the 21st century, could thrive on culture, creativity, and art alone. However, the daily experiences of living in the Ruhr, as well as the poverty and unemployment statistics mentioned earlier, stand in stark contrast to this suggestion.

Referencing "Detroit" in the Ruhr

Some of the templates used in the attempt to advance the creative economy and the supposed "creative class," and to place the Ruhr in a more "global" discourse, sound suspiciously like Detroit's more recent attempts at trying to redefine itself as a global city, tourist destination, and center for arts and creativity. The central story that is being told in the Ruhr, and that will sound familiar to Detroiters, is essentially one in which the deindustrialized urban landscape becomes a *frontier* open to newcomers' discoveries. These discourses became especially prevalent in the context of the European Capital of Culture

RUHR.2010 and related both to the region as a whole and to specific areas within the region that were targeted for redevelopment. This excerpt from an article in *Art Magazine* addressing the transformation of Dortmund-West, one of the city's redevelopment areas that is supposed to transform itself from a working-class neighborhood shaped by the industry into a "creative quarter," is in many ways exemplary for how the discourse is led: "It is quite possible that at some point there'll be fat-reduced Latte Macchiato here. And galleries selling cool paintings. And tapas-bars in which graphic designers open their laptops.... But it does not quite look like that yet" (Schlüter, 2010, p 20, author's translation). The article addresses the fact that while the area has not transformed as a whole, the first indicators of change are supposedly visible: artists are moving into the area, participating in the process of redevelopment. The kind of reinvention and economic uplift that is alluded to in these statements and in the discourse in the Ruhr as a whole is also prevalent in stories about Detroit's comeback. Around the same time that *Art Magazine* published the article about the Ruhr as "Der wilde Westen" ("The Wild West"), Toby Barlow explained Detroit along similar lines in the *New York Times*: "Detroit right now is just this vast, enormous canvas where anything imaginable can be accomplished" (Barlow, 2009). Typically, in such narratives, the post-industrial landscape becomes a blank slate open to new inscription. In these terms, the differences between the Ruhr and Detroit in coping with deindustrialization do not matter: both places can be made void of their past history and current situation by being construed as empty canvasses dependent on their redefinition by—largely white and affluent—outsiders.

Such stories and hopes appear to be rather similar in deindustrialized cities across the Western hemisphere. At the same time, two rather large and significant projects in the Ruhr Valley have explicitly made use of "Detroit"—and not England's Black Country region or Upper Silesia in Poland, both of which would share a similar legacy of coal mining, to list just two examples—as a trope to comment on ongoing developments in the region and to urge action in a specific direction. These are interesting to look at from a comparative angle, mainly because of their different strategies of using and referring to "Detroit." Certainly, and while their names might suggest this, these projects—the state-funded Bochum-based arts undertaking *Detroit Projekt*[7] (*Detroit Project*) and the manifesto *Von Detroit Lernen* (*Learning from Detroit*) published by the Recht auf Stadt (Right to the City) movement in the Ruhr[8]—are not research projects dealing with the City of Detroit or anything that happens in the City of Detroit. The initiator of the former, Urbane Künste Ruhr (Urban Arts Ruhr), is a public cultural agency focusing on art in public spaces and curated by Katja Aßmann. The agency was installed in the aftermath of RUHR.2010 and works as a follow-up organization of this project.[9] The latter collective describes itself as a rather loosely organized network of urban activists, journalists, researchers, artists, and social workers in different parts of the Ruhr—basically, a citizen initiative with a rather loose organizational structure. Thus, it is evident that the initiators of these projects are not experts either on Detroit or on urban development in the Ruhr; rather, a variety of backgrounds come into play. Urban Arts Ruhr and the Right to the City movement in the Ruhr are, by and large, regionally based. In contrast to the former project, the latter does not receive large-scale state funding; it is a leftist movement concerned with social and cultural change initiated by inhabitants of the region.

Learning from Detroit

The manifesto *Learning from Detroit*,[10] its title clearly referencing "Learning from Las Vegas," was published in September 2014. It originated in a 2013 conference dealing with the meaning of Lefebvre's conception of a "right to the city" in the Ruhr Valley. The conference was based on the idea that such a right needs to be spelled out differently in the Ruhr than in growing, bustling places such as Hamburg or Munich. The manifesto goes along with a longer conceptual paper giving explicit examples of the Ruhr's challenges titled "Realize Ruhrgebiet,"[11] which I will also be taking into account in my following close reading.

The manifesto is rather short and uses "Detroit" as a prime example of a postindustrial city, while stating that deindustrialization in the Ruhr has not reached its final point yet. Instead of criticizing post-industrial "Detroit" for anything that it has supposedly "done," and instead of referring to anything that is supposedly happening (or not happening, for that matter) in the City of Detroit as international media often likes to do for the purpose of self-aggrandizement, the manifesto asks what the Ruhr might be able to learn from Detroit. This suggests an interest both in dialogue between the two places and in using "Detroit" as a resource for the Ruhr.

Upon closely studying the text, it quickly becomes evident that the manifesto is highly critical of the Ruhr's current strategies of celebrating the industrial past: "We no longer want to see the pictures of glorified and romanticized workers"—images that are often used to advertise and promote the Ruhr and its heritage. It also criticizes the ongoing emphasis on the Ruhr's metropolitan character and the idea of a "changing region," neglecting the unemployment and poverty, features that characterized, for example, the slogans used by the European Capital of Culture RUHR.2010 mentioned earlier. The manifesto even goes so far as to state that "the Ruhr area does not exist," but that rather than cooperating, the cities usually considered part of the region are taking away each other's resources in a rather useless debate about where new "flagship projects" should be erected ("cannibalistic parish pump politics"). All of these examples show that the initiative does not agree with the prominent storyline of the Ruhr as a successful example of urban transformation.

The manifesto appeals to the idea of social justice when arguing that public funds should be devoted to the improvement of the social structure of the Ruhr instead of to large-scale building projects, such as those realized in the context of RUHR.2010:

> Those who build flagship projects next to impoverished areas so that their shine may one day reach the poor as well, are not just ignorant but cynical.... No one should have to search the trash for something useful in the shadows of those major projects.

The Right to the City initiative would like for the Ruhr to accept long-term shrinkage and deindustrialization as facts, and to open unused spaces to artistic and other activity without bureaucratic hassle. Overall, the text counters ongoing efforts to promote the region's transformation and argues that what is usually celebrated as a success—the Ruhr's process of reinventing itself—has not improved the situation for all citizens of the region alike.

The essence of what could be learned from Detroit, and, according to the text, specifically from the Detroit Summer initiative, mainly relates to what the text calls "non-commercial urbanization," namely, do-it-yourself (DIY) projects as well as artistic and social projects making use of available spaces in the city, and citizen-run social organizations based on solidarity and the idea of sharing (see Kinder, Chapter Six; Howell and Feldman, Chapter Eleven). The members of the movement feel that such activities are too often limited in the Ruhr due to legal concerns.

Based on the idea of a basic income for every citizen, independent from the availability of jobs or the ability of an individual to participate in the working world, the members of the movement aiming at a

Ruhr-specific "right to the city" want to participate in the political discussion around the future of the Ruhr.[12] This goal means speaking up for the idea and becoming active ("We are getting involved. Now!"), instead of letting others take the important decisions regarding the region's future development. Looking at the group's specific agenda, it becomes evident why "Detroit" is a useful trope for them to relate to. Not only is Detroit a city that has developed specific approaches to dealing with shrinkage, however problematic those may be for the city, but it is also known in Germany for its extensive urban agriculture projects that the initiative also wants to push in the Ruhr. In Germany, urban agriculture is, by and large, a middle-class pastime, and it is one arena where the City of Detroit has lately been given a lot of positive credit by the German media (eg Kwasniewski, 2013).

In essence, and while neither the manifesto nor its extension "Realize Ruhrgebiet" relate very specifically to Detroit or to how exactly the process of "learning from Detroit" could happen, these documents present an alternative vision of the Ruhr's future. They express a harsh criticism of the entrepreneurial city that has become prevalent in many discussions of the Ruhr's future, as well as, for example, in the context of RUHR.2010. The documents criticize projects that focus on the "creative economy"—such as those that were intensely "pushed" during the year of the European Capital of Culture—which are focused solely on economic aspects instead of on art.

The reliance of this initiative on ideas by Lefebvre in these terms is not too surprising. While Lefebvre's ideas in his own manifesto remain rather vague and do not spell out in detail what would be entailed in the "right to the city," this catchphrase is used in many places undergoing processes of urban and economic transformation. Often, citizens in such places will argue that they have lost power in processes of decision-making that affect their communities (eg Purcell, 2002). Without breaking down what exactly the "right to the city" could look like, the idea is used as a cure-all medicine to suggest that power can supposedly be transferred back to the people (cf Purcell, 2002, p 100).

Along with these ideas, and in contrast to the reliance on economically driven attempts to install "flagship projects" in the Ruhr, the manifesto calls for citizen involvement in order to overcome poverty and deal with abandoned commercial and other facilities. It also urges citizens and politicians to develop a vision that accepts the departure of the industry from the region and that no longer funds such old industries instead of focusing on the conditions that the industry has left behind: "We want to face them directly: the poverty, the social segregation, the out-migration, the vacant sites and the boredom." These activists do not want to deny the downsides of the region's economic transformation, but rather use "Detroit" as a model of how these can be confronted and successfully overcome—without, however, stating clearly how "Detroit" could be helpful in this undertaking.

The Detroit Projekt

In contrast to the manifesto focusing on a process of learning from Detroit, the *Detroit Projekt*, coincidentally (or not) initiated by an organization that is significantly closer to the idea of an entrepreneurial future for the Ruhr than the citizen initiative discussed earlier, uses a different approach—quite literally, *not* learning from Detroit. This project, which took place in the City of Bochum, home to the Opel/GM plant, between 2013 and 2014, draws a decidedly negative picture of Detroit. The project's slogan makes this fact evident without a doubt: "This is not Detroit." This slogan, on the one hand, refers to the idea that GM cannot treat Bochum in the same way that it has treated Detroit. On the other hand, though, the project goes much further than this and uses Detroit as a negative example of economic and social transformation that the City of Bochum should not ever be looking to. The project website claims that:

> Detroit is not only the city where the future of the Opel factories is decided. The people of Detroit have already faced what we do not want to experience: the closing of the automotive and steel industry, moving away and leaving behind a landscape of ruins. But Bochum is not Detroit: Bochum re-invents itself![13]

Instead of giving credit to the perseverance of Detroiters and their strategies of dealing with the large-scale departure of the auto-industry, as well as establishing solidarity between the citizens of Bochum and the citizens of Detroit, the project uses "Detroit" as a solely negative, absolutely horrific vision of what could happen in Bochum. At the same time, the text makes use of Detroit to cast a positive light on the situation in the Ruhr. It highlights how "Bochum re-invents itself"—as if Detroiters would just silently and passively accept their fate and not even get the idea of finding (creative or other) strategies to deal with the transformation.

Upon studying the project more closely and upon a detailed reading of its website and program, it becomes evident that Detroit, the city that is so prominently featured in its official name—the *Detroit Projekt*—is not really part of its program at all. The readings, concerts, parties, and arts projects taking place in the Ruhr do not make an effort to actively create a productive link between the Ruhr Valley, or Bochum, and Detroit. They do not really comment on what is going on in the City of Detroit, even though some of the events refer to Detroit directly or indirectly, for example, the "Motown BBQ." The connection to Detroit is still only vague, and it does not seem as if there was space for an open dialogue with "Detroit," or between citizens of Detroit and citizens of Bochum. Nevertheless, the project as a whole was not as top-down as it might sound. There were several instances where citizens of the Ruhr could actively participate and bring in their ideas for the future of their city, such as in a photo competition asking participants to show where in Bochum the future becomes visible.[14] Whether this helps build a connection to Detroit, though, remains questionable.

It seems almost ironic that a project named *Detroit Projekt* is so adamant on becoming *not* Detroit, and on *not* learning from the city. The project concentrates on promoting a solely negative image of the city that lends its name to the project, using it as a scary future vision that the City of Bochum should not have to confront. While the project describes its goals as the initiation of a discussion around the future of the city, the future of work, and the future of art, the main result of this engagement is already fixed in the slogan: "Under no circumstances should Bochum become like 'Detroit.'" What exactly this means, or how exactly the project wants to achieve this goal, remains vague, at best; it is up to the reader of the website—and probably the audience of events taking place within the project—to decide.

The project, with its support by the German Federal Cultural Foundation and the Kunststiftung of North-Rhine Westphalia, could have provided an ideal opportunity to initiate cooperation between artists and institutions across the Atlantic Ocean (for an example of a Dutch cultural fund supporting such partnerships see Wiersum et al, Chapter Fifteen); it could have fostered citizen-based dialogue about the long-term meaning of deindustrialization and ways of coping with these challenges. However, it does not even include many Ruhr-based artists—something that it actually has in common with RUHR.2010, the project that was to promote the creative economy as well as the arts (and artists) in the Ruhr and that Urban Arts Ruhr as a whole has more recently come under scrutiny for (Bolsmann, 2014).

Conclusions

While both projects discussed in this chapter are very different from each other, they clearly point to current tensions determining the possible futures of Germany's Ruhr. The official, marketing-related campaigns, among them the *Detroit Projekt*, hints at the pressures of disassociating oneself from the idea of the Ruhr as a depressed post-industrial landscape and to put oneself on the map of successful cities that have quite literally "made it." In this project, "Detroit" stands as an icon of a kind of post-industrialism that Bochum needs to free itself from. It is absolutely unclear whether the citizens of Bochum or the Ruhr actually had any associations with "Detroit" at all before this project was initiated and implemented the slogan "This is not Detroit." In that slogan, Detroit is used as what Dora Apel (2015, p 6) has called "the central locus for the anxiety of decline." Ironically, though, it may quite possibly have been the slogan "This is not Detroit" that in the first place provoked a growing interest in the city among the citizens of the Ruhr, who, of course, wanted to understand what the fuss was all about.

By contrast, the more locally centered "Right to the City" Ruhr initiative, which set its goal toward *Learning from Detroit*, points to the dissatisfaction among the citizens—at least those citizens involved in the project—with regard to growing social injustice and poverty. While the region is setting up expensive marketing campaigns, opening newly refurbished cultural "flagships"—such as a former brewery cooling tower gone museum[15]—and building luxury housing,[16] initiatives such as this one would like to redirect the community's focus on pressing social problems that cannot be compensated by marketing alone. This is, of course, not an unusual agenda for a citizen initiative. However, it also makes clear that not all citizens necessarily identify with the way their home region—if it is a coherent region—is advertised in official campaigns, such as those of RUHR.2010. This becomes evident not only in the text *Learning from Detroit*, but also in the public discussion about whether the Ruhr is, in fact, the metropolis that the makers of RUHR.2010 tried to sell it as.[17]

Both projects, *Learning from Detroit* and the *Detroit Projekt*, are misleading in their use of "Detroit" as a buzzword. Both projects are not about anything that is going on in Detroit, but, rather, they both use one specific dimension of Detroit—citizen engagement and urban agriculture in the first example and the supposed "ruins" of Detroit and the city's economic decline in the second example—in order to advance very specific ideas about the future of the Ruhr. If anything at all, the only thing this might make clear is that much like the future of Detroit, the future of the Ruhr is not fixed in these terms: the path to the future is open, but it does not happen on a "blank canvas." It has to be place-based and, in these terms, supported by the citizens. It is most likely that solutions to problems such as long-term unemployment, educational challenges, disinvestment, and the lack of opportunity have to be based on local conditions and cannot easily be transferred from one place to another. Different structures of local and regional governance will have to be taken into account, alongside cultural specificities, while, at the same time, not discounting the idea of learning from each other, possibly even building on the idea of a "right to the city," if such a right can, indeed, be spelled out in detail.

Notes

[1] When these projects use the word "Detroit," they oftentimes use it as a buzzword and do not necessarily base their assumptions on very detailed background research in or about the City of Detroit.

[2] See: http://www.it.nrw.de/statistik/a/daten/bevoelkerungszahlen_zensus/zensus_rp1_dez13.html (accessed January 15, 2016).

[3] See: http://www.metropoleruhr.de/fileadmin/user_upload/metropoleruhr.de/Bilder/Daten___Fakten/Regionalstatistik_PDF/Arbeitsmarkt/Tabellen_05_2015.pdf (accessed January 15, 2016).

[4] The West German Broadcasting Agency (WDR) also reported about this topic, see, for example: http://www1.wdr.de/themen/aktuell/armutsbericht-nrw-100.html (accessed January 15, 2016).

[5] See: http://www.shrinkingcities.com/index.php?id=2&L=1 (accessed January 15, 2016).

[6] For a more detailed discussion of this idea, see Reicher (2011).

[7] See: http://www.thisisnotdetroit.de (accessed December 23, 2015).

[8] See: http://www.rechtaufstadt-ruhr.de (accessed December 21, 2015).

[9] See: http://www.urbanekuensteruhr.de/de/about-us (accessed December 21, 2015).

[10] See: http://www.rechtaufstadt-ruhr.de/learning-from-detroit/ (accessed December 21, 2015).

[11] See: http://www.rechtaufstadt-ruhr.de/files/2014/08/Realize-Ruhrgebiet.pdf (accessed December 23, 2015).

[12] At the moment, the idea of a basic income is negotiated in a number of cities in Europe, many of them located in the Netherlands. One city that has worked with this idea is Utrecht. The concept is closely monitored there, and has made quite an impact. For more information, see, for example: http://qz.com/473779/several-dutch-cities-want-to-give-residents-a-no-strings-attached-basic-income/ (accessed December 24, 2015).

[13] See: http://archiv.urbanekuensteruhr.de/en/projects/das-detroit-projekt:-opening.35/ (accessed December 23, 2015).

[14] See, for example: http://www.ruhr-guide.de/ruhrstadt/bochum/fotowettbewerb-mein-bochum-unsere-zukunft/22770,0,0.html (accessed December 24, 2015).

15 The "Dortmunder U" that was opened in the context of RUHR.2010, see: http://www.dortmunder-u.de (accessed December 24, 2015).

16 The "Phoenixsee" (see: http://www.phoenixseedortmund.de/Home.html [accessed December 24, 2015), a man-made lake, is replacing a steel plant in Dortmund. Around this lake, luxury housing has been and is still being built. This has led to several public discussions about such developments and the "right to the city" in Dortmund as well.

17 While I do not have statistical evidence for this, I was involved in several projects during that year, one of which was an international summer academy for students dealing with the Ruhr's future development and with its role within Europe (see: http://www.kulturwissenschaften.de/home/veranstaltung-265.html [accessed December 24, 2015]). In this context, there was a public discussion with one of the main heads behind RUHR.2010. The gist of the discussion was that the students absolutely did not want the Ruhr to be redefined as a metropolis.

You may not know my Detroit

jessica Care moore

If you've never slid down the GIANT SLIDE on a
potato sack
you may not know my Detroit.
If you've never eaten a Coney at 3 a.m. you may not
understand why it doesn't matter
how many games we win or lose
we wear our D HATS and tats year round.
Our streets were built to the rhythm of a
hand clap sound
I am a Detroit Lion on Linwood, a rebellious Tiger on
Tireman
a Stanley Cup carrying Red Wing on Rutherford.
a Detroit Piston constantly putting up new nets around
forgotten
white backboards and orange squares.
Rebellious cities never had it easy.
Innovative freeways aren't always paved in gold
Still, that thin strip of M-8 we call *The Davison* became a
conduit to every future highway in our nation
and so is the assembly line steel & wheels of our cars.
Detroiters always kept this country moving.
Revolutionary people don't always get good press but it
is in our DNA/it is our bloodline gift
to survive.
When the surface of your skin has potholes blasting
Temptations' records through
your pores

When your fingertips are blessed
by international water and you are now under the world's
media microscope
constantly checking your arms for track marks and close
ups
of how you might look once the
high was gone.
You are simply one city/built above crystals You are the
river of freedom
You are the tenacity of Malcolm
The truth of Sojourner.
We are the fish fry at grannies The Swim-Mobile
The Brightmoor Soccer Team/Dynamo's Deli on
Plymouth/The Boggs Center
The Aker School For Gifted Children
The old school sweet of Dutch Girl Donuts
The west side Sweet Potato Sensation cakes across the
street
from the mural covered beauty
we call Artist Village.
We exist in the brilliance of our young debaters, our
champion athletes, our self empowered rockers, our
young farmers & dancers and scientists and Future social
activists.
We are 5 E Gallery and Arise Detroit and
Black WOMEN Rock! We are N'namdi Gallery and
The Charles H. Wright and Goodwells and the opposite
of white flight
Our babies are Ice Dreamers
Young souls on ice
Detroit hockey players up early
at Butzel on Wyoming and Lyndon.
We are cultivating young visual artists at Cultural Roots
Art Camp
inside Mama Makini's home every summer on Prentis.
We are Coach Shaheed's Basketball Camp at Renaissance
We are all necessary coaches who act as fathers and
moms who create safe sanctuaries and
rite of passage programs for our daughters
Beautiful Detroit sistas. We are not urban fiction.
When the pulse of *our* city stops beating
the soul of American music and manmade industry dies

a metropolis with a broken heart
a split in half baseball field for months
a train station with broken stained glass eyes
that can still reflect we are a city with pride
our neighborhoods fighting for their namesake.
We may have abandoned homes but we
are not an abandoned people.
I hear outsiders talking about a New Detroit
I remember the beauty of Old Detroit

Detroit is the old black.
Block parties/the Cass Co-op/and late night car races
Hip Hop Shop and 7 smile strip
Tigers baseball games on a radio, around a neighborhood
bonfire
loud enough for the entire block to listen.
I was raised inside this sound.
I walked down Joy Road to get to school
I found lifelong friends on Ward Street/Stahelin
Pinehurst/Mendota/Manor/Littlefield Tireman/
Plymouth/West Chicago/Rosedale Park Mack and
Bewick/Gratiot/Harper/Conner Cadieux/Mansfield/
French Road/Heidelberg
Jefferson/Van Dyke/St Aubin Bagley/Porter/Church/
Holbrook/Evergreen Vernor/Marston/North End/
Livernois Chandler Park/Rouge Park/Palmer Park
I was raised on
Hamilton Bus Stop stories
The Purple Gang glory
Hudson's and Kresge's Five and Ten
When Belle Isle was open and alive way past ten!
We are the spirits rising inside Alice Coltrane's holy
ghost harp
We the *ooh baby baby* that made Smokey's smile melt tears
We the Wonder Bread smell of Stevie's harmonica
An international legend making city.
We are used to stones being thrown against our glassy
lakes.
Detroiters don't do fake.
We do work. We make art. Out of our neighborhoods
We made Anita Baker/Mike Banks/Juan Atkins/Jeff
Mills and Derrick May.

We made the Queen of Soul/and John Doe.
We made Proof and Slum Village/and white M & M's
We made Jackie Wilson/David Ruffin
The Supremes and The Winans family.
We make characters like Dreadlock Mike and Willie
Jenkins who told me:
We made jump rope from wire. We used to make everything.
We birthed two of the Fab Five and claim the whole
team
We the Bad Boys and the Errol Flynn.
Don't talk about a city's feet
when these are shoes you can't fit in.
We don't sleep in late
We don't wait for someone else to do it
We surrounded by masters
We the graves they love to walk over
We the people the census don't always count correctly
We are the sum of our grandmothers' prayers
and our Native ancestors' wishes
My brothers had to take out the garbage. I busted suds in
the kitchen.
We southern rooted. Country. Alabama/Mississippi/and
Georgia.
We grassroots soldiers.
We Damon's Records and Spectacles on Grand River
We the after-hours.
Concrete and Flowers
We know peace and
Joe Louis black power.
We the blue collar inside the rainbow of humanity
We the assembly line of work ethic and Union muscle
Jays Chips and Faygo Red hustle
We are EASTERN MARKET ON SATURDAYS
We a city of Masjids/Synagogues/Temples
And Baptist Church preachers
We fly hijab/wrapped sisters on Friday/and some of the
finest Church suit brothas
you'll ever see on any given Sunday
Muhammad Mosque Number 1/Fellowship Chapel/
Greater Grace/Hartford Memorial/We Triumph
We Bakers Keyboard Lounge and the legacy of Berts

Some of us young enough to know that there is young
genius being brewed in this city
in the keys of Jon Dixon/in the trumpet of Kris Johnson
in the writing of dream hampton/inside the sax of
Ladarrel and
De'sean/the voice of Steffanie Christi'an/Thornetta
Davis/and Monica Blaire.
We Dwele and Miz Korona/Black Milk/Wajeed,
Invincible & Ideeyah
We DJ Dez/Hot Waxx/Sacari/Nick Speed/One Belo
We are Khalid's *Center of the Movement*/Piper Carter's
Foundation of Women In Hip Hop
Detroit has spirits.
Not just the statue in front of the Coleman A. Young
Building
We got real time spirits & Ancestor spirits
All of them protect our city. Stand as guardians.
Our historians have names/buy coffee at Avalon
Still eat Coney dogs at Lafayette
Drink Detroit Red
Go to Sweetwater for the wings
Enjoy the dark lights at Union Street Value the Cass Café
Detroit is easily translated into
French and South African Apartheid and
The Berlin Wall crumbling down
Jewish and African holocausts
Black men in Italian suits
Shades painting live at the Torino Music Festival &
Underground Railroads Stops
Stop
and find a major city in this country find a musician on
this planet that doesn't
Respect Our History
MLK didn't preach his dream here first for no reason
Woodward Avenue is the spine of movements.
Michigan Avenue baseball left arm pitching
Grand Boulevard right leg walking
The steel & grind of Techno still breathing just east of
downtown
We wipe away the tears of clowns
America would not be America if not for the Motown
sound

The integrity and heart of our people are not bankrupt
We are rich with history. Raised on tradition
Our Daddy's lessons and our Momma's intuition
We have coaches and teachers and parents & activists and
leaders on the frontline
of this river/front.
We ride bikes down the Dequindre Cut. Maybe you've
heard of us.
We are the people inside the Michigan hand
Indigenous Detroiters & we love our land
We make artists with international fans
I'm from a Detroit hood, so I'm a part of the plan
Somebody gotta show the young ones
How to get up 75
We are not ghosts
We make art work in this city
We
Are
Alive.

(Copyright, Moore Black Press, from the book, *Sunlight through Bullet Holes* by jessica Care moore. Reprinted with permission.)

Section Two
Practices from Detroit

NINE

Evolution of municipal government in Detroit

John Gallagher

The second section of the book focuses on new practices found in Detroit. It features chapters written by writers who are either engaged in these new activities, or by insightful commentators who have witnessed and written about the city for a long period of time. John Gallagher fits into this latter category; his close to 30 years of writing about economic and urban development for the *Detroit Free Press* puts him in a unique position to assess many of today's new social and spatial practices. The trend that he focuses on in this chapter is the spinning off of pieces of Detroit's government into public–private partnerships, non-profits, or other forms of governance outside the City of Detroit's direct control. Gallagher takes an optimistic, if cautious, assessment of the shift in places such as Eastern Market, Cobo Center, or Belle Isle away from city control. His arguments are rooted in the structural and historic decline of the city, as illustrated in earlier chapters by George Galster and Ren Farley. Gallagher describes how, amid rapid population and economic decline, the city became unable to provide the funding to support the institutions, parks, and amenities within its borders. While he acknowledges the improvements that such partnerships bring, he is also aware of the tensions, many of them racial in origin, which have been produced or exacerbated because of this.

Gallagher outlines several factors that contribute to the more successful operation of these places, including access to different sources of funding and dedicated management (points that are reiterated in the conversation with Dan Carmody, President of the Eastern Market Corporation, in Chapter Nineteen). However, as others have noted in this book (see Victor, Chapter Twenty), Gallagher also reminds us that we should not assume that these transformations represent the only story taking place in Detroit and that there is a growing gap between the city's economic and geographic core (where most of these spin-offs take place) and its periphery. There are many caveats we need to be cautious of, including the fact that many of these spin-offs took place while Detroit was under an emergency manager who was not democratically elected by the people. The idea that these pieces of Detroit were "taken" away from its citizens will be picked up further in the conversations with Sandra Hines (Chapter Seventeen) and Yusef Bunchy Shakur (Chapter Twenty-four). That Gallagher ends his chapter with a discussion of the region's troubled history with race and racism and the implications that this has for spinning off pieces of municipal government also underscores his nuanced and balanced approach to journalism and to understanding the impact of these governance shifts.

John Gallagher is a veteran journalist for the *Detroit Free Press*. He is also the author of four books, including *Reimagining Detroit: Opportunities for Redefining an American City* (Gallagher, 2010a), which was named by the *Huffington Post* as among the best social and political books of 2010. His most recent book, *Revolution Detroit: Strategies for Urban Reinvention* (2013, Wayne State University Press), starts with the premise that Detroit can offer powerful lessons on dealing with urban decline and a broken municipal model. Gallagher was born in New York City and joined the *Detroit Free Press* in 1987 to cover urban and economic redevelopment efforts in Detroit and Michigan, a post that he still holds. John and his wife, Sheu-Jane, live along Detroit's east riverfront.

Introduction

It may be hard to credit today, when Detroit's city government has been shrunken by years of cutbacks followed by the nation's biggest municipal bankruptcy, just how robust Detroit's City Hall operations were in the 1950s. In those years, a middle class that seemed to expand and grow more prosperous every year demanded newly built houses that filled out the city's remaining empty corners and created a flourishing tax base that paid for all sorts of services, both essential and desired. Detroit's population was growing toward 2 million. The cityscape was crowded—14,000 people per square mile. With almost one third of Michigan's population living within its borders, Detroit exercised an outsized influence on the state's politics and economy. When the legendary Mayor Coleman A. Young, the city's first African-American chief executive, took office in 1974, the city operated 117 skating rinks, 18 city pools, and five "swim-mobiles," portable metal tanks that were filled with water and traveled to neighborhoods so kids could take a dip. The police department carried more than 4700 uniformed and civilian employees on its roster and had helicopters in the sky. Under the city's long-time planning director, Charles Blessing, Detroit mapped such groundbreaking urban renewal projects as Lafayette Park, an aesthetically significant enclave designed by famed architect Ludwig Mies van der Rohe. There were many such manifestations of a city on the move (Bomey and Gallagher, 2013).

By the time Young left office 20 years later, the city had closed all but a handful of its skating rinks and several of its city pools. The police helicopters were gone. About 2000 fewer police officers patrolled the city streets. As the years passed and the city's fiscal crisis deepened, more service cuts and layoffs followed. A succession of mayors demanded and got union acquiescence to pay reductions and furloughs. However, this cost-cutting failed to stop the inexorable downslide. The total assessed value of Detroit property—a good gauge of the city's tax base and its ability to pay bills—has fallen a staggering 77% over the past 50 years in inflation-adjusted (2012) dollars. City leaders tried repeatedly to reverse sliding revenue through new taxes. Despite adding a new income tax in 1962, a new utility tax in 1971, and a new casino gaming tax in 1999—not to mention several tax increases along the way—revenue adjusted for inflation fell 40% over the 50 years from 1962 to 2012. Meanwhile, higher taxes were helping drive residents to the newly built suburbs and were driving away business, further sapping the city's tax base. Today, Detroit still does not take in as much tax revenue from its multiple sources, including casino taxes, as it did from property taxes alone in 1963 (Bomey and Gallagher, 2013).

Layoffs, service cutbacks, and the piling on of more municipal bond debt, these were the tactics repeated across the landscape of the American heartland as cities large and small battled the impacts of suburbanization and deindustrialization. However, in Detroit, as in some other cities, another less-publicized strategy emerged—that of spinning off pieces of the municipal government into a series of private conservancies, public authorities, and non-profit corporations that could deliver municipal services when the cash-strapped city itself could not. These spin-offs proved controversial, but they were also remarkably successful, within certain limitations. It is the purpose of this chapter to examine these spin-offs and how and why they succeeded, as well as the limits of this type of municipal intervention.

Creative solutions for the delivery of municipal services

The trend began in Detroit in 1999 when the city's art museum, the Detroit Institute of Arts, left direct city management and became managed by a non-profit board. In 2002, General Motors and the philanthropic Kresge Foundation combined to fund the newly created Detroit Riverfront Conservancy, created to build and operate the city's planned RiverWalk waterfront promenade rather than having the city's parks and recreation department attempt the task. Shortly thereafter, the non-profit Detroit 300 Conservancy, formed to celebrate the city's 300 birthday in 2001, gifted the creation and operation of the central Campus Martius Park to Detroit—again a site owned by the city but managed by professional outsiders. In 2006, the city's Eastern Market, a Saturday farmers market, and the Detroit Historical Museum were both spun off into non-profit entities: the Eastern Market Corporation (see Carmody, Chapter Nineteen) and the Detroit Historical Society. In 2009, a new regional authority took over operation from the city of Cobo Center, the city's convention facility. Later, the city's workforce development agency, which had operated so inefficiently that the state of Michigan nearly cut off its funding, became the non-profit Detroit Employment Solutions Corp. The city's visionary framework for recovery, titled Detroit Future City, was drafted not by the city planning department, but by an outside working group funded by the Kresge Foundation and staffed by a variety of academic and professional planners. Moreover, during Detroit's municipal bankruptcy, both the city's public lighting department and its water department—the latter serving about 2 million customers in both the city and suburbs—were reorganized as public authorities. Perhaps most controversially, the city's historic Belle Isle Park was shifted from the city to the Michigan Department of Natural Resources under a long-term lease. These were just some of the operations spun off into quasi-public non-profit management entities or, as in the case of Belle Isle, another government unit (Gallagher, 2013a).

The reasons were manifold. Park facilities at Belle Isle had deteriorated for many years because the city lacked funds to keep things up; even park bathrooms were padlocked because there were not enough city workers to clean them. At Cobo Center, the aging facility, first opened in 1962, was proving so inadequate for modern shows that the planners of the iconic North American International Auto Show were threatening to go elsewhere with their annual event. Eastern Market was similarly tired and outdated, with many of the farmers' stalls empty and a good deal of the produce offered on Saturday wilted. Creators of the RiverWalk and Campus Martius Park were too politically savvy to say so openly but it was universally presumed that only independent conservancies freed from the politics and the whispers of corruption of direct city control would be able to do their jobs. Featherbedding was another problem; at the Detroit Historical Museum, the workforce shrank from 60 before the spin-off to 25 afterward with no loss of functionality; indeed, the museum and many of the other spun-off departments and functions transformed themselves from failures to successes once freed of direct city management (Gallagher, 2013a).

None of these spin-offs happened easily. Indeed, the city's municipal unions and their allies on City Council and elsewhere in city government often resisted bitterly. Partly, their objections were based on fears of job losses, but there was also a philosophical objection that the city was giving up too much and getting too little in return. To critics, these arrangements smacked of selling off the city piecemeal; they recalled the late Mayor Coleman A. Young's remark that "You don't sell off the jewels for the price of the polish." Most of the transfers took place only after bitter debate over losing control to outsiders.

But happen they did, and the improvements at the various entities generally proved immediate and dramatic. At the Cobo Center, the new regional board launched directly into a $277-million expansion and upgrade that was completed in mid-2016. So impressive were the results that the annual auto show signed up for a new long-term contract with the facility. Campus Martius and the RiverWalk have won national recognition for their creative placemaking. The spun-off workforce development agency quickly found itself back in the state's favor as it placed hundreds of candidates with local businesses, including a Ford Motor Co. supplier and the Meijer retail stores opening in Detroit.

Factors contributing to more successful operations

There's no single reason why the non-profit bodies running Cobo, the Detroit Institute of Arts, the RiverWalk, and other assets work so well under a new structure. Rather, it appears to stem from multiple factors (Gallagher, 2013a), as outlined in the following.

More efficient operations

The Detroit Historical Museum now operates with fewer than half the employees it had in 2006 when it left direct city control. Savings were gained in the building operations department, which was reduced by 75%.

At Cobo Center, operating expenses were reduced by 28%, from an estimated $20 million in the year prior to the authority's assumption of control to $14.5 million three years later. Over that time, Cobo's utility costs dropped from about $4.8 million in 2010 to about $2.8 million in 2012, a reduction of nearly 42%.

Cobo operates with roughly the same number of employees today as before, even though the authority picked up several new functions that were based elsewhere in city government, including finance and accounting, payroll, human resources, marketing, and sales.

Long-time experts said that the freedom from direct city control allowed these new entities to operate more as a private business. "These new authorities are able to create more flexibility in job descriptions and setting standards for acceptable performance, and I think that has had an impact," Sheila Cockrel, a long-time City Council member and now a consultant, said in a 2013 media interview (see Gallagher, 2013b).

New revenue sources

Often, new funding sources opened up once an operation was freed from direct city control. For example, the Cobo regional authority benefits from regional hotel and liquor taxes; the RiverWalk has been built largely with donations from the Kresge Foundation and General Motors, and Eastern Market has benefitted from foundation gifts from Kresge and others.

Focused management

Prior to its 2006 spin-off from city control, Eastern Market bounced among at least three city departments. None focused primarily on the market. However, once under the control of the non-profit Eastern Market Corporation, a new professional management team was put in place. The market was its sole focus. The same thing happened at Cobo, where the new Cobo regional authority hired a leading national firm involved in convention center management to run it. The RiverWalk has been built and managed under similar professional management.

"The spin-offs are able to procure faster with less bureaucracy, get better prices," Cockrel said. "These institutions aren't bogged down with the financial chaos that has impeded efficient operation in Detroit for so long. People get paid on time" (Gallagher, 2013b).

New capital projects

New funding sources and more focused management has allowed almost all of the spun-off entities to undertake major capital improvements. In mid-2016, Cobo finished a $277-million expansion that added a riverside atrium, a new entrance, better loading dock facilities, new lighting, escalators, and other systems, a major new ballroom, and additional meeting rooms and banquet facilities.

At Eastern Market, more than $15 million has been poured into renovating market sheds, plus millions more for the district, including a $10-million federal transportation grant to construct a network of greenways linking the market to the east riverfront and Midtown. The RiverWalk, the Detroit Historical Museum, and other operations have all undertaken major improvements, such as the recent extensive renovation of the historical museum.

Even critics of the new arrangements often concede that the spun-off entities were able to accomplish tasks that would probably have stalled if left to the cash-strapped and understaffed city departments. As former City Council President Charles Pugh said in 2013 of the new RiverWalk created by the Riverfront Conservancy: "There's no way we could have done that."

Key conditions must be met

However, caution is called for. Most of the successful spin-offs dealt with services that had a clear focus, a specific geographic location, and a discreet mission with relatively clear boundaries, such as operating a convention center, a museum, or building the RiverWalk. It also helped that there was often a dedicated revenue stream to support the new management structure, such as the hotel and liquor taxes that supported Cobo's improvements or the regional tax approved in the tri-county region to support the Detroit Institute of Arts.

It also helps if the tasks involved are technical, such as providing street lighting or operating a single Downtown park, rather than those that involve solving broader social problems such as police work. Indeed, Brady Baybeck, a Professor of Political Science at Wayne State University, told the *Detroit Free Press* that the model has worked well in Detroit because it has been applied to some obvious situations: "My assessment of Detroit is that they're picking the low-hanging fruit that can sustain themselves through revenues or through contributions," he said (Gallagher, 2013a).

Critics also note that the authorities and conservancies that manage the assets are not led by democratically elected public officials, but by people appointed by boards or, in some cases, by elected officials. That means that the city needs to balance the potential for service improvement with the potential for diminished accountability or democratic control.

All these issues took on their most dramatic cast during Detroit's municipal bankruptcy of 2013–14, when US Bankruptcy Judge Steve Rhodes and Kevyn Orr, the city's emergency manager appointed by Governor Rick Snyder, ran Detroit as virtual dictators, bypassing mayoral and City Council control entirely. The fact that the bankruptcy reorganization was accomplished with relative swiftness and with fewer cuts to municipal pensions than expected made acceptance of this temporary lapse of democracy more acceptable to many, but certainly not to all.

An irony of this reinvention of Detroit's municipal government is that the city's new mayor, Michael Duggan, who took office at the beginning of 2014, has said repeatedly that he dislikes the process of spinning off municipal services and that he intends to stop it. He has even drawn some of the functions back closer to mayoral control, such as the Detroit Employment Solutions Corporation workforce development agency, which coordinates closely with Duggan's economic team even as it still operates as a separate non-profit. Duggan has said often that he cannot guarantee results if he cannot control a given service and the people who run it, and so he is determined to gather the reins of control back into mayoral hands.

How this will work out in years to come is yet to be seen. Clearly, though, Detroit provides one of the nation's most dramatic examples of an evolution of municipal government in response to stress, as well as some of the most creative solutions for the delivery of municipal services among older industrial cities.

At this point, two questions present themselves. First, how applicable are these tactics used in Detroit to other cities? Second, does Detroit's notorious racial divide—more than 80% of the city is African-American, while the suburbs are largely white—make this process of reinvention easier or more difficult?

As to the first question, Detroit certainly enjoys some advantages that may not be available to other cities. Despite the city's reputation for Rust Belt vacancy and decline, the Southeast Michigan region as a whole, encompassing the immediate three-county area, including Detroit plus several exurban counties, remains overall quite wealthy, a legacy of the region's rich industrial past. Vast fortunes were made in Detroit during the industrial heyday of the 20th century, fortunes that underwrote many of the region's museums, libraries, universities, and hospitals. Several major philanthropic foundations based in Metro Detroit, including the Kresge Foundation and the Community Foundation, have been there to pour money into revitalization projects in the city. Most notably, these efforts included the "grand bargain" during Detroit's bankruptcy that saw multiple foundations donate more than $300 million into a pool to shore up the pensions of city government retirees and "rescue" the artwork of the Detroit Institute of Arts from possible sale to satisfy creditors. Not all other cities are so lucky in their philanthropic institutions. Certainly, many smaller cities—Flint, Gary, Allentown, dozens or hundreds more—probably lack the long-term wealth or the sizeable philanthropic entities that can engage in such spirited urban rescue missions. Then, too, the ability of state government to appoint emergency managers or to otherwise control the process of reinvention at the local city level may be more or less helped or hindered by state and local laws elsewhere. Finally, it could be said that Detroit's very distress, its status as the nation's poster child of urban decline, became something of an advantage from around 2010 onward. Everyone from the Obama White House to entities like the Ford Foundation to Detroit's local billionaires wanted to save the city. Artists fleeing rising prices in Brooklyn often made their way to Detroit, the "next" Brooklyn. Saving Detroit became the thing to do, and other cities probably do not enjoy that same advantage (Bomey et al, 2014).

As to the second question of race relations, it must be concluded that the metro region's long, sad history of racial discord has influenced the reinvention of Detroit's city government at every step, albeit in complex ways. The very need to reinvent Detroit's municipal structure in the first place stems in large part from the racially motivated flight from the city to the suburbs, which drained away the city's tax base. Then, too, as the African-American population swelled to such numbers as to take over City Hall, the city's municipal workforce came to employ thousands of black middle-class urban professionals. These municipal workers were threatened by the spinning off of municipal operations to the outside conservancies and authorities. Indeed, many of the bitterest struggles over spinning off these entities centered on whether municipal workers would lose their jobs once their operation had been released to non-profit control. In early 2016, Detroit employs fewer than half the municipal workers it did 50 years ago, and while most of that reduction was due to the shrinking tax base and not the spinning off of operations, the fear of further losses made the spinning-off process that much more difficult.

It is also clear that some operations probably, or at least arguably, ought never to be spun off. Scandals in Michigan in 2015 over the inadequate food served to state prison inmates calls into question whether the food contracts should have been let to a private operator. The use of private security guards in Downtown Detroit, personnel employed by billionaire Dan Gilbert's Rock Ventures after Gilbert moved his corporate headquarters to Downtown in 2010, has sparked considerable debate over the privatization of public spaces (Doucet and Smit, 2016; see also Kreichauf, Chapter Four). Indeed, the whole debate over whether charter schools have represented any real improvement over public schools remains unresolved.

Then, too, there are other ways to reinvent municipal government besides spinning off pieces of it. Under Mayor Mike Duggan, the city has been upgrading its woefully underperforming information technology operations, for example, introducing new smartphone apps to make it easier for citizens to report dangerous buildings or to pay for parking at a Downtown meter. Cities everywhere have been utilizing such technological improvements to streamline their operations.

It is fair to say that Detroit went the route of spinning off municipal operations only because, first, it was forced to by the realities of its loss of tax base, and, second, the city enjoyed an usual degree of support from well-funded philanthropic foundations and legacy corporations who call Detroit home. That these spin-offs have succeeded so well is a tribute to the ingenuity and grit of Detroit and its supporters. However, no one should think that this Detroit model proved easy to achieve, or is necessarily a path for others to follow.

TEN

Detroit's emerging innovation in urban infrastructure: how liabilities become assets for energy, water, industry, and informatics

Dan Kinkead

Detroit has many aspects that, all too often, are conceived of as liabilities. These include vast amounts of vacant land, empty and abandoned buildings, and undervalued property. Dan Kinkead sees these characteristics not as liabilities, but rather as assets for leveraging new and innovative urban practices. His chapter focuses on innovative infrastructure, such as renewable energy production or industrial adaptive reuse. In it, he provides specific examples of where a variety of stakeholders are coming together on specific projects that form part of holistic approaches to a multitude of challenges. The examples presented in this chapter are varied and involve both changing practices in specific sites throughout the city and new techniques of data gathering and mapping that are helping to both better understand the city and meet some of the challenges that it is facing, including the threat from speculators mentioned in Chapter Five by Joshua Akers.

Dan Kinkead is an architect and urban designer. He is a principal for urban design at the national design firm SmithGroupJJR, and visiting architect in residence at the Cranbrook Academy of Art. Before his current role, Dan was the Founding Director and Director of Projects for the Detroit Future City Implementation Office. Dan's career has included a design principal role at Detroit-based Hamilton Anderson Associates, and an urban design role at Skidmore Owings & Merrill, LLP, in New York. He graduated from Harvard University with a master of architecture in urban design, with distinction, and from the University of Kentucky with a bachelor of architecture. Kinkead's work has been published in domestic and international design media, including a recent contribution to *Remaking Post-industrial Cities: Lessons from North America and Europe*, edited by Don Carter (Routledge, 2016).

Introduction

Detroit is often defined by emotive and consumable illustrations of its struggles. The physical manifestations of its historic depopulation and disinvestment are equally startling. With a 60% decline in peak population, over 23.4 square miles of accumulated vacant land, and its recent emergence from the largest municipal bankruptcy in US history, Detroit is broadly recognized for the negative characteristics of global economics, and socio-political distress (United States Census Bureau, 2010; Motor City Mapping, 2014; see also Galster, Chapter Two). Yet, more recent assertions, including the Detroit Future City (2013) *Strategic Framework Plan*—a comprehensive recovery tool launched in 2013—are beginning to articulate a new future for the city. Moving beyond the conventional tropes of urban redevelopment, it reveals a coordinating playbook for a range of community, government, institutional, and business partners to maximize their impact through collaboration, and create a more fiscally, socially, and environmentally sustainable city.

Accordingly, the characteristics representing the physical dimension of Detroit's challenges are beginning to yield curious advantages. This chapter reveals, though a series of examples and projects, how perceived liabilities that represent Detroit's decline are becoming intrinsic assets for its recovery. With available land, relatively low capital cost thresholds, and opportunities for initiatives to yield system-wide impacts, a renewed entrepreneurialism and ethos of localized innovation is manifest in a range of endeavors. Chief among them are emerging innovative infrastructures. Whether renewable energy production, storm-water management, industrial adaptive reuse, or accessible digital tools, these infrastructures sit at the intersection of urban resilience, intrepid civic stewardship, and ingenuity.

In the process, historically powerful racial divisions remain, but are beginning to give way to shared strategies and actions for recovery. In many cases, conscious and deliberate methods for inclusion and shared outcomes, as well as resident-driven initiatives, are mediating a new dimension of racial and cross-sector collaboration. While questions about authorship and privilege are appropriately present, increasingly candid exchanges on these issues are an implicit outcome of the innovative infrastructure itself. From environmental justice and green infrastructure achieved through vacant land reutilization, to redevelopment and digital access to once-isolated information, many initiatives are manifest through Detroit's crucible of race and recovery.

As Detroit directly engages its own challenges, it is also demonstrating how similar regional, national, and global issues may be addressed. From improved impacts on the city's globally significant water source, to broader information access, as well as the conversion of the city's Fordist economic apparatus into hubs for innovative, skilled, and inclusive production, Detroit is delivering highly relevant, comparatively low-cost, and translatable strategies and tactics—at multiple scales.

Innovative urban infrastructure

What follows are early cases of how Detroit is adapting to create new city systems through collective enterprise. Each is born of substantial need, but also thoughtful coordination to fulfill the shared objectives of participatory plans such as the Detroit Future City *Strategic Framework Plan*, and community aspiration. Many of Detroit's perceived liabilities are reframed as assets; the city's vacant and abandoned land becomes land of opportunity from which a range of stakeholders may start businesses and create innovative projects. The results are not simply "different" infrastructures, but rather holistic strategies improving performance, addressing long-standing environmental justice concerns, and yielding new economic opportunity. Each of these initiatives, while different in impetus and focus, is born from similar and unconventional partnerships that often include residents, entrepreneurs, educational institutions, and activists.

Renewable energy

From small-scale, site-specific photovoltaic power generation, to larger district-wide arrays for community power, Detroit's power supply is on the verge of increased diversification, environmental performance, and resilience through university partnerships, community-driven strategy, and growing industry-wide awareness of the renewable energy opportunities for Detroit. Here, underutilized vacant land, and former industrial sites and facilities, are becoming the locus for renewable energy production.

While renewable energy production at scale in Detroit remains an elusive enterprise, the emerging piloting efforts and strategies illustrate growing confidence. With increased interest and collaboration—from the United States Department of Energy to motivated residents—Detroit is poised to regain significant ground lost to other cities in reduced environmental impact, and illustrate how urban space can be reused to create localized renewable energy in recovering cities across North America.

The Beltline Solar District

The Beltline Solar District is motivated to provide greater renewable energy offerings to Detroiters by adaptively reutilizing available vacant industrial buildings and land. The Beltline Solar District will also demonstrate how utility-scale renewable energy providers can improve the environment, employ Detroiters, and complement ongoing renewable energy production from the region's investor-owned power providers (Van Buren, 2015).

Led by Diane Van Buren, a resident and finance, development, and planning consultant, the Beltline Solar District—a partnership of committed residents and technical experts—is preparing to implement a catalytic 5 megawatt solar array and storage facility within vacant buildings and land along the Beltline industrial and rail corridor on the city's near east side. This once-robust industrial corridor and rail spur is now home to a smaller, but active and eclectic, assembly of businesses to which the power would be provided. The District, near Van Buren's home, is shaped in partnership with these local businesses, the City of Detroit, and surrounding neighborhood residents. The initiative intends to set a new standard for renewable power generation in Detroit, break down barriers, reduce costs and unknowns, and enable others to contribute. The efforts would also complement DTE Energy's renewable energy production, which is largely through wind-turbine power along the great lakes, with limited production in Detroit.

With 230,000 square feet (5.3 acres) of existing vacant land, 200,000 square feet (4.6 acres) of car ports, and 750,000 square feet (17.2 acres) of building rooftops, the District is planning initial implementation across a 36-month "performance period" that includes the following (Van Buren, 2015, p 3):

- economically feasible utility-scale photovoltaic system that can be installed for a cost of $2 per megawatt or less;

- effective policies, finance tools, and systems to streamline the implementation process;
- a triple bottom line assessment of the community benefits of the pilot;
- district incorporation into a future citywide master plan development; and
- collaboration with DTE Energy to fulfill a solar program of up to 20 megawatts of photovoltaic power and 1000 new related jobs for Detroiters by 2020.

Sampson-Webber Solar Power Garden

Initiated through a partnership between Detroit Public Schools (DPS) and Lawrence Technological University (LTU), an integrated renewable energy, food production, and rainwater harvesting initiative is being developed for the Sampson-Webber K-8 school on the city's near west side. The project, started in 2014, is currently midway through implementation and is intended to be complete by 2017. The result will be an energy farm, learning gardens, and an outdoor classroom with photovoltaic energy and rainwater harvesting systems.

Working hand-in-hand with students, parents, community members, and faculty, Associate Professor Constance Bodurow, Engineering Professor Don Carpenter—both of LTU—and their joint architecture and engineering studios have leveraged Ford College Community Challenge funding and other support to design and construct a small-scale photovoltaic array and garden in an unused portion of the Sampson-Webber school yard. DPS students worked with LTU graduate students in engineering and architecture to learn about renewable energy, water conservation, and food production. They are also participating in the project's construction, and gaining valuable skills (Bodurow, 2015).

The first of its kind for DPS, this innovative program includes a shared long-term vision for the site, school, and surrounding neighborhood. Opportunities for this integrated learning environment provide powerful lessons for students, bring challenged communities together, and provide a prototype for citywide deployment. Accomplished with limited funding and dedicated stewardship from LTU, the program demonstrates how partnerships can yield small, but remarkably impactful, outcomes for children who might not otherwise be exposed to emergent technology, or have sufficient access to fresh food for their families.

Blue and green infrastructure

Like many other developed cities of Detroit's vintage, storm–water and sanitary waste are combined for treatment before being released. These systems are often expensive to operate and to improve, and they struggle to manage the ever-increasing number of high-volume rain events. Detroit's combined sewer system, when overwhelmed, directly discharges untreated combined sewage into the Detroit River, and by extension the Great Lakes. Such sewage includes human waste as well as fertilizer run-off from lawns and automotive detritus from paved surfaces.

At the core of the Great Lakes, Detroit sits at the center of 84% of the North American fresh surface water supply, and 22% of global fresh surface water supply (USEPA, 2015). Detroit's sewage output has direct and undeniable impacts on this globally significant body of water, bounded by 48 million people. In 2011, Detroit had 36 direct discharges of untreated and partially treated sewage (Detroit Future City, 2013, p 186).

While expensive large-scale subterranean concrete vault systems have been contemplated to mitigate such discharges, the substantial cost of these systems has pre-empted their implementation in Detroit. Instead, two large-scale blue and green infrastructure projects are now being implemented in the city by utilizing available vacant land to mitigate combined sewer overflows. These initiatives leverage federal–local and public–private partnerships to realize the functionality of a new urban form that integrates sizable open space areas with natural systems. The result will not only be improved and cost-effective infrastructure, but also long-term open space utilization that improves Detroit's supply and demand mismatch. This, in turn, supports increased residential and employment densities in areas where robust fixed systems are present to support them. In addition, agglomerating economies can be achieved, and effective high-volume systems (such as mass transportation) can be effectively utilized and supported.

Upper Rouge Tunnel Green Infrastructure Initiative (URTGI)

In 2010, recognizing the overwhelming cost of an ambitious storm-water storage tunnel project below the city's northwest side, the Michigan Department of Environmental Quality (MDEQ) approved a $50 million investment in blue and green infrastructure over a 19-year period from 2010 to 2029 to ultimately manage the same volume of water, but with natural systems at-grade. Currently, within the

2013–17 time period for the project, $15 million has been approved to mitigate 2.8 million gallons of storm water in the original area in which the tunnel was contemplated (Green Infrastructure, 1). This amount, which matches the two-year 24-hour peak rain event amount to which engineers are required to design, is now being addressed through a large-scale blue and green infrastructure project throughout the city's Brightmoor neighborhood.

Here, within the few parts of the city exhibiting some degree of topographical change (Detroit is quite flat), sits the Rouge River, which flows to the Detroit River and the Great Lakes. This means that storm water can be more effectively separated and conveyed, naturally, through this hydrological system. The area also includes some of the highest concentrations of vacant land. In some cases, significant numbers of sites can be assembled into larger sites. The residents of Brightmoor, long identified as intrepid innovators, are embracing a new form of living that includes expansive open space and many uses, such as urban agriculture and renewable energy (Archambault, 2009).

To meet the MDEQ project goals, the Detroit Water and Sewerage Department (DWSD) and its team of consultants have initiated the project and identified high-priority areas in which the volume of storm water saved will have a more substantial positive benefit than in another area due to natural hydrology. Moreover, the green infrastructure techniques used will be integrated into the neighborhood, helping to improve its physical condition, while providing space for recreation, increased agriculture, and community functions.

With final rounds of vacant home demolitions to be completed in 2015 and 2016, the URTGI area will have sufficient site area for potential storm-water run-off reduction of 44.8 million gallons. While no one hopes for the kind of disinvestment and depopulation experienced in Brightmoor, the realization of positive natural systems within the space of such loss demonstrates how cities like Detroit can leverage unique circumstances to improve resilience and system performance that benefit residents, the city, and the Great Lakes.

Great Lakes Restoration Initiative (GLRI)

As the URTGI project was being assembled, a smaller research-driven green and blue infrastructure pilot was being initiated by the Southeast Michigan Council of Governments (SEMCOG), and a range of community partners along the city's lower east side. Together with the Detroit Future City Implementation Office and the Detroit Economic Growth Corporation, SEMCOG gained US Environmental

Protection Agency funding, and matching funding from the Erb Family Foundation and the Kresge Foundation, to ultimately create a $2 million targeted blue and green infrastructure pilot project in the DWSD's Near Eastside Drainage District. The project has been implemented in two main areas with two respective partners: Recovery Park, a socially motivated urban farming enterprise testing large-scale storm-water retention techniques; and the Eastside Community Network, a community development organization integrating smaller-scale individual lot techniques that may be translated to a range of vacant lots throughout the east side. Like the URTGI, the GLRI pilot is using the two-year, 24-hour storm as the design target, but the objective here is to evaluate the impact of different techniques in achieving this target (SEMCOG, 2013).

Both projects demonstrate how urban areas that have suffered disinvestment and depopulation can reduce extremely high fiscal and environmental costs associated with gray infrastructure, and directly impact the health of residents and the Great Lakes by including low-maintenance green systems that have an array of ancillary benefits, including reductions in air pollutants and high heat events due to a depleted urban tree canopy. While similar projects are increasingly common in US cities, the scale and significance of the potential impact differentiates Detroit.

Building infrastructure: reindustrialization

Often catalogued as "post-industrial," cities such as Detroit are perceived to be perpetually confounded with an anachronistic economy and built infrastructure—facets of a highly extractive, one-dimensional, and unsustainable model. However, for Detroit, the most obvious vestiges of its flawed mono-economy—its industrial buildings—are quietly becoming infrastructural advantages. Detroit is distinguished from most of its industrial cohort of "legacy cities" by a global identity, and an equally deep stock of vacant industrial facilities, totaling over 4.3 square miles in floor area alone (Interface Studio, 2010, p 3). With high capacity power, water, and structures, set within accommodating zoning, these facilities are a major part of Detroit's evolution, yielding a more diverse and durable core of manufacturing—one in which a wide array of products, participants, and techniques are driving Detroit's new industrial economy.

Here, Detroit's burgeoning innovators are leveraging low-cost ready-made infrastructure for production, and a growing national and international appetite for authenticity in manufacturing. The sociocultural, economic, and physical intersections yield a new life for Detroit's buildings, and a new opportunity to create a more inclusive, granular, and resilient localized economy. If Fordist scales of production and divisions of labor instrumentalized its workforce and contributed to Detroit's downfall in a global economy, more skilled, hands-on, and remarkably less extractive production processes are emerging as intrinsic qualities to provide a more fertile economic environment and a reduced number of footless enterprises. What follows are a few examples that begin to convey some early legitimacy to this premise.

Detroit Bikes—13639 Elmira Street

Through the reutilization of a 50,000 square feet formerly vacant factory on the city's west side, Detroit Bikes began producing bikes at scale in 2012. Employing and training Detroiters, and contributing to broader bike culture in a city that now operates the second-largest weekly mass bike ride in the country, "Slow Roll," the growing company is deliberate about its location outside Downtown–Midtown, leveraging former production equipment from the auto industry, and the desire to create handmade, affordable, and high-volume US bike frames. As stated by Zak Pashak, Founder and President of Detroit Bikes:

> This is a bike built by the car industry, really ... these are the skill sets of auto industry people in an auto industry town. These are the machines from auto industry tool and die shops, and a lot of the people that work here did, at one point, work in the auto industry. (Quoted in Davis, 2015)

Shinola and College for Creative Studies—Argonaut Building

Shinola, a luxury product line manufactured in Detroit, and the College for Creative Studies, a renowned multidisciplinary design school, are anchor tenants for the adaptively reutilized General Motors Argonaut Building. This former "skunkworks" for General Motors was once the home to industrial design and prototyping led by Harley Earl, the company's design leader. Today, the once-vacant structure is the center of Shinola's fabrication of watches, bikes, and leather goods, where its Detroit-resident workforce is trained by expert manufacturers, creating enduring and intrinsic skills. Initiated by the College for Creative Studies, the adaptively reutilized facility anchors many of the program's most innovative design studios. It is noteworthy that both Shinola and

Detroit Bikes also leverage Detroit's robust global logistics chain—a less known, but critical, facet of the auto industry.

Pony Ride and Russell Industrial Center—Corktown and Milwaukee-Junction

Providing space and equipment to emerging firms for fabrication, these now locally iconic incubators support an array of start-ups with shared resources and networking (see Cooley, Chapter Twenty-one). Here, entrepreneurs, including those gaining funding and support from new sources such as the New Economy Initiative and the Goldman Sachs 10,000 Small Businesses Program, are utilizing the industrial space and collective networks within the facilities to advance their work. These incubators not only play a critical role as the starting point for many entering the entrepreneurial ecosystem, but those such as Pony Ride cultivate a strong impetus for social advocacy (Rajagopal, 2016).

Recovery Park Food System—8201 St. Aubin Street

The medium-scale food system start-up is dedicated to growing food in the city to provide jobs and training to those with substantial barriers to employment. It is one of many socially conscious food production enterprises stimulating the economy in a city that maintains over 30% of its region's food-processing employment (Detroit Future City, 2013, p 56). As stated by Gary Wozniak, Recovery Park's leader: "We're taking a look more at commercial indoor agriculture so that the jobs are year round"; "We can get three, maybe four growing seasons working indoors" (quoted in Hennen, 2012). The group is also preparing to reuse an area of the city's near east side for greenhouse production in 2016.

Information infrastructure

To equip any city to make the substantial recovery Detroit must make, those contributing must have access to the necessary information to make informed decisions. However, in the wake of Detroit's long decline, the resulting reduction in effective systems for information dissemination about property, budget, and crime was palpable. Recent changes, however, have begun to address these challenges, and illustrate how entrepreneurialism and transparency can thrive in such an environment, creating important advancements in and instilling a sense of shared authorship of and accessibility to the city's future.

Today, as Detroit's public sector regains its footing under the leadership of Mayor Mike Duggan, substantial improvements—both within the city and outside—mark a more innovative and robust mixture of advancements that are allowing Detroit to actually leapfrog other cities in their systems management.

Mapping, evidence, and strategy

It may not be a coincidence that Detroit's greatest struggles emerged at a time when the city itself seemed to have the least overall capacity, but in that space of challenge, an array of civic advocates and technologists have stepped in to provide the essential resources necessary for all Detroiters, from the highest-level leaders to the resident, to make the most informed decisions.

From this work has emerged data and mapping tools, with national currency, being developed in Detroit. Here, the information once owned by a select few is now increasingly in the hands of many. Certainly, "digital divides" persist, but the increasing democratization of information in Detroit is helping. The intense interest in understanding more about Detroit's condition given the enormity of the challenges it has faced has yielded tools such as Data Driven Detroit's Open Data Portal and "Motor City Mapping," and Loveland's "Why Don't We Own This?" and "Site Control," each equipping users with valuable information about property, regulation, and ownership. Accessible at home or on public library computers, most facets are free for use, while some have minimal fees. Loveland's "Why Don't We One This?" site is now used in many cities across North America—all stemming from Detroit's decline and the vacuum of capacity into which organizations like Loveland have stepped (Data Driven Detroit, 2015; Loveland Technologies, 2015).

Such advancements are uniquely important now as offshore speculators seek to make gains in a recovering Detroit with a very low price threshold for property. Here, Detroit's tax-foreclosure crisis yielded over 25,000 properties for auction in 2015, accommodating bids as low as $500 per property in second-round bidding (Olberholtzer, 2015). With consistently high numbers of properties available in these auctions year after year, the diversity and accessibility of clear land management tools and information can provide wider participation in processes historically woven within closed power structures.

A Field Guide to Working with Lots

If Detroit Open Data provides Detroiters with candid insight into government, and Site Control outlines better land information, *A Field Guide* from the Detroit Future City Implementation Office equips residents with analog and digital information about how they can improve vacant land in their neighborhoods. While Detroit's vacant land portfolio is expansive, it is also remarkably disaggregated across the city, typically manifest in one or two vacant lots on a given block. Such lots can often be a source of blight in neighborhoods, but they can also be beautiful spaces that stabilize neighborhoods, bringing residents together and improving ecological performance (Detroit Future City Implementation Office, 2015).

A Field Guide to Working with Lots provides an informative tool to residents to improve vacant lots in their neighborhoods. It includes a lot design catalog of 35 different treatments, and a workbook that walks residents through the entire lot-improvement process, from side-lot disposition, to permitting, design, plant selection, grading, and maintenance: "Options are grouped by the people involved, experience level, maintenance, storm water benefits, and cost" (Link, 2015, p 20). The tool is intended to be highly accessible, from its content to its methods for distribution, including libraries, churches, city district offices, and the Internet. To support catalytic efforts by residents to improve their lots, the Detroit Future City Implementation Office launched a mini-grant program in late 2015 to fund a range of resident-led improvement projects across the city. Tools such as the mini-grant can contribute to a more stable and equitable environment for self-provisioning in Detroit.

Conclusion

While Detroit's resulting social, economic, and physical challenges from over a half-century of disinvestment and depopulation remain significant, some are revealing opportunities for the city's inclusive and innovative recovery. If Detroit's past was linked to monolithic industry, conventional top-down decision-making, and the exploitation of resources, its future represents a more aware and diverse set of partners, and an ethos of intrepid civic stewardship.

Detroit may not be the vanguard of innovative infrastructure, but instead, to other cities, it is a noteworthy illustration of how fertile ideas and partnerships can be forged within an environment of struggle and change. If the process of Detroit's municipal bankruptcy has stripped away the final veneer of its conventional and unsustainable past, it has also revealed the need for a more inclusive and integrated future. While substantial infrastructure developments in cities were the sole domain of governmental concerns, contracts, and plans, they are becoming increasingly linked to the very citizens, businesses, and institutions that they are to support, and much more diversified in their application. This yields increasing ideation and creativity while more directly linking decision-makers, implementers, and end users. More contributors and integration naturally yield important benefits, such as public inquiry, information sharing, and implicit evaluation. They also yield new challenges to ensure that regulation and policy can keep pace, and fragile cross-sector partnerships can be supported. The results are noisy, messy, and transformative.

ELEVEN

Visions in conflict: a city of possibilities

Sharon Howell and Richard Feldman

Just as Dan Kinkead sees new possibilities emerging in Detroit, so, too, do Sharon (Shea) Howell and Richard Feldman. However, rather than focusing, as Kinkead did, on infrastructure or resilience, or on how bottom-up initiatives can become part of the planning system, as Khalil Ligon will describe in Chapter Twelve, Howell and Feldman's possibilities are much more rooted in social revolution and formed out of the visions of activists such as Grace Lee Boggs (see Chapter Twenty-five). They see Detroit as a space to begin anew, with genuine grassroots movements taking hold out of the destruction of the industrial era. Such a vision puts them at odds with many in the city's establishment, and these conflicts about the future of the city are outlined in this chapter.

They argue that Detroit's corporate visions are focused on taking back control of the city and that the imposition of an emergency manager and the declaration of bankruptcy in 2013 were central to this strategy. In contrast, their vision is rooted in local production and local, democratic control. Central to this is their People's Plan, formed by more than 60 different organizations to counter the Plan of Adjustment put forward by the city's "corporate powers." Tapping into the city's lengthy history of resistance, Howell and Feldman argue that these two visions are now "at war." Their chapter focuses on resistance and struggle in three important areas: land, water, and consciousness. Readers of this chapter will find many arguments that challenge or contradict many of the celebrated initiatives, narratives, and practices in Detroit. Such critical commentaries on the injustices of Detroit's contemporary "revitalization," as well as visions for a more inclusive and just city, are important today as the city emerges from bankruptcy and new narratives focused on Downtown's "success" are constructed.

Richard Feldman and Shea Howell are members of the James and Grace Lee Boggs Center to Nurture Community Leadership. They have been active in community-based struggles in Detroit for more than four decades. Richard Feldman has also worked in a Ford assembly plant and is active in the United Auto Workers. Shea Howell is a Professor of Communication at Oakland University. Over the years, they have written many articles together. Their most recent essay, "A Detroit story: ideas whose time has come," was published in 2014 in *Grabbing Back: Essays Against the Global Land Grab* by Alexander Ross (AK Press). Many of the visions and practices put forward in this chapter will be elaborated upon further in Section Three of this book, "Conversations from Detroit."

Introduction

Detroit is a city shaped by possibilities. In the early decades of the 20th century, the possibilities of good-paying jobs and freedom from Jim Crow attracted thousands of African-Americans from the South to join those of European descent in providing the labor and skills for the emerging industrial might of the city. Mexican-Americans and people from throughout Central America developed vibrant communities in the face of European hostility, including the coerced deportations of thousands of people during the Great Depression (Zielin, 2011). Arab-Americans also came seeking work, creating some of the largest communities in the country. In this cultural mix, by mid-century Detroit was a Mecca for African-American culture, political thought, and action. White flight, aided by federal and state programs, and accelerated by the 1967 uprising, opened the way for black political power in the mayor's office, public services, the halls of the state legislature, and the US Congress (Bates, 2014).

As automation and capital flight combined to eliminate most of the jobs that had attracted people in the early part of the century, hostility from the surrounding white suburbs intensified. State and federal dollars became scarce. People, factories, stores, and homes disappeared. Decline dominated the media coverage of the city. As Herscher (2012, p 6) explains, Detroit is characterized as being "in such deep decline, it is scarcely recognizable as a city at all."

Yet, some of us understood these changes to be opening new possibilities. We realized that the deindustrialization of Detroit was part of a larger transition, as great as that from hunting and gathering to agriculture, or from agriculture to the industrial age (Boggs and Kurashige, 2011, pp 29–47). The "triple revolution" of rapidly changing technology, more destructive methods of warfare, and advancing human rights combined to create a new moment of possibility for revolutionary change in our cities, our country, and ourselves (Ad Hoc Committee on the Triple Revolution, 1964). These changes were intensified throughout the subsequent decades as capital flight and global competition increased.

As Andrew Herscher comments, decline tells only part of the story. The disappearance of the industrial economy and the capitalist values that shaped it also created "spaces and opportunities for the alternative means of achieving viable urban lives", as crisis brings a new "openness" (Herscher, 2012, p 15). Grace Lee Boggs, well-known Detroit philosopher-activist for more than 70 years, often remarked: "Detroit is the place and space to begin anew." As a city steeped in the values of African-American culture, Detroit's people had resources of memory and imagination "to make a way out of no way." Grace Lee Boggs explained how abandonment becomes the grounds for new creativity: "The thousands of vacant lots and abandoned houses not only provide the space to begin anew but also the incentive to create innovative ways of making our living—ways that nurture our productive, cooperative and caring selves" (Boggs, 2009).

Two visions

The corporate power structure does not share the view of Detroiters creating the possibilities of a new kind of city for the 21st century. Rather, the city is seen as incompetent, corrupt, incapable, and needing to be saved. L. Brooks Patterson, the executive of neighboring, prosperous Oakland County, captured this attitude in a recent interview in the *New Yorker*, saying "What we are going to do is turn Detroit into an Indian reservation where we herd all the Indians into the city, build a fence around it, and then throw in the blankets and corn" (Kate, 2014).

Crime, not creativity, is the usual portrayal. Creative innovation is, almost always, cast as the province of young, white, college-educated men. They are positioned in the mainstream media as the people who would save Detroit from itself (Herscher, 2012, pp 7–8). The recent election of the first white mayor in over half a century, Mike Duggan, reflects this thinking from the surrounding suburbs.

Yet, it is precisely in this area of creative possibilities emerging from the "outsiders" that we at the James and Grace Lee Boggs Center to Nurture Community Leadership have concentrated our efforts for more than 40 years. We understand the re-creation of urban life from the bottom-up places of Detroit as part of the new radical movements for liberation emerging globally (Solnit, 2004). Change, initiated from the ground up, is the only way to solve the many crises we now face. Shifting away from top-down initiatives and efforts to stimulate job growth, we advocate local production of the goods and services required to support life based on principles and practices that develop people and place. This kind of visionary organizing, emphasizing values and the creation of alternative structures and sources of power, is an expression of the emerging forms of new radical politics, perhaps best embodied by the Zapatistas. It emphasizes developing political forms for creating power, rather than concentrating on seizing state power (Boggs and Scott, 2012). While distinct to times and places, this radicalism moves beyond oppositional, mass-based politics, to new forms of resistance and the creation of alternative structures, languages, and methods of organizing (Solnit, 2004).

The Zapatistas center this perspective in the differences between change imposed from the top down and change emanating from the bottom up. They say:

> Throughout the world, two projects of globalization are in dispute: the one from above that globalizes conformity, cynicism, stupidity, war, destruction, death and amnesia. And the one from below, that globalizes rebellion, hope, creativity, intelligence, imagination, life, memory, building a world where many worlds fit. (Subcomandante Marcos, 2003)

Bankruptcy

For those of us struggling to create a new city though the imagination and energy of people in neighborhoods, the declaration of bankruptcy in Detroit at the end of 2013 was a pivotal moment. Two visions that were able to coexist in the wide expanse of the city were brought into direct conflict. These two visions are now at war (Clark, 2015). Basic questions of who the city is for, who benefits, who bears the pains of change, and who decides are now in front of us.

Corporate powers are attempting to regain control of the city and shape it for their own benefit. The declaration of bankruptcy and the imposition of an emergency manager were central to that effort. Bankruptcy was the essential, necessary step toward the "revitalization" of the city on corporate terms (Brogan, 2015). It became the means to displace African-American political power, attack unions, and shift city assets into private hands (Feely, 2013). It has provided the means to develop a whiter, wealthier Downtown core, surrounded by darker, poorer neighborhoods. These neighborhoods, home to outsiders, will require increasing military measures to control (Boggs, 1963).

Even the most conservative of commentators acknowledges that the bankruptcy restructuring is leading to "two Detroits." Nolan Finley (2014) observed:

> Near the top of the list of the challenges Detroit faces as it starts its post-bankruptcy era is avoiding becoming two cities—one for the upwardly mobile young and white denizens of an increasingly happening downtown, and the other for the struggling and frustrated black residents trapped in neighborhoods that are crumbling around them.

Finley grudgingly acknowledges that "racial tensions" are simmering.

The vision of the city advocated by the Boggs Center and those with whom we work flows from Detroit's rich history of social struggle. It imagines a city developed on principles of equality, justice, regenerative local production, and a culture of compassionate care. It is a city that many Detroiters believe is emerging in the cracks of the old. As Detroit-based lyricist, performance artist, and activist Invincible, in the work Emergence, says: "We're on the verge of an earth shift, while we're searching for purpose, parallel universes are bursting at first you can't tell on the surface" (see: www.emergencemedia.org).

History of resistance

The emergence of new ways of thinking and acting in opposition to capitalist values has a long history in Detroit. Detroit has been at the forefront of creating collective resistance to the dehumanization and destructiveness of industrial capital.

This history of resistance is widely acknowledged in the city. Its riverfront holds a public memorial to the women, men, and children of the Underground Railroad who came to Detroit as their last stop before freedom from slavery. That memorial sits in Hart Plaza, named for Senator Phil Hart, the "Conscience of the Senate." Street names remember some of the most powerful labor leaders and human rights advocates in the country. Martin Luther King Jr and Malcolm X spoke to large crowds in the center of town. The United Auto Workers, founded in the struggle for the dignity of labor in the 1930s, calls Detroit home. Detroit provided African-American leadership in politics and the arts and has been at the forefront of environmental justice and sustainable living efforts. It became the home of Rosa Parks, James and Grace Boggs, and General Baker. It gave the highest honors in the city to Angela Davis and Nelson Mandela shortly after their release from prison. It gave birth to American Revolutionary theory through the Dodge Revolutionary Union Movement, the Republic of New Africa, and the National Organization for an American Revolution. It surrounded these political formations with artists, music, poetry, presses, and publications. It is a movement city.

As Laura Gottesdiener (2015, p 6) eloquently described:

> The city is often credited with inventing and mass-producing the twentieth century, while its workers simultaneously took the lead in revolting against the injustices of the era. Its factories put the world on wheels and labor laws on the books. Its workers and thinkers sparked and fanned a number of this country's most influential resistance movements.
>
> Detroit: every article about you should include a love letter, a thank-you note, a history lesson, for without you …

Tempered by time and experience, resistance to the bankruptcy and its aftermath was and is widespread. The Boggs Center is part of a citywide coalition of more than 60 organizations who projected a People's Plan to counter the Plan of Adjustment put forward by the corporate powers. The People's Plan reflects the widespread commitment by citizens to resist corporate domination and to project alternative solutions. It begins:

> The restructuring and rebirth of Detroit will not be delivered by a state-imposed emergency manager, nor through Chapter 9 bankruptcy proceedings, foundation contributions, closed door deals, or other devious and misleading corporate schemes. Detroit's rebirth will be the result of the people's unrelenting demand for democratic self-governance, equal access to and management of the natural and economic resources of the city.

US Social Forum/shrinking the city

This people's vision was crystallized in 2010 when the US Social Forum burst onto the streets of Detroit. This forum grew out of the World Social Forum (WSF). The WSF began in 2001 in Porto Alegre, Brazil, as a counter to the World Economic Forum. Although receiving almost no mainstream press, by 2008, these global gatherings attracted more than 180,000 people, leading to the decision to host coordinated, regional gatherings across the globe. The slogan of the WSF, "Another World Is Possible," counters the widely quoted neoliberal idea that "there is no alternative" (Goodman and Amin, 2015). In 2008, the first US Forum added, "Another U.S. is Necessary." We added to this our vision of "Another Detroit is Happening." On T-shirts, banners, and posters, Detroit was seen as the heart of a global movement challenging neoliberal capitalist development schemes (Holmes, 2010).

As 20,000 people gathered to celebrate grassroots imagination, theory, and practice, the newly elected Mayor of Detroit, former National Basketball Association (NBA) star turned businessman Dave Bing, announced plans to shrink the city. Bing, spokesman of the corporate-philanthropic elite, talked of a different "dreamscape: a downtown light rail line, a new hockey stadium, shiny charter schools to complement a slimmed down 'traditional' district, an industrial farm on the East side, and new housing enclaves" (quoted in Abowd, 2010).

In contrast, Forum-goers saw the seeds of the alternative Detroit. As one commentator said, people saw:

> not only the site of capitalism's brutality, [but] also of a community's resolve to face it. "For a very long time, there's been an underground, more sustainable version of work being done that has come about out of necessity," says (Lottie) Spady. That necessary work precedes the Forum, and will continue when it's over. (Quoted in Abowd, 2010)

Over the next five years, the conflicts between these two visions intensified.

The remainder of this chapter concentrates on three areas where we at the Boggs Center have been engaged: contesting land, water and consciousness. Each reflects the kind of resilient, visionary organizing central to our efforts to create a more just future. This organizing begins with the question: what are the values that we need to encourage as we move toward a more just, responsible, and ecologically sensitive future? It places resistance as an essential process in opening up new political possibilities. We argue that through these struggles, Detroiters are creating a future that will preserve and protect all life. Developing alternative programs, practices, and policies becomes a way to create community power.

Contested land

Detroit's 139 square miles contains vast areas of open land. Abandoned by people and industry, the land remains. It has literally provided the ground to re-imagine a city capable of feeding itself. As Gerald Hairston, the father of the urban gardening movement said, "The city that feeds itself, frees itself."

The urban gardening movement has long been recognized as holding the potential for creating another kind of city (Solnit, 2007). However, open land, farmed for use of friends and neighbors, does not fit well into the capitalist logic. In capitalism, excess land is not an opportunity, but a problem. The view of land as a commodity was clearly articulated by developer John Hantz and his proposal to create an urban, industrial-scale farm inside the city. In 2009, Hantz wanted 10,000 acres. In exchange for getting land cheaply, he would put it to "productive use." Hantz was completely transparent in his motivation.

He told the *Wall Street Journal*, Detroit "cannot create value until we create scarcity. Large-scale farming could begin to take land out of circulation in a positive way" (Dolan, 2012). For the next four years, people opposed the land giveaway and large-scale food production. Ultimately, Hantz settled for less than 200 acres and had completely given up on food production. Instead, he planted hardwood trees.

Through the resistance to Hantz Farm, people clarified the political importance of urban gardening as a community-building process. They challenged the view of land as a commodity, emphasizing it as essential for community restoration, giving young people a sense of process, and creating healthy, more ecologically balanced neighborhoods. This political perspective infuses the food justice movement. The Detroit Food Policy Council and Detroit Black Food Security Network advanced thinking and conversation about food justice through this resistance.

Urban agriculture has moved from a "fringe idea" to the center of discussions about new ways to rebuild the city. In 2014, a study by the Detroit Food and Fitness Collaborative found that "The city's food system including supply from local farms and market gardens, processing, distribution and market demand currently produces

$3.6 billion in revenue and directly employs more than 36,000 people" (Lee, 2015).

The local food system is now the third-largest employment sector in the city. With a realistic 30% growth rate over the next few years, the study noted that "the local food production ecosystem would make it the second-largest source of jobs in Detroit behind only the government sector—and imagine the opportunities for entrepreneurs and suppliers as well" (Lee, 2015).

This resistance to Hantz also generated two progressive policy initiatives to guide development: community land trusts and community benefits agreements. Under the leadership of the People's Platform, community activists, working at the district level, are pursing ways to turn these ideas into policies that would go a long way toward limiting the kind of displacement and disruption of lives that is currently a normal process of development. In October 2016, the People's Platform successfully raised nearly $200,000 to purchase 14 occupied homes that were facing auction. Through the community land trust initiative, all previous owners are able to remain in their homes.

Water, human rights, and public trust

Detroit takes its name from the French term for straits. It is the place where the upper Great Lakes narrow, placing it in the center of roughly 20% of the world's fresh surface water. Yet, it became the first American city to be cited for human rights violations because of the massive water shut-offs to over 100,000 people who could not afford ever-escalating water bills.

As the bankruptcy agreements concluded, the Detroit Water and Sewerage Department was placed into a court-mandated regional authority. Suburban interests, fueled by decades of racism, insisted that any regional deal protect them from paying for those in Detroit who were behind on their water bills.

Thus, the emergency manager ordered massive water shut-offs. This policy was met with immediate resistance (NAACP, 2014b). Some people refused to let trucks turn off their water. Others turned the water back on after the trucks left. Activists and churches set up water stations. Neighbors shared water through hoses and outdoor kitchens. Activists were arrested blocking the shut-off trucks from leaving the station and mass marches supported by NetRoots Nation and Roots and Remedies brought thousands onto the streets (Levy, 2015).

Neither the mayor nor the City Council would intervene. Their lack of response to the need to protect water as a human right and public trust brought international condemnation (Holloway, 2014). The irony of this struggle is that since 2005, Michigan Welfare Rights and the People's Water Board have had an alternative Peoples Water Affordability Plan, passed by the Detroit City Council, but never implemented. That plan, structured to charge for water by percentage of income rather than use, would have provided a means not only to keep water flowing to homes and families, but also to provide for much-needed infrastructure repair (Guyette, 2015a).

This struggle has pushed the conversation about our responsibilities to preserve and protect the natural world upon which all life depends. The complete failure of the corporate elite to respond to this crisis in any meaningful way has underscored the inability of old paradigms to solve today's problems. For example, in the face of more than 24,700 shut-off homes put on the mayor's philanthropic community's plan, only 300 customers were able to keep up payments (Guyette, 2015b).

In May 2015, faced with the realization that local political interests were not willing to reconsider this failed strategy, activists called for an international summit to generate legal, legislative, and movement strategies (Unitarian Universalists Service Committee, 2015). Far exceeding expectations, delegates came from 47 states and 10 nations. Out of this effort, national and statewide legislation was crafted and local organizing was energized (Howell, 2015). The implementation of this legislation seems increasingly likely, as in June 2015, the City of Philadelphia adopted a plan based on that advocated by Detroiters (Owens, 2015).

What time is it? Creating consciousness/creating structures

Detroit holds the bones of the old industrial era, visible in every neighborhood. Even the most forlorn structures reflect the resilience and urge for life. Trees grow out of abandoned rooftops. Gardens grow in old tires and reclaimed wooden beds. The sense of old ways dying and giving way to the new and unexpected is everywhere. It is commonplace for people to talk about the end of the industrial era. People know we are moving from one paradigm to another.

The awareness of participating in an unusual moment of human evolution is fostered by a political culture that encourages ideas, thinking, and rethinking. This culture has its roots in our radical pasts. Study groups, skill development, native-language newspapers, and publications of those whose lives and voices were never recorded or recognized in the mainstream media all flourish here. Political analysis surrounds political action. Many of these actions are providing models of new ways to live and make a living. They are the source of new stories about the people of the city and of new language to understand ourselves and our time.

On Detroit's east side, the Hope District provides a health clinic, gardens, orchards, and technical support, and is turning local crops into potato chips for sale to local anchor institutions. It hosts Peace Zones for Life to provide community solutions to conflict (see Hines, Chapter Seventeen). Avalon International Breads (see Victor, Chapter Twenty) casts itself as a community-building bakery, inspired by the thinking of James and Grace Boggs. Back Alley Bikes developed a cooperative for-profit arm called The Hub to provide bikes and bike repair while supporting youth learning programs. The Boggs School (see Chapter Twenty-three) is expanding place-based education through its public charter, developing student "solutionaries" and addressing critical community issues as the core of their curriculum. These are a few examples of the emerging models of local economic activity, educational innovation, and cultural work that are emerging guided by community values. These activities are enlarged by a vibrant arts and cultural life that articulates visions of a better world. Invincible/ill Weaver captures much of this spirit in performance art and multiracial, intergenerational, and collective organizing. Invincible works with Detroit Summer and co-founded the Detroit Future Youth Network to support social justice activities with media-based projects. They are currently touring nationally with "Beware of the Dandelions," the most recent project of Complex Movements.

This respect for the creation of ideas to change reality has been a core aspect of the radical culture of Detroit. African-Americans established newspapers and printing companies, and later radio. The United Auto Workers (UAW) ran its own radio station. Radical publications of poetry and plays through Broadside Press, the Fifth Estate, and Paradigm Press made materials available to people in churches and communities. The Boggs Center, Hood Research, East Michigan Environmental Action Council, the People's Platform, and several progressive formations offer publications, educational meetings, and performance spaces, popularizing analysis and actions.

Recognizing the central connections among modes of production and cultural and political change, Detroit has hosted two groundbreaking conferences, exploring the theory and practice of new work and emerging economies. In 2011, the Boggs Center organized Re-imagining Work, and in 2014, New Work, New Culture. Several hundred people from across the nation came to Detroit to talk about miniaturization of production, community-based strategies for economic activity, and the new democratic possibilities emerging from these shifts. Windmills, 3D printing, underground gardens, and regenerative practices were explored as ways to challenge the growing inequalities of the extractive economy of capitalism.

Detroit is now the home of the Allied Media Project and Conference (AMC). Bringing together over 2000 independent, justice-seeking media makers every June, the AMC is becoming a force in creating interlinking movement activists. Influenced by the work of the urban agricultural movement, they have extended the metaphor from food justice to digital justice, establishing the first Digital Justice Coalition in the country, providing skills and opportunities for independent, activist media (DeVito, 2015).

There is a broadly shared understanding of the people's vision of the future of our city. It is explicitly anti-capitalist and anti-racist. It runs counter to the corporate-led visions for Greater Downtown, which celebrate the city's middle-class "renaissance." It projects the possibilities of a new kind of city, based on values that reflect compassion, respect, equality, and care. In Detroit, people are not only re-imagining city life, they are creating values, processes, and practices to bring a just future to life. The possibilities are endless.

TWELVE

Reconstructing Detroit: the resilient city

Khalil Ligon

In this chapter, Khalil Ligon discusses the role in which non-municipally led community development strategies can play a role in revitalizing Detroit. She argues that Detroiters who have persisted and remained in the city despite all its problems should play a central role in shaping its future. Rather than focusing on "resilient" cities, Ligon sees resilience coming from Detroiters themselves. In the absence of any strong and visionary leadership, they have taken matters into their own hands. Such sentiments featured strongly in Kimberley Kinder's chapter (Chapter Six) on do-it-yourself urbanism and will be a central focus of many of the conversations in Section Three. What sets Ligon's chapter apart is her ability to easily move between the two worlds of planning and the grass-roots community initiatives she describes in this chapter.

Ligon's approach to urban planning, design, and development has been framed by the experience of witnessing her own neighborhood's dramatic decline. She grew up (and still resides in) the area near the Coleman A. Young International Airport in Northeast Detroit (see Chapter One). The first time we met, she described how the closure of McNichols Road by the airport severed her community in two, separating people from businesses, schools, and churches. She then saw first-hand the effects that such a planning decision had on her community. Today, she is one of the few residents still living on her street. As a result of seeing this transformation, her professional life has been dedicated to championing community planning efforts such as the ones she describes in this chapter, some of which she has been personally and professionally involved with. They offer opportunities for shared and inclusive visions and stand in contrast to the developer- and corporate-led projects in Downtown. Her central message is that city officials need to listen to, and empower these community initiatives if Detroit is to avoid repeating past mistakes and injustices.

Khalil Ligon is chief executive officer of Vista Vantage Consulting Group, L3C, an urban planning and environmental design firm based in Detroit. She has developed award-winning community plans and leads a variety of sustainability initiatives to advance green infrastructure, climate adaptation, and food systems development. Khalil is active throughout the community, serving on various boards, including the Detroit Eastside Community Collaborative (DECC), the US Green Building Council, and the Detroit Greenways Coalition. She holds a master's degree in urban planning from Wayne State University.

Introduction

Music. Fashion. Automobiles. Democracy. Detroit has been the epicenter of innovation throughout history. One could argue that Detroit is one of the nation's most significant cities in the past century (see Galster, 2012). Although Detroit has a long history of industrial innovation across multiple sectors, its political and social failures would eventually blemish its rich legacy and force a reckoning still necessary today (Sugrue, 1996).

Detroit used to be a city brimming with life and vitality. Thoroughfares once bustling with people and streets lined with trees and neat homes now resemble apocalyptic movie scenes. Weeds burst through untraveled streets, while trees and wildflowers engulf sidewalks and open fields. Vacant, dilapidated, and charred houses and storefronts loom ominously, neglected and abandoned by property-owners and city leadership alike. Requests for resources to demolish or, at a minimum, secure open, dangerous structures fall on deaf ears. Some blocks are razed over, dotted by a single home, often meticulously maintained in its isolation. Well-populated streets pepper a landscape overwhelmed by urban decay.

Detroit has a land mass that could hold three major cities—Boston, Manhattan, and San Francisco.[1] However, unlike each of those metropolises, Detroit has a fraction of the population density. This contrast illuminates the unique challenges that Detroit faces when juxtaposed against cities with triple the number of people in a much more constricted landscape. This distinction greatly affects planning and development decisions, which are typically influenced by density (or the lack thereof).

Detroit's current conditions have incited a slew of discussions, debates, and sometimes diatribes about the best approach to land-based decisions. Infrastructure, like streets and utility and sewer lines, were built to accommodate a population in excess of 1 million. Currently, Detroit has just under 700,000 residents. From a spatial and economic standpoint, how best to use land is an issue that remains largely unresolved. Catalysts for the destruction of a once globally and historically significant city can be traced back to multiple race riots dating as far back as 1863 and the urban renewal policies of the 1950s. This chapter examines a potential way forward that can be found in non-municipal community redevelopment strategies that place a high value on neighborhood-level expertise to help shape meaningful policies and plans. The people who have persisted in Detroit neighborhoods have come up with creative ways to address neighborhood decline, often without political support or government resources (see Kinder, Chapter Six). Despite the shift in landscape, economy, and political leadership in post-war Detroit, its people have demonstrated a resiliency that could inspire a new model for revitalizing the city.

A history not to be repeated

Since the 1950s, hundreds of thousands of Detroiters have fled the city for the suburbs, spurred mostly by increased personal wealth, racial discrimination and fear-mongering, and urban renewal. As the city's population declined, so, too, did its tax base (see Galster, Chapter Two). Businesses closed, neighborhoods emptied out, and one could argue that the city's political leadership did little to stop it. Once the fourth most populous city in the nation, Detroit's population would decline dramatically over the next several decades. While the city's consistent mismanagement of resources is well documented, derisive state policies have equally contributed to Detroit's decline. In 1999, the state of Michigan eliminated the requirement for municipal employees (eg, public safety officers and city department heads) to reside in the city, further accelerating the loss of population and resources. The elimination of residency meant that those employed to protect, manage, and operate the city were no longer required to be personally invested in the city, despite collecting their income from the city (see conversation with Sandra Hines, Chapter Seventeen). This is just one of many leadership foibles that proverbially drove Detroit into the ground.

Detroit's first wave of population decline was by its white residents. Eventually, this would be coined "white flight" and attributed as a singular cause for the unhinging of Detroit. Federal housing policies facilitated this mass movement through generous mortgage subsidies and infrastructure development. Government resources went largely to the expansion of expressways at the expense of public transportation investments, fueling suburban sprawl. The Davison Expressway, the nation's first sub-grade freeway, was built in Detroit (MDOT, 2015) and would be one of many that would alter the course of history for the city. Notably, black residents were denied access to these resources, regardless of financial capacity (Sugrue, 1996).

Black people who migrated to Detroit were relegated to the overcrowded east side of the city (Galster, 2012). Racially polarized housing policies, including redlining, made it difficult for them to purchase homes, even if they had the means (Sugrue, 1996). Indicative of what would later be celebrated as the resilient spirit of Detroit's people, black residents in the city built communities filled with businesses, schools, and homes. However, government-financed white flight quickly drained Detroit of its people, political power, and resources.

Once vibrant corridors of black-owned businesses were displaced by urban renewal projects that slammed up against them. Paradise Valley, Harmonie Park, and Black Bottom are just a few of the places where the growing majority of Detroit citizens operated successful companies. However, the development of expressways to accommodate the expansive amount of cars produced and driven obliterated these areas. The intentional decimation of these corridors is, to this day, visually evident. A drive down Harper, Gratiot, Grand River, Mack, Woodward (north of Midtown), and even through some parts of Downtown reveals glaring evidence of this era of decline (see Chapter One, Figures 1.4 and 1.5).

Left behind, looking forward

Over a 50-year period, Detroit's population went from being 80% white to 80% black. This dramatic shift in the racial composition of the city would come to have a significant impact on the city's landscape during that same time span. The remaining population in Detroit, here by choice or because they could not afford to move elsewhere, would work unceremoniously to maintain neighborhood character and vivacity with limited resources.

In the absence of visionary and compassionate leadership, many Detroit citizens have taken matters into their own hands. Desiring a better quality of life, residents co-opt land and property left derelict by egregious owners to grow food, hold community events, and sometimes operate businesses. This social innovation, bred from necessity, has widely become the norm, and is reflected in community and citywide land-use planning (see Kinder, Chapter Six).

Why must citizens bear the undue burden of maintaining communities? The responsibility of the citizen has grown beyond simply paying property taxes and maintaining their own property to the regulated standards. Now, citizens use their personal resources to address limited or deficient city services. Mowing vacant parcels, boarding up vacant houses, and community policing, are all activities typically conducted by the municipality. Yet, citizens who initially stepped up to fill a void are being encouraged by city leaders to continue these efforts, often with no financial relief or subsidy.

Limited government support, boundless community vision

Many residents living in Detroit during the 1980s, 1990s, and early 2000s found ways to deal with gruesome social conditions and deficiencies in city government and resources. Before the burst of city-led development in Midtown and Downtown Detroit, it was not uncommon for community-focused development groups to spearhead initiatives to spur local economies and address shortfalls in housing, jobs, education, public health, the environment, and other community issues. Non-profits offered workforce development programming to help train former autoworkers and adapt their skills for emerging industries. Residents formed block clubs and other types of community associations to address crime and blight (see Hines, Chapter Seventeen). Despite the absence of a tuned-in government, residents in Detroit found ways to improve the quality of life in their communities. Residents helped form community-specific coalitions, like Osborn Neighborhood Alliance, Grandmont Rosedale Community Development Corporation, Jefferson East Business Association (now Jefferson East, Inc.), and U-SNAP-BAC, to address geographically focused issues. Such alliances have endeavored to improve local economies, build and renovate homes, improve public health, and eliminate blight. Unfortunately, some improvements and needs were far beyond the capacity—financial and human—of the residents undertaking such work.

By the 1980s, Detroit was a predominantly populated by black people. Post-riot tensions were high as the city remained politically and economically isolated from the inner- and outer-ring suburbs. Crime was at an all-time high, as the crack epidemic collided with failing school systems and high unemployment. Detroit was often referred to as the "murder capital" of the country.

During the 1990s, local government sought to restore parity to fragile relationships with suburban and regional political leaders. While neighborhood development was virtually non-existent, expansive projects began to take shape in Downtown and Midtown, causing a shift in growth that would foreshadow future advancement.

In the early 2000s, political and governmental mishaps began to take center stage in the national media. Scores of schools were closed. Elected officials were embroiled in scandal and corruption. Vacant buildings impaled a vast majority of the city and few neighborhoods resembled the mid-century era of prosperity that Detroit once embodied.

By 2010, the city was clearly on the brink of economic collapse. The cost of maintaining decades-old infrastructure and demolishing thousands of abandoned properties overwhelmed the city, coupled with record-high unemployment and a broken school system (itself contributing significantly to neighborhood blight with scores of decommissioned schools). Mismanagement of public funds and exorbitant debt propelled the city into bankruptcy and state oversight. Public officials were proposing to raze whole neighborhoods and relocate residents to more populated areas of the city. It was this imprudent policy approach that prompted numerous community-led planning initiatives and widespread mistrust of city-led right-sizing efforts.

Coming up with new ideas for Detroit's ruins may be its saving grace. Citizens, practitioners, and governing leaders have created innovative approaches to reconstructing the city. Citywide and localized planning efforts have generated new frameworks for land use and placemaking; the abundance of vacant land presents boundless opportunities to explore new sustainable and low-impact development. Countless initiatives aim to improve existing conditions through blight remediation, climate adaptation, storm-water management, and adaptive land reuse. Groups like Eco-D and the Detroit Climate Action Collaborative are spearheading projects to increase sustainability and climate resiliency through citywide design and development practices.

In an unprecedented fashion, practitioners and citizens are now working together to devise measures to design socially, economically, and environmentally equitable urban places. The bridging of lived experiences and technical expertise is shifting planning practices and policies, as demonstrated through the Neighborhood Strategic

Revitalization Framework developed by Community Advocates of Detroit (CDAD) and the Local Support Initiatives Corporation's (LISC's) Building Sustainable Communities. Grassroots organizations are leading collaborative efforts to revise inflexible land-use codes, zoning, and master plan language.

Reconstructing the resilient city

Detroit is undeniably growing in popularity, as evidenced by coverage in the national media and influx of people migrating to the city. With the spotlight on Detroit, now is the time to diligently, carefully, and thoughtfully apply lessons learned from failed policies and embrace the inventive planning practices being employed at the neighborhood level.

Development has been largely imbalanced throughout the city. Downtown, Midtown, and Central City have seen significant levels of private and public investment, new infrastructure installed, the relocation of national franchises, resources for budding entrepreneurs to open storefronts, and a boom in residential development (see Kreichauf, Chapter Four). Meanwhile, people living in neighborhoods that are not self-organizing and leading their own development initiatives find themselves on the fringes of Detroit's revitalization. A less clear strategy for community development outside Central City pits neighborhoods against each other for both attention and resources. Local leaders instigate these sentiments by "targeting" neighborhoods, a process that seems neither fair nor democratic. This prioritization does not consider the unique values inherent in every community or equitably distribute resources. In order to ensure that Detroit's resurgence does not repeat the mistakes of this city's past by disenfranchising its residents, city leaders should look to the examples being set by community-planning efforts.

Community Advocates of Detroit and the Lower Eastside Action Plan

Several land-use plans developed at the neighborhood level utilized CDAD's Revitalization Framework. Most notable is the Lower Eastside Action Plan (LEAP). The LEAP process focused on Detroit areas south of Interstate 94 and east of Mt. Elliot. This area purportedly had the highest concentration of vacant land in the city and was one that elected officials targeted for extensive bulldozing. In 2010, LEAP employed a distinctive planning approach, bringing together residents, business-owners, and institutions with technical practitioners—planners, architects, engineers, lawyers, demographers, and data analysts. Over the course of 18 months, LEAP engaged thousands of residents in an iterative series of conversations to cultivate parcel-level ideas for repurposing vacant land and regenerating economic growth without the forcible relocation of people from their neighborhoods. The LEAP planning process, piloted from 2010 to 2012, is now considered a model initiative, garnered an Environmental Protection Agency (EPA) National Smart Growth Award, and continues to influence decision-making at the municipal level.

The Detroit Eastside Community Collaborative and Detroit Greenways Coalition

Highlighting community assets through resident engagement processes is a core component of creating inspiring neighborhood plans. However, after many years of decline and disenfranchisement, planning initiatives have beleaguered many residents. The Detroit Eastside Community Collaborative (DECC), launched in 1992, began as a consortium of community development organizations and institutions dedicated to revitalizing Detroit's east side through various housing and economic development initiatives. Today, the organization's focus centers on creating mobility in neighborhoods through the development of non-motorized bike paths, trails, and greenways. DECC developed the city's first planned greenway, a nine-mile path from East Eight Mile to the Detroit Riverfront. DECC's grassroots approach spawned similar efforts citywide and led collaborative initiatives to increase the amount of bike lanes installed throughout the city. DECC works with local community groups to host events intended to get people outside and active. Cycle Into Spring, DECC's signature fund-raiser, brings hundreds of cyclists together annually to bike through the east side along the Conner Creek Greenway. Its Earn-A-Bike program pairs students with professional bike experts to learn how to build and repair bicycles. DECC also sponsors health and recreational programming, including kayak tours along the Detroit River, youth and adult walking clubs, outdoor fitness classes, vacant-lot replanting, and community health fairs.

DECC also advocates for policies that support non-motorized paths and the creation of bike lanes. DECC exemplifies the public–private partnerships that community groups undertake to bring about change in Detroit neighborhoods. Greenway construction, maintenance, and programming are supported through community crowd-funding and philanthropic donations.

The Detroit Greenway Coalition (DGC) partners with groups like DECC to serve as a collective voice for advancing greenways throughout the city. Since its formation in 2007, DGC has worked with community groups and public officials to build an interconnected system of greenways and bicycle lanes with a goal of making Detroit a world-class city for biking and walking. DGC has worked with city officials to develop numerous policies to support biking, including a Complete Streets ordinance, a citywide non-motorized plan, and the installation of over 150 miles of bike lanes. Since 2001, Detroit has boasted a 400% increase in bicycling (Schwartz, 2015), evidence that grassroots-led initiatives can have a significant and positive impact on infrastructure development.

US Green Building Council and Better Block

In 2002, the US Green Building Council (USGBC) launched its Detroit chapter. The group focuses on promoting sustainable building standards by transforming the way buildings are designed, constructed, and operated.[2] Since its inception, the Detroit USGBC chapter has worked with city officials, business-owners, and community groups to expand awareness and understanding of sustainability principles and implement more resilient building projects. Its consortium of professionals has worked to increase Leadership in Energy and Environmental Design (LEED)-certified building projects throughout Detroit and the region. Currently, there are over 100 LEED- and Energy Star-certified buildings in the city.

The USGBC started working with local community groups in 2012 to launch Better Block Detroit, a series of semi-permanent place-based interventions that educate and empower communities to radically transform the built environment and promote healthy and vibrant neighborhoods. Through Better Block, the USGBC has worked in four different neighborhoods to promote sustainable development through placemaking and tactical urban design. Better Block projects have demonstrated what is possible when Detroiters are permitted and equipped to implement their vision for restoring neglected urban areas.

Detroit Environmental Agenda and Detroit Climate Action Collaborative

Climate change, widely known to be driven by man-made greenhouse gas (GHG) emissions, will presumably have a significantly adverse impact on Detroit. The city is comprised largely of impervious surfaces and industrial activities that contaminate air and water alike. Detroiters Working for Environmental Justice (DWEJ), the city's oldest environmental justice agency, works collaboratively across sectors to raise awareness about environmental and public health impacts, especially among the city's poorest residents. DWEJ also advocates for policy changes to address environmental issues across the city. Most notable are its Detroit Environmental Agenda (DEA) and Detroit Climate Action Collaborative (DCAC).

The DEA unified the city's leading environmental and social justice groups to compile and share information regarding the "role a healthy environment plays in creating a city where people want to live, work, and raise a family."[3] With a goal of elevating the environmental ethic in the city, the DEA produced a research report that highlighted the current environmental conditions of the city and plausible action strategies to address them, as well as a voter guide compiling the responses of political candidates on high-priority environmental issues. The DEA is also leading efforts to establish an Office of Sustainability within the city's executive branch. Such an office will extend the capacity of local government decision-makers to address long-standing environmental issues by coordinating grassroots and municipal courses of action.

The DCAC endeavors to create the city's first climate action plan (CAP) and complementary climate ordinance. These tools are intended to reduce GHGs citywide and mitigate the impact of climate change in Detroit. Extreme weather events, like heatwaves and flooding, impact all Detroiters, but overwhelmingly affect poverty-stricken residents. As the city has limited resources to address the effects that climate change has on residents and infrastructure, preventive measures are of critical importance. The DCAC convened business leaders, researchers, and community groups to develop a multi-point plan, outlining tools, strategies, and policies that the city can implement to address the local risks of climate change. The CAP is set to be released by 2017 and will highlight land use, policy, and program interventions. CAPs are widely regarded as useful tools that cities can use to pinpoint local climate change impacts and tailor adaptation and mitigation strategies that align with the regulatory capacity of the municipality (Snover et al, 2007).

EcoDistricts

EcoDistricts are neighborhood-scale communities where green, sustainable practices are implemented to create jobs, protect natural resources, and meet the basic needs of residents. The EcoDistricts model employs a global regenerative planning and development approach that facilitates, promotes, and implements sustainable building and infrastructure projects. In 2014, EcoWorks convened a group of Detroit's foremost community planning, governmental, and service agencies to learn about the model at an EcoDistricts Incubator. Under the eco-D banner, participants attended the incubator in Portland, Oregon. While there, eco-D members networked with practitioners from across the country, toured local sustainability projects, and developed a framework and governance strategy for implementing EcoDistricts in Detroit. Today, the eco-D initiative facilitates the formation of green neighborhoods through a suite of peer-learning exchanges, technical support, and financial resources to implement community plans. Partnering with the Michigan State Housing Development Authority (MSHDA) and City of Detroit, eco-D helps communities desiring to become EcoDistricts by coordinating new and existing sustainability resources. In 2015, eco-D helped Detroit garner a national Target Cities designation to help implement community plans to become resilient. The process of eco-D selects two communities each year to help establish EcoDistricts. It is believed by eco-D and its partners that through this highly collaborative, community-centered approach, Detroit can become a 21st-century model for urban sustainability and resiliency.

Conclusion

Although the city has not fully recovered from the substantial disinvestment and population loss fueled by racism and suburban sprawl, there is a growing sense of urgency for Detroiters, native and new, to rethink community design and develop high-quality living, working, and recreational centers for all. The initiatives referenced herein highlight the sustained interest and willingness of residents to collaborate with decision-makers to co-create sustainable, resilient communities across the city.

Emerging from the largest municipal bankruptcy in US history, Detroit leaders would be best served to not repeat past mistakes. In order to achieve economically, environmentally, and socially just policies, public officials should employ tactics successfully used in non-municipal community redevelopment strategies. Working with and valuing the lived experience and legacy knowledge of the city's long-term residents will help create the kind of equitable development that makes Detroit a great place to live again.

Detroit is hardly a blank canvas. Instead, it is a tapestry of blended and shared experiences that incite both critique and adulation. Creating a citywide sustainability and resiliency strategy should begin with the cultivation of a shared vision for Detroit's future among city leaders and residents. As the city is overhauling its planning department and revamping the city's master plan of policies, embedding such principles and approaches are tantamount to laying a new foundation for what land-use policies can achieve. Establishing a centralized sustainability office that can connect and coordinate the various efforts happening across the city would also bolster their impact and better leverage resources. Planners should be responsible for encouraging people to dream beyond what is seen, and, more importantly, empowering and equipping them to make those dreams a reality. Placemaking should not be just about designing cool landscapes for middle-class consumption. Rather, it should be about creating places for people to live in the best way imaginable.

Detroit needs leaders who will step up and be less concerned with being popular and more interested in being effective. Making decisions for the common good requires a willingness to take risks, share resources, and make uncommon decisions. Leaders that can spur collective action and support a culture of stewardship, responsibility, and accountability will ensure that history does not repeat itself here. When this type of compassionate and visionary leadership meets the commitment and dedication exemplified through community planning and development, we can have the world-class, inclusive, and well-designed city that we have long desired. Should the city follow through on implementing the many sound ideas generated at the community level, Detroit will be poised to become a replicable smart growth archetype for urban resiliency.

Notes

[1] See: http://detroitography.com/2015/04/10/map-can-detroit-really-be-compared-to-any-other-city/
[2] See: http://www.usgbcdetroit.org/index.php/about
[3] See: http://detroitenv.org/our-principles/

THIRTEEN

Reawakening culture among Detroit's resident majority

Jessica Brooke Williams

While significant attention has been given to professional placemaking and cultural activities in the Greater Downtown Detroit area (see PPS, 2014), far less attention has been paid to cultural activities and organizations in the city's disparate neighborhoods. In this chapter, Jessica Brooke Williams examines cultural instability and neighborhood economies among what she calls Detroit's "resident majority." She defines this term as those who identify as "black," "African-American," or those of African descent who have populated Detroit throughout generations and have comprised the majority of the city's population for almost the last 50 years. The chapter examines five major Detroit planning documents since the Second World War. Today, Williams argues that art, if used primarily as a utility, can be a true catalyst for community revitalization because it provides the opportunity to help rebuild cultural sustenance among Detroit's resident majority. As was also explored by Khalil Ligon (Chapter Twelve), intentionally extending urban planning efforts is important to shaping these cultural efforts. The effects of cultural practices, as demonstrated by the example of the Heidelberg Project (see also Guyton, Intermezzo II) can contribute to shared experiences (healing, learning, growing), values, and goals among Detroit's resident majority.

Jessica Brooke Williams is a graduate of Wayne State University's Master's of Urban Planning program. She is a scholar of American and African diasporic history and art, with a BA from the University of Michigan. Between 2007 and 2012, she was a Project Coordinator at the Heidelberg Project while also serving in positions at other human service organizations, including United Way and the Skillman Foundation. Williams is a member of Detroit's resident majority and is currently a practicing urban planner in program evaluation, land use, and economic development in Detroit.

Culture and its interpreted context

Culture is often used as frontage to help differentiate the environment of one place from that of another. That culture, moreover, is *expressed* through the behaviors, practices, and beliefs upheld by a group of people with shared experiences and values. These expressions often, if not always, include some visual, auditory, or physical art form interwoven in daily life, and play a continued role in defining that culture and its evolutions. The world's strongest civilizations are explicitly known for exemplifying unification through artistic expression, whether through paintings, written word, customary garb, song, or dance. Through art, people find an association with one another, experiencing similar mental and emotional interpretations of life, and therefore having stronger connections to each other and the land they live on.

In Detroit, a positive, unifying culture among the City's resident majority faintly exists, and is a measurement of cultural displacement, spanning across time. The enslavement and disenfranchisment of African peoples in America and the Great Migration north from southern states where some African and indigenous practices were sustained (eg Congo Square and Mardi Gras in New Orleans, LA), as well as the abandonment of major manufacturing industries, leading to the dismemberment of once healthy neighbourhoods, inconsistent educational opportunities, and limited access to resources, all contribute to imbalances in cultural sustenance among the resident majority in Detroit. There is, however, an undeniable strength clearly exemplified by the resident majority in their ability to remain among derelict buildings and poor city services, whether by choice or not. Some remain committed to dutifully maintaining their property, as well as property abandoned by others, to sustain integrity and hope contrary to ruin (see Kinder, Chapter Six). Still, Detroit neighborhoods remain disjointed, not simply by structural vacancy and decay, but by fragmented behaviors, practices, and beliefs. The lack of positive, shared experiences and values impacts the establishment of strong neighborhood economies.

Fortunately, reconnecting the resident majority to experiences that will inspire a stronger sense of self, others, and the land around them is possible through reoccurring planning efforts that are infused with the awakening influences of art and creative utilitarian practices. Although this argument is focused on the experiences of the resident majority and does not intentionally examine any other ethnic group living in Detroit, as the fastest-growing and third-largest population in Detroit, the cultural fortitude of the Latin population in Detroit is not to be entirely ignored. Although Latin population in Detroit do not share the same story of cultural displacement in America as the resident majority, and are intentionally not examined further in this chapter, some Latinos have experienced similar migration patterns to the north for better economic opportunities for generations. Furthermore, despite shifts in place, they have sustained their cultural identity through continued practices that often, if not always, utilize some type of art form and reinforce economic sustainability. Therefore, these sustained practices should be acknowledged and thoughtfully sought out as an example by planning professionals and the resident majority alike.

Detroit's ambivalent relationship with creative placemaking

The most common urban renewal practice where art is used with the intention to engage residents is known popularly as creative placemaking.[1] In Detroit, various creative placemaking efforts are continuously organized by public, private, and non-profit organizations with the intent to create thriving places to live, work, and play. Oftentimes, creative placemaking is linked to larger economic and job growth strategies, and are becoming ever-more popular in large urban cities in need of economic resurgence, like Detroit. Strategically equipped statewide organizations, like Creative Many, are committed to "advancing the arts, culture and creative industries" in Michigan toward strengthening the economy, communities, and educational opportunities for children.

Nonetheless, in a White Paper on the practice of creative placemaking written by Anne Gadwa and Ann Markusen (2010), they present findings on the limitations of the creative placemaking practice. The inability of creative placemaking efforts to significantly engage residents across demographics are due to challenges of "community skepticism" and "displacement," among several others. These challenges, in particular, affirm the need for more thoughtful and insightful uses of art that engage residents, uninhibited by systemic or capitalist structures and ideals.

Further exploring creative placemaking in Detroit with these challenges in mind, more recent and robust efforts using art are evident at a higher rate and volume in neighborhoods adjacent to Detroit's Greater Downtown area, like Corktown or Midtown, as well as neighborhoods like Grandmont Rosedale, Palmer Woods, and Bagley Community that sit farther away from the Downtown area but contain similar assets (ie colleges, universities, hospitals, major businesses, bordering and affluent suburban cities). Murals, art festivals, and community gardens are a few of the more common creative placemaking activities that take place in these same neighborhoods to engage residents in sustaining shared community ideals. More distinct, large-scale, and recurring public art programming, like the Detroit Design Festival and De-Electricity, are known to attract thousands in attendance each year, and only take place in the areas closest to Downtown and Midtown, or in areas where a continuous influx of young families and professionals are found, like West Village and Indian Village. At times, these recurring events and other large-scale mural efforts that commission both local and international artists to redefine the visual appeal of the built environment and begin a new story of Detroit's present and future, can be viewed as "outsider art"—casting an identity on the city and resident majority that is not altogether shared or acknowledged. In 2013, 27 artists from around the world were commissioned to create large-scale murals in the newly constructed parking garage in Downtown Detroit called The Z. The murals were created under private investment and with the intent to turn the parking garage into a "destination" (see Crain's Communications, 2013). Although the colorful array of graffiti-like murals stir feelings of awe and fantasy, there is little to be said for its content creating cultural sustenance for the resident majority, nor is the garage highly accessed by this same group.

In neighborhoods geographically disconnected from the Greater Downtown area and with little to no assets, there is limited access and opportunities to implement large-scale creative placemaking strategies known in other areas of the city. However, as mentioned earlier, the non-profit sector is a key player in developing creative place-making strategies in these neighborhoods that focus primarily on the functional, rather than commercial, use of art to support neighborhood economies and prevent displacement among the resident majority, and has been doing so in partnership with local artists, arts institutions, and philanthropic organizations. For example, non-profit organizations like Detroit Black Community Food Security Network (DBCFSN) (see Yakini, Chapter Eighteen) are partnering to reconfigure vacant land on the west side of Detroit into creative, healthy, and economically viable alternatives through urban garden programming unique to the needs of the resident majority. Nonetheless, the stark difference between the efforts of DBCFSN and those mentioned earlier that take place in more traditionally attractive and stable neighborhoods is the degree to which residents identify with these efforts and create shared experiences of and shared values toward a stronger and viable neighborhood.

The implications of imbalances in the overall impact of creative placemaking efforts in Detroit correlate with the socio-economic identity of the residents experiencing them. The level of exposure to and understanding of art and its capabilities dictate its overall impact. The socio-economic identity of residents living in neighborhoods with significant assets does not mirror residents living in neighborhoods with minimal assets. Higher numbers of college-educated residents with disposable income are concentrated in neighborhoods with greater assets, whereas higher numbers of residents with low income, little to no college education, and limited exposure to historical and customary practices are concentrated in neighborhoods with fewer assets.

A history of master planning in Detroit

With creative placemaking as a basis, urban planning in Detroit can create more robust opportunities to use art to renew cultural roots for residents who are historically disadvantaged in order to move toward more resident-driven decision-making on the land they live, work, and play on. The devotion of the urban planner in Detroit, and city planning departments overall, should be to assist the resident majority in establishing more opportunities to build community in order to better implement larger land-use plans. Where resident knowledge, experiences, and opinions of the land around them *should* act as the core of planning processes and decisions, instead, traditional and contemporary planning techniques continue to be unrepresentative of the resident majority's voice. The lack of resident-majority voice creates further disconnect between each other and the land around them. Furthermore, traditional and contemporary planning efforts are still very much rooted in interpretations of objectives outlined in a city's master or comprehensive plan. In Detroit, master plans have historically interpreted culture as a "district" or "center." This idea of culture simply as a "place" or "destination" cannot motivate action in uncovering ways to make more distinct and critical opportunities for residents to connect with one another and the land they live on. Master planning in Detroit must also acknowledge culture as a feeling of community that is conceived of shared experiences and values that are fluid and intrinsic.

Detroit has four documented master plans beginning in 1951, with subsequent plans about every 20 years. Detroit also has one citywide strategic plan created in 2012 through a partnership with the City of Detroit and The Kresge Foundation. In the brief exploration of each plan to follow, the intent is to reveal the history of plan making in Detroit as it relates to resident engagement in planning processes, development plans for culture, the disconnect between the intent of the resident engagement process and the cultural needs of the resident majority in order to connect with the process, and the evolution of resident engagement toward realistically establishing strong neighborhood economies throughout Detroit.

The 1951 plan: the booming years

Detroit's 1951 master plan was created during a time when the population peaked at 1.9 million (Detroit, City of, 1951). The planning process lists the involvement of 21 public agencies. The Arts Commission—a consortium of members appointed by the city to oversee operating agreements between the City of Detroit and the Detroit Institute of Arts—was the only agency or organization listed that was representative of the arts and/or culture in Detroit. The extent to which each agency participated is not explained. Aside from listing the Arts Commission as a participating public agency, a separate area of the master plan outlines general development plans for the Civic Center, Cultural Center, and Riverfront. Planning for these spaces demarcate the intention to nurture cultural and social competency. Civic engagement in the planning process is stated in the introduction as follows: "The plan and its objectives have been reviewed by citizens and civic groups in conferences and public hearings before the Commission" (Detroit, City of, 1951, p A). Further detail on conferences and public hearings are not documented in the plan.

The 1973 plan: a period of shifts in space and place

During the execution of Detroit's second master plan in 1973, Detroit was still the fifth-largest city in the US (Detroit, City of, 1973). Auto manufacturing remained its leading industry. Additionally, the birth of the Motown Recording Company in 1959 led to major cultural influences. Motown music not only drew significant fanfare, but also shaped social movements, with songs that promoted a need for peace and social justice during a time of extreme racial prejudice and civil unrest. Detroit also housed the second-largest number of active theater venues in the US, second to New York. However, Detroit's population had shrunk by over 330,000 people since 1950—a rate of over 16,000 people per year. Motown moved its operations to California in 1972, while the auto manufacturing industry implemented budget shifts as post-war technology innovations led to systematic strategies for reduced costs and maximized revenue. Shifts in industry locations to cheaper suburban land resulted in shifts in public welfare as fewer employment opportunities shrank the tax base support in Detroit and discriminatory housing practices prevented certain racial and socio-economic groups from mobilizing to suburban housing areas to fulfill employment needs. The installation of the cross-city expressway system caused harmful effects on communities across Detroit. The freeway partitions led to resident displacement and the loss of once-thriving neighborhood connectivity.

The 1973 master plan was simply an amendment to the 1951 plan, largely following similar outline, language, and land-use policies as before. Amendments were based on the land-use changes that had taken place since the last master plan was implemented, including the expressway system and its tangible impacts on housing, transit circulation, and industry. Further distinctions of these changes are outlined under the term "urban change," which dissects the city into three land-use development phases; Old City (development before 1900), Middle City (development during 1900 to 1930, and the change of these areas with the auto industry), and New City (development currently expanding/contracting from Middle City development). Each phase is examined to demarcate the waves of land-use development to suggest distinct policy approaches for each phase of land use for shaping a holistic framework for conservation and redevelopment.

Under Article 203 Urban Form, the plan vaguely articulates civic engagement by stating: "Large numbers of citizens and virtually every agency and department in the City of Detroit has participated in its evolution." Further explanation of resident demographics and participation methods is not provided.

1990: fragmentation without representation

In 1990, Detroit's total population was 1,027,974—a decrease by over 400,000 people since 1970 (Detroit, City of, 1992)—while the resident-majority population became even more dominant due to the discriminatory practices mentioned earlier. Leading occupation types of residents were, respectively: technical, sales, and administrative; operators, fabricators, and laborers; service; and administrative support.

Of the resident-majority population, 32% of families lived below the poverty level. Detroit's third master plan evolved the strategic approach of planning by geographic phases found in the 1973 master plan, by dividing Detroit into nine geographic sectors; East Central, Near Northwest, North, Northwest, Riverfront, Southwest, West, and Woodward—an approach proving that thinking around resident and land relationships was evolving. Where possible, each sector was then dissected into several subsectors based on neighborhood, schools, or major roads (ie Evergreen, Rosedale, Hubbard, Harmony Village, Pershing, etc), or based on further geographic divisions (ie East Central, Middle East Central, Lower Woodward, Upper Woodward, etc). Each sector was given a "rezoning concept," and each subsector presented further detailed information on redevelopment.

In addition to each geographic sector of policies, the master plan includes Article 201 social goals, Article 203 physical development goals, and Article 202 economic goals. Article 201 focuses on policies that create and maintain positive neighborhood and family environments that will support a productive, informed, and concerned citizenry and community. More specifically, Article 201 demarcates policies in the areas of recreations, arts, and culture. Policies 201-16, 201-17, 201-19, and 201-20 collectively state the need to increase resident exposure to and participation in art activities, encourage ethnic and neighborhood art events, facilitate improvements in the working and living conditions of artists, and increase financial support for arts to expand and stabilize the industry.

Policies 202-9 and 202-10 recognize the impact of commercial recreation and cultural events as economic development tools. In addition to policies addressing vacant land, redevelopment, preservation, and relocation, Policy 203-30 designates a profound strategy to encourage the provision of public art as part of every major public and private development. This strategy creates cohesion with Articles 201 and 202 by further articulating areas to increase resident exposure to art, activate artists' employment opportunities, and create spaces that are esthetically pleasing to support commercial and cultural activity. The article also states that the correction of land-use problems is found in collective actions taken by property-owners, businesspeople, and neighborhood groups. Although information on engagement in the planning process is not specified, as stated in the city's second plan, Article 201 Social Goals, Policies, and Strategies recognizes creating and maintaining positive neighborhood and family environments, with further distinctions of arts, culture, and ethnic needs reiterated in policies under Recreation, Arts, and Culture.

2009: ideas for growth amid decay

Consistent with the 2009 American Community Survey (ACS) one-year estimates, Detroit's total population was 911,000, a predicted loss of 116,974 people since 1990—the smallest population decline over a 20-year span in comparison to population losses between implementation of the 1950, 1973, and 1992 master plans (though this would prove to be an overestimation of the city's population, as the 2010 census recorded a population of 713,777). During this time, the leading industries in employment of the workforce population in Detroit were as follows:

- Education service, health care, and social assistance = 26%.
- Service and sales = 25%.
- Retail trade = 12.4%.
- Arts, entertainment, recreation, accommodation, and food service = 12%.
- Manufacturing = 11%.

The percentage of employment by industry is indicative not only of deindustrialization, but also of the shifts in demographics. By this time, baby boomers experienced their first wave of retirement. Millennials, the children of baby boomers, were moving to areas outside of Detroit for different or better job opportunities, and immobile, low-income families were suffering from limited job opportunities and high dependency on social services. These three major demographic shifts influence taxpayer power or lack thereof, resulting in poor city services, the abandonment of intended land-use policies, and higher rates of neighborhood decay. Housing cost burdens for renters were 67% and 53% for owners with mortgages. By 2009, vacancy rates were estimated to reach nearly 25%.

Drawing distinctions from the 1992 master plan, Detroit's fourth master plan of policies was a result of incremental strategies taking place since 1994 (Detroit, City of, 2009). The plan evolved with the emergence of common practices in community-based planning processes, which were inherent in post-industrial cities where planning for growth was a counterproductive phenomenon, but attempts to gain community feedback rallied new hope to discover opportunities for growth. The plan's intentions were to act as guidance for actions to take place over the next 10 years by providing greater clarity in and easier access to land-use regulatory policies. The master plan organized citywide policies into 17 elements,[2] also referenced in neighborhood cluster recommendations. Engagement in the planning process is, again, summarized with vagueness, and the number of those engaged, the engagement methods used, and the specific locations of engagement were not stated. Instead, the following is mentioned: "During the spring and summer of 2003, a series of engagement workshops took place, coordinated by the City's Neighborhood City Halls."

2012: a partial future

Finally, and contrary to the four master plans evidenced earlier, the development of Detroit's Strategic Framework Plan in 2012, led by Detroit Future City, reflected not only an engagement process indicative of a shift in population and industry, but also shifts taking place in the urban planning profession and recognition by philanthropic and non-profit organizations in particular of the need to rally new ways to engage residents in learning and decision-making so that plans are better utilized. The reported total population count, according to the 2010 census, was 713,777, nearly 200,000 fewer people than predicted in 2009. At this time, there are also 150,000 vacant and abandoned parcels, or, in other words, 20 square miles of vacancy scattered throughout the city (Detroit Future City, 2012). The substantiality of vacant land and buildings resulted in low property values, decreased economic opportunities, and highly disparate real-estate development.

Unlike the 2009 Master Plan of Policies, as well as other previous master plans, the Strategic Framework Plan is not a legally mandated document, nor was it created under statutory procedures and formats and executed by the municipality's planning agency. Instead, the plan was organized as a "unified vision and is intended to be used as a guide for implementers, investors, and regulators participating in the revitalization of Detroit." The Detroit Economic Growth Corporation (DEGC)—a non-governmental entity—led the efforts of designing and implementing the initiative, and overseeing the planning team, which included local, national, and international personnel in planning design, economics, engineering, and the like. Additionally, the DEGC was vested and vetted by the interests of local and national philanthropic institutions that also act as key stakeholders in the redevelopment of Detroit—The Kresge Foundation being the predominant grant-making institution of the Framework, with a long history of investment in arts and culture across the country.

The plan drew on five elements—Economic Development, Land Use, City Systems, Neighborhood, and Land and Building Assets—of which all were encompassed by engagement strategies. More interestingly, the 24-month-long public process with residents and civic leaders, beginning in 2010, further elaborated the distinct democratic approach of the plan-making process. Civic engagement was detailed as the foundation of the city's future, and a diverse and lateral division overseeing community engagement efforts was outlined. A steering committee of 12 civic leaders across fields like business, philanthropy, and faith-based institutions, a civic engagement team led by a local partner, process leaders to gain citywide feedback, and the Mayor's Task Force were involved in the strategic approach of gaining input.

A combination of methods was used for civic engagement. Engagement types included an oral history film project, a 24-7 online game, telephone town halls, and a "roaming table" that went inside neighborhoods across the city to gain resident feedback. Data representative of the reach of these engagement methods used over the course of two years are outlined in a monthly timeline report within the plan. According to the data provided, by September 2012, 163,600 "connections" had been made, and over 70,000 survey responses and comments had been received. Gender, race and ethnicity, age, and geography (rates of vacancy) of registered participants within Detroit that provided the respective information were recorded:

- Gender: 61% female; 38.5% male.
- 47% African descent; 30% European descent; 14% Latino.
- 32% age 55–74; 23% age 35–54; 21% age 18–34; 14% age 17 and under.
- 35.3% of participants lived in areas of moderate vacancy, 26.2% in areas of low vacancy, 13.8% in the Greater Downtown Detroit area.
- 12.8% were non-Detroit residents and 11.3% of participants lived in high-vacancy areas.

These figures, alongside others mentioned earlier, reveal an engagement process far more robust than witnessed in past planning processes. However, limitations in engaging the resident majority at a majority level still reside, as displayed in the aforementioned participant statistics. This further presents implications for challenges mentioned earlier about creative placemaking strategies. Therefore, the need to think more critically about the cultural identity of the resident majority based on the context of their experiences rather than within the context of larger, more broad (and sometimes vague) urban American culture while attempting to revitalize major urban cities like Detroit takes precedence.

Toward shared experiences, values, and goals

There are numerous art forms and environments that can be utilized to help the resident majority heal, learn, and examine the identity they share with each other and the land around them, and be inspired to sustain that connectivity in a positive way that impacts larger community welfare. In order for these art forms to be utilized in a way that is transformative to both the resident majority and the field of urban planning, learning in modern civic participatory methods must undergo a "white wash" with art-centered experiences that are functional, relative, and significant to the resident majority in spaces inclusive of where they dwell and interact with each other most. Buoyantly so, there are pockets of neighborhood-based efforts emerging in Detroit's resident-majority neighborhoods, as well as in similar places across the nation, that are focused on using art and space in unconventional ways to stimulate and sustain community realignment. These efforts are being driven by residents, national organizations, and everything in between, and are profound studies for the larger urban planning field to learn from. Nonetheless, these efforts are still emerging practices and not altogether a concrete design to be inserted into larger resident engagement plan-making processes in distressed environments. The continued and more robust assessment of these practices deserves and requires the thoughtful collection of data, critical research, incremental analysis, and cross-sector collaboration to sustain funding and momentum.

As mentioned earlier, there are numerous grassroots examples of residents and community-based organizations that have taken the initiative to reconfigure cultural imbalances experienced by the resident majority in Detroit. Another significant example of this can be found in the works of the Heidelberg Project (HP) (see Guyton, Intermezzo II). Spanning over 30 years, the HP is a non-profit organization that continues to use art as a catalyst for positive change, and continues to be widely documented through film, photography, and literature. Utilizing two city blocks in one of the oldest resident-majority neighborhoods in Southeast Detroit, the HP showcases art installations made from found objects that provoke thought, discussion, and healing on issues of systemic racism, capitalism, substance abuse, and mental instability, primarily experienced by the resident majority. The HP's visitors have come from over 120 countries as the art installations also speak to universal and balanced differences among human life and living. Although the HP does not focus primarily on the functional use of art, the context and content of the art displayed present learning in an unorthodox fashion, revealing trauma in a way that is strikingly relative to all people, despite skin color or country of origin. For examples, *Souls on High* is an installation crafted from several pairs of old shoes, tied together at their laces and dangling casually from tree branches at the center of Heidelberg Street (see Figure 13.1). The piece intends to interpret experiences had by people of African descent, specific to the brutality and trauma of hangings as both slaves and free people, and as victims or witnesses. However, as the name of the installation suggests, and in its placement high above in trees, at an angle that encourages viewers to look up, the piece also pays homage to all souls (people) and their journey throughout life, often supported by the soles of the shoes they have worn that carry them throughout and above negative experiences.

Figure 13.1 *Souls on High* art piece in the Heidelberg Project by Tyree Guyton

The HP's off-site programs also reach students in the classroom at local elementary schools, as well as major colleges and universities across Michigan and the world. An Educator's Kit for K-12 classrooms was designed with partnership support from the Erb Family Foundation. Institutions like Wayne State University, the University of Michigan, and College for Creative Studies continue to utilize HP's lecture opportunities and site tours to engage graduate and undergraduate students in the relationship between history, art, and land as producers of cultural relevancy in the present.

Outside of Detroit, there are examples of art-based planning and cross-sector partnerships in resident engagement alongside larger planning goals that may serve as opportunities for replication in Detroit. For example, in Harlan County, a rural mountainous region of Kentucky abandoned by a once-thriving coal mining industry with a history of racial divide, performance art is being used to engage residents in healing and decision-making on land use. Community-wide stage plays that interpret historical issues and movements toward dispelling these issues are performed at the county's community college and local gym and auditorium. To add shared value to this experience, the actors in the play are actual residents expressing their real experiences in Harlan County through script.

Another example of art-based resident engagement can be found in Honolulu, Hawaii. The arrival of corporate food-cropping industries, beginning in the 1970s, spread throughout the land. The result was the loss of many family farms, which, in turn, repressed the cultural and communal practices of indigenous peoples, and shifted their economic dependency on to these same corporate entities. To support healing and rebuilding from this loss, organizations like the Bishop Museum are utilizing the museum's collection and staff of orators to sustain knowledge and practices of venerable Samoan customs. The few remaining and remote indigenous family farms are also used for education and the advocacy of customary practices.

As these art-based examples can be found throughout the world, and continue to take place throughout Detroit, there is often little to no ties to larger city planning efforts and little funding support. They do not feature in official master plans, which have guided planning and (re)development in cities such as Detroit for decades. Consequently, the lives of these programs are short and their impact is minimal. However, as there is an evident increase in the number of large, international, philanthropic initiatives emerging that are focused on arts and culture (ie Knights City Challenge, ArtPlace), the opportunities for cross-sector collaboration involving local city government are infinite, and the ability for these initiatives, and others to come, to focus primarily on reconfiguring cultural sustenance among disadvantaged populations is absolute.

Conclusion

There are many existing and emerging art-based participatory practices that command collaboration and support by the urban planning profession at a municipal level (see Ligon, Chapter Twelve). As time, opportunities, and funding have largely been limited, there is less evidence as to their long-term impact. However, as examples from this chapter, and others from this volume, have demonstrated (see Care moore, Intermezzo I; Guyton, Intermezzo II; Putnam et al, Chapter Twenty-Three; Boggs, Chapter Twenty-Five), (re)establishing cultural sustenance among disadvantaged populations in order to impact the larger successes of city planning goals is important to a just city. Master and comprehensive planning methods, such as the ones documented earlier in this chapter, have yet to completely evolve beyond conventional Eurocentric, theory-based principles. However, the ever-present systemic issues facing populations like Detroit's resident majority warrant a need to shift these principles toward more inclusive, functional, culturally sensitive, and resident-driven planning processes if land-use plans intend to thrive and be relevant.

Along with the study of individual household characteristics, understanding art as a functional tool and learning the historical context of its use by civilizations around the world and across time by urban planning students and practitioners can create inevitable ties to the quality of resident engagement processes in plan-making and greater success in plan implementation and strong neighborhood economies. Given generations of cultural displacement experienced by the resident majority, the process of healing must first take place with the understanding that constant, unorthodox engagement methods rooted in art and organized in applicable spaces are credible. Creative place-making has begun to create a powerful context for shifts in attitudes about the ability of art to play a critical role in renewing the quality of place. However, there is far more growth needed regarding how culture is interpreted by city planning departments. Such an understanding will, in turn, have a significant impact on funding opportunities and the long-term sustainability of culturally relevant, art-based programs. This approach has the potential to lead to genuine improvements in the resident engagement processes in spaces with higher concentrations of the resident majority and fewer traditional "placemaking" assets.

Notes

1 Creative placemaking is an evolving field of practice that intentionally leverages the power of the arts, culture, and creativity to serve a community's interests while driving a broader agenda for change, growth, and transformation in a way that also builds character and quality of place.

2 The 2009 master plan's citywide policies included the following 17 elements: Arts and Culture; City Design; Community Organizations; Economy; Education and Libraries; Environment and Energy; Health and Social Services; History, Legacies, and Preservations; Industrial Centers; Infrastructure; Intergovernmental Relations; Neighborhood and Housing; Parks, Recreation, and Open Space; Public Safety; Retail and Local Services; Transportation; and Mobility Zoning Concepts.

FOURTEEN

Make sure you are helping: experts, solidarity, and effective partnering with locals

Drew Philp

From Williams' "resident majority," we move on to another local perspective from Detroit. In 2009, Drew Philp bought an abandoned house on the East Side of Detroit for $500, renovated it, and turned it into his home where he currently resides. Detroit attracts no shortage of attention and many people come to the city with the intention of helping. Living where he does, Drew often encounters such people, an experience he illustrates in the chapter's opening vignette. However, Philp questions some of their intentions; using William Easterly's distinction between "searchers" and "planners," he differentiates between people coming in to implement their own ideas versus those who arrive willing to listen and contribute to the efforts of those who are already there. Through a combination of his own experiences and his work as a writer, journalist, and educator, Philp reflects on five common practices of overlooked and unexamined biases he is keen for people to avoid when entering into a new place and seeking to contribute to life and activity therein. His message resonates with many other voices in the book; the idea of the "blank slate mentality" that many outsiders have when entering Detroit will be picked up in conversations with the founders of the Boggs School (Chapter Twenty-three), which is coincidentally in the same neighborhood as Philp's home. While this critique is often aimed at visitors and new incoming and often wealthier residents, scholars, researchers, and educators can also learn from Philp, and other Detroiters, about how to enter a community, engage with it, and, hopefully, contribute to the activities and endeavors already going on there.

Drew Philp is a freelance writer and journalist from Detroit. His work has appeared in the *Detroit Free Press*, *Metro Times*, *Bakersfield Californian*, and *The Guardian*. His *Buzzfeed* article "Why I bought a house in Detroit for $500" was read more than 1.5 million times. His memoir of building his house and living in Detroit, *A 500 House in Detroit: Rebuilding An Abandoned Home and An American City* will be published by Scribner April 11, 2017.

Introduction

> Once [Gay] People began to say who they were, you found it was your next door neighbor or it could be your child, and we found people that we admired. That understanding still doesn't exist with race. You still have separation of neighborhoods where races are not mixed. It's the familiarity with people who are gay that still doesn't exist for race and will remain that way for a long time as long as where we live remains divided. (Ruth Bader Ginsberg, quoted in Millhiser, 2014)

I had my shirt off and I was on my back, under my truck. The starter had gone and I'd been wiping rust out of my eyes all morning trying to break the seized bolts. Someone pulled up behind me and honked the horn. I came up with my framing hammer. This was East Detroit, Poletown to be exact, and I didn't know anyone who would be doing that. My roommate wouldn't be back for hours, and like a rude prom date, whoever was back there wanted me to come to them. They wanted something from me.

The neighborhood was prairie land, long forgotten by the municipal government, most aid agencies, and the Church. The street I was living on was named after the saint of the Catholic Cathedral three blocks away, closed, so the tithing of the faithful could be used elsewhere. Most of the houses had closed too, been torn or burned down, and the animals ran wild—rabbits, pheasants, foxes (see Figures 14.1). Behind my house was a brimming junk forest—abandoned grain silos, dumped boats, hot tubs, lewd foliage. I found it quite nice for a walk. But there was a murder every day in Detroit, dozens of suspicious fires a week, and 11,000 untested rape kits, hence the hammer.

I shimmied out from under the truck and came up with my makeshift weapon, ready for anything. When I saw what was behind me I was mostly confused. A golden minivan sat in the driveway, and behind the wheel was a white woman with long straight hair in a headband wearing some kind of prairie dress. Her stuffy clothing and stiff countenance pegged her as devoutly religious, if cloistered, but she didn't seem to pose a threat. I put the hammer down, wiped my hands, and walked over to the van.

"Hi! We're here delivering lunches. How many do you need?" The driver thrust a brown paper bag through the open window. There were more people in the back and they looked like they had just walked out of Pat Robertson's closet: button-down shirts buttoned to the top, khaki pants, reasonable shoes. They looked scared. Each of their heads rested against the headrest, eyes forward, all hands lay clearly visible and sweaty on armrests like a nervous traffic stop. It was only the driver who ever looked me in the eye. Detroit was 83% black, America's blackest city, and all of them were white.

"Um, I guess my roommate might want one too," I said. "Wait, who are you guys? Did someone call you? What are you doing here?" "We're here to serve the poor," the woman said and handed me another paper bag. I looked inside: a baloney sandwich, a fruit cup, some Cheetos, and a Hostess Sno–Ball. "Thanks, I guess." I didn't really know what to do next, so held out my hand for her to shake it. She looked at it like I had shoved an eel into her car. "God bless." She drove away without shaking my hand. She wouldn't touch me. I opened the tailgate on my truck and sat in the bed, swinging my feet over the sandy driveway as I ate the lunch, growing angrier and angrier. When my roommate got home, I handed him his. I never saw those people again.

Figure 14.1 Dubois Street north of Gratiot (Photo, Brian Doucet)

The problem of charity

I'm white and not a generational Detroiter, so I often feel the responsibility to help shepherd folks, often white themselves, who want to "help save Detroit" and are on a journey of discovery of how to do good. The burden often falls on people of color and the marginalized to explain race and class in America, and I think white folks who may be a bit further along on that journey have a duty to help others, if just to release some of the weight on the already overloaded. A lot of my experience comes from mistakes I've made myself. But this story in particular, if a bit dramatic, helps to illustrate some key issues with the problem of charity and "helping" Detroit. It can be tessellated to places all over the world.

This city is at a crossroads, and we have a unique opportunity to change things here—for the better— and honor the past by altering the future. Many people speak about "bringing Detroit back" as a shorthand for getting back to some golden age. Yet, during this "heyday," a six-foot-high concrete wall was constructed near the city's northern border of 8 Mile Road to help keep black people out of all-white housing developments (Karoub, 2013; see also Figure 14.2). Is this what we want to go back to? If the future is to be different, we must avoid past mistakes.

Figure 14.2 Dividing wall erected in the 1940s to separate an existing African-American area from a new white-only development near 8 Mile and Wyoming (Photo, Brian Doucet)

With almost two thirds of our population having left, Detroit is *the* city of leaving. Detroit is also now a city where parachute journalism, service day-trips, and quick jaunts to observe or participate in the spectacle of exodus capitalism have become fashionable (see, eg, Burns, 2015; Cowley, 2015). When we come in quick and leave, when we're not around to see the consequences of our actions play out—for good or ill—this can create some problems, as this is our number one problem.

Sometimes, charity can do more harm than good. In a perfect world, people would stay put, buy into communities, and learn from their own experiences. If we want to create real change, this is how to do it. This is not always possible or realistic. But there are some ways to mitigate, and possibly overcome, these issues for those that truly care and truly want to help in the short and medium term.

The story that leads this chapter was my first real experience on the other side of charity, the receiving end. It made me confused and angry: these people did not think I could feed myself? These people thought it proper to assume I needed help? And is it not kind of rude to pull up, honk the horn, and expect someone to come see what you want? Was the lunch actually nutritious? And was I worthy enough to feed but not touch?

I *was* hungry, I was certainly broke, but I was just minding my own business, not looking for a handout. My neighborhood does have hungry people, but there are also some securely comfortable people as well. And what does it have to say about my humanity that someone was willing to come visit my house but not perform the most basic of human interactions, the handshake? I'm a little rough around the edges, but surely I'm still a human being and not a wild animal. I don't bite. The event got me thinking, who was this lunch really meant to benefit? Was it truly for me? Or was it for the conscience of those handing it out? I began to feel like part of my humanity, my integrity, my free will, my individualism had been stolen from me.

Searchers versus planners

In his excellent book *White Man's Burden: Why the West's Efforts to Aid the Rest Have Done So Much Ill and So Little good*, William Easterly (2006) writes about two types of approaches to development: searchers and planners. Easterly's analysis focuses largely on foreign aid to the Global South, but the framework works well both for devastated American cities and on a personal level.

Planners come with ideas of how things should be done. They arrive with a certain set of goals, a certain set of tools, and a very specific mission, like feeding the hungry, making an art project to "brighten" the neighborhood, or planning a protest around a specific issue. From the outside, they see a problem and wish to solve it with solutions developed from outside the community, often by experts.

Searchers enter a community believing people are the experts on their own problems. They look for ways to support and facilitate solutions that the community members themselves have already developed. They throw their out-sized resources behind those community-developed solutions, and, most importantly, they help to raise people of color (in cities such as Detroit) and the marginalized to positions of power, leadership, and decision-making.

Planners say, "This is how we're going to do it." Searchers say, "How can we help?" With this framework in mind, the remainder of the chapter will reflect on five common practices of overlooked and unexamined biases that we want to avoid when coming to help others. They are drawn from several examples in Detroit, including my own story from the beginning of the chapter.

1. Don't amputate dignity

A handout, especially when unasked for, can strip people of their dignity, pride, and self-respect. That brown bag left me feeling less of a man, as if these people thought I could not provide for myself and my family, as if I was a stray dog. In Detroit and many places like it, the struggle for self-sufficiency has a long history and we must be wary of undermining this. Don't get me wrong, there are people who occasionally and genuinely need a leg up. I have myself. But it's one thing to run around forcing generosity upon folks and assuming people need you, and another to offer the opportunity for folks to choose their destiny themselves.

2. Don't assume anything

The people handing out lunches assumed something about me, namely, that I was hungry or too poor to feed myself. They didn't ask; they just handed me a lunch. Assumptions create resentment, and are often wrong. Even when they are correct, they can create bitterness as they often expose the power dynamic between donor and recipient. Assumptions often rely on stereotypes for their initiation, and end up reinforcing them. Assumptions can often sneak up unnoticed, and matters of culture that lie unexamined can often undermine genuine efforts. It's best to have not only a solid grounding in the touchstones of the culture you will be working with, but also, and perhaps more importantly, an understanding of the traits and customs of your own culture and identity, especially if it is the dominant one.

Whiteness, in particular, often lays unexamined. American culture has a habit of thinking that whiteness is the sun that all other racial planets revolve around, that other cultures' traits are deviations from this baseline. This is not the case. Whiteness contains certain traits and touchstones unique to the group, and often unhelpful ones, that must be examined before and during any work of this kind.

3. Don't give busy people homework

This is going to get a bit metaphorical here, and it's paltry in this instance, but belies a larger trend I've experienced in Detroit. The folks handing me lunch made me stop what I was doing and come to them. As I've experienced it, this is often more pronounced with art projects, community meetings planned from the outside, and organizing jaunts. If folks haven't bought into the community and are there for just a moment, these meetings are often useless, don't add up to results, and can feel like homework for those often overloaded with the stress and extra work that comes from living in tough areas and the unfair disadvantages that saddle the marginalized. At their worst, they can cause burnout for folks trying to organize themselves.

Involved people feel the need to keep up with what is happening in their neighborhood, and when everyone wants to do an art project on an abandoned house for example—something that people may not, and often don't, want—these meetings can become endless and get in the way of actual solutions proposed by the community themselves. An important facet to remember is, "Was I asked to come do this? Or am I asking a community for something?" Good intentions and benevolence don't supersede results. You might need to walk around and speak to people sitting on their porches to see if the idea is viable or necessary before calling a big meeting about it, where people may come to feel beset by and reactionary to changes in their neighborhood that you may not be around to see the results of.

4. Might it do more harm than good?

I was hungry, and it was lunch, but was it all that nutritious? Was the temporary abatement of hunger through processed meat and sugar

255

worth a stab at my dignity? Is that for someone who's dignity is not at stake to decide?

Sometimes, the results of charity have unintended, unhealthy, consequences. In one egregious example, a group of outside activists, supported by local ones, came to my neighborhood to protest the trash incinerator, the largest in any city in the US. It's a good cause. Using a community space, they made protest paraphernalia—hundreds of spray-painted sunflower pickets, miniature incinerators, signs. When the protest was over, they left, without having cleaned up their mess, and all those signs made it back to the community space. In a bout of staggering irony, we didn't have any other options for what to do with the trash. So it went into the incinerator and into my community's lungs. They didn't have to share in the acrid smoke because they were off gallivanting to their next good deed.

This is another common occurrence with neighborhood public art projects. The art is made, the artists leave, and, over time, the art rots. This leaves a mess for those left to clean up. Just as you don't want to give busy people more homework, don't leave what may become trash for someone else to clean up despite how important it was when you started.

5. Treat people like adults

This is the most important point. Treat people like adults—and like people. Just because you have a traditional education doesn't mean that equates to the skills necessary to succeed in places like Detroit. People are the experts on their own problems, and, in certain instances, this makes them smarter than you. Follow their lead.

And for God's sake, don't work with people you won't touch! Don't work with people who you wouldn't live next to yourself, and don't ask people to do anything you wouldn't do. Don't be rude, and don't bring anyone to work in a community you're unsure of. One hesitation, when it comes to something as simple as a handshake, can ruin everything. Sometimes, it ends up sticking with a person for years.

How to create meaningful change

We all make mistakes. I've made quite a few myself. Mistakes are human and are OK as long as we are learning from them. Being around to see the results of your own actions is the best way to learn from your own mistakes. When we cannot stick around forever, we have a particular responsibility to be as prepared as possible. This means understanding the history and current weeds of oppression in any community you'll be working in, but also understanding the subtle role those dynamics play out within you, personally, and your actions in progress. In the communities in which they are foisted upon, development projects, art projects, and organizing projects will be judged by results, not good intentions.

There's a simple test to determine if your organizations and projects are acting as searchers or planners and are result- and not ego-driven. Ask yourself, is what I'm creating a reflection of the world I want to live in?

If we don't want a world in which straight white males run everything, are we building our organizations to reflect this? If you wouldn't put—or wouldn't be allowed to put—that art project in your own neighborhood, is it necessary for here? Why aren't you doing it in your own community? Would you want someone to come to your neighborhood and leave what you might not term as art, but clutter? Would you want someone to assume you need charity? Why not?

Ask yourself, would you eat the proverbial food you're handing out? Would you be willing to live next to your art project forever? Are you getting in the way? Will you be creating more problems? And if your project may create good things *and* problems, who's to decide if the balance is worth it?

Let people from the community lead. Detroit is full of exciting ideas and visionary leaders. Look for solutions already being developed by the community members themselves, and support them. Trust the people and the community you're working with. They know. They live it every day.

FIFTEEN

New Strategies DMC, takin' it all back home: lessons from Detroit for arts practices in the Netherlands

Friso Wiersum, Bart Witte, and Nikos Doulos

In the Netherlands, the Utrecht-based Expodium arts collective is an example of a group that saw inspiration in the do-it-yourself mentality in Detroit. They were frustrated by the top-down way in which the arts are used in urban development in the Netherlands. Often, this takes the form of artists being used as "placemakers" to make a neighborhood or space more attractive for capital investment and gentrification. Seeking to counter this approach, Expodium took inspiration from the practices and ideas emerging from Detroit and obtained funding from the Netherlands to set up an artist residency there. Rather than trying to implement their vision in Detroit, the goal was to learn from the practices in the city and to engage with artists and the local community. In total, five Dutch-based artists traveled to Detroit. During their stay, many got to know Drew Philp, and Expodium's approach to entering Detroit would fit more within the concept of a "searcher" rather than a "planner" (see Chapter Fourteen). Equally important, they were also able to invite a grassroots community leader in the field of urban agriculture from Detroit over to the Netherlands to share their insights and lessons with planners, community leaders, and policymakers.

In such an edited volume, it is also important to showcase perspectives of outsiders who have come with these mentalities, but who have also learned from their experiences in Detroit. As the three members of Expodium illustrate in their chapter, their time in Detroit shaped the way in which they subsequently engaged with Dutch planning and urban development back home, though they already operated from a different standpoint than many other artist groups in the Netherlands. How they engaged with their own neighborhood in Utrecht was also reminiscent of ongoing practices in Detroit.

Expodium consists of Friso Wiersum, Bart Witte, and Nikos Doulos. They are an arts-based collective and consider themselves to be an urban "do tank," as opposed to just a "think tank." Through a variety of methods of artistic research, they generate vital information about urban areas and, at the same time, activate those areas and their users. They document, archive, contextualize, and frequently publish information and knowledge generated through their practice. They collaborate and work with diverse groups, including: international networks of artists, architects and academics, housing corporations, local governments, museums, universities, festivals, and art institutions. Expodium's most recent publication, *Unmaking, or How to Rethink Urban Narratives*, takes the permanent reconfiguration as the conditio sine qua non of the contemporary city. It is a book on the city as they perceive it; a place to rethink and re-imagine the existing built environment. *Unmaking* is available via Expodium's website (www.expodium.nl).

Introduction

To begin with, Expodium never "discovered" a pristine Detroit; we were aware what we could encounter there, and it was precisely this that led us to building a residency program in the "Motor City." Expodium's practice of using interdisciplinary research by artists, scientists, and activists to devise tools for artistic interventions took us there. Knowing about the particular circumstances in Detroit and the ensuing use of particular methodologies, Expodium wanted to expand its own toolbox with Detroit practices. We showcased that toolbox in a curated cultural program, targeted at artists and urban thinkers alike, in order to influence debates and discussions on urban matters.

Between 2009 and 2011, Expodium, a Utrecht-based arts collective, ran an artist residency program in Detroit. Five cultural workers, each of them working with Expodium in a different way, spent nine weeks in Detroit. In this chapter, we reflect on the lead-up and construction of these residency programs, on what actually transpired while in Detroit, and, most importantly, on what lessons we took back home with us to the Netherlands from Detroit.

Expodium and the city

In 2006, Expodium decided to change from being an exhibition space to being a long-term research platform, focusing on the theme of urban development. At that time, newspapers were publishing stories about a new urban era, which was marked by the fact that more than 50% of the global population was now living in cities. We quickly found that in the Netherlands, the arts was used in a top-down way, often to promote the aims of large stakeholders such as the government, developers, or housing associations (Boie and Pauwels, 2010). We realized that the role of the artists was nothing new and that artists have been instrumental in urban change for many years. However, our focus lay in understanding the relationship between artists and professional planners, architects, and urban designers under the context of changing attitudes toward social welfare and the relationships between the state and the individual. We were, and are, interested in how such challenging cooperations evolve and how we as cultural agents can help shape these wider relationships. These questions would eventually lead us to Detroit, where the presence of both strong arts communities and the necessity of a do-it-yourself (DIY) approach to urban projects would bring us key insights and lessons for our practices in the Netherlands.

Expodium and Utrecht

However, before our work took us to Detroit, we examined places closer to home. Even before the economic crisis, similar stories of industrial and demographic decline were present within "Rust Belts" in Europe. In the Netherlands, declining populations, shrinking economies, and a retreating welfare state became characteristic of areas such as the former mining region of South Limburg or the plains around Groningen. However, one of the most challenging and noticeable areas of decline in Europe was found in parts of the former East Germany. In 2006, Expodium launched a series of events involving German city planners and invited them to the Netherlands to share their findings. Somewhat later, Expodium joined in a research and lecture series on "Shrinkage" after the publication of a government-sponsored think-tank study entitled "Krimp en Ruimte" ("Decline and Space") (PBL, 2006). The insights gained from actors in regions and eras of urban decline prove to be powerful counter-narratives to, and possible strategies for dealing with, neoliberal fairytales of eternal growth.

One year later, in 2007, we directed our attention toward an actually-existing manifestation of this fairytale: the Utrecht shopping center Hoog Catharijne. The financially profitable mall, designed in the 1960s had become a lively, if not boring, shopping center during the day and a shelter for the homeless during the night. In contrast to many American shopping malls, Hoog Catherijne is situated in the city center, rather than in the suburbs. The shopping concourse at Hoog Catherijne was built one level above the street and provides direct access to the main railway station, also situated at the same level. The city's homeless used to sleep either in some of the empty corridors throughout the mall or in and around the loading bays and storage areas at ground level, which, because of the mall's elevation, had become largely devoid of street life. Grand redevelopment plans were announced in the mid-2000s for the mall, station, and the surrounding streets. Before the renovation work was to commence, Expodium researched the original plans, the unexpected usages, and popular views on Hoog Catharijne. Expodium did so by inviting artists to spend time in residence in Utrecht and hosted a show in an empty store—the now-infamous adjective "pop up" was not in fashion yet—in the shopping mall. Our publication based on this work, "HC on the move," offers unique critiques on city planning models in a medium-sized town in the Netherlands (Expodium, 2008). However, more generally, the publication's questions of ownership of public space (the shopping mall is privately owned), economic expansion and social impact (traditional neighborhoods were demolished for the construction of the mall), the importance of local history (during the post-war decades, Utrecht lost half of its medieval city center), and the role of city governance are touched upon.

In addition to the redevelopment of Hoog Catherijne and Central Station, Utrecht was experiencing one of Europe's greatest urban expansion plans. Leidsche Rijn, an entirely new part of the city, eventually to house 90,000 people, was being developed on the western edges of the city. As Utrecht's population is around 300,000, this represents a significant addition to the city's population and area. The municipality and developers involved in Leidsche Rijn jointly invited Stichting Kunst in Opnbare Ruimte (SKOR; the foundation for art in public space, non-existent today) to curate an art program during the initial years of the area's construction. Entitled "Beyond Utrecht," this project was to serve as an outsider's view and as an appealing narrative for those critical of the concept of top-down city planning, which historically guided urban developments in the Netherlands. What was different about "Beyond Utrecht" was that it involved artists and the arts directly in the process of placemaking. Taking a critical stance toward these roles for the arts, Expodium organized independent tours through this building site as part of our bottom–up approach to city planning and the independent role that the arts should play in urban change. We were inspired by the infamous publication "T.A.Z.: The Temporary Autonomous Zone" of Hakim Bey (1991) on socio–political tactics of creating temporary spaces that elude formal structures of control. Through initiatives such as this, with arts strategies relating to urban planning, the "free" and often more radical role that artists can play in this process and our willingness to share insights via public programs eventually led us to build an arts residency project in Detroit.

New Strategies DMC (Detroit Motor City)

In 2008, the Expodium team developed plans for a residency program in Detroit. We obtained grants from the Mondriaan Fonds and Stichting DOEN (Mondriaan Funds and DOEN Foundation), which enabled us to host cultural workers in Detroit for a period of nine weeks. The set-up was to send pairs of these cultural workers to Detroit each year. The aim was for these cultural workers to connect with existing projects that were already ongoing in Detroit. These included groups such as the Yes-Farm, 555 gallery, Design 99, Hatch, and Detroit Collaborative Design Center. In order to become acquainted with the local situation, we encouraged our artists to become embedded in the existing arts scenes and groups. The intention was that these residents would be able to work on projects that made an essential contribution to communities in Detroit, as Expodium strongly believes in the capacity of the fine arts to develop innovative visions concerning changes and developments in contemporary society.

In order to prepare the cultural workers for their residence period in Detroit, we prepared some background information to familiarize them with the challenges both facing the city and its inhabitants, and to help them with their own preparation. In it, we explained that Detroit's situation can be read as a visual manifestation of the new post-industrial city, a hybrid of a paradoxical alignment of the urban and the rural. Detroit-based cultural initiatives respond creatively to the city's current situation and are set to play an imperative role in the redevelopment of the city (Expodium, 2009a). In addition, we asked the cultural workers to work toward a series of interventions and presentations while still in Detroit, and come up with an effective format to translate and communicate their experiences and practice back in the Netherlands (Expodium, 2009b). Also, the artists were obliged to keep an up-to-date blog on their experiences, practices, and findings during their stay in Detroit. This blog hosts an interesting collection of materials that the artists submersed themselves in while residing in Detroit, as well as personal observations and reflections on Detroit, on the idea of residencies, and on similarities and differences between Detroit and other cities.

In total, five Dutch-based artists participated in this program. Nikos Doulos and Joao Evangelista visited the city in the summer of 2010. The focus of their visit was to map forms of agency within the existing social structures. They did so through a set of formal and informal encounters, connecting notions of care, ideas about sharing, and thoughts on self-sufficiency. Thus, they also expanded Expodium's network and laid the foundations for the next artists. The following summer, Chris Meighan and Jonas Ohlsson participated in the program. Their work examined matters of artistic practice. Finally, in the fall of 2011, Friso Wiersum visited Detroit and looked at the political and historical situation in the city. All residents set up a series of events in Detroit. These centered on themes that included discussing the artist's specific work, the role of being a critical outsider, and questions of agency. These events could take the shape of artist performances, presentations, convivial dinners, a film series, a night of DJ'ing, and physical interventions.

The artists translated their experiences in Detroit into various different projects and initiatives. The first two residents initially shared their findings during an exposition in Expodium's working space in Utrecht. This project, "Visual Translation: Archive of Impressions," was centered on a selection of 273 prints (consisting of Detroit newspaper articles, photos, and blog posts), divided into themes such as "sense of belonging," "new systems of energy production," and "bartering mechanisms." A second presentation by these artists involved the use of a classic American yellow school bus that took people to an old farm in the Leidsche Rijn area of Utrecht, addressing the urban–rural relation. The main output inspired by their time in Detroit, however, was a guidebook depicting their findings in the Motor City and functioning as a tool of opening up discussions on autonomy, agency, and rights to the city beyond the realm of Utrecht and Detroit (Evangelista and Doulos, 2011).

The second generation of artists shared their insights in a different way: Chris Meighan made a short movie on the "Michigan Left" road traffic design, developed in Michigan, which replaces an at-grade left turn with a right turn, followed by a U-turn—including his personal answers to his question "why being an artist" (Meighan, 2011), while Jonas Ohlsonn incorporated his Detroit experience into his existing artistic presence, ranging from graphic design to audio lectures. The last cultural worker to take up the residency program in Detroit was Friso Wiersum, who presented his findings in Utrecht during a series of events titled "21st century ill digital toys." These events touched upon topics such as "ruin porn," the art of watching, urban farming, and future memories (Wiersum, 2010).

Bringing it home: lessons from Detroit

Each artist gained personal insights and used their Detroit experience to shape their own individual practices, but what did this collectively mean for the practices, philosophy, and community relationships for the arts collective of Expodium? While addressing this question, it is also important to reflect on the changing political climate in the Netherlands during the period when the residency took place. During this time, the Netherlands underwent a political shift from a country characterized by its open and tolerant culture, toward one where openly xenophobic politicians began to gain ground and local and national arts funding was under threat (see Siegal, 2013). The cultural consequences were clear; some municipal arts budgets were reduced by up to 60% and many political leaders began to question the arts' and artists' contributions to society. Artists either had to compromise or had to find other ways than public grants to maintain their profession.

It is in such governance narratives that we find parallels between Detroit and the Netherlands. The bottom-up initiatives that are essential to keeping large parts of Detroit livable, particularly for residents outside of the Greater Downtown, the DIY mentality and practices in many neighborhoods (see Kinder, Chapter Six), and the cooperative manner of formal and informal cultural centers, with their ensuing desire to maintain a presence in public spaces, echoed Expodium's changing cultural practices and attitudes toward its surroundings. One of the biggest changes we made was our decision to leave our offices in the city center and relocate to the neighborhood of Kanaleneiland. For some time, Expodium had a small residency in this post-war neighborhood. The area, while developed as a middle-class community of low- and medium-rise apartments, as well as single-family homes, had quickly deteriorated into one of the city's poorest areas. When built, it was almost exclusively social-rented housing. Since the 1970s, the population changed from a largely Dutch, middle- and lower-middle class mix, to a low-income area with one of the city's largest concentrations of non-Western inhabitants. Architecturally, the neighborhood was built in a modernist style, with a separation of functions and ample open and green space. Recently, however, many of the flats have been demolished and replaced with new, owner-occupied homes aimed at enticing young professionals to settle and "upgrade" the neighborhood.

During the renovation process, the municipality and social housing corporations invited cultural entrepreneurs to live in the soon-to-be-demolished flats in order to accelerate the placemaking process, and thus gentrification. This symbolizes the Dutch belief in malleability, and represents the old top-down approach to city-making that dominated much of 20th-century planning. Expodium was one of the early cultural "change-makers" to precede this scheme. From our experiences in Detroit, we were aware of the risks and conflicts associated with treating Kanaleneliand as our "blank canvass." We had seen how other artists and incomers tried to impose their ideas on a local population that was racially, economically, and culturally very different from the new incomers. Rather than treating this initiative as a virgin territory to act upon, Expodium held firm to our belief in organic and locational development. That implied keeping account of the local histories, the fights and struggles of (former) local residents, and the plans that never materialized. We observed that "hipster" newcomers to Detroit added insult to injury when occupying houses of former neighbors and not caring about those relationships. City developers, and artists alike, face the same challenge when they are adding to change in urban landscapes.

Thus, one of the first acts of Expodium at their new residency project in Utrecht (which partially ran parallel to the residency project in Detroit) was to invest time in getting to know the neighbors: the present neighbors, the neighbors that had recently left, and the ones arriving. In Kanaleneiland, with its modernist architecture, that meant reclaiming public space as life had hitherto been sliced up in private segments. One of the very concrete examples that Expodium brought home from Detroit was the notion of the front porch as a transitional space between public and private realms. So, we constructed one adjacent to our residency flat and new offices (see Figure 15.1). This simple act proved to be an emblematic gesture in the neighborhood: little boys playing football on the street came along to help the Expodium crew mix concrete and cut wood, little girls found a platform where to practice their dance moves, and smoking neighbors a place to smoke when it was raining. At the same time, Expodium was approached by another local resident who asked why the permission to build this porch was granted as his applications to rebuild his flat were all rejected. Expodium could only answer that they never obtained permission as it was never asked for. Behind these different strategies lie worlds of policymaking and growing gaps between policymakers and "normal" citizens. Whereas Expodium is an artist-run art space with a name known to the housing corporation that owned the flats, this person was not. Local Utrecht questions of privilege thus resemble questions of access to networks in Detroit (and by privilege, we basically refer to the act of debating with the authorities on the relevance of the porch for the local community, a privilege that was subsequent since the porch was already there—built and functioning). The housing corporation came to us and we have to credit their openness to subvert the existing regulations and allow it to stay. It is that tactic of creating counter-narratives that stemmed from a multiplicity of examples in Detroit. By addressing the urgency for a semi-private collective space, we proceeded with creating one outside of the regulative boundaries.

Figure 15.1 Working to install a new "front porch" on an apartment building in Kanaleneiland, Utrecht (Photo, Expodium)

The porch, parasitical in its initiation, became a mediative tool for negotiations and remains a symbolic totem of a horizontal way of dealing with the city. The Kanaleneiland residency program was forced to close down after a new series of budget cuts in 2013. The porch found a new owner who promised to continue to maintain it and share it with the rest of the inhabitants of the neighborhood.

Public space and industrial history in Utrecht

Yet another consequence of Expodium's residency in Detroit was the emphasis Expodium and the residing artists put on DIY attitudes. Whether building an engine that could work on recycled vegetal oil from the nearby Chinese takeaways or guerilla planting vegetables in the surroundings of the Kanaleneiland residency, Expodium looked to examples encountered in Detroit for enabling self-reliance. Urban farming, a necessary practice in many parts of Detroit, is one area where our lessons from Detroit were of use for both our own practices and movements developing in our home city. In the Netherlands, urban farming tends to revolve around middle-class practices and has been seen in policy circles as a useful, if temporary, way to occupy underused spaces. Our take on the practice, influenced by our experiences in Detroit, brought new insights to these debates in the Netherlands and invitations from different groups in Utrecht focused on greening the city and promoting social cohesion through urban farming. We were invited to join the "Edible Utrecht" council, and through this, continued to influence the debates and develop our networks in the city.

Those networks proved valuable for the next chapter for Expodium. After budget cuts to the arts, the national government further cut budgets for welfare and other social services. Concomitant to these cuts were the calls for a "participation society" (*participatie samenleving*) where citizens and governments were meant to cooperate in social practices. This has resulted in a less-regulated and more privatized society. When the city council published a new vision for the Werkspoorkwartier, a small and often overlooked industrial area in Utrecht, they invited creative entrepreneurs and creative hubs to "participate" in the remodeling and rejuvenating of this zone. Expodium realized that their experiences in Detroit, with historical industrial heritage, the myriad of personal biographies from "the Great Migration," and abandoned industrial sites, could be of added value to this process of city renewal. Where Detroit still has nostalgia for the "wonder years" of the car industry, Utrecht was ignoring its industrial past and focusing on a post-industrial future centered around the university, tourism, and consumption. Large parts of the city and its inhabitants were left aside in this new vision, including many of the foreign "guest workers" who came to work in factories in areas such as the Werkspoorkwartier (the area was named after the eponymous Werkspoor company, a railway manufacturer based in this part of Utrecht).

One of Expodium's best-known artistic acts in this former industrial zone was the preparation and production of an opera on the historic context of this industrial zone. In it, we focused on the arrival stories of international migrants to Utrecht and the economic globalization that caused the closure of factories and steelworks. The "opera" was performed twice in 2015 and attracted a great diversity of local residents, thereby invoking pride in this almost-forgotten part of Utrecht's history.

However, Expodium's activities in the Werkspoorkwartier are evolving further. The 2015 program "Unmaking the Netherlands" aimed to create a knowledge production hub between experts from both visual arts and urban planning. It is an arts and education program predominantly targeted toward members of the local artistic community who seek to enrich their ability to contribute to social change through arts practices. In it, we question how creative practices can utilize public space for the benefit of positive social change. It is based around three open-ended thematic pillars: play, urban cannibalism, and the walking culture. This concept would never have seen the light if it were not for the Detroit experiences. Expodium was very much inspired by Detroit artists and art collectives who shared and influenced public spaces in the city. Play as an artistic notion is nothing new, but the spaces in Detroit offered unique opportunities to the arts and toward public events. Within Expodium's notion of *urban cannibalism*, we understand the city as an organism that feeds and destroys itself by absorbing all it can absorb from within and beyond its city limits. Thus, *urban cannibalism* surpasses the idea of the human stage in which we anthropocentrically assume we make the city. The walking culture—even though developed artistically for the Kanaleneiland residency—confronts the built city landscape with the eternal departure point for any interpretation: our body. By inviting the walker to escape from the standardized city rhythms, he or she will discover the city anew. Despite a physical landscape built primarily for the automobile, Detroit's economic landscape forces many of its inhabitants to walk great distances on a daily basis (26% of Detroiters do not own a car [UMTRI, 2014]).

Conclusion

Expodium dedicated much attention to "malleability" and its counter-narratives in its artistic programs prior to the Detroit residency project. Despite the recent funding cuts, arts and the way in which artists can shape urban space have traditionally taken a very top-down approach in the Netherlands. The Detroit residency project offered Expodium, and the artists involved, the opportunity to physically, mentally, and socially experience and understand the counter-narratives, bottom-up initiatives, and DIY urbanism present in Detroit. They have since become an integral part of Expodium's core ethos: locality matters, history matters, people matter. Thus, rather than being an art space with artistic presentations for the artistic crowd, Expodium transformed into a knowledge production hub (firmly rooted in the art scene) connecting locals and often marginalized communities to international developments in urban planning and the arts. The DIY or even DIT (do-it-together) mentality of many Detroiters has been leading in that transformation. In the Netherlands, such practices are increasingly borne out of necessity as budget cuts and changing political attitudes toward the arts mean that such models will be increasingly common and necessary. Expodium also believes in the transformative power of people; the ways in which ordinary Detroiters worked together to build their communities and change their environment is perhaps the biggest lesson we have taken from Detroit.

INTERMEZZO II

My Detroit

Tyree Guyton

Quotes by Tyree Guyton:

> "When I was five years old, my great-grandmother Katie told me that I would be a great man."
>
> "At the age of nine, my grandfather put a paintbrush in my hand and it felt like my hand was on fire."
>
> "*What* I am saying is that here, in this city, 2 + 2 = 8."

2 + 2 = 8

The world came to Detroit looking for a chance to be part of the American dream in the early 1950s. At its peak, the city had almost 2 million inhabitants—one of the largest cities in the country at that time.

The time for me was the early 1960s. As a kid growing up on Heidelberg Street, it was great! It was a wonderful place to live, raise a family, and we always had fun. People took great pride in their neighborhoods and jobs were plentiful. The Big Three, which defined the city's largest employers—Chrysler, Ford and General Motors—were always hiring, so one was sure to land a good job. In fact, the Big Three was the reason why the City of Detroit became so largely populated. All races flocked to the D in search of jobs in this booming industry. All of the young kids, myself included, dreamed of owning a car—a dream that was obtainable as most families had at least one car and some had two.

Through the eyes of a 12 year old, there was very little blight. The economy was strong and monies circulated throughout the neighborhoods. It seemed that everywhere you turned, there was a small business, which made each neighborhood sufficient.

The Motown sound was in the air and people were dancing in the streets. I recall hearing Marvin Gaye, the Supremes, and Temptations throughout the radios and record players on every block. At the same time, the Vietnam War was happening and many returned to the States wounded and crazy as hell in the mind. I watched as two of my own brothers tried to fit back into a society that was also at war—black people and white people and the great separation in the City of Detroit. They never made it.

I was 12 at the time of the infamous 1967 insurgence (the riots). I thought the world was coming to an end. Things seemed out of control. Images of angry dogs and water hoses treating people of color like animals were very frightening. All of a sudden, the color of my skin was not the right color. I often wondered how a so-called white God was going to save me when there was so much hatred for black people. This began the time when I challenged religion.

Black people were fighting for equal rights with the efforts of Dr Martin Luther King Jr, Malcolm X, and the black power movement. The Black Panther organization used to walk through the neighborhood, armed and ready to defend our communities. This movement was created in the 1960s and originated out of Oakland, California. I recall thinking how strong and cool they looked in their berets and sunglasses. Later, I would learn how well-meaning and significant this group really was, but back then, I just remember thinking that I wanted to be a part of this group of black people who could legally bear arms. I became angry, confused, and sometimes felt that it would be easier to be a white person because they always seemed to have the advantage. I felt the riot was justified and thus played a part in looting and vandalism.

As I grew up, and like most young black men, I took a job in the automobile industry. I worked at Ford Motor Company and made a good living, but after six years, I knew that I wanted more out of this life—a paintbrush was calling my name. I enrolled in the College for Creative Studies in the early 1980s and after two years dropped out. I was discouraged by my college professor, who told me that I did not fit in. At the time, I had separated from my wife but had two small children to care for, so I moved back to Heidelberg Street and lived with my children in the basement of my grandparent's home, which would later become the Dotty Wotty House.

In 1986, I had an epiphany while standing on the porch. I saw that I needed to move off the canvas and bring my work on to the street and thus began the Heidelberg Project. For me, the Heidelberg Project became a medicine, first for myself, and then for all those who chose to experience it. Some loved it, others hated it, but it was alive and it began to thrive.

Throughout this 30-year journey there have been many highs and lows, lots of joy and lots of pain, demolitions, and fires, and it is not over yet. However, one of my greatest joys was walking across the stage of the College of Creative Studies to receive an honorary doctorate of fine arts in 2009. Reflections of my great-grandmother's words flooded my mind and I knew that I was on to something great.

As I reflect back on this 30-year journey, I have come to realize many things. Not only was the Heidelberg Project a medicine for me, it also became my teacher. I have come to learn that everything is meant to be. We are part of this great creation called life. Everywhere we look, whether Detroit or other cities around the nation and the world, we seem to be in a shift—a radical change, a revolution. We see this in every facet of life: our economy, our educational system, our political system, our religious system. Has there ever been a pope that steps down from his position? I mean, let us really think about this, God's representative on Earth has stepped down. What does this tell us? Even the weather patterns are out of control, with conditions that are often hard to explain. Universally, these conditions should make us think deeper.

As I see it now, everything is in divine order. Nothing escape the pattern of spirit law. We are all playing our parts in this maze called life, throughout the world. In the real world (not the imaginary worlds in our mind), everything is happening simultaneously and you do not know what will come next. So, I find myself always questioning the true process of creativity in everything.

Plato said, "Time is the moving image of reality." What if we find out that it is all a dream? What is life today in the 21st century? How do we fix the problems of this world today? What if it is really not broken except in our minds?

The new becomes old and the old becomes new again. I believe my job as an artist is to create magic out of chaos. All things had their moment in time and now it is time for something new. I believe that we must start with the newness of our minds and use our imagination to help create a new Detroit. We have got to be reborn again into a higher state of consciousness where we can see new possibilities. I have come to a place in my life where I believe that everything is in perfect harmony. However, as history demonstrates, there will always be casualties. It is the way of the world.

As I study life and ponder why things are as they are, I find myself searching beyond what I see and understand with my eyes. Everything has a season, and right now it is Detroit's time to baffle the world! Thomas Jefferson said "When the people fear their government, there is tyranny, when the government fears the people there is real liberty." The city (Detroit) is a microcosm for a changing world. I believe that we are being prepared for an even greater, more miraculous change. You cannot heal the land until you heal the minds of the community. The present state of the "now" factor is the true reality that awaits us today, but are we ready? A change of consciousness, NOW, is the only real success for Detroit. Change the minds of people and you change the whole world. The new renaissance is in the people. When I created the Heidelberg Project, people said that it didn't make sense, $2 + 2 = 8$. Does it always have to make sense if it works?

Section Three
Conversations from Detroit

SIXTEEN

Lowell Boileau

Artist and founder of DetroitYES

This final section of the book features interviews with inspiring and engaged Detroiters who have strong visions for the city and how to make it more inclusive, just and fair. Many of these voices do not regularly feature in either academic debates nor wider policy, planning or political conversations about the city. I consider it an honor and privilege to be able to feature these voices within this book.

Our first conversation is with Lowell Boileau, a Detroit-area-based artist and founder of the DetroitYES website. A fine art painter by training, Boileau began documenting the abandoned buildings of Detroit in the mid-1990s, long before it was fashionable or popular to do so. His *Fabulous Ruins of Detroit* web tour was an Internet sensation when it was launched in 1997. What sets this site apart from many others is the contextualization and explanation that comes along with his work. He has been described as a "longstanding documentarian" by Nate Millington (2013) and an "unofficial city historian" by Dora Apel (2015). Boileau lived in Highland Park between 1972 and 1999, and after moving with his family to Farmington in 1999, maintained a studio in the Michigan Building in Downtown. A visit to his web tour reveals "the story of modern day Detroit [that] will unfold in all its complexity." His original Fabulous Ruins site has evolved into DetroitYES, a forum to discuss all things Detroit (see: www.detroityes.com).

Your Fabulous Ruins of Detroit *web tour was one of the first places that showed Detroit's ruined landscape; what prompted you to set up that site?*

It was a mix of mischief and concern. On the concern side, I am a champion of Detroit. I didn't feel that the story of Detroit was being

277

fairly portrayed. I wanted to kick back against that by explaining, through the ruins, how the City of Detroit came to be what it had become. I wanted to bring to attention that some very important historic and architecturally significant properties were in danger of loss; that a loss of our heritage was at stake. There was a mischief side too. As far as city officials and most locals were concerned, they wanted to deny the ruins, shun them, and forget about them. I had travelled to many historical ruin sites, like Efes in Turkey, Rome, and Athens, and they all had guidebooks. "Rome has ruins, Athens has ruins, ours are bigger," I thought, so why not make a guidebook to the Detroit ruins and tell why they exist?

Why do you think there has been so much interest in your work?

I touched a nerve. There's a lot of nostalgia in the tour. It unlocked intense emotions that surprised even me. After I launched the Fabulous Ruins tour, the *New York Times* did a big coverage of it. The site was also a Yahoo Pick of the Year in 1998, back when that meant something. I received thousands of emails with people pouring out their hearts about Detroit, some in tears.

What makes your work different from all the other art, photos, and websites depicting Detroit's ruins?

I was telling a story while always searching for context and meaning. I wanted the tour to be something that could bring understanding, not just be gawking at a train wreck. There were reasons why the train wrecked, why it came off the rails, and why it was staying off the rails. Whether it was from federal tax policies, the building of expressways, or the big one, racism, all those different elements were creating an incredible loss of buildings, history, and even lives.

So how do you contextualize your work and show these factors?

In the original Fabulous Ruins tour, I have a section called "How can this happen," which offers a preliminary answer and invites the audience to add theirs. I also added subsequent web tours to illustrate physical evidence of the cause of decline. For example, a famous wall still stands out by 8 Mile Road that was built for the purposes of racially dividing a 1940 housing development (see Figure 14.2). There is the stark contrast one sees today when crossing Alter Road from Detroit into Grosse Pointe. These are physical vestiges of racism. Or, one sees the remains of the old Jewish west-side community, with its abandonment and former synagogues, which are now, almost to a one, inner-city churches.

Can you explain why you changed the name of your website from the Fabulous Ruins to DetroitYES?

I didn't want my project to only be about Detroit's ruins, so I rebranded it as DetroitYES. My interest was: let's talk about it. Let's figure out how we can heal Detroit. I'm an artist; I have grand visions. I want to fix Detroit. So I set up a discussion forum. When you log into it, there is a greeting screen that says "Detroit: What went wrong? How can we heal it? Where do we go from here?"

I want to talk about two specific buildings. The first is the Michigan Theater Building, where you have your studio and office. Why is this an important building to understand?

Because it was used as a set in the movie *8 Mile*, the Michigan Theater has become an icon of Detroit. People from around the world come to see it. But most don't realize that down below it once stood the workshop where Henry Ford created his first car, back in 1896. He drove it out onto the streets of Detroit and began the creation of the wealth of Detroit from which this 4000-seat movie palace and office building arose. By the 1970s, with the effects of the automobile having played out by giving rise to expressways and new suburban theaters, this theater was dying. Why? No parking! What irony! The office building was facing extinction for the same reason. So they gutted the theater, leaving the canopy and upper balcony, and made it into a parking lot, which at least saved the building. Now, in one spot, you have the story of Detroit: the automobile giveth and the automobile taketh away.

The other building is the William Livingstone House. What makes that an important building?

The William Livingstone House was Albert Kahn's first independent project as a young architect. Over time, its Brush Park neighborhood became tough and impoverished. Like other nearby Gilded Age houses, it was carved up into cheap apartments and began to crumble. In the ruins photography community, it acquired the name "Slumpy" because of its notable slumping turret. In 2007, as part of a nearby gallery exhibition, I created a "possibilist" painting of the house where I "restored" it to its glory with an ongoing open house party. I called it "Open House" (see Figure 16.1) and hung it side by side with a photo of the house in its actual state, all torn open and abandoned. I hoped to inspire its restoration. Alas, it was demolished.

Figure 16.1 Lowell Boileau, *Open House* © Lowell Boileau

What do you mean by possibilist?

The painting "Open House" is not of a picture of a reality, but it could be possible. Traditional realist painters, with "photo realists" being the most extreme example, try to exactly recreate a scene. My idea was about a possibility. I aimed to inspire, not recreate. I'm not a realist, I say, I'm a possibilist.

What do you think about the way that Detroit's Downtown revitalization is having an effect on the rest of the city?

I think it's having an immense positive psychological effect. The area from Downtown to New Center is the pounding historical, cultural, and spiritual heart of Detroit. The heart needs to be healthy for the rest to be healthy. Overall, the revival is a huge positive. It is the new cover on our book and the world does judge books by their covers.

You talked earlier about this vision for healing Detroit. What do you think is needed to heal Detroit?

There are big divisions in our metropolis, creating waste and disadvantaging the City of Detroit and other struggling areas. I have a four-item plan.

The first is "Tear Down Those Walls." I want Detroit to become one united metropolitan community. The financial burdens borne by our older troubled communities, who are stuck caring for our poor and dealing with crime, need to be shared by our wealthier ones. Cops who are busting kids for pot in suburbs need to be redeployed to troubled areas to pursue real criminals.

The second is "Build That Wall." Metro Detroit needs a "sprawl wall" to stop further development into rural lands and encourage development of the many abandoned properties inside that wall.

The third is "Turn Red Lines Green." Areas redlined with high insurance rates need to have those rates lowered to the average rate of the entire region. One of the biggest detriments facing people willing to move into the city, particularly young people, is exorbitant insurance rates.

The fourth is "Tear Down This Wall." Create a Schengen-style treaty to remove the border between Detroit and Windsor so that we can have a truly open international metropolis.

Is the narrative about Detroit changing now?

In recent years, there has been a big perception shift. Detroit has become a darling in media eyes because everyone loves a comeback story and there is definitely a big comeback happening here. Poor Chicago has become the bad boy when talk of cities plagued by crime arises, not Detroit. Suddenly, we get a pass, even though our rates are still hideously high. We'll take it.

This comeback story, is that one-dimensional? Does it reflect the reality across the city?

With Detroit, it's two steps forward, one step back. There are still bad things happening amid the progress but I think, especially after the bankruptcy, that there is a greater collective understanding of the significance of the City of Detroit's health, and that a healthy Detroit is needed for the health of the whole metropolitan region and even our auto companies' image.

A lot of people come to Detroit and think it's a blank canvas; what are your thoughts to that mindset?

To some extent, it is a bit of a blank canvas. You can come to Detroit and you can get a beautiful abandoned house. You can't get it for $1 anymore, but for a few thousand dollars, you can get a stake here, become part of the solution, and build a neighborhood. I've always described Detroit as a city of islands. There are all these pockets of activity and positive things happening. You can go in, build your own island, and eventually connect it to the greater matrix of a better Detroit.

What makes you so optimistic and so positive about the city today and the direction that it's going?

There are some very solid fundamentals about Detroit that have always been here. We have always had a very creative core, not just in the fine arts, but in the industrial arts too, and an ability to problem-solve things. But I always caution people not to dwell on or in our past glories. Instead, ask how do we take that legacy and heritage and use it as a strength for redefining what the city's going to become? Most other cities—Chicago, Los Angeles, Seattle, and others—have defined purpose and direction, with established power structures. In Detroit, all those cards are up in the air; it's a very exciting time to be in Detroit.

Note

This conversation was conducted on January 26, 2016, in the home of Lowell Boileau in Farmington, Michigan.

SEVENTEEN

Sandra Hines

Detroit Coalition Against Police Brutality

The Detroit Coalition Against Police Brutality is one of America's first and leading organizations fighting police brutality. The Coalition was founded by educator/activist Gloria House, PhD, and Marge Parsons in 1996, and was led from the late 1990s on by Ron Scott, who passed away in November 2015. Detroit has a long history with police brutality, as Sandra Hines discusses using her own personal experiences.

After the city's 1967 Rebellion, precipitated by consistent and pernicious police brutality against African-Americans, Detroit moved quickly to become a predominantly African-American city. Yet, the police force remained dominated by whites. In 1971, the Detroit Police Department created the anti-crime taskforce Stop the Robberies Enjoy Safe Streets (STRESS). In two years, the STRESS unit was involved in the deaths of more than 30 individuals, predominately African-Americans. Ending the STRESS program was one of the campaign promises of Coleman Young, who was elected as the city's first African-American mayor in 1973. While Young worked to integrate the police department, the continuing economic decline of the city meant that major problems remained. As Sandra Hines describes, the immediate impetus for founding the Coalition grew out of the police killing of Malice Green in November 1992, six months after the uprisings in Los Angeles against the acquittal of the police involved in the Rodney King beatings (see Azikiwe, 2006).

Since its founding, the Coalition has been active with the Detroit Board of Police Commissioners, which provides civilian oversight of the police department, by attending its regular meetings and bringing issues and incidents of police brutality to the Board. In Scott's obituary, it was argued that the Coalition's work and Scott's advocacy were important factors in Detroit avoiding the kind of anti-police brutality uprisings seen in cities such as Ferguson or Baltimore (Fournier and Dickenson, 2015). Sandra Hines has been active in the Coalition for many years and is currently its President. She hosted a radio show with Ron Scott, *Fighting for Justice*. For more on the Coalition, see: www.detroitcoalition.org

---

Can you start by describing some of the history of police brutality in Detroit?

The Coalition was born to respond to police control over poor and black people. Historically, instead of living by the dictum "to protect and serve," the police have been there "to command and control." Over the years, because of where Detroit was located, many black people came from the South to the North. It is a city that a lot of black people chose to come to because of the car industry. They could get work and a home, so it was viewed as being a Mecca for black people. They thought that they weren't going to be met with racism. But there was a racist regime here that was pretty much doing the same thing as in the South. The only difference was that here they were able to get work and eventually people were able to buy homes.

Police brutality was used as a mechanism to keep black people in their place and to keep control over neighborhoods. I grew up in the early 1960s, around 10 minutes from Downtown. On weekends, the police would beat one of our neighborhood fathers up. Everyone knew that somebody's father was going to get beat up by the police. We would walk up the street as little kids and say, "oh, your daddy got beat up"; "your daddy got a broken arm." And we would laugh because we were ignorant. We didn't know that was something to keep our people in line. That's where we saw the riots in 1967, or really Rebellion. Rebellion is what it was. The Coalition was born out of the idea that black people was just tired and fed up with being misused and abused here in the city.

Was there a specific event that led to the formation of the Detroit Coalition?

There was a young man, not too far from here, named Malice Green. Malice Green was killed by Detroit police officers Walter Budzyn and Larry Nevers. The people referred to them as "Starsky and Hutch," which was a television program about two police offers who were rough and tough and would come in and straighten the neighborhood out. They picked up Malice Green during a traffic stop. They chose Malice this particular night and what happened was that the people came out—people were already tired; it was brewing and brewing and people were fed up. Budzyn and Nevers used their flashlights to beat Malice to death in front of the people. They literally beat his brains out of his head. After that, people were fed up and that's how the Coalition was born.

Dr Gloria House and Marge Parsons, who was an activist at this time, were attending a conference on young black men. At the end of the conference, Marge and Gloria agreed that addressing police brutality would go a long way toward addressing the challenges faced by young black men.

What is some of the work that the Detroit Coalition does?

We started having meetings and the Coalition became known as the organization that was on the forefront of ending police brutality in the city. We also started developing relationships with lawyers and people who were interested in making this become a reality. So we started meeting with the families who had been victims of police brutality. As a result of our meeting, protesting, demonstrating, and organizing, we became a real major force here in this city to deal with police brutality. Almost to the point where we were able to change the culture of the police.

How did you do that?

By attending the Police Commissioner's meetings, which was something we helped organize and establish. We stressed that the police couldn't police themselves, so that is how the Police Commission became a reality. We pressed the issue that people have to control the police as well as the police having to control the people. We started basing our theory and philosophy on Sir Robert Peel, who established progressive policing principles in 1800s' Great Britain. The police were established to protect the people but, in reality, the people also had to develop a relationship with the police department. He said, "The police are the people and the people are the police." In the 20 years that we have been in existence, we were able to establish a close relationship with the police, as well as establishing a way for people who felt that they had been brutalized or victimized to have somebody to back them up and to support them to get justice for their loved ones that were killed or abused by police.

What are some of the causes you are involved in today?

We are looking at police car chases. We feel that the car chases should be illegal. Usually, the people they are chasing, they end up killing themselves or some innocent person and the police that started the chase does not get charged or disciplined at all. But there are people who lose their loved ones; it's usually over something like a stolen car, something where they can get the license plate and pick them up later.

One of our other bigger cases is Reverend Edward Pinkney, a Benton Harbor minister. He is currently under house arrest because he's fighting for justice in Benton Harbor. Whirlpool Corporation wants to completely control what happens in the city of Benton Harbor, socially and economically, and Reverend Pinkney went up against them with the people and, ever since, he's been in jail on trumped-up charges. We are working to try to get Reverend Pinkney out of house arrest and free.

Ron Scott. Can you speak about some of his visions and ideas?

Ron was a king! His role as a facilitator of better police–community relations was very significant. He always thought that people had to talk to one another; they had to come together and discuss what the problem was and how you could come up with solutions. He believed in communicating as opposed to making negative snap judgments about people. It was a major blow when he died. We are now reeling from his death and are trying to make sure that we can keep his legacy going. He put in too much work and too much time to let it go.

What have been some major accomplishments of the Coalition?

We are well known over the country, not just in the City of Detroit. We are one of the leading organizations in police brutality. We created the doorway and opened the path so that now other communities see that they need a Police Commissioners board to address some of these challenges. Like these national cases, if they had had a Police Commissioners board, some of that stuff may not have happened. Cases like Ferguson, Chicago.

How do you measure success for the Coalition?

We were one of first groups that actually organized a Coalition against police brutality. We were the first organization that really made a difference in the policies and laws pertaining to police violence toward citizens. The biggest victory is that we actually laid the trail for other cities to form their own police brutality organizations.

I want to end by talking about Detroit more generally. What are your thoughts on the negative images of Detroit that get projected around the world?

That's all political. That is the image the corporate power structure wants us to have because we had black power. You have to understand that we had the first black mayor ever here in the City of Detroit, who reigned for 20 years. They didn't want us to have black power. So in order for them to take that away from us and destroy the image of Detroit, they created an image of us as being downtrodden and poor, and just gave us a negative whooping backwards and forwards so that they could take this city back.

How would you describe what's been happening politically in Detroit today?

It is a complete takeover! It's still being played out. They brought in emergency managers to destroy our schools, destroy our cities. The only cities that have emergency managers are the black ones: Detroit, Highland Park, Benton Harbor, Saginaw, Pontiac. All the cities run by black leadership. They wanted that and took it away. They stripped black people of the power. It was the only place in the US where we had real power, where we were literally in control of everything. And they were determined to take it back and they did. And so they set it up and people say it's a conspiracy. They are absolutely right.

What are your thoughts about the new developments in Downtown?

That's all a part of the takeover. "We are going to bring Detroit back." Bring it back to what? "Take it back" is what they really mean. "Detroit is coming back." Coming back from where? Coming back to us, and "us" don't look like me. They did whatever they could to destroy black power. They have been very successful.

And the new middle class moving into Downtown and Midtown?

They made it easy for them! They gave them incentives, money; they can stay in an apartment for some length of time before they had to pay rent. They gave them all sorts of gifts to move back here to be a part of the takeover. What about rewarding the people who have managed to stay here all these years? Where are the rewards for them? For us?

You've talked a lot about the police, politics, and the institutions of Detroit. What about the people? Is it a divided city or are there things that bring black and white Detroiters together?

Even though there is a lot of racism, there is also a lot of unity in this town. There are some things that people, both black and white, will embrace about this city. Like the fireworks, parks, restaurants, the music, Motown. The music would bring people together. Our concerts, festivals. People don't feel threatened when they come to festivals and community events. Winterblast, Campus Martius, and the ice skating. Our community is becoming a community where we don't really view ourselves as being black or white. We view each other as being a community that has a rich history we can be proud of. If we push more in the direction of that message, I think that is what we should move forward in doing so. I see our young people doing that. You see they are willing to be a human being as opposed to being a black human being or a white human being.

Note

The conversation with Sandra Hines took place at the Boulevard Temple Care Center, West Grand Boulevard, Detroit, on January 25, 2016.

EIGHTEEN

Malik Yakini

Detroit Black Community Food Security Network

The next five conversations all revolve around the topic of food. We start with Malik Yakini from the Detroit Black Community Food Security Network (DBCFSN). The organization was formed in 2006 in order to address food insecurity among Detroit's African-American community and to organize members of that community to play a more active role in local food security and food sovereignty.

The primary location for growing food is the D-Town Farm, a seven-acre site in Rouge Park. D-Town is one of the largest urban agriculture sites in Detroit. Funded through the Kellogg Foundation, they are involved in both the production and selling of food in the City of Detroit, as well as working to educate local communities and visitors to Detroit.

Malik Yakini serves as the executive director of the DBCFSN. He has been an activist for more than 40 years and has lived in the same house on the west side of Detroit since the 1960s. He was politicized and radicalized as a teenager and came of age during a very volatile time period in Detroit, characterized by protests and walkouts at the schools he was attending. His adult life has been dedicated to uplifting the community that he is a part of. For more information, see: http://detroitblackfoodsecurity.org or www.d-townfarm.com

---

Can you explain the concept of food security and why it's such an important issue in Detroit?

Food security is generally understood as being a condition that exists when all the members of a community have adequate amounts of culturally appropriate food. When we started the DBCFSN, we were familiar with the term *food security*. But as our awareness of that term grew, we realized that what we were actually looking at was *food sovereignty*, more so than *food security* because food security only speaks to people having adequate amounts of food. As one of my teachers and comrades, Raj Patel, says, "you can have *food security* in prison." So we are really struggling for something much broader than that, which is control of the systems that provide our food. This includes how that food is grown and transported, and justice with how that food is accessed.

The concept of food sovereignty, why is this an important issue for Detroit's African-American population?

In Detroit, as in the rest of the US, we have these overarching systems of oppression: one being the system of capitalism and the other being this system of white supremacy. And so those two things, which are intersectional, combine to decrease access to high-quality food for Detroit's African-American population. They also limit our ability to shape the food system that provides that food.

I look at the African-American experience within a larger historical context. I'm not just looking at Detroit in 2016; I'm looking at the history of African people in America on a timeline, or continuum. We had this huge migration of African-Americans from the South to industrial cities, ramping up in the 1920s and continuing through the 1960s. Many were coming for better economic opportunities. But many were also escaping the harsh, overt racism of the South. So we formed communities because of segregation, but they were often somewhat self-reliant. We owned more of the businesses in these communities back then because we didn't have the opportunities to purchase from businesses in other communities. Fast-forward to today's time period, we have the same community of people who have been on this historical journey for this higher level of human life who are now in a situation where we have very little control over the markets in our community, and the types and quality of food that is brought into our community.

What do you mean by "very little control over the markets?" What kind of food is available in neighborhoods in Detroit?

In most neighborhoods in the City of Detroit, there are not robust opportunities to access high-quality food. In 2007, a chain of national supermarkets called Farmer Jack closed its locations in the city. That was the last in a series of supermarket chains to close in the City of Detroit.

When I was a child in the 1960s, there were at least seven national supermarket chains, all of which had multiple locations throughout the city. So you were always within walking distance of a major full-service grocery store. With the closing of those grocery stores, we are left with smaller stores that all too often, and I want to be careful in terms of how I word this because I don't want to overgeneralize, but all too often, we find these smaller stores are selling inferior-quality produce. All too often, we have sanitary problems in stores. All too often, we have a level of disrespect from the store-owners and the people working in the stores toward the African-American population that they are serving.

We have two major kinds of stores that people can access food from in Detroit. One would be called a grocery store or supermarket. There are no national chains, although we have 70–80 smaller supermarkets. However, within many neighborhoods, there is no grocery store. Then there are these smaller stores called party stores. They primarily sell cigarettes, alcohol, or lottery tickets, and other things that can only nominally be considered food: potato chips, ramen noodles, and other very highly processed and packaged foods. In many of those smaller stores, you have what I call "wordless transactions." You go into the store and there is a sheet of bulletproof glass between the clerk and you. You put your item into the turnstile and they ring it up. You see the price on the register facing you. You put your money in the slot and they give you your change. There's no acknowledgment of you as a human being.

With that context in mind, what is the vision of the DBCFSN?

Our vision is that we have the City of Detroit where residents and visitors are treated with dignity and respect from the venues that they go to to purchase food, whether that be grocery stores, party stores, gas stations, or anywhere else. The other part of our vision has to do with having a localized food economy where the residents of the community see some economic benefit from the money they spend on food. Right now, millions of dollars are spent per day on food in the City of Detroit but most of that functions as an extractive economy. The money is not circulated within our economy to create jobs, ownership, or community empowerment, or to create a sense of wealth. It is extracted from our communities in much the same way that colonial powers extracted resources from the countries that they colonized. So our vision would be that we have a more localized food economy that is not functioning in an extractive manner, but is functioning to circulate wealth in our community in order to empower the people who are spending the money.

In the City of Detroit, we have a tremendous amount of vacant land—it is estimated that about a third of the city's 140 square miles is vacant land. Given this opportunity, part of our vision is that we produce as much of the food that we are consuming as we can. If we are able to grow 10% of the fruits and vegetables consumed in the City of Detroit, it would instantly inject millions of dollars into the economy. It would create jobs and opportunities for entrepreneurship and ownership. It would create this greater sense of community, wealth, stability, and empowerment.

How do you put this vision into practice?

We have several programs. The largest and most labor-intensive is D-Town Farm, which is a seven-acre farm that grows 30 different vegetables and fruits using organic methods. We sell that food at farmers' markets and at the farm itself. At one level, we realize that given the totality for the need for locally grown produce in the City of Detroit, what we are doing is miniscule. But we think that what is more important is that we are planting seeds into people's consciousness as to the capacity to provide for themselves. One of the things that an oppressive system does is suggest to people that they don't have the capacity to provide for their own needs. They believe that this is the exclusive province of corporations or the government. At D-Town Farm, shifting people's thinking about food is equally as important as the actual food that we grow.

How do you measure success?

That is an interesting question that comes up a lot. I don't have a definitive answer but I'll give some broad parameters—also with the understanding that the food system intersects with every other system in society, so it's not like we can only work in food and change health outcomes for people because food intersects with poverty and health care and other factors. But we think that success might include the following: increasing the venues in which people can obtain high-quality, fresh, healthy food within a community, as well as the degree to which people's eating habits have been changed as a result of having access. But, there's a larger question, which is what does a healthy community look like? That has to do with people having employment. We think that the food sector is important to this; it is either the first- or second-largest employer in the Metro area. So part of what a healthy community might look like is that we have more jobs paying livable wages in the food system. Another indicator might be that agricultural projects contribute to the esthetics of communities. Blighted areas where trash is dumped have a negative impact on people's self-image.

Speaking about Detroit more generally, in an earlier conversation, you said that Detroit is often portrayed as a "poster child" for urban decay. What is your reaction to the city being depicted in this way?

The thing is that there can be parallel realities or parallel truths. The photos we see of decaying Detroit and abandoned buildings, that's real. People didn't come here and make that stuff up. There's a huge amount of that in the City of Detroit. And it's true that Detroit is probably the barometer, in some ways, of the decline in capitalism generally. At one point, Detroit was the hope for the *American Dream*, with the auto factories, the significant homeownership, and the middle class in the city. But as the auto industry declined and Detroit didn't have a diverse economy, that's led to tremendous poverty and blight in the City of Detroit. Yes, all those things are true but that is only part of the truth. What we find is that many journalists, documentary-makers, and photographers come to Detroit and engage in ruin porn. They find the worst of the worst and then they photograph that and they shoot those images out to the world, and so many people think that Detroit is this sort of wasteland of miles of abandoned fields and derelict buildings, and that's only part of the picture. We still have very vibrant neighborhoods; we have pockets of affluence in the City of Detroit. We have lots and lots of grassroots efforts to make communities better and often those things are overlooked. In terms of my reaction, I would like to see a more balanced and fairer portrayal of Detroit that recognizes the crisis that we are in, but also uplifts the efforts of the people who have stayed here. It's not like everyone has abandoned Detroit; many of us have been here the whole time and we don't just give up. People have a great interest in what we are doing to respond to this because our response in some way creates the template for how people throughout the world will have to respond. So that gives us this tremendous responsibility. Many of us have that awareness that the work we are doing is much larger than the City of Detroit; it is work that is impacting humanity as a whole.

Detroit is changing rapidly and there is a lot of gentrification taking place around Downtown and Midtown. What are your thoughts on what is happening there and how it impacts the rest of the city?

That's interesting because one of the initial stages of an area being gentrified is the renaming of that area and the reframing of it. For many years, that area was considered to be the Cass Corridor. The Cass Corridor was known for alcoholics, drug addicts, prostitution, cheap hotels, and so I reluctantly use the term "Midtown." I use it, but I say "so-called Midtown." Maybe, eventually, I'll submit and just start using it, but it is a bit uncomfortable for me because I know it's part of the process of getting people to think differently about an area, and to disconnect the historical memory. What's happening in so-called Midtown is disturbing to me because of the vast inequity that exists between Midtown and most other areas of the city. Let me say this clearly, we think capitalism is a really terrible system, a dangerous system, and, in many ways, gentrification is just an extension of the logic of capitalism. So if the only driving factor is profit, then you're going to constantly have gentrification and the removal of people; those who have access to wealth will always be in control and those who don't have access to wealth will be victimized. So, at some point, we've got to evolve to another way of thinking economically that puts people and the health of the environment above profit.

Many of us say that there are two Detroits developing now. There are areas where tremendous amounts of capital are being poured into. But in this neighborhood [the Northwest Detroit Neighborhood where the interview was conducted], there is no capital being poured in. I'm very disturbed by that. I'm not anti-development, but I'm anti-inequity in development and concentrating development in certain areas with the idea that somehow that prosperity will trickle down to the rest of us. I've seen no historical reason to believe that it works and I have no reason to believe it will work this time. We see public subsidies for this gentrification; the new hockey arena that's being built is essentially being publically subsidized, with the idea that if we can create this huge development, that somehow that's going to create some prosperity for the rest of Detroiters. I have absolutely no confidence that that kind of top-down economics works. In my view, if we want a prosperous local economy, the way to do that is not to create these huge mega-developments, but by creating small neighborhood developments that can employ people and create vibrancy in the neighborhood.

Are you hopeful for the future of Detroit?

Let me say, in a broad sense, I'm always hopeful and if I wasn't, I wouldn't be doing what I'm doing. But I have serious concerns because we are at a precipice or potential turning point. If things continue on the same trajectory that I see now, in 20 years, black people in Detroit will have very little power. On the other hand, we are at a point in history where perhaps we can turn the tide on some things;

the Black Lives Matter movement is a sign of hopefulness. The work of Yusef—in some ways, Yusef himself—represents hopefulness (see Yusef Bunchy Shakur, Chapter Twenty-four). This idea that you can come from being a gangster—and he's not a made-up gangster; he's a real-life gangster. To go to prison and reform yourself and to come out and be an asset to the community as opposed to a predator on the community is a sign of the possibility of human redemption.

So I always hold out hope for the possibility of human redemption and the possibility of transformation. Social movements are very interesting and there can sometimes be one turning point that can really cause people to move in a different way. You never know which child is potentially the next Malcolm X. I hold out hope because I have a deep-seated belief. Martin Luther King said the arc of the universe bends toward justice.

Note
This conversation was held on January 26, 2016, in the offices of the DBCFSN, on Puritan Road in Detroit.

NINETEEN

Dan Carmody

Eastern Market Corporation

Eastern Market was founded in 1891 and is one of the largest food markets in the US today. One of the reasons for that, as Dan Carmody will explain, is that similar markets in other cities have been gentrified out of existence. Eastern Market is spread over six blocks, with five principle structures. The Eastern Market district is a 400-acre local food district that includes numerous food wholesalers and producers, as well as other businesses. The Saturday market is open year round; during the summer, up to 40,000 people come to the market on Saturdays. There are seasonal retail markets on Tuesday and Saturday from June through September and there is also a wholesale market during Michigan's growing season.

Dan Carmody has been President of the Eastern Market Corporation for almost a decade. He moved to Detroit in 2007 after living and working in cities such as Chicago and Manchester, UK. He has dedicated his life to Rust Belt cities. Since 2006, the market has been run by the Eastern Market Corporation, a non-profit public–private partnership. It is still owned by the city, which appoints seven of the 21 members of its board.

Detroit is often referred to as a "food desert." What are your thoughts on this term?

I don't like the term "food desert." First, it's wrong to call Detroit a "food desert" when you have our market, as well as the Detroit Produce Terminal on the city's southwest side; both are portals through which some of the best food in the country enters Detroit. There is a rich selection of independent grocers in the suburbs; they have no problem coming into Detroit, picking up produce, and taking it back to the suburbs. "Food desert" doesn't convey the deviousness of how we devise a food system that can get really good-quality food near people with higher incomes, but not necessarily to neighborhoods near the market where people with low incomes reside. It also demonizes Michigan agriculture, which produces 150 different crops of food, which are not getting to our most vulnerable residents. It also belies the fact that there is plenty of bad food in those neighborhoods. "Food deserts" strike me as "we just need to get a bit more quality food and people will buy it." Or it's deemed as a food access problem. As I see it, we also have a food demand problem. We have a healthy food consumption problem. Driving consumption is about both supply and demand. Calling Detroit a "food desert" is an oversimplification.

What about the role of urban agriculture and community gardens?

The urban gardening movement's most key breakthroughs are not in the amount of food that it produces; it's in changing people's attitudes. It's about citizens coming together to improve their neighborhood without much help from anyone else. It is estimated that nearly 20,000 Detroiters will be involved in the 1500 gardens expected to be planted this coming spring. That's profound. And these 20,000 people are changing their relationship with food. They pull that carrot out of the ground and begin to think that might be normal rather than the Twinkie from their local convenience store. That, too, is key. For me, urban agriculture's power as a teaching tool and a community organizing tool exceeds its impact as a food production tool.

How do these ideas fit into the philosophy and vision of the Eastern Market Corporation?

The vision of the Eastern Market Corporation is to shepherd Eastern Market to help create a healthier, wealthier, and happier Detroit. To that end, we are a cluster-based economic development organization working to effect change and strengthen regional food systems. We are also a place-based economic development organization working to strengthen the public market district itself. The Eastern Market district is one of the few remaining local food districts in the country because it wasn't gentrified out of existence into bars, boutiques, and lofts over the last 50 years, as many of our North American contemporaries were.

Can you explain a bit more about this healthier, wealthier, and happier paradigm?

Sure. On the healthier side, we're trying to help address the national epidemic of diet-related disease. We're trying to celebrate food. Our health-care costs are so high and our food costs are so low; there is a relationship in that of "you get what you pay for." We try to program more education classes in the market. We try to build alternative distribution networks from our wholesalers in the market into neighborhoods. We have also been national leaders in monetizing support for people to buy fruit and vegetables, making it easy to use federal food benefits in the market, but also working with partner originations on food incentive programs like Double Up Food Bucks [see: http://www.doubleupfoodbucks.org/], which provides up to $20 of matching funds per person during Michigan's growing season for people who use federal food benefits to buy produce.

On the wealth of the city, bottom up, we try to create an ecosystem to support the incubation and acceleration of food business. We do this through four ways: access to the market; access to low-cost production spaces through our shared-use kitchen and our pending white box plus and co-packing acceleration programs; access to mentoring and expertise; and access to capital through programs like the Goldman Sachs 10,000 small businesses program. We've had some pretty substantial successes; 150 companies are selling products at the market that weren't here when the city was running it. Back then, the city just allowed the sale of fruits, vegetables, plants, and flowers. We now have cookies, pierogis, sausages, jams, jellies, pastas. All of those represent local companies employing local people.

Top down, we try to bring specific economic experience to larger and more established companies that want to stay in Detroit. We have the opportunity to do that here in Detroit; that's where the largely vacant land to the east and northeast of the market comes in handy, in order to provide a space for new food businesses. The food cluster is identified by national economic development cluster-based experts as having the broadest range of skill sets with the highest percentage of entry-level, living-wage jobs.

And happier: it's using the market as a place where people come together and enjoy each other. Whether that's through our market or through our events. We try to animate Detroit with arts and engage people in a number of ways so that they feel better about themselves and their community.

Eastern Market used to be run by the city. Today, Eastern Market Corporation is a non-profit public–private partnership. What makes this a good fit for governing the market?

The public sector in a resource-starved environment can't focus on specific tasks as one might like. Previous to us taking over management, the market was part of the Recreation Department of the City of Detroit. There were some really capable people there. They had over 150 properties, mostly playgrounds and parks, which were central to their mission. But they had a rapidly diminishing budget. So the idea that this whole separate focus on the food system or market management would rise to the top of their central mission was never going to happen. From the 2000s on, there has been a lot of interest in food. There has been a lot of corporate and foundation support for activities in the market. I think those funders would have been reluctant to put their money into the city as it was sinking toward bankruptcy and ultimately going through bankruptcy. Our governance structure has allowed us to raise a lot of outside capital that can come through our organization as a non-profit conduit, which may not have happened with the city. We raised $17 million, $11 million of which was new money we obtained from non-governmental sources. The market is owned by the City of Detroit but we are trying to benefit private vendors, and so you have that rub between "Where does that public good end and where does that private benefit start?" So a non-profit is a healthier place for that discussion to happen.

You mentioned that Eastern Market survived because it wasn't gentrified out of existence like so many other food markets. Are you feeling the pressures of gentrification today?

With gentrification, there is no easy answer. The classic case we have to work with is *Detroit versus Everybody*, which is essentially a T-shirt shop. A T-shirt shop in a food district is, by definition, gentrification. A T-shirt shop owned by two young black male entrepreneurs may not be the classic case of gentrification. We have to remain open to multiple interpretations of what's good investment and what's denigrated as gentrification. Most of those Rust Belt towns I've been in are in dire need of investment waves also known as gentrification. Gentrification is development with displacement; our goal is to do development without displacement.

How do you do that?

We use tools at our disposal such as a community development corporation (CDC) to assist the private sector in holding space at below market prices. That helps to be able to accommodate a mix of tenants better than a purely for-profit model would. With 20% of the commercial real estate market held below rapidly increasing market rents, the District could 1)retain businesses that helped give the market its authenticity, 2) continue to attract edgy businesses, and 3) keep a tenant mix that includes those that serve low and moderate income residents of adjacent neighborhoods.

As we develop the market, we can't stop this wave of investment that is coming at us; it is already coming our way. That's the wave of investment that destroyed other local food districts around the country as the real estate became more valuable for uses besides food businesses. So how do we maintain authenticity, which we define as our role as a working food district and our place where economic democracy thrives, for as long as we can? To retain our authenticity as a working food district, we have no other choice but to expand the district to create space for new food enterprises if we want to be anything more than just a niche food production area. On the other hand, we need to intervene to ensure continued economic democracy. We've been able to retain the market district's tenancy, which appeals to a wide variety of the population because rents have been reasonable and low. We are still not sure if those rents are headed for the stratosphere or if it's just an illusion, but we need to be prepared to have an intervention strategy so that retail space remains affordable for a wide variety of businesses.

Finally, I'm wondering what you have learned from experiences in other places and what insights Detroit can offer to the rest of the world?

Putting equitable development and fairness as a centerpiece of community revitalization is an important lesson. How you remedy that is a little murkier. What I like about the food system sector is that of total entrepreneurial activity, about a third is food-related these days. It's a lot easier for people to participate as a food entrepreneur rather than a tech entrepreneur if you don't have an advanced degree. A wide range of people are capable and may possess that old family recipe that can be successful in the marketplace without having to invent something in a lab. This provides economic hope for people with low economic means that I don't see across all economic sectors. I think Detroit is also in the middle of experimenting about how we repurpose derelict urban land. We have a huge opportunity.

Any final insights to add?

Look at the satellite imagery around Eastern Market today and compare it with old photos from 1949 when it was a tight fabric. You see the effects of the last 60 years. We've proven in Detroit that when three things align—federal problems to encourage flight, race relations to encourage segregation, and monoculturalism in our economy that didn't give us a diverse job base—they are more destructive than atomic bombs or carpet-bombing. European cities that were leveled in the World War II by bombs made here in the "Arsenal of Democracy" are now thriving while ironically Detroit, the place that manufactured those weapons has been devastated.

Note

The conversation with Dan Carmody took place on Saturday, January 23, 2016, in the offices of the Eastern Market Corporation.

TWENTY

Jackie Victor

Avalon International Breads

When Jackie Victor and her then partner, Ann Perrault, opened Avalon International Breads on Willis Street in June 1997, they challenged the narrative that Detroit was closed for business. They were one of the first new businesses to open in Midtown and the success of their bakery helped to change the narratives about Detroit.

However, Avalon operates from a distinct business philosophy, which focuses on a triple bottom line of earth, community, and employees. They have offered a living wage and health benefits to their employees, 90% of whom live in the City of Detroit. While both Jackie and Ann grew up in Metro Detroit, they have lived in the city since 1990 and 1980, respectively.

Jackie and Ann were friends with Grace and Jimmy Boggs (see Chapter Twenty-five), and Grace's philosophy, inspired by Hegel, of understanding the contradictions that emerge when new solutions are found is evident in Avalon's relationship with the city and with Midtown. Avalon, a triple-bottom-line business founded by two activists, has been a catalyst for gentrification. While Jackie is incredibly proud of how her business helped to midwife the changes taking place in Midtown, she is careful to remind anyone that this, in turn, creates its own contradictions and that we should not be under the illusion that everything in Detroit is getting better, especially beyond the narrow confines of *The 7.2*. However, the experience of Avalon and the philosophy of its co-founder offer some insightful visions as to ways in which a more inclusive Detroit can be built.

You grew up in the suburbs of Detroit. What was your relationship with the city?

My grandfather emigrated from Russia and opened a small department store in what was then Hastings Street, in Paradise Valley. At that time, Hastings Street was a thriving community. So I grew up with these idyllic stories of Detroit. My parents moved out to Bloomfield Hills when I was one. When my grandfather saw their house for the first time, he cried and said "Who would have through that an immigrant like me, with no education, could come here and that his son would have this?" My father was an attorney working in the Guardian Building Downtown. My mom was a classical musician, so we would see concerts Downtown. I grew up going back and forth and viewing this progression of economic disparity from the back seat of a car driving on The Lodge (M-10 Freeway). I remember seeing things changing from green, to something that was a little more run-down, to something that was like it had just been hit. I remember asking why. My parents did not have a good answer because there wasn't a good answer without addressing issues of race and class. So I grew up with these burning questions that were uncomfortable for me. I couldn't write them off like others from my generation in the suburbs who could live with that disparity.

When I went to the University of Michigan, I got politically radicalized and got to know issues of race, class, and cultural imperialism. In one class, a professor brought in Grace and Jimmy Boggs as guest speakers [see Chapter Twenty-five]. They would have been in their 50s or 60s then. I heard them speak and remember thinking: if people like that are in the city, I want to live in the city too. But at that time, nobody at the University of Michigan was talking about Detroit. At that time, the narrative about Detroit was that it was going to be saved by the Renaissance Center [see Chapter One]. But when Jimmy and Grace spoke, they said that Detroit was going to be rebuilt block by block, relationship by relationship, garden by garden, community by community, contradiction by contradiction. My head spun. They pulled it all together for me. So, in a sense, I followed them here. I was part of an early organizing group of Detroit Summer and that kind of stuff. I met Julia Putnam (see Chapter Twenty-three) when she was in the first group. But most other people I grew up with in the suburbs stayed there; I remember at my 20th high-school reunion, I was one of two people from my graduating class of 435 who were living in the city.

How did you end up starting Avalon?

I used to shop at the food co-op that was on the corner and it was the nexus of the community in the Cass Corridor. Most of this block was pretty vacant. During this time, I met the co-founder of Avalon who became my life partner for almost two decades, Ann Perrault. She was friends with Jimmy and Grace. At a certain point in our relationship, we decided that we wanted to do something together. At the University of Michigan, I used to volunteer at a local co-op bakery called Wild Flour; it was such a wholesome and beautiful environment, I remember thinking that this is an honest way to make a living, and it was next door to their co-op! When I moved into the city and shopped at the co-op, I used to think "How cool would it be to have a bakery with that kind of a vibe, right next to this co-op?"

People saw the Cass Corridor as a dangerous place, but that was never my experience. My experience was that there was a lot of poverty here; a year before we opened, there was a tent city down the road with 300 people living there in the middle of winter. But there were also a lot of artists and significant art and education institutions. But those institutions were 100% disconnected from anything else that was going on. People were getting off the expressway, driving to the hospital; driving off the expressway, driving to Wayne State. Nobody was stopping anywhere to buy anything. There was almost no retail. So there was millions of dollars coming in every day and then going back out to the suburbs. Ann and I both wanted a change of career and we were talking about what we wanted to do and she said "let's do that bakery you always talked about." We knew nothing. We weren't business people. We weren't even capitalists. We weren't bakers; we loved food and we loved cooking. At one point, the space next to the co-op opened up. Perfect! It was $500/month in rent and completely empty. It had no windows, only one light bulb hanging from the ceiling and a pipe where the toilet was, that's it. We wrote a business plan, and studied with a Buddhist priest who had worked for Deloitte and Touche and talked about "right livelihood" business and triple bottom lines.

Why do you think you were so successful?

The narrative at that time was: Detroit is closed for business. And we just blew it up! So maybe it wasn't closed for business. Jimmy used to say "don't wait for the man to get you a job. Bake your own bread, fix your own shoes, and build your own bikes." We took that to heart and took it literally. Our vision was that we would have this business, and then it really became ground zero for the renewal of Detroit. That is how it started. What we found right away was that, rich or poor, the number one thing people said was "Thank You for opening a place to spend my money." But that means more than just consumerism. It means there's no place to have exchanges, get your bread, and get a cup of coffee. There was no common space. So it meant a lot to a lot of people right away (see Figure 20.1).

Your vision of the triple bottom line. Can you talk about it some more?

This idea of earth, community, and employees. People weren't talking about this back then. Our idea was to have a business that not only valued a financial bottom line, but would be a business that had three bottom lines. The first would be earth, which would mean, at the very least, using 100% organic flour in everything we made. Right relationship with the community was, in part, providing something that was of use in this under-served community. Our customer service mission is providing an oasis of healing and compassion in a world that is sorely in need. It's been my vision that our customer service is our community mission. We've given lots of money, product, time, and space to lots of other organizations. We've also been just a gathering place where people meet. The right relationship for our employees has always been the trickiest. It started with deciding that we were not going to pay the minimum wage, but rather the livable wage, or come as close as we could to the livable wage to stay successful economically. We had health care and benefits before many small businesses were providing that.

What role do entrepreneurs play in shaping cities and communities?

Considering the fact that we don't have government that serves the people in many ways anymore, entrepreneurs are very important. The government gave up on cities 40 years ago. People also just willingly moved out of the city and took the resources out of the city with them. It didn't really start to reshape until entrepreneurism started coming back. And that includes Dan Gilbert. Entrepreneurs play a huge role in part because government plays such a small role the moral leadership in in our country at this time. And that's a great thing because businesses like ours can have a huge impact with very little resources and shape a certain tone and flavor in a way that a city more dominated by the government might not. But it's necessary but not sufficient, because if it were sufficient, we'd have public schools we can send our kids to, the neighborhoods would all be safe, and the roads would be fixed. You have to have government too.

What about the large investments that are now pouring into the city?

I'm not being a cheerleader for Dan Gilbert but I sometimes think activists can be a little quick to criticize. Anyone who dumps $2 billion into an urban area and creates a certain economic intensity, I don't think you can say that's all bad. It comes with its own contradictions and some of those contradictions are very bad. Some of those contradictions mean that some of those who used to be able to live in Downtown can't live in Downtown anymore. We started this resurgence in Midtown. It was very grassroots and it's taken on a life of its own and now a lot of people are being priced out of this neighborhood. Obviously, gentrification happens everywhere, but as Grace would say, that's also the dialectic.

This leads to my next question on your thoughts about the role your business has played in shaping Midtown?

I am really proud and privileged to have midwifed a business that then midwifed this renewal right around us. The businesses on the block are all owned by Detroiters and people who have been here for generations. What makes this block great is that it's really one of the few integrated, down-to-earth, authentic little commercial districts. Now, there are literally hundreds of new businesses and tens of thousands of new residents.

What do you think about the contradictions that this has raised?

How do I feel about a store around the corner selling $3500 bikes and $900 watches when we still can't buy socks and children's clothes in the whole city? Do I wish there was an in-between? Yes I do. This is America, a capitalist economy, that's what allowed this place to thrive. But I think the problem right now is that we missed that in-between thing.

Is Detroit becoming less divided economically today?

I would say it is becoming even more divided. I always say this to anyone: never have the illusion that Detroit is getting better. There are 7.2 square miles that are getting really good for the people who have the privilege of living there. It's not like it is all high-income; some people are just able to live here. But the schools, and the neighborhoods? There are neighborhoods that are like the Wild West. There are kids who live in those neighborhoods who have never been to Midtown, much less the Riverfront, much less the Dequindre Cut, much less the public library. It's a completely polarized city. The more people who come in and repopulate *The 7.2*, the more everyone's feeling so good about it, and I feel good about it sometimes too. But what I feel really bad about is that the majority of Detroiters are not benefiting from this renewal. I mean, I think the lighting is working better. Duggan, I will give him credit, said "I will turn the lights back on." And I think that's an important, symbolic first step. But the high levels of poverty, the illiteracy? Those things aren't going away.

What will it take to solve some of these problems? Is getting the lights back on important?

Streetlights are important for public safety and quality of life. Infrastructure is important. But what's going to make it better. Some small things and some big things. The urban agriculture movement and the thousands of community gardens. Those kinds of things make actual, significant impacts. And the public–private collaborations are also necessary. The Riverfront Conservancy, what they've done with the Riverfront and the Dequindre Cut has made the city a better place to raise children in and to live in for everybody. The Eastern Market, a public–private partnership, has made the city a better place to live in [see Dan Carmody, Chapter Nineteen]. Then there are other things that only the government can solve, and education is one of them. Detroit schools are broken. So who is going to fix them? Every non-profit has come and said they are going to fix it. I'm sorry, the government has to fix public schools.

Do you think that the context in which businesses like yours were able to grow and thrive is under threat with all the investment now coming into Greater Downtown Detroit? Will it be possible for Avalons to open up in five years?

That's a great question. Right now, it is still such an underserved city that there is so much room for new businesses. But I think entrepreneurs, retailers in particular, are going to have to start looking in new markets and at different ways of doing things. I'm watching businesses open up everywhere in the city. I think the challenge is for people to be leaders and not just followers. Why Avalon is Avalon is that we didn't just take anyone's word for it. So it's certainly harder in *The 7.2*, but we have 140 square miles in this city, so if people are interested and willing to look at different business models that serve different demographics, there is no shortage of needs. It's going to make it more challenging in one sector or area, but that doesn't make it impossible.

Figure 20.1 Avalon International Breads, interior (Photo, Brian Doucet)

Note

The conversation with Jackie Victor took place at the Avalon Bakery on Willis Street in Detroit on January 26, 2016.

TWENTY-ONE

Phil Cooley

Entrepreneur, owner of Slows Bar-B-Q and Ponyride

Even more so than Avalon, Slows Bar-B-Q has been celebrated by journalists as being central to the city's recent revival. However, while Slows (and Phil Cooley) have received much praise, they have also been criticized as leading to the gentrification of Corktown and pricing others out of the neighborhood.

Cooley also owns the nearby restaurant Gold Cash Gold and Slows has expanded to multiple locations, including in Midtown and in Grand Rapids. One of his newest ventures is Ponyride, which provides space for entrepreneurs to accelerate and incubate their ideas, in what Cooley describes as a safe and supportive environment where people are not afraid to try new things, or even to fail. The Ponyride location was a tax-foreclosed building; Cooley purchased it to try to change the narrative of tax foreclosure and as "a study to see how the foreclosure crisis can have a positive impact on the community."

Phil grew up an hour north of Detroit. After graduating college, he spent time working as a model and lived in various cities around the world. He returned to Michigan and settled in Detroit a few years before opening Slows. In addition to this work, he sits on the advisory board of the American Civil Liberties Union (ACLU) of Southeast Michigan and is an adjunct professor at Lawrence Tech. For more on Ponyride, see: www.ponyride.org

You moved to Detroit in the early 2000s and started investing in Detroit more than 10 years ago. What drew you to the city?

I moved here because of hip hop, techno music, the garage rock scene, Tyree Guyton. I loved the Talking Heads and Suicide and lot of things that came out of the 1970s in New York City. I was reading and thinking about some of the thought process of Peter Schjeldahl, *New York Times* art critic, at that time. His idea was to move to a city, go to the bars, meet like-minded people, and start a movement. I lived in all these major cities and they were great and beautiful, but expensive. And I never felt I was part of the community, so I came here looking for New York's SoHo of the 1970s. And I found that. I found some of the most creative and talented people. I found citizens here that worked together because they had to, and that was important to me.

So you found 1970s' SoHo here in Detroit. Is that now under threat as the city is seeing new capital pouring in?

Creativity needs community, affordably, and connectivity. I feel that, to some extent, Tyree Guyton could probably benefit from having more people around. But at the same time, a lot of folks have felt priced out. When we look at what we have to charge in rent, we lose money on our properties. We charge around $1/square foot, so 1000 square feet is around $1000 a month. To a lot of Detroiters, that's gentrification. "It's too expensive," they say. We already lose money on it and we don't want to lose more money on it. I don't know what to say? People will pay it. So it's a tough conversation about how can you sustain the arts and creativity here.

Slows is often credited as being a catalyst for the revitalization of Detroit, and has even been called a "poster child" for the city's transformation. What are your thoughts as to how Slow's has influenced Detroit?

We sometimes get way too much credit for what we've done and other times people hate us for no reason. I think we were impactful, along with our neighbors. Are we the "poster child" for the revitalization of Detroit? Maybe the poster child, but we are certainly not the reason. We are one very small portion but, yeah, we get a lot of people who give us a tremendous amount of credit, which is flattering, but we are one restaurant. We employ 100 people; we are very proud of that. But we can't do that by ourselves.

When you opened, you were front-page news in September 2005. That's pretty unusual for a restaurant. Why was it such a big deal?

I think we were the only restaurant to open that year and so that's why we were on the front page. The reality of functioning cities is that they have to have dense neighborhoods with taxpayers and more than one restaurant. After our success, it was shocking for some people to hear that we wanted more businesses to open up next to us. A lot of other people had this prevention mentality of "oh no, this was our city and we have the one restaurant that all people should go to." We are a region of 4.5 million people, so there's room for more! I think that opening Slow's instilled confidence in some folks, which was important.

One of your latest ventures is Ponyride. Can you talk about the vision and philosophy behind it?

This is one of the most risk-averse places in the world and we were the opposite of that during the Industrial Revolution. Now you've got every lawyer and economist saying "we can't lose this in this quarter; we have to cut back here and there." There is so little innovation and experimentation; so little room for failure. I make lots of mistakes and so does everyone else. So I want to see what happens when people learn from their mistakes and grow from their mistakes instead of sweeping them under the rug or not even being willing to try. This is just about experimenting and community. Detroit is like the stone soup folk story; that's what makes the city so great. We don't have a lot here but we all work together and everyone brings one thing and then all of a sudden the soup's better because everyone had input. When people can have safe space to approximate in and work together in, these lines will blur. They won't steal from each other; they'll learn from each other.

What role do entrepreneurs play in shaping cities?

The important thing is that we are one of many. And I love the Big Three, but if you're going to wait for them to create 250,000 jobs, you're foolish. Entrepreneurs, that's where our growth is coming from. Corporations are shipping all their shit overseas because they can get cheaper labor. And so when we talk about manufacturing, this is why we look at Ponyride. It's not just because we have the infrastructure, which we do, but we also have the DNA—the people. We design, build, and engineer things.

You've renovated some abandoned buildings. Slows also sits across from the city's most famous ruin: the Michigan Central Station. What are your thoughts about the fascination that many outsiders have about the ruins of Detroit?

I've been through a lot of the buildings and I get it. There is beauty to the abandoned train station. But it also represents a lot of difficult things for our community and I think a lot of people exploit those things to tell dishonest stories about Detroiters, which is unfair. But I don't want to judge people. If someone comes here to see the ruins, I'm not going to scream and yell at them. But I know that's the first thing a lot of people see because it is so often communicated to the rest of the world. But, of course, there is so much more. There is great opportunity there, too. Look at the Ruhr Valley in Germany and what they've done with their post-industrial infrastructure [see Sattler, Chapter Eight]. They looked at it and said "What can we do with this?" Their citizens got together and collaborated with a lot of outside and inside talent, as well as government, and everyone worked together to create something great. So, hopefully, this is a landscape where there are great possibilities in different ways. Hopefully, we'll see more buildings like Ponyride get rehabbed.

Note
This conversation with Phil Cooley took place on January 23, 2016, at Ponyride in Corktown, Detroit.

TWENTY-TWO

Wayne Curtis and Myrtle Thompson-Curtis

Feedom Freedom Farmers

The term "urban garden" may be too narrow to describe the work that Wayne Curtis and Myrtle Thompson-Curtis do with their Feedom Freedom farm on Manistique Avenue on the far east side of Detroit. In 2009, they planted their first seeds in a formerly abandoned lot next to their home. Today, they grow food on roughly one acre of land. It is shared with the community and sold within the neighborhood, as well as at Eastern Market.

For Wayne and Myrtle, growing food is an act of revolution that is closely connected to their consciousness as African-Americans oppressed under capitalism. Urban agriculture is done out of necessity and is an act of taking control of their lives under an economic system that has rendered much of Detroit's population expendable. Feedom Freedom evolved into a teaching garden, and through numerous roundtable discussions, they organize cooking workshops and their Art in the Garden Program. They also run garden learn and play events with children and their caregivers in order to teach about food and how they can contribute. Wayne is a former Black Panther member and comes from a long tradition of activism rooted in Detroit's economic and racial struggles. Myrtle has lived her whole life on the east side of Detroit. For more, see: http://feedomfreedom.anderswift.com/

What made you decide to focus on a community garden?

Myrtle: I wouldn't say that what we do is anything phenomenal. It's been done since time began. I don't buy into the idea that in order to stay alive in this world, I need money for everything. We do what we do because we resist. It is also an act of love for ourselves, and our love for others. So when I do what I do, I'm not trying to get rich out of it; it's not going to save Detroit. You can grow all the food you want; it's not going to save Detroit because we are tied to this system. But it is an act of saying that I think differently than all these laws and policies that are being enacted. I am tapping into my consciousness. As a human being, I understand that food is meant to keep me alive, it's not meant to make me rich. For us, growing food is an act of revolution. It's a revolutionary act of love, not just for ourselves, but for others.

Wayne: Our consciousness was the reason then and it's the reason now: our ability to come together and get rid of old capitalist ideas of individuality. Under capitalism, individuality couldn't exist unless you had some money. So you didn't need nobody because you had the ability to consume and get things you needed in the market. In our neighborhood, that type of concept is almost non-existent because of the transformation of the working class, the lack of jobs, and the dismantling of the welfare state.

How does growing a garden contribute to community?

Wayne: So growing a garden is not just growing food. It's growing a lot of other things, hearts, and minds. It goes beyond hobby because hunger pains always have to be answered. So growing food is connected to all these inconsistencies to control us. I was reading that there was a man arrested for growing okra. In some places in the world, the same system arrests people for collecting rain water. We're the same as them, almost a million miles away. They created the crisis that brings in bottled water. They create the crisis where you have canned air. "We are going to disrupt your ability to become solutionaries" is the same thing as "we are going to resolve your problems." So how do we develop the consistency to deal with that? Feedom Freedom, D-Town, the Boggs Center, that's what all of us are doing. It's a constant struggle, it's not a hobby. It's for real because it sustains life.

Why is providing fresh food so important in Detroit?

Myrtle: Because of a lack of places to get fresh, healthy, affordable food. There is still a lot of work to be done getting people to understand what that really means because the marketing for convenience foods is just so prevalent. Returning to more simple practices or things that make more sense, there's still a lot of work to be done in that area.

Wayne: We are growing consciousness about growing food. We are growing consciousness about what we call "settlers" coming into our neighborhood with a different perspective than the one that we have. Our consciousness was raised within us through struggles and resistance.

Why are there so many ideas and visions of resistance coming out of Detroit?

Myrtle: Detroit has a long history as a black liberation town. Detroit is a place of unions and struggle. When I think of Detroit, I think of a place of constant change and folks constantly fighting for their dignity to be held in tact. People fighting the effects of capitalism, the auto industry failing, segregation, desegregation, racism. In my lifetime, I've felt the effects of all of that. It's a place where I know that people are proud to be who they are no matter what was happening; 1960, 1970, 1980, you had people who were proud to be from Detroit because it made people scared of you, or many people respected you, or many people wondered "How the hell did you survive it?" When I think of Detroit, I think of a place where there was always this black power struggle and folks being proud of that and having access to things that were culturally appropriate. I grew up in an integrated neighborhood. Then it became a segregated neighborhood. Then it became a devastated neighborhood. That has been what I have seen and what we've been fighting for a long period of time. No matter what it might look like, no matter how raggedy it might look, it is still Detroit and you are still going to take care of it.

Wayne: My grandfather was part of the Marcus Garvey movement. He was part of the strikes at Ford when the foundry was first built. He was part of the indignity of how he was treated as a black man here in this town. A time when people did not expect jobs unless you worked in a restaurant or shined shoes. The contradictions of the workers and the political-economic system of industrialization, which caused internal contradictions within the working class because everyone is scrambling for money. Which creates racism; which created the riots in 1948, 1964, 1967. So capitalism has produced its own contradictions within its working-class population, which has caused us to scramble for survival with each other.

A lot of people are moving to Detroit and many are interested in urban agriculture. What impact does this have for you and your community and what message would you give to people who are coming to Detroit?

Myrtle: I can give you one example. A young lady moved back to the city last summer and she wanted to grow food for the neighborhood. She wasn't a wealthy lady. She had a husband and two kids and she said "I want to create a community garden for my neighborhood." She lived on one of the less-populated streets. My suggestion for her was: "first, make sure that people in your neighborhood want you to grow food for them. And don't be upset when it becomes a lot of work with very little help." But I told her the first thing I would do is talk to the folks in the neighborhood; just have some conversations.

A lot of people come to Detroit and they want to learn from it. What vision or message would you want to impart to people?

Myrtle: That's a hard one. How and where do you enter? Do you come to glean? What do you leave and what do you take with you? For me, the biggest messages are undoing racism and undoing capitalism and really understanding what revolution is. It's an evolution process. That's something to think about. It sounds like an easy question, but I can't just give a flip-easy answer. It takes having those conversations as to what do you expect to learn that you haven't already? I travelled with Grace many times and young folks would ask this question and the answer is not easy and sometimes there isn't an answer, just another question. But it's asking that permission, can I enter?

Wayne: We are not a fishbowl. We are not fish. In a fishbowl, people come in and they look at it as separate from themselves. They should realize we are not a fishbowl and that they are a part of it, whether they realize that or not. They are a part of this, unless they are going to become part of the ruling class. They should understand the process of developing consciousness under capitalism. You're here one day and you have a job and money and you can buy a diamond ring and act

Figure 22.1 Wayne Curtis and Myrtle Thompson-Curtis discussing their work with students from the Netherlands (Photo, Brian Doucet)

as an individual not needing anybody unless they have money. Then you're in a situation where you don't have access to jobs and money. Then you're in another situation where you just don't have anything at all. All that develops consciousness. Then you leave that situation and you become *solutionaries*. You become *cultural transformationists* because you realize you have to change the environment that you live in just to grow some food.

Note

The conversation with Wayne Curtis and Myrtle Thompson-Curtis took place on January 24, 2016, at the Boggs Center in Detroit.

TWENTY-THREE

Julia Putnam, Amanda Rosman, and Marisol Teachworth

The Boggs School

The James and Grace Lee Boggs School is a community-based public charter school on the east side of Detroit. It employs a placed-based model of learning, which is learning rooted in the local. This means that it stems from history, geography, community members, businesses, and the challenges and possibilities in the community. After five years of planning, the school opened in 2013. It has 112 students from Kindergarten through grade 7. Around 60% of the students come from within around a mile radius, and most of the rest come from across the city, with a few kids coming in from the suburbs. The core values of the school are: high levels of critical thought; creativity and learning; excellence in teaching; authentic and trusting relationships; community empowerment; and equity within both human relationships and the natural world. The core purpose is: to provide the tools to achieve ambitious goals and live lives of meaning, to nurture a sense of place and develop a commitment to a better Detroit, and to grow our souls by developing a connection with ourselves, each other, and the earth.

Julia Putnam, Amanda Rosman, and Marisol Teachworth are the three co-founders of the school. They were influenced by the philosophies of Grace and Jimmy Boggs and the school was born out of many conversations with the Boggs and others about the role of education in a city like Detroit. As a teenager, Julia participated in the Detroit Summer program, a multiracial, intergenerational collective working through the Boggs Center (see Chapter Twenty-five) to transform communities by confronting problems with creativity and critical thinking. Currently, Julia is the school principal, Amanda is the executive director, and Marisol is the programming director. For more information, see: http://www.boggsschool.org/

What made you think about starting up a placed-based school in Detroit?

Julia: When I was in school, I was learning how to get A's and that was pretty much the highest people expected of me. I was obedient enough to produce that, but I didn't feel it was meaningful. The purpose of school was that I would get good grades in order to be able to get into a good college and into a good job, and therefore have the means to leave the city because there was nothing here for an upwardly mobile person. A lot of the ways in which Detroit schoolkids measured their success was whether they were able to leave Detroit when they were done with school. We wanted to think about what it would mean to redefine success. When our kids graduate, do they have the means to believe they have contributed to the betterment of Detroit and their future?

Amanda: A lot of the conversations that led up to the formal planning were around not only what is the point of education, but also what does progressive education look like in a place like Detroit, where there are no factory jobs available?

What should it look like?

Julia: We are trying to figure that out every day.

Marisol: One of the things that we did was come up with a mission. Our mission was to nurture creative, critical thinkers who contribute to the well-being of their communities. From that grew our values and our purposes [see editor's introduction]. We were thinking about when our students are moving on to the next phase of their lives. What are those people like? Who are they? What are their relationships like? What can they do? How have they interacted with their community?

Julia: One of the things we know and believe is that in a post-industrial city, the work and learning has to be relevant. It can't be just about how you can get a job to work for someone else. It really is about being creative, thinking critically about the problems that exist and how we're going to address them.

How have Jimmy and Grace's visions and ideas been reflected in the school?

Julia: I met Jimmy and Grace when I was 16. They started the Detroit Summer youth program to redefine, rebuild, and re-spirit Detroit from the ground up. I tell people that my education began then. It wasn't until I did Detroit Summer that I felt I could contribute to Detroit being a better place. We have a quote from Grace in the foyer: "we all have the power to create the world anew." She called the kids *solutionaries* because they are the ones to come up with solutions for what we are facing.

I've heard the term solutionaries *a lot in Detroit. Can you explain what it means?*

Julia: One of Grace's ideas was that our theory of change used to be that you just protested enough and you get enough people angry enough and that will effect change. But she got the idea from Margaret Wheatley that change doesn't happen from critical mass, but the critical connections you make with people. Slowly but surely, things evolve into something different than they were. *Solutionaries*, as opposed to revolutionaries who are just violently overturning something, are using their creativity and critical thought to think about what the solutions might be and how we can work together. One of the reasons Grace loved Detroit so much was that she saw the city as a place where people had stopped waiting for other people to come in and solve their problems. By necessity, Detroiters had to figure out how to take care of themselves. I think that is what's so inspirational about Detroit for other people.

How do you measure success?

Julia: We are constantly talking about that and trying to balance the need for kids to have real academic skills. One of our purposes is to give the kids tools to live purposeful lives of meaning and reach ambitious goals. For us, that can be varied.

Amanda: One way to measure success is to ask: is the community better because of our presence? That's a place-based focus. We are working on expanding our campus, so we talked with the neighbors to give them a chance to express concerns. We learned that they are really happy with the school being here. So we are really working to establish those relationships.

What does place-based education look like in a city such as Detroit?

Julia: Detroit is exciting for a lot of outsiders, but it is very challenging for people who have grown up here. The message I got growing up here was: "Detroit was once a wonderful city and it is no longer. And who knows when it will be good again." That made me question what it meant for me and my future. What we want for our kids who go to the school is to feel really rooted in this place.

Marisol: It's about connecting people to place. We do that by taking walks in the neighborhood and asking a lot of questions, which is something we did all the time in Detroit Summer.

How do the students see Detroit?

Marisol: It depends on who you ask. But I think most students see this community as really beautiful.

Julia: Another measure of success would be whether the kids see it as beautiful because of something they've done. Some of the kids have been here since before we opened and actually helped in the first year to renovate and tear down the weeds in the playground. That tells them that they have agency too; they don't have to wait for someone else to come and make something good.

Detroit is changing rapidly and there are a lot of new developments taking place in Downtown. What impact does this have on your school and your students?

Julia: Our kids don't feel it.

Amanda: I don't think that kids who aren't exposed even know that those things are going on. I think that it even creates a problem because there's more frustration. People talk about what's going on in Downtown and you can't see it in the neighborhood. And they know that someone is putting effort into Detroit and it's not for them.

Marisol: This reminds me of a story last year when one of our teachers took two neighborhood boys to dinner in Downtown by Campus Martius. They were just shocked at what Downtown Detroit looked like. There were so many restaurants; so much going on, even a music festival. So these kids—who were born and raised in Detroit—had no idea that there was this Detroit. They asked: "Who is this Detroit for? It's not for me and I have lived here my whole life."

What are the challenges you face with running this school?

Julia: If you believe, as Grace said, that "you have the power within you to create the world anew," then you are constantly bumping up against all the assumptions, all the existing structures and ways of doing things. And when you say, "no, we're going to do something differently," but you don't exactly know what different needs to look like yet and you are making the path as you go, it feels very daunting and exhausting. One of the things that Grace said to us when we asked her blessing to name the school after her was "yes" but with the challenge that we must always be thinking beyond what we even believe is possible because, otherwise, we will recreate the structures that we are trying to challenge. We've all been indoctrinated into what school is and so when things get difficult, we will default to that.

What advice would you give to people who want to come to Detroit and contribute to what is happening here?

Julia: Go slow.

Amanda: We've learned that people do not necessarily have training or experience in how to enter a community respectfully. There's a strong blank slate mentality, which is offensive. There are a lot of people who come and tell us what they would like to do in our school.

Marisol: The savior mentality: this neighborhood needs this, or these kids need this. Gain the background knowledge, what are you going into? What are people already doing? Where are there already roots? How are community members and organizers planning and thinking about neighborhoods that they live in.

Julia: I also wonder if the community needs what people are coming to offer. "You need what I have to offer you"; that's not usually framed as a question, but rather as an assumption. "And you should feel grateful to me that I'm even here to offer my presence." Maybe. But maybe wait and see and look and learn and listen. Maybe there are people already doing that. When urban farming got really popular, a lot of people came in and got involved with that. But there are people who have been farming and gardening in Detroit for a really long time. Is another garden what a community needs?

Amanda: Having felt all of this, these are the pitfalls, but we'd be nowhere without the people who stepped out of wherever with no personal gain but to help us.

Julia: Jimmy used to say: "It is only in relation to other bodies that any of us is somebody." And people have come here because they felt inspired by what we were doing, not because they pitied us. There's a huge difference.

Where is Detroit going to be in five years?

Julia: Can we do 25 years? I don't know. That's what is exciting for me about Detroit. I don't know what is going to happen. It could get worse before it gets better.

Amanda: That was something that troubled Grace, when people would say "Detroit is coming back." That is fraught with issues because the old Detroit was problematic and look where we ended up. If we are going back to what Detroit looked like in the glory days, that's a problem.

Marisol: What I feel hopeful about for the future of Detroit is that there are a handful of people, Boggs School students, who have been nurtured into critical thinkers who have the tools to make great decisions and will be contributing to a better Detroit.

Julia: In five years, we are going to have pretty powerful 11th-graders.

Note
The conversation with Julia Putnam, Amanda Rosman, and Marisol Teachworth took place at the Boggs School on Mitchell Street on the east side of Detroit, January 25, 2016.

TWENTY-FOUR

Yusef Bunchy Shakur

Author and neighborhood organizer

Yusef Bunchy Shakur's life story is one of incredible transformation, redemption, and inspiration. He grew up near Linwood and West Grand Boulevard, on the lower west side of Detroit. By the age of 13, he had been kicked out of every Detroit public school he went to. As a teenager, he helped co-found the Zone 8 gang, one of the most notorious gangs in the City of Detroit. He then went to prison for a crime he did not commit. In prison, he met his father. It was that relationship that had a tremendous impact on transforming and redeeming his life, like his father did prior to him arriving.

When he emerged from prison, he walked out as a revolutionary, not the gangbanger he went in as, dedicated to black liberation and to making his neighborhood a better place. Shakur has published two memoires, *The Window 2 My Soul* (2010, Urban Guerrilla Publishing) and *My Soul Looks Back* (2012). He is a well-sought-after speaker, both in Detroit and further afield. His most inspirational work can be found in the role he plays in the neighborhood where he grew up and continues to live. Shakur organizes an annual neighborhood festival backpack giveaway in the yard next to his house. Between 500 and 800 backpacks are given away each year to local children. The backpacks are filled with school supplies and books, and free food for all participants is provided. The giveaway brings together more than 1000 people through a peaceful event where neighbors can engage with each other and where children can be children and run around having fun without the thought of being shot or beat down. In addition to this event, Shakur has led a neighborhood-warming project during the winter to help provide resources in different parts of the city in what he describes as "neighborhood deserts."

Shortly after our conversation, he launched a project aimed at resisting gentrification by working toward transforming an abandoned house into a community center, which will not only provide amenities and resources for the neighborhood, but also act as a place to support indigenous leadership. Between February 1 and 15, 2016, Shakur stayed in this house, which lacked heating or electricity, in order to fund-raise and raise awareness of his campaign to resist gentrification, and to show that people have a human right to resist oppression, but also that the people of his community have their own vision for the development of their neighborhoods that does not include the displacement of people. He was able to raise $20,000 dollars and received a matching donation of $25,000, so his sacrifice did not go in vain. While Shakur's neighborhood is currently one of the poorest in the city, it is situated less than five minutes from Midtown and New Center and the threat of gentrification and displacement of the poor and African-Americans is very real. More about Yusef's transformation and the work that he does can be found at: www.yusefshakur.org

---

How would you describe the Detroit you grew up in?

The Detroit I grew up in was after 1967, which was the benchmark for white supremacy and for white people leaving the City of Detroit. You had the physical and social collapse of neighborhoods because when white folks left, the resources left with them. It undermined the communities—and keep in mind they we're already struggling. But when that became the social norm of white flight and black exploitation, the black communities were forced to scatter into a mode of survival of the fittest. These are the conditions I was born into. Drugs became a prominent thing during this time. Heroine was already there, but in the 1980s, crack cocaine became king. It took the place of General Motors, Ford, and Burger King; it provided jobs for a permanent underclass that was locked out of the job market. It became an economic backbone for what would become third-world neighborhoods. It was part of this shift in the black community, where the slogans or mindsets of "I'm black and I'm proud" and "we're fighting the man" all evaporated. The new slogan became "I gotta get money"; the new lifestyle is extreme individualism. Gangs become the new social force for youth to find meaning in our oppressed lives. It captured my imagination and the streets were my outlet for anger, my hurt, and my pain.

Your journey is one of incredible transformation, inspiration, and hope. What's your philosophy today?

My philosophy and vision is that I'm a New African Revolutionary Nationalist. I believe that black people are oppressed; black people have the right to our own independence. But to get there, the cornerstone of my philosophy is *restoring the neighbor back into the hood* by evaluating these third-world neighborhoods and diagnosing the conditions that created the third-world neighborhoods we are surviving in, which is white supremacy, capitalism, and black inferiority. Our work of restoring the neighbor back to the hood is fundamentally rooted in rebuilding and re-spiriting our community through love and demonstrating a sense of power through controlling our destiny by building liberated zones. By building liberated zones, we are combating all the social ills that are working to destroy us and put us on the path of liberation, because if you look at the devastation in our community, it's because of a lack of power, which black people don't have. So, ultimately, part of our philosophy is that we have to gain power. If you look at it historically, it wasn't slaves that were brought to America, it was noble men and women who were reduced to slaves to build up white power. But we had our own power base and independent government of nations, and coming to America we became a unique nation, a New African nation.

You talked about putting the neighbor back in the hood. What does this mean?

It's analyzing my life and utilizing my life as a catalyst of the deterioration that our family and our community has be subjugated to over hundreds of years, and saying we can't continue to allow ourselves to be pawns in our oppression. Instead of not giving a fuck, we need to care more because when you internalize your oppression, it breeds a self-defeating mentality of not giving a fuck. The streets are not going anywhere because on one corner, you got gangbangers, drug dealers, and thugs who represent a social norm of internalizing their oppression and becoming pawns of white supremacy and capitalism; on the other corner, we should have fathers, mothers, revolutionaries, and business-owners who are demonstrating that they care and present a form of resisting the social norm that is devaluing our community and human life, so, ultimately, we don't have enough balance in our community. It is designed that way. By taking this position, we are infusing into our communities self and community love.

We've created a Peace Zone that the late Ron Scott has described on our road as establishing a liberated zone (see Sandra Hines, Chapter Seventeen); we've created love, we've created hope. Fundamentally, you can't have any movement without love, hope, and revolutionary ideology.

How do you put this philosophy into practice?

Putting it into practice first started with myself. You can't go out and change the world until you change yourself. The Cuban revolutionary Che Guevara said that the cornerstone of making a new society is by first creating a new human being. I bring that into practice through my transformation and redemption; I had to work on myself and continue to work on myself: to be a better father, man, and revolutionary. I met my father in prison. He taught me how to be a better man to a woman and to be a peaceful person in my community. So if I have a dispute, I don't have to result to a gun; I don't have to result to a knife. So it's about removing the hurt. As we say in America, "hurt people hurt people." But I've been fortunate to make the transition to "healed people heal people." So we do an annual backpack giveaway, literally right here at my mom's house [see Figure 24.1]. For me, inviting people to my house and community is inviting you into my home, showing you that I love you, showing you that I care. To have my mother cook for thousands of people, these are some of the instrumental things that take place in putting revolutionary theory into practice, and then consistently being able to do that over 10 years has bred respect and power to help fuel change.

Figure 24.1 The backpack giveaway organized by Yusef Bunchy Shakur (Photo, Nick Kozak)

When you speak to Detroit youth, what messages do you give to them?

Hope is real. Change is possible. And that they have to realize the pawn that they have become in this game of capitalism. That their lives have become expendable as a result of white supremacy. They have to overstand that these terms are very nuanced to them but they are real in their world. Many don't even realize that they are capitalists. They don't even know they live in an economic system that thrives on extreme individualism; that's why they want those Michael Jordan shoes. That's why they are willing to kill, rob, or steal to get some shoes that only cost pennies to make in another country. They're disengaged from a knowledge base that is ultimately exploiting them because they are rooting their humanity upon these materialistic things. So even though they are not a slave like their ancestors, they're now a slave to a new system of materialism.

You started off by saying 1967 was really pivotal for the Detroit you grew up in. What do you think caused the decline of the city?

The reality is that it was doomed to decline because of racism and white supremacy. It was doomed to decline because of capitalism. These are systems that are rooted in destroying human lives and exploiting people. So why wouldn't we expect devastation. When you talk about the collapse of the auto industry, why wouldn't' you expect it? That's what capitalism does. And it has to reinvent itself because, ultimately, when it has no more bodies to eat, it turns on itself. It's important that I speak in that way because what happens is that people get blamed for the problems of capitalism and white supremacy. We are just going through a period where we say "the city was bankrupt." The city wasn't bankrupt; capitalism was bankrupt! Imperialism and white supremacy were bankrupt.

What are your thoughts about the pieces of Detroit's government, such as Eastern Market, leaving the city's control?

They haven't left by the will of the people. They were snatched. We live in a country that, from a world view, is supposedly anti-dictatorship. But in Detroit, you strip a people of their ability to elect their mayor and you impose a financial manager, which is nothing but a dictator. That's nothing but a hypocrisy. But again, back to values, we have to develop the grassroots movement, the grassroots leadership to build true people power. For me, that's where my philosophy has to come in by overstanding that we have to engage people where they are at now in order to move them into a different place of seizing power by helping them heal and transform themselves into better human beings.

There is a new narrative about Detroit, one of revival and renewal. What are your thoughts about this and about how gentrification impacts your community?

That's the unique thing about oppression. It can fool you. Oppression can be so sophisticated that you can think that you are not oppressed or exploited. As long as you have the oppressors telling the story and writing the narrative, it will always be portrayed in their best interest. So when we further evaluate it and say the "revitalization, the redevelopment, or the rebirth of this new Detroit," what Detroit are we talking about? Obama was here recently and he spoke proudly: "I see a new Detroit." That's a white Detroit. It's not black Detroit. You go through black Detroit you see devastation, you see oppression, hurt, and exploitation. The seeds of this new Detroit are nothing but an acceleration of gentrification. We see nothing but devastation at the expense of black communities and bodies. We have a campaign that we are going to launch where I plan on staying in a house down the street and the goal is to resist gentrification. We are right next door to Midtown, New Center, all these new white development areas. But what has happened is that this community here in particular has been economically, politically, and socially neglected. So, as a result, it has become prime real estate. So you see the opportunity of the new West. Here's an opportunity to build something new in this community. But what happened to the people who are still here. Our lives don't matter? This is where the slogan of Black Lives Matter comes into play. It's a slogan to acknowledge that "hey, watch it with that bulldozer, you are bulldozing away people and a legacy of people."

Do you worry that your neighborhood will gentrify and the African-American community will be displaced?

It's not a worry, it's a reality. It's what is taking place and what's happening. The campaign I'm launching is a direct result of dealing with that situation. But the campaign is also about supporting indigenous leadership. We have to continue to build the hope of the people that you have the power to resist and the power to develop your own vision. Resistance is a human right.

So what would be the narrative you would want to share about Detroit?

The narrative has to be rooted in the idea that these problems are not new or isolated problems. The leadership we have at the forefront, they are opportunistic leadership, handpicked by the media, corporate America—blacks and whites—they are maintaining the negative renegade narrative that supports the capitalist elite rooted in white supremacy. This is history replaying itself. You went from a time of the redlining of communities, where you couldn't economically afford to pay for things; that was straight blanket white supremacy.

Today, we are blind to the fact that we live in the richest country and we have extreme poverty, extreme homelessness, and extreme joblessness. And robbing has become a social job for many. Congressmen will never tell you that there will not be enough jobs for every American. They will never tell you, but that's the reality. So for a guy who has been incarcerated, what else do you expect him to do when his past comes back and he's out on the street? In changing the narrative, we have to overstand it from a historical standpoint, and from what lens? From my lens of black liberation, a lens of the Black Panther party, a lens of Malcolm X, Ella Baker, these individuals spoke to the condition as well as developing the platforms and the work of fighting and dying for black liberation. Overstanding that the counter-intelligence program from the American government sabotaged and attempted to destroy our movement. In doing that, they assassinated our leaders, falsely incarcerated our leaders to become political prisoners. What happened? They took away our leadership. When they took away our leadership, they took away our parents. So a child without a parent, he or she is going to grow up in a renegade environment that is going to produce renegade behavior, anger, and hostility. Now I'm mad at my dad; where have you been dad? What's happened? It's hard to digest. If it's hard to digest, how do you think you're going to get the best result? So the narrative has to be one of resistance, liberation, self-determination for black people, and the efforts at eliminating and destroying white supremacy and capitalism.

With all that in mind, are you hopeful for the future?

I'm hopeful because I believe in liberation. I'm hopeful because I'm confirmed in my belief that black people have the right to self-determination. A hopeful people is a people that is on a path to liberation. A hopeless people is on a path to self-destruction. The day my hope is removed is the day I voluntarily accept my oppression. And you may as well put a bullet in me.

Note

This conversation with Yusef Bunchy Shakur was held on January 25, 2016, at his home on Ferry Park Street in Detroit.

TWENTY-FIVE

Grace Lee Boggs

Activist (1915–2015)

Detroit is the space and place to begin anew.
Detroit is a city of hope.
Revolutions are about creating new societies in the places and spaces left
vacant by the disintegration of the old.

These words and visions, told by Grace Lee Boggs, underpinned the way she saw Detroit and how it would shape the world to come. It is fitting to end our conversations about Detroit with a woman who believed that change and revolution came from creating new economies, relationships, and ways of thinking from the ground up, not by seizing power. In her later years, the concept of revolution changed to one of (r)evolution, meaning that revolution happened over time, through people changing their relationships with themselves, each other, and the world around them. For Grace, evolution and revolution stand in a dialectic relationship with each other.

I had the privilege to meet with Grace several times, and to bring groups of students from the Netherlands into her home. One of my final conversations with Grace took place in April 2014 and is featured in the following text.

Grace lived to be 100, and passed away in October 2015. For most of her life, she was a revolutionary. Some of her early work was with the Marxist C.L.R. James in the 1940s and 1950s. She moved to Detroit in 1953, with her husband James Boggs, a fellow activist and African-American from the South who migrated to Detroit to work in the auto factories. Grace and Jimmy would later have an intellectual break with C.L.R. James and with Marxism. In Detroit, they worked together on issues of civil rights and the black power movement. Living in Detroit influenced the Boggs' thinking on the role of automation (which was making much of Detroit's labor force redundant), capital flight, and racism. Jimmy passed away in 1993.

For Grace, revolution and transformation are not "magical process[es] but hard work that required taking responsibility for ourselves and our communities" (Kelley, 2015). The creation of self-governance structures and the rethinking of work through local production were central to hers and Jimmy's ideas of revolution. This is why the role of urban agriculture and community gardens (see Feedom Freedom, Chapter Twenty-two), and place-based education (see Boggs School, Chapter Twenty-three), among others, were essential to her ideas and struggles. For Grace, transformations and revolutions came not from changing who is in power (or protesting against those in power), but from communities and movements who claimed their own spaces in which to realize the world they wished to achieve. For Grace, this meant focusing on the question of 'how to grow our souls' to produce a new "American Dream whose goal is a higher Humanity instead of the higher standard of living dependent on Empire" (Boggs and Kurashige, 2002, p xiv).

Grace Lee Boggs authored several books, including *Living for Change: An Autobiography* (University of Minnesota Press, 1998) and *The Next American Revolution: Sustainable Activism for the Twenty-first Century* (Boggs and Kurashige, 2011). She was also the subject of the documentary *American Revolution: The Evolution of Grace Lee Boggs*, released in 2013 and produced by Grace Lee. Her visions and activism survives through the Boggs Center to Nurture Community Leadership, which is situated in the home she and Jimmy moved to in 1953 and in the thousands of people who have been inspired by her and are putting her ideas of (r)evolution into practice (some of whom are featured throughout this book). For more information, see: www.boggscenter.org

---

You've lived in Detroit for more than 60 years. How would you describe what has happened here?

When I came to Detroit in 1953, the Packard plant had not yet moved to Wisconsin. The Chrysler Jefferson plant, where my husband worked, employed 17,000 people. If you threw a stone up in the air, on the way down you would hit an autoworker. It was just amazing. Within a year, things started to change. Auto production started up again in Germany and Japan. Automation and robots began to replace human beings on the line. Eventually, the Chrysler Jefferson plant employed only 2000 workers and the Packard plant moved to Wisconsin. If you threw a stone up in the air, on the way down it would hit a vacant lot.

And the question was: what do you do with that vacant lot? People who had come from the South during the war to work in the plants saw a vacant lot as promise, rather than blight. That migration changed the history of Detroit. It gave it the possibility of bringing the country back into the city. In my opinion, the transition from agriculture to industry was as monumental as the one from hunting and gathering to agriculture. Jimmy felt that he lived through three epochs: agriculture in the South; industry in the North; and post-industry and high-tech. It is that idea of cycles of civilization and the evolution of humankind that characterizes Detroit and helps us to understand it.

We see so much devastation in Detroit, yet you are so hopeful about the city, why?

I remember the meetings we organized back in the 1980s and people would come and while everyone was talking about hopelessness, they were also talking about the things they were doing. I think this is one of the most important things to understand: that when things go bad, a lot of people give up. But some people do not; some people see the crisis as opportunity and those people become the leaders of the future. That's related to the whole question of where leaders come from and where new epochs come from.

Are you leading this?

The role that the Boggs Center has played is to name what is taking place. It's really important to recognize what is happening because naming it gives it reality. But it is the people who are leading it.

That's very different from the view that sees politicians as leaders. What role does the city play in this?

I think the best example of the city and city government is what Coleman Young did. When the crisis hit Detroit, there was a lot of violence because there were no jobs. Coleman said "let's demolish a neighborhood to build an auto plant. Let's bring back the past and that comeback mentality." That's what official leaders have.

Why is urban agriculture, for you, an act of revolution?

Because we face planetary extermination if we keep on the old way of trying to live on industrial production. I don't know if you know the book *The Great Transformation* by Karl Polanyi. He talks about the transformation from the idea of earth to the idea of land; how we've been looking at things that are essential to live and how that transforms everything. This is the return to another philosophy.

What does that mean?

It's to see earth as earth, and not as land. To be able to free ourselves from thinking in terms of commodities, where we commodify everything. If you begin thinking in terms of commodities, eventually you become a prisoner to wants. You can't distinguish between needs and wants. Marx understood that when he said "all that is holy is profane. All that is solid melts into air." It's how you define reality.

In the film Requiem for Detroit?, you are quoted toward the end of the film as saying: "the American Dream is dead, long live the American Dream." Can you talk about that?

Julien Temple made the film. We were seated here in the living room and he suggested that we go upstairs and sit outside. As I looked up and down the street and saw the cars going, I saw the contrast between the cars and trees. Detroit is fantastic in June. It's so green; the trees are so huge. It's just a completely different world. All of a sudden you see that industrial society is just a phase in the history of humankind.

Think of the folks who built the Packard plant and what they thought was important. And when you see today how that's just brokenness and concrete, you realize that the age of production turned into the age of consumption, which jeopardized the planet and all life on it. When you see this, you begin to look at history in a very different way. That is an example of how giants fall.

Is Detroit a leader in this thinking today?

I think it is increasingly recognized as a leader for the post-industrial age. All we need to do is look at what is happening to the planet to realize that the industrial age is not the final epoch unless it becomes the end of all.

If Detroit is a leader in this thinking, what insights can it offer the rest of the world?

I think Detroit helps us to see that expanding production is not the be all and end all of human life. I remember when I was in the Bay Area, where they did a showing of the film [*American Revolutionary: The Evolution of Grace Lee Boggs*] and I did a Q&A. I left my wheelchair and people where clapping and cheering. People want a spiritual leader. They know that production is not the end of everything. It has been very jeopardizing.

Detroit is attracting a lot of attention today. Why do you think people are moving here?

The reason why people move into Detroit is twofold. One, there is a lot of space and it's very cheap. And two, they want to be part of being pioneers in what is taking place. They are mostly young people, mostly artists, and they are creating new ways of living together. They are very multi-ethnic and multigenerational. They are very different and we don't know what is going to happen. It's a cultural change.

Detroit has historically been a racially divided city. How does this new influx of people impact race in the city?

I think it's helping all of us, blacks as well as whites, to see race differently. What I see if you look at the history of our organization is how we have moved from being primarily concerned with the black movement to becoming really multi-ethnic and how we have moved to a new vision of what human beings are about. We have moved from a materialistic thing to an almost humanist approach. I don't know if you are aware of this or not, but Saturday nights in Detroit are wonderful. Young people just love going Downtown. They feel very free. It's very multi-ethnic, multigenerational. It's very lively. You would never expect that out of Detroit.

Your life has been dedicated to revolution. How does that come about?

It can be very dangerous. All sorts of fakers can come in. But people want it desperately. They want to grow their souls. People know we are at the stage where we have to grow spiritually. And this has happened once before, in the two centuries before Christ, during the transition from the Bronze Age to the Iron Age, when all the great religions were born. And all of them have some form of the Golden Rule in them. We are now in a post-industrial age and approaching something very different. The revolution we are on the threshold of is a very different kind of revolution and leap forward in the history of humankind.

How will this happen?

The way it's just happening right now! In Europe, because you've had so many kings, I think it's very difficult for people to understand that revolution is not about taking power. You think that is what revolution is about: 1917, you take power. The idea that revolution is a way of life is hard for them to grasp. That's what Detroit helps us to see.

Revolution as a way of life; can you articulate that a bit more?

To recognize that the reason why 1917 took the form that it did was because the Tsar was such a son-of-a-bitch and he was running everything. But in America, we don't have a country where that's happening. And particularly as people in power become less and less functional, things begin to change. I think that you need to think of revolution in cultural terms rather than in terms of power and government. I mean, think of the kind of change that takes place in the transition from hunting and gathering to agriculture; the things that took place between elders and children; that took place in the relationships with education. All those cultural changes that are essential to revolution would have been obscured because your concentration has been so focused on taking power.

I think when we look at the revolution in the US, it's going to take place not through taking power in Washington or anything like that, but different areas will begin to manifest their strengths. The Bay Area will be very different from the Rust Belt. The South will be different from the North. It's already happening all over the place.

Many of the other people in this book, such as the founders of the Boggs School, Wayne and Myrtle Curtis, Yusef Bunchy Shakur, Malik Yakini, are they part of this revolution?

Yes, they are.

Note
This conversation with Grace Lee Boggs took place at her home in Detroit on April 9, 2014.

TWENTY-SIX

Conclusion: Detroit and the future of the city

Brian Doucet

Listening to the voices of people like Grace Lee Boggs, it is easy to be inspired and filled with a sense of hope. Hers was a powerful voice projecting an alternative narrative to that of urban failure. The initiatives that have grown out of conversations at the Boggs Center, or through the passionate visions and tireless work of activists and community and civic groups, offer genuine alternatives for a more inclusive, fair, and socially just future. I am honored and privileged to have been able to share conversations with people like Yusef Bunchy Shakur, Malik Yakini, Sandra Hines, and the many others who are involved in initiatives that are making a real difference to Detroit and its residents.

These voices offer an alternative to the narrative that dominated Detroit for decades, that of decline and abandonment. But they also need to be placed in context. Contributions by George Galster, Ren Farley, Joshua Akers, John Gallagher, and others offer sobering reality checks as to the severity of Detroit's challenges and the inability of its current political and economic systems to tackle some of the city's biggest problems. Only by highlighting complex and diverse perspectives can simplistic narratives be challenged and the contradictions of Detroit's economic, social, racial, and political conditions be revealed.

Yet, Detroit and many other cities around the world are still portrayed in simplistic, one-dimensional narratives, which is why scholars, practitioners, and others need to continually challenge those messages by asking difficult questions and offer alternative ways of interpreting the city.

In Detroit, the dominant narrative for decades was as a metonym for urban failure. The peak of this narrative came in the years after 2008, with the global financial crisis, the US subprime mortgage crisis, and the bailout of the auto industry: Detroit's prominence as the poster child for urban decay took it to a world stage. Filmmakers, journalists, photographers, and academics from around the world put Detroit's problems into global limelight. It was in these years that numerous coffee-table books depicting the city's ruins were published (Austin and Doerr, 2010; Marchant and Meffre, 2010; Moore, 2010; Taubman, 2011), as well as films such as *Detropia*, which relied heavily on ruin imagery.

However, beginning around 2012 and accelerating since the city exited bankruptcy, a new narrative of Detroit emerged. No longer are the stories coming from Detroit all bad (see Austin, 2014; Coyle, 2014). *National Geographic* even ran an article about Detroit being "cool again" (Ager, 2015). People, academics included, began talking in a language of "renaissance", in a way that had not been seen since the 1970s (Neill, 1995). In many circles, the Grand Bargain and resolution of Detroit's bankruptcy were heralded as a model for success and something other cities could emulate. Rather than being seen as a symbol of urban failure, this new depiction of Detroit is of a comeback city full of energy and entrepreneurial spirit.

There are many visible signs of renewal: several billion dollars is being invested Downtown, as long-abandoned skyscrapers are being renovated, many by billionaire Dan Gilbert (see Akers and Leary, 2014). A new light rail line along Woodward Avenue will bring mass transit to the largest urban region in America without a subway, streetcar, or commuter train (notwithstanding the People Mover). Public spaces, such as Campus Martius, have been the focus of intensive placemaking initiatives, often at the request of Downtown's new corporate leaders. In a celebratory article espousing the opportunities for young people in the new Detroit, Maria Tomlinson (2015) states that "This city has everything Millennials could ever want. It's a growing city, just as we are. As we are out trying to find our path in life, so is Detroit." This new narrative of Detroit is taking on the form of a city that has become a playground for artistic, culinary, and cultural consumption, as illustrated by a recent *Toronto Star* article titled "Detroit is America's great comeback story" (Bain, 2016). The author states:

> Stop being sorry for Detroit. Stop being scared of Detroit. The story here is no longer automobile industry collapse, decline, decay and blight. It's about a glorious city that

birthed the Model T and Motown, that's coming back better, stronger, artier.

One of the biggest champions of this new comeback narrative has been Richard Florida. In 2012, he produced a series of short videos entitled *Detroit Rising*. In them, he stated that:

> I think what Detroit offers is for young people or interesting people or engaged people ... it offers something for them, and it doesn't have to advertise ... I think what's really interesting is this incredible shift back to the city.[1]

The comeback that Florida and others such as Tomlinson and Bain speak about is becoming a new and ever-more prominent narrative about Detroit. While Detroit has been known as a "renaissance" city at various periods in its history, this current reincarnation of the term appears to have more traction, both nationally and internationally (Glaeser, 2011). It also fits within wider discourses celebrating a new urban age, both in the US and internationally. While not always mentioning it by name, this narrative celebrates the ways in which gentrification and similar forces make cities attractive places for middle-class living, consumption, and recreation.

Today, however, the comeback is only one part of Detroit's story. But just as it has been important to deconstruct the narrative of urban failure, so to is it essential to critically examine the new "renaissance." Questions of who benefits from it, who is included and who is excluded are central to many of the contributions to this book. Regeneration, gentrification, and renewal are, indeed, taking place, but they have very distinct economic, racial and social geographies as to who is taking part in this revival. This "comeback" can primarily be found in *The 7.2* square miles of Greater Downtown Detroit. This, and a few other pockets scattered around the city, constitute the boundaries of the city's current "renaissance" (Doucet and Smit, 2016; see also Kreichauf, Chapter Four). When people celebrate the successes of the new Detroit, this is the Detroit they are referring to. While Maria Tomlinson states that Detroit is "growing," there is little evidence to show that this is actually happening either outside *The 7.2* or in statistics for the overall city (between 2000 and 2010 the city lost a quarter of its inhabitants).

Greater Downtown is a cleaner, safer, and brighter place with more amenities than a few years ago. However, it is only those who are privileged enough to have the means to be able to live, work, and play there who truly reap its rewards. Most of the new restaurants that

Bain's *Toronto Star* article showcases are beyond the means of average Detroiters. This new wave of investment, which is gaining momentum, socially and spatially excludes much of the city. Greater Downtown is pulling away from the rest of Detroit at a rapid pace. With a new narrative that celebrates Detroit as a "comeback" city and a new urban playground, one must ask: what exactly we are celebrating when *parts* of the city have been opened up for white, middle-class consumption while the rest of the city and its inhabitants are excluded from it?

Detroit's Downtown renewal is fraught with tensions and conflicts about access to the city, power, and privilege (see Howell and Feldman, Chapter Eleven). Rather than merely being a spatial quantifier, *The 7.2* is a brutal demarcation of prosperity and renewal on the inside, and poverty, foreclosures, and abandonment on the outside. In Richard Florida's films, most of the people he speaks to are white, and the places he stops on his tours are within *The 7.2*. There are very few African-Americans depicted in the films, despite the city's population being over 80% black; nor are there any visible signs of poverty, despite Detroit still being one of America's poorest cities. *The 7.2* comprises roughly 5% of the city's population and 5% of its surface area. Narratives focusing on the perceived successes of *The 7.2* rely heavily on the physical results of formerly abandoned buildings being transformed into tech start-ups or hip cafés, without adequately addressing the causes of the city's decline or rooting it in wider social, economic, or racial contexts. They also ignore the ways in which such investments actively contribute to growing inequality and divisions within cities (Doucet and Smit, 2016).

So, a new narrative of a "comeback" or "renaissance" city has emerged and is beginning to supplant the dominant narrative of urban failure. Both, however, lack complexity and contextualization. Critical urban thinkers need to challenge and critique this new narrative of success and celebration. This new renaissance narrative is larger than Leary's (2011) concept of a *Detroit Utopia* discourse, which focused on individuals (predominantly white), entrepreneurs, and risk-takers. Since 2011, this narrative has expanded to include the larger, corporate remaking of the city as well, and ties into wider back-to-the-city narratives that are built upon the celebration of new middle-class urban spaces (cf Glaeser, 2011).

In their book *Splintering Urbanism*, Graham and Marvin (2001) argue that cities are fragmenting because of the "emergence of myriads of specialized, privatized and customized networks and spaces." In Detroit, Greater Downtown has become a city unto itself. The physical, social, employment, leisure, and even marketing infrastructures of Detroit are now more fragmented, with the core rapidly pulling away from the periphery. Therefore, it is highly problematic to talk about a new "renaissance" in Detroit by only focusing on these networks while ignoring the other 95% of the city.

Detroit has many lessons to offer the world. However, it would be wrong to conclude that the redevelopments taking place Downtown, despite their high profile, offer genuine solutions to the wider issues of poverty, social exclusion, foreclosures, access to water, and racial divisions that continue to plague the city. However, it is not a stretch to envision a time in the near future when Greater Downtown's "renaissance" is seen as a model for other cities to emulate. For decades, "Detroit" was a byword for urban poverty, blight, and failure. If the Greater Downtown continues to be portrayed as a success story that gets translated to represent the entire city, it is not inconceivable to imagine Detroit becoming a symbol of how a city can emerge from the deepest of economic holes into a great place to live, work, play, and invest. When focused exclusively on the Greater Downtown, such a narrative is easy to construct and is based around comparatively simple questions of image reconstruction, placemaking, and the creation of new, middle-class consumption space. However, when we situate that part of the city, and those who occupy it, within a wider context, the new narrative of a "renaissance city" becomes easy to deconstruct and we are confronted with much more challenging questions about power, politics, class, and race.

When these perceived economic successes are unquestionably celebrated and viewed as formulas for successful cities, the underlying structures that drive social and spatial divisions are ignored. Under such an approach, difficult questions of who profits from these spaces, who has access to them, and how they reproduce or create divisions within cities are rarely confronted. This is not just a Detroit issue; the trickle-down, property-led redevelopment, with a generous dose of gentrification and the *creative class*, has become a standard model that cities around the world employ (often following the advice of scholars such as Richard Florida) in order to attract inward flows of capital, affluent residents, and tourists into core parts of cities.

Those who champion this model do not have long-term answers to the questions of economic, social, spatial, and racial divisions, which continue to be found in cities because, as Jackie Victor (Chapter Twenty) stated in her conversation, there are no good answers without addressing issues of race and class. What is happening in *The 7.2* brings investment and capital to the Greater Downtown; it is not an answer to the major challenges facing Detroit and most Detroiters. Importantly, the question of investment for whom is seldom asked by those who are celebrating today's urban renaissance. Moreover, even if (or when) *The 7.2* expands into neighborhoods such as Yusef Bunchy Shakur's (see Chapter Twenty-four) and beyond, the spatial boundaries between prosperity and exclusion will merely shift, rather than reduce, with those unable to afford to stay becoming displaced.

The inability of Greater Downtown's "renaissance" to adequately address structural issues of race, class, poverty, politics, and economics is the primary reason why its key champions do not feature in this book. As they do not confront these issues directly, they offer quick-fix solutions, which, in the words of George Galster (Chapter Two), treat the symptoms rather than the cause (see also Akers, Chapter Five). What has interested me, as a scholar and educator concerned about the spread of gentrification and the growing level of inequality, injustice, and polarization in our cities, are the voices, analysis, practices, and perspectives of those who are directly engaging with these complex issues and questions. Even chapters by those who operate within *The 7.2* offer critical reflections and insights into the role of, and the need to address, wider structural forces.

Perspectives within this book

The main fault lines within this book are not between the corporate and activist visions, but rather between the variety of different perspectives on Detroit that acknowledge, to varying degrees, the importance of structural forces of class, economics, race, and politics. With regards to the current trends in the Greater Downtown, there are two major discourses within this book. The first sees this investment as necessary but in need of being managed and controlled to ensure that it is as inclusive as possible. This is predominantly, but not exclusively a white perspective. Contributors such as George Galster (Chapter Two), Reynolds Farley (Chapter Three), John Gallaher (Chapter Nine), and Dan Kinkead (Chapter Ten) are, in many ways, hopeful about what this current wave of Downtown development can bring to the city, while, at the same time, stressing that this alone is not sufficient for a just and inclusive city.

The second discourse views these processes as a threat and part of a continued takeover of the city. This is often infused with strong racial overtones and is a dominant African-American perspective from contributors in this book. Many argue that this Downtown comeback is highly contentious; as several conversations noted, the wording, in and of itself, of Detroit "coming back" is problematic and disturbing to African Americans, in particular, as the old Detroit was fraught with racial injustices and the new Detroit "coming back" excludes many of its residents and neighborhoods (see conversations with the Boggs School, Chapter Twenty-three; Malik Yakini, Chapter Eighteen; Yusef Bunchy Shakur, Chapter Twenty-four; Grace Lee Boggs, Chapter Twenty-five).

As Yusef Bunchy Shakur attested, gentrification is a real concern for many low-income people, particularly African-American residents of Detroit's inner-city. René Kreichauf's chapter (Chapter Four) also demonstrated the unevenness and inequalities inherent in Greater Downtown's current transformation.

Similar fault lines can be seen around the issue of Detroit's bankruptcy. Reynolds Farley argues in Chapter Three that Detroit's future is brighter after its emergence from bankruptcy. He cites the restructuring of local government that took place (which saw roughly 20% of the city's workforce made redundant), as well as new funds for police and fire departments (which included provisions for higher salaries). As he and John Gallagher (Chapter Nine) articulate in their chapters, bankruptcy has accelerated the transferring of many city assets into partnerships with the private and non-profit sectors. These authors see this as positive because it opens up new funding streams (a point discussed with Dan Carmody, President of the Eastern Market Corporation, one such spin-off [see Chapter Nineteen]) and relieves the city of the need to make capital investments in improving and upgrading these facilities. Farley argues that this enables the city to concentrate more on its core services, such as the police and fire departments.

However, to many others, bankruptcy represents a taking back of power and control from the people of the city. This is perhaps best articulated in the chapter by Sharon Howell and Rich Feldman (Chapter Eleven). The arrival of an emergency manager, combined with the filing for bankruptcy, were, according to them, necessary steps for the corporate elite of the city to realize their capitalist vision for Detroit and remake the city on their terms. Bankruptcy was a mechanism to attack African-American political power and unions, and to transfer city assets into private hands. Their counter-vision, forged in decades of resistance, is rooted in equity, justice, local production, and compassionate care. In a sentiment articulated by many of the activists and community leaders interviewed for this book, they argue that these two visions are now at war.

Not everyone in this book would argue that the differing visions for the city are at war. However, they all acknowledge the painful divisions that exist within the city, and that these will not be healed by new developments Downtown or the gentrification of low-income neighborhoods. There is an understanding that these divisions are part of the wider society in which they find themselves. Some contributors are extremely critical of the direction in which the city is going; others are more hopeful. However, they are all able to put what is happening in Detroit into the wider context of social, spatial, economic, political, and racial change that often extends far beyond the boundaries of the City of Detroit.

Policy insights

The different chapters in this book offer neither a recipe for success nor an easy pathway for Detroit and other cities like it to become less divided and more inclusive places. That is because there are no easy answers. Those who promote easy answers to complex cities should be looked at with caution and confronted with those difficult questions.

As many of the issues in Detroit get to the very core of inequality and divisions within cities and societies, coming up with simple policy recommendations and suggestions as to how they can be implemented is a difficult, if not impossible, task. If cities like Detroit reflect the wider socio-economic, racial/ethnic, and political divisions within society, then these are all areas that need to be addressed. In many cases, these are political questions, rather than issues for (local) policymakers alone. However, for policy and practical insights, two major points throughout the book are worth reiterating. The first is that many contributors to this volume have articulated that Detroit's decline is largely a product of forces outside its borders. As I explained in the introduction to this book, this is why, when taking students to Detroit, I start my visits in the suburbs. Chapters by George Galster (Chapter Two), Reynolds Farley (Chapter Three), and Joshua Akers (Chapter Five) illustrate this geography. Political fragmentation, the suburbanization of jobs and households, global economic shifts, Michigan state laws, and many other forces outside of the City of Detroit have contributed to Detroit's decline over many decades. Galster's (2012) housing "disassembly line" best illustrates this point: Detroit, or any city for that matter, is powerless to shape the external forces that affect it. This perspective contrasts with the view put forward by many others, such as Edward Glaeser (2011), who argue that the uncompetitive and unentrepreneurial nature of Detroit's economy, combined with incompetent and corrupt political leadership, contributed to its decline.

For policymakers, a major insight from this book should be that genuine structural solutions to urban problems cannot come solely from within the city itself. In some cases, this requires regional cooperation, rather than competition, in areas such as housing policy, economic development, education, and transportation, among others. There have been small moves in Southeast Michigan recently, particularly in regional public transit, toward more cooperation. Unfortunately, this view goes against the grain of many dominant policy directions, and the dream of a growth boundary to curb sprawl, as advocated by both George Galster (Chapter Two) and Lowell Boileau (Chapter Sixteen), remains a long way off. This is by no means exclusively a Detroit, or even American, issue; even in countries with a strong tradition of centralized planning, such as the Netherlands, cities are increasingly competing, rather than cooperating, with each other in these areas (Doucet, 2015c).

The second key point for policymakers centers on the question of who is part of the conversation and who is able to influence the shape and direction of cities. For all the talk about participatory and inclusive planning, there are many perspectives and visions presented in this book that are excluded from mainstream planning and decision-making. Their visions are clear and offer genuine alternatives for more inclusive cities, but they rarely become part of the conversations that shape urban space. For policymakers, planners, and politicians looking to build inclusive and just communities, actively searching for, and listening to, these voices and reaching out to groups and individuals who do not normally take up the call to "participate" is an important step.

While many people may claim to speak for the most disadvantaged or excluded in society, this is very different than ensuring that they have a stake in the future of the city and that their voices are central in these urban conversations. This perspective is summarized by Selina Todd (2016), Professor of Modern History at Oxford University:

> The poor are always other people, in need of charity or discipline. They are the socially and economically "excluded", according to Tony Blair, a group that needs to be spoken for, rather than listened to; who require "inclusion" in existing institutions, rather than equal power in deciding how those institutions will operate.

This lesson also builds on David Harvey's (2008) idea of "the right to the city." The essential part of this is not simply the right to live in a city, but rather, as Harvey states: "the right to the city is far more than the individual liberty to access urban resources: it is a right to change ourselves by changing the city."

Many contributors to this book are already exercising their right to the city: Wayne and Myrtle Curtis are cultivating a garden next to their home as an act of revolution; the Detroit Black Community Food Security Network is shaping perspectives on food and working toward food sovereignty and food justice; the Boggs School is putting into practice new visions and meanings of education; and Yusef Bunchy Shakur is practicing his vision of "putting the neighbor back in the hood" on a daily basis (see also the examples in Chapter Six from Kimberley Kinder and Chapter Seven from Jason Roche). However, for the most part, they operate outside the normal circuits of planning and decision-making and they have very little control over the wider systems that shape their lives and their communities. The decision to include so many non-academic contributions in a scholarly book was deliberately made to bring these important visions into urban conversations that rarely hear directly from their perspectives. Those who have been inspired by what they have read should look for similar visions in their own communities, listen to and respect their perspectives, and work with them to bring their voices into the conversations that make and shape cities. This is particularly true for professionals working in planning, local government, housing, and other related fields.

Concluding thoughts and final questions

The different chapters in this book have all, to varying extents, examined the role of class, race, economics, power, or politics in shaping and explaining Detroit. Due to this, many chapters end up posing more questions than they answer. Many also offer hope: hope that if these issues are confronted, the root causes of inequality and injustice can also, in turn, be addressed and Detroit can become a more inclusive city.

Many popular narratives of Detroit set it out to be something distinct and separate from the rest of society. Dora Apel (2015) argues in her book *Beautiful Terrible Ruins* that our fixation with Detroit's ruins is a coping mechanism for dealing with the decline of modern society. In such a perspective, she argues, we view the ruination of one of modernity's most powerful and influential cities at a safe distance, thereby keeping it separate from ourselves. Yet, as Apel and many contributors to this book have explained, such perspectives are convenient ways of ignoring some of the harsh realities of capitalism. The image of Detroit as a metonym for urban failure that I outlined in Chapter One also works as a way of *othering* Detroit: "our city may have its problems," the narrative goes, "but at least we are not Detroit."

However, Detroit is not detached from its surroundings. In Chapter Twenty-two, Wayne Curtis stated that Detroit is not a fishbowl because a fishbowl implies something separate from the people coming to look into it. Unless we are part of the ruling class, he argued, we, too, are a part of Detroit's condition. As George Galster explained (Chapter Two; see also Galster, 2012), the growth of the suburbs and the decline of the city are two sides of the same coin. This is why what happens in Detroit matters; the visions, struggles, conflicts, and lessons from this highly divided city are important because their economic, political, racial and social structures are central to how our societies are organized. For my students, this is perhaps the most powerful lesson of all; those who are able to see this not only look at Detroit through new perspectives, but are also able to critically reflect on the power relations and fault lines within their own societies as well. Seen from this perspective, there are far more parallels with Detroit than things that set it apart from their own cities.

With that in mind, I want to end with a question that I often pose to students. Rather than asking "What will it take to 'fix' Detroit?" I challenge them to think of what conditions are necessary to ensure that the poverty, racial injustice, and inequality they have seen in Detroit are no longer possible. Only by reframing the question in this way can we genuinely address the issue of divided cities and societies.

Note
[1]   See: http://www.citylab.com/http://www.citylab.com/work/2012/05/detroits-creative-potential/2068/

References

Abowd, P. (2010) Another Detroit is happening, but which one do we need?, *Truthout*, June 18. Available at: http://truthout.org/archive/component/k2/item/90215:another-detroit-is-happening-but-which-one-do-we-need

Ad Hoc Committee on the Triple Revolution (1964) The Triple Revolution. Available at: http://www.educationanddemocracy.org/FSCfiles/C_CC2a_TripleRevolution.htm

Ager, S. (2015) Taking back Detroit. *National Geographic*, May, pp 57–83.

Aguirre, J.R.A. and Reese, E. (2014) Introduction—foreclosure crisis in the United States: Families and communities at risk, *Social Justice*, 40, 1.

Ahmed, A. (2015) UN panel: "Detroit water cutoffs violate human rights." Available at: http://america.aljazeera.com/articles/2014/6/25/detroita-s-disconnectionofwaterservicesviolateshumanrightssaysun.html (accessed August 17, 2015).

Akers, J.M. (2013) Making markets: think tank legislation and private property in Detroit. *Urban Geography*, 34, 1070–95.

Akers, J.M. (2015) Emerging market city. *Environment and Planning A*, 47, 1842–58.

Akers, J.M. and Leary, J.P. (2014) Detroit on $1 million a day. *Guernica*, July 28. Available at: https://www.guernicamag.com/daily/joshua-akers-and-john-patrick-leary-detroit-on-1-million-a-day/

Anderson, E. (2000) *Code of the Street: Decency, Violence, and the Moral Life of the Inner City*, New York, NY: WW Norton & Company.

Anderson, R. (2012) Interview: Director, City of Detroit Planning and Development.

Apel, D. (2015) *Beautiful, Terrible Ruins*, Rutgers: Rutgers University Press.

Archambault, D. (2009) Brightmoor may be the most distressed place in Detroit. It may also be the most hopeful, September 29. Available at: http://www.modeldmedia.com/features/brightmoor0909.aspx (accessed November 20, 2015).

Austin, B. (2014) The post-post-apocalyptic Detroit. *New York Times Magazine*, July 11. Available at: http://www.nytimes.com/2014/07/13/magazine/the-post-post-apocalyptic-detroit.html?_r=0

Austin, D. and Doerr, S. (2010) *Lost Detroit: Stories behind the Motor City's Majestic Ruins*. Charleston: The History Press.

Authority, T.C.H. (1946) *The Slum ... is Rehabilitation Possible?*, Chicago, IL: Chicago Housing Authority.

Avari, J. (2013) This Canadian city could be the next Detroit. *The Globe and Mail*, December 9. Available at: http://www.theglobeandmail.com/globe-debate/this-canadian-city-could-be-the-next-detroit/article15820368/

Azikiwe, A. (2006) From the frontlines: a report on the Detroit Coalition Against Police Brutality. *Pan-African News Wire*, June 19. Available at: http://panafricannews.blogspot.nl/2006/06/from-frontlines-report-on-detroit.html

Azikiwe, A. (2015) Detroit recovery? Don't believe it. Available at: http://www.workers.org/articles/2015/08/18/detroit-recovery-dont-believe-it/?utm_campaign=shareaholic&utm_medium=facebook&utm_source=socialnetwork (accessed September 1, 2015).

Babson, S. (1986) *Working Detroit: The Making of a Union Town*. Detroit: Wayne State University Press.

Bain, J. (2016) Detroit is America's great comeback story. *The Toronto Star*, September 10. Available at: https://www.thestar.com/life/travel/2016/09/10/detroit-is-americas-great-comeback-story.html

Barlow, T. (2009) For sale: the 100$ house. Available at: http://www.nytimes.com/2009/03/08/opinion/08barlow.html?_r=0 (accessed January 15, 2016).

Barrabi, T. (2014) Detroit water crisis: shutoffs resume after month-long moratorium. *International Business Times*, August 27. Available at: www.ibtimes.com

Basten, L. and Utku, Y. (2011) Laboratorium des Strukturwandels. In C. Reicher (ed) *Schichten einer Region: Kartenstücke zur räumlichen Struktur des Ruhrgebiets*, Berlin: Jovis, pp 158–81.

Bates, B.T. (2014) *The Making of Black Detroit in the Age of Henry Ford*, Chapel Hill, NC: University of North Carolina Press.

BBC (British Broadcasting Corporation) (2014) #BBC trending: North East England hits back with pride. *BBC News*, May 12. Available at: http://www.bbc.com/news/blogs-trending-27377878

Beauregard, R.A. (2003) *Voices of Decline: The Postwar Fate of U.S. Cities*, New York, NY: Routledge.

Beauregard, R.A. (2006) *When America became Suburban*, Minneapolis, MN: University of Minnesota Press.

Beckett, A. (2014a) The North-East of England: Britain's Detroit? *The Guardian*, May 10. Available at: http://www.theguardian.com/uk-news/2014/may/10/north-east-avoid-becoming-britains-detroit

Beckett, A. (2014b) Andy Beckett: why I compared the North East to Detroit. *The Journal*, May 13. Available at: http://www.thejournal.co.uk/news/north-east-news/andy-beckett-compared-north-east-7114480

Bell, R., Ellefson, J., and Rivera, P. (2015) 7.2 Sq. Mi (2nd edn). Available at: http://detroitsevenpointtwo.com/

Berman, M. (1988) *All that is Solid Melts into Air: The Experience of Modernity*, New York, NY: Viking Penguin.

Bernt, M. and Rink, D. (2010) Not relevant to the system: the crisis in the backyards. *International Journal of Urban and Regional Research*, 34(3): 678–85.

Bernt, M., Cocks, M., Couch, C., Grossmann, K., Haase, A., and Rink, D. (2012) Policy response, governance and future directions. Shrink Smart Research Brief No. 2, March, Helmholtz Centre for Environmental Research—UFZ, Leipzig.

Berry, B. (1977) *Urbanization and Counter Urbanization*, London: Sage Publications.

Bey, T. (1991) T.A.Z.: The Temporary Autonomous Zone. Pacific Publishing Studio. Available at: http://hermetic.com/bey/taz_cont.html

Binelli, M. (2012) *Detroit City is the Place to Be: The Afterlife of an American Metropolis*, London: Picador.

Bodurow, C. (2015) [SW]LABNZE prototype project, Detroit.

Boggs, G. (2009) Detroit: city of hope. In These Times. Available at: http://inthesetimes.com/article/4247/detroit_city_of_hope

Boggs, G. and Kurashige, S. (2011) *The Next American Revolution: Sustainable Activism for the Twenty-first Century*, California, CA: University of California Press.

Boggs, G. and Scott, R. (2012) The urgency of now: a conversation with Grace Lee Boggs and Ron Scott. Video, University of Michigan Detroit Center, July 24. Available at: https://www.youtube.com/watch?v=yIlrY6zgzys

Boggs, J. (1963) *The American Revolution: Pages from a Negro Workers Notebook*, New York, NY: Monthly Review Press.

Boie, G. and Pauwels, M. (2010) *Too Active to Act*, Amsterdam: Valiz Publishers.

Bolsmann, A. (2014) Urbane Künste Ruhr in der Kritik. Available at: http://www.derwesten.de/wp/staedte/gelsenkirchen/urbane-kuenste-ruhr-in-der-kritik-aimp-id9202230.html (accessed January 15, 2016).

Bomey, N. (2015) *Detroit Resurrected: To Bankruptcy and Back*, New York, NY: W.W. Norton.

Bomey, N. and Gallagher, J. (2013) How Detroit went broke. *Detroit Free Press*, September 15.

Bomey, N., Snavely, B., and Priddle, A. (2013) Detroit becomes largest U.S. city to enter bankruptcy. *USA Today*, December 3. Available at: www.usatoday.com

Bomey, N., Gallagher, J., and Stryker, M. (2014) How Detroit was reborn. *Detroit Free Press*, November 9.

Boyer, B.D. (1973) *Cities Destroyed for Cash: The FHA Scandal at HUD*, Chicago, IL: Follett.

Boyle, K. (2004) *Arc of Justice: A Saga of Race, Civil Rights, and Murder in the Jazz Age*, New York, NY: Henry Holt & Co.

Bradley, B. (2015) The blight-fighting solution for saving 40,000 Detroiters from eviction. *Next City*, November 9. Available at: https://nextcity.org/features/view/detroit-foreclosures-tax-auction-loveland-technologies-jerry-paffendorf

Brake, K. and Herfert, G. (2012) *Reurbanisierung. Materialität und Diskurs in Detuschland*, Wiesbaden: VS Verlag für Sozialwissenschaften.

Brenner, N. (2004) *New State Space: Urban Governance and the Rescaling of Statehood*, Oxford: Oxford University Press.

Brenner, N. and Keil, R. (2011) From global cities to globalized urbanization. In R. LeGares and F. Stout (eds) *The City Reader: Fifth edition*, New York, NY: Routledge, pp 599–608

Brogan, SJ. (2015) 2 years after filing, bankruptcy put Detroit on track, *Detroit Free Press*, July 18, Available at: http://www.freep.com/story/opinion/readers/2015/07/17/detroit-bankruptcy/30322441/

Brownley Raines, A. (2011) Wandel durch (Industrie) Kultur [Change through (industrial) culture]. Conservation and renewal in the Ruhrgebiet. *Planning Perspectives*, 26(2): 183–207.

Burns, G. (2015) One of a kind Airbnb to offer travelers authentic Detroit experience. *MLive*, October 26. Available at: http://www.mlive.com/news/detroit/index.ssf/2015/10/one-of-a-kind_airbnb_to_offer.html

Callahan, B. (2014) Detroit and Cleveland are among the 25 worst-connected U.S. cities. Connect Your Community 2.0. Available at: http://connectyourcommunity.org/detroit-and-cleveland-are-among-the-25-worst-connected-u-s-cities/ (accessed July 16, 2015).

Cantor, L. (2007) *Tigers Essential: Everything you need to know to be a real fan!*, Chicago: Triumph Books.

Castells, M. (1991) *The Informational City. Economic Restructuring and Urban Development*, Oxford: Blackwell.

Castells, M. (1996) *The Rise of the Network Society*, Malden, MA: Blackwell.

Checkoway, B. (1980) Large builders, federal housing programmes, and postwar suburbanization. *International Journal of Urban and Regional Research*, 4, 21–45.

Chieppo, C. (2014) New Orleans' winning strategy in the war on blight. *Governing Magazine*.

Christoff, C. (2013) Detroit citizens protect themselves after police force decimated. *Bloomberg News*, May 30.

Chronopoulos, T. (2014) Robert Moses and the visual dimension of physical disorder efforts to demonstrate urban blight in the age of slum clearance. *Journal of Planning History*, 13, 207–33.

Citizens Research Council of Michigan (2013) *Detroit City Government Revenues*, Report #382 (April), Lansing: Citizens Research Council of Michigan.

Clark, A. (2015) The threat to Detroit's rebound isn't crime or the economy. It's the mortgage industry. *Next City*, December 7. Available at: https://nextcity.org/features/view/detroit-bankruptcy-revival-crime-economy-mortgage-loans-redlining

Clement, D. (2013) The spatial injustice of crisis-driven neoliberal urban restructuring in Detroit. Open Access Theses, Paper 406.

Coggans, L. (2014) Blight battle. *Memphis Flyer*, March 20.

Cooper, M.H. (2015) Measure for measure? Commensuration, commodification, and metrology in emissions markets and beyond. *Environment and Planning A*, 47.

Corrigan, Z. (2015) Gentrification of downtown Detroit producing huge profits for the rich. Available at: https://www.wsws.org/en/articles/2015/01/06/gris-j06.html (accessed August 19, 2015).

Counts, J. (2014) Welcome to Gilbertville (formerly Detroit). Available at: http://beltmag.com/gilbertville/ (accessed July 19, 2015).

Cowley, S. (2015) A Detroit florist's vision turns an abandoned house into art. *New York Times*, October 14. Available at: http://www.nytimes.com/2015/10/15/business/smallbusiness/a-detroit-florists-vision-turns-an-abandoned-house-into-art.html?_r=2

Cox, K. (1993) The local and the global in the new urban politics: a critical view. *Environment and Planning*, 11: 433–48.

Coyle, J. (2014) Daring to dream in Detroit. *The Toronto Star*, December 13. Available at: http://www.thestar.com/news/insight/2014/12/12/detroit_fights_its_way_back_from_the_brink.html

Craddock, S. (2000) *City of plagues: Disease, poverty, and deviance in San Francisco*, Minneapolis: University of Minnesota Press.

Crain's Communications (2013) First look at the Z: it's not your typical Detroit parking deck. October 11. Available at: http://www.crainsdetroit.com/article/20131011/NEWS/131019961/first-look-at-the-z-its-not-your-typical-detroit-parking-deck

Cwiek, S. (2014a) Judge rules there's no guaranteed right to Detroit water service without paying bills. *Michigan Radio*, September 29. Available at: michiganradio.org

Cwiek, S. (2014b) Orr looks to private sector for help with Detroit water department mess. *Michigan Radio*, March 21. Available at: michiganradio.org

Darden, J.T. and Thomas, R.W. (2013) *Detroit: Race Riots, Racial Conflicts, and Efforts to Bridge the Racial Divide*, East Lansing, MI: Michigan State University Press.

Darden, J.T. and Wyly, E. (2010) Cartographic editorial—mapping the racial/ethnic topography of subprime inequality in urban America. *Urban Geography*, 31, 425–33.

Data Driven Detroit (2015) Homepage. Available at: http://datadrivendetroit.org (accessed November 25, 2015).

Davey, M. (2013) Going, in uncertainty, where no other big city has. *New York Times*, July 20, p A10.

Davis, R. (2015) Motor City to bike city: inside Detroit's bicycle renaissance. November 22. Available at: http://www.nbcnews.com/news/us-news/motor-city-bike-city-inside-detroits-bicycle-renaissance-n467316 (accessed November 25, 2015).

Davy, B. (2004) *Die Neunte Stadt. Wilde Grenzen und Städteregion Ruhr 2030*, Wuppertal: Müller und Bussmann KG.

Deppe, S. (2015) Kreativwirtschaft im Ruhrgebiet macht weniger Umsatz. Available at: https://www.ruhrnachrichten.de/leben-und-erleben/kultur-region/Neue-Studie-Kreativwirtschaft-im-Ruhrgebiet-macht-weniger-Umsatz;art1541,2649400 (accessed January 15, 2016).

Desan, M.H. (2014) Bankrupted Detroit. *Thesis Eleven*, Vol. 121(1): 122–30.

Detroit 7.2 (2015) *7.2 SQ MI: A report on Greater Downtown Detroit* (second edition). Available at: http://detroitsevenpointtwo.com/resources/7.2SQ_MI_Book_FINAL_LoRes.pdf

Detroit Blight Removal Task Force (2014) *Every Neighborhood has a Future ... and It doesn't include Blight*, Detroit: Rock Ventures.

Detroit Board of Realtors (2009) Average home price in Detroit: 1994–2009. Encyclopedia Britannica blog webpage, May 19. Available at: www.britannica.com

Detroit Future City (2012) Detroit Future City strategic framework. Executive summary. Available at: http://detroitfuturecity.com/wp-content/uploads/2014/12/DFC_ExecutiveSummary_2nd.pdf

Detroit Future City (2013) *2012 Detroit Strategic Framework Plan*, Detroit: Inland Press.

Detroit Future City Implementation Office (2015) A field guide to working with lots. Available at: http://dfc-lots.com

Detroit Home Prices and Values (2014) Zillow real estate webpage. September 30. Available at: www.zillow.com

Detroit Residential Parcel Survey (2009) Homepage. Available at: http://www.detroitparcelsurvey.org/

Detroit Water Brigade (2015) Homepage. Available at: www.detroitwaterbrigade.org/

Detroit Works Long Term Planning Steering Team (2012) Detroit future city: Detroit strategic framework plan. December. Available at: https://detroitfuturecity.com/framework/

Detroit, City of (1951) *Detroit Master Plan*. Detroit: DCPC.

Detroit, City of (1973) *The Detroit Master Plan*. Detroit: DCPC.

Detroit, City of (1992) *Detroit Master Plan*. Detroit: DCPC.

Detroit, City of (2009) *City Master Plan*. Detroit: DCPC.

Detroit Progress LLC (2012) About: Detroit progress/wholesale/investment/foreclosure/properties. Available at: http://www.detroitprogress.com/.

Deuber, L. (2013) Warum deutsche Städte nie pleite gehen. Available at: http://www.wiwo.de/politik/ausland/detroit-ist-insolvent-warum-deutsche-staedte-nie-pleite-gehen/8520010.html (accessed January 15, 2016).

Deutsch, L. (2012) Collateral damage: mitigating the effects of foreclosure in communities, *Temple Political & Civil Rights Law Review*, 22, 203.

DeVito, L. (2015) 17th Allied Media conference kicks off. *MetroTimes*, June 18. Available at: http://www.metrotimes.com/Blogs/archives/2015/06/18/17th-allied-media-conference-kicks-off

Dolan, M. (2011) Detroit mayor scales back his overhaul plan, for now. *Wall Street Journal*, June 29. Available at: http://online.wsj.com

Dolan, M. (2012) New Detroit farm plan taking root. *Wall Street Journal*, July 6. Available at: http://online.wsj.com/article/SB10001 424052702304898704577479090390757800.html

Dolhinow, R. (2010) *A Jumble of Needs: Women's Activism and Neoliberalism in the Colonias of the Southwest*, Minneapolis, MN: University of Minnesota Press.

Doucet, B. (2013) Four days in Detroit: a Dutch urban geography fieldtrip to the Motor City. *Belgeo*, 2013-2.

Doucet, B. (2014) What we really find when we compare Detroit with the north-east of England. *The Guardian*, May 15. Available at: http://www.theguardian.com/local-government-network/ the-northerner/2014/may/15/compare-detroit-and-north-east-of-england

Doucet, B. (2015a) What Grace Lee Boggs taught my students. *The Detroit Free Press*, October 8. Available at: http://www.freep.com/ story/opinion/contributors/2015/10/08/what-grace-lee-boggs-taught-my-students/73580646/

Doucet, B. (2015b) Detroit's gentrification won't give poor citizens reliable public services, *The Guardian*, February 17.

Doucet, B. (2015b) Faillissement Detroit Spiegel voor Nederlands Beleid. *Stedenbout en Ruimtelijke Ordening*, 96(1): 38–41.

Doucet, B. and Smit, E. (2016) Building an urban "renaissance": fragmented services and the production of inequality in Greater Downtown Detroit. *Journal of Housing and the Built Environment*, 31: 635.

Doussard, M. (2013) *Degraded work: The Struggle at the Bottom of the Labor Market*, Minneapolis, MN: University of Minnesota Press.

Downie, L., Jr (1974) *Mortgage on America*, New York, NY: Praeger Publishers.

Dwyer, J.G. (2011) No place for children: Addressing urban blight and its impact on children through child protection law, domestic relations law, and 'adult-only' residential zoning, *Alabama Law Review*, 62.

Easterly, W. (2006) *White Man's Burden: Why the West's Efforts to Aid the Rest have done so much Ill and so little Good*, New York: Penguin Books.

Eddy, M. (2013) In Germany's rust belt, a polished but ailing city. *New York Times*, December 24. Available at: http://www.nytimes. com/2013/12/25/world/europe/in-germanys-rust-belt-a-polished-but-ailing-city.html?_r=0

Editorial (2013) United strategy needed to cure Detroit's cancerous blight. *Detroit News*, December 19.

Einhorn, R. (2001) *Property Rules: Political Eonomy in Chicago, 1833–1872*, Chicago, IL: University of Chicago Press.

Eisinger, P. (2015) Detroit futures: can the city be reimagined?, *City & Community*, 14(2): 106–17.

El Khafif, M. and Roost, F. (2011) Keine klassische Metropole. Einführung in die Lage und Dimension des Ruhrgebiets. In C. Reicher (ed) *Schichten einer Region: Kartenstücke zur räumlichen Struktur des Ruhrgebiets*, Berlin: Jovis, pp 16–37.

Elliott, M. (2011) We need to ask: is gentrification happening in Detroit? Available at: http://www.modeldmedia.com/features/gentrifyfeature1211.aspx (accessed August 12, 2015).

Elphinstone, J.W. (2007) Home buyers look for deals at auction. *The Washington Post*, August 28.

Erbe, B.M. (1975) Race and socioeconomic segregation within a metropolitan ghetto. *American Sociological Review*, 40 (December): 801–12.

Evangelista, J. and Doulos, N. (2011) Detroit: back to the future: archive of impressions. between illusion and delusion, urban and rural, living and leaving. Available at: http://newstrategiesdmc.blogspot.nl/

Expodium (2008) HC on the move. Video registration of a "safari" through the surroundings of the shopping mall. Available at: https://www.youtube.com/watch?v=5rfbC-bJUjM

Expodium (2009a) Detroit residency guide. Internal document.

Expodium (2009b) Application 2009. Available at: http://www.mondriaanfonds.nl/en/

Falls, J. (1989) *The Detroit Tigers: An Illustrated history*, New York: Walker & Co.

Farley, R. (2011) Black–white residential segregation: the waning of American apartheid. *Contexts*, 10(3): 36–43.

Farley, R. (2015) The bankruptcy of Detroit: what role did race play? *City and Community*, 14(2): 118–37.

Farley, R., Danziger, S., and Holzer, H. (2000) *Detroit Divided*, New York, NY: Russell Sage.

Feeley, D (2013) Which Way Out of Detroit? *Solidarity*, November/December. Available at: https://www.solidarity-us.org/node/4027

Field, J. (2013) Gilbert owns Downtown Detroit, but who owns the most private land in the city. Available at: http://michiganradio.org/post/gilbert-owns-downtown-detroit-who-owns-most-private-land-whole-city (accessed August 18, 2015).

Finley, N. (2014) Where are the black people? *Detroit News*, December 15. Available at: http://www.detroitnews.com/story/opinion/columnists/nolan-finley/2014/12/14/black-people/20322377/

Flanagin, J. (2015) The Brooklynization of Detroit is going to be terrible for Detroiters. Available at: http://qz.com/453531/the-brooklynization-of-detroit-is-going-to-be-terrible-for-detroiters/ (accessed September 18, 2015).

Florida, R. (2002) *The Rise of the Creative Class (and how it's Transforming Work, Leisure, Community and Everyday Life)*, New York, NY: Basic Books.

Florida, R. (2012) Detroit rising. The Atlantic Citylab. Available at: http://www.citylab.com/special-report/detroit-rising/

Fournier, H. and Dickenson, J.D. (2015) Detroit community activist Ron Scott dies. *Detroit News*, November 30. Available at: http://www.detroitnews.com/story/obituaries/2015/11/30/ron-scott/76556578/

Freund, D.M.P. (2007) *Colored Property: State Policy and White Racial Politics in Suburban America*, Chicago, IL: University of Chicago Press.

Frug, G. (2001) *City Making: Building Communities without Building Walls*, Princeton, NJ: Princeton University Press.

Gadwa, A. and Markusen, A. (2010) Executive summary to Creative Placemaking. White Paper for the Mayor's Institute on City Design.

Gallagher, J. (2010a) *Reimagining Detroit: Opportunities for Redefining an American City*, Detroit: Detroit Wayne State University Press.

Gallagher, J. (2010b) Matty Moroun and his big slice of Detroit. *Detroit Free Press*, May 11.

Gallagher, J. (2013a) Detroit jewels shine with help from non-profits. *Detroit Free Press*, April 3.

Gallagher, J. (2013b) Reimagining Detroit. *The Cairo Review of Global Affairs*, Fall. Available at: http://www.thecairoreview.com/essays/reimagining-detroit/

Gallagher, J. (2014) Sugrue: trickle-down urbanism won't work in Detroit. *The Detroit Free Press*, February 23. Available at: http://www.detroitchamber.com/sugrue-trickle-down-urbanism-wont-work-in-detroit/

Galster, G. (2012) *Driving Detroit: The Quest for Respect in the Motor City*, Philadelphia, PA: University of Pennsylvania Press.

Ganser, R. and Piro, R. (2012) Parallel patterns of shrinking cities and urban growth: spatial planning for sustainable development of city regions and rural areas. *Ashgate*, 73–82.

Gibbs, A. (2013) Detroit's Belle Isle becomes a state park after Michigan signs lease deal. *Huffington Post*, October 2. Available at: www.huffingtonpost.com

Giermann, H. (2015) Defensive architecture creates unlivable cities. *ArchDaily*. Available at: http://www.archdaily.com/601152/ defensive-architecture-creates-unlivable-cities/ (accessed December 31, 2015).

Glaeser, E. (1998) Are cities dying? *Journal of Economic Perspectives*, 12(2): 139–60.

Glaeser, E. (2011) *The Triumph of the City*, New York, NY: Penguin Press.

Glaeser, E. and Gyourko, J. (2005) Urban decline and durable housing. *Journal of Political Economy*, 113(2): 345–75.

Goldberg, D.T. (1993) *Racist Culture: Philosophy and the Politics of Meaning*, Oxford and Cambridge, MA: Blackwell.

Goldstein, M. and Stevenson, A. (2016) Market for fixer-uppers traps low income buyers. *The New York Times*, February 20.

Good, D.L. (1989) *Orvie: The Dictator of Dearborn: The Rise and Reign of Orville L. Hubbard*, Detroit: Wayne State University Press.

Goodman, A. (2005) Central cities and housing supply: Growth and decline in US cities. *Journal of Housing Economics*, 14: 315–35.

Goodman, A. and Amin, S. (2015) African economist Samir Amin on the World Social Forum, globalization & the barbarism of capitalism. Video, *Democracy Now!*, March 27. Available at: http:// www.democracynow.org/2015/3/27/african_economist_samir_ amin_on_the

Gordon, C. (2003) Blighting the way: urban renewal, economic development, and the elusive definition of blight. *Fordham Urban Law Journal*, 31: 305.

Gotham, K.F. (2009) Creating liquidity out of spatial fixity: the secondary circuit of capital and the subprime mortgage crisis. *International Journal of Urban and Regional Research*, 33: 355–71.

Gottdiener, M. (2010) *The Social Production of Urban Space*, University of Texas Press.

Gottesdiener, L. (2015) A foreclosure conveyor belt: the continuing depopulation of Detroit. *Common Dreams*, April 20. Available at: http://www.commondreams.org/views/2015/04/20/foreclosure- conveyor-belt-continuing-depopulation-detroit

Gowan, T. (2010) *Hobos, Hustlers, and Backsliders: Homeless in San Francisco*, Minneapolis, MN: University of Minnesota Press.

Graham, S. and Marvin, S. (2001) *Splintering Urbanism: Networked Infrastructures, Technological Mobilities and the Urban Condition*, Abingdon: Psychology Press.

Gregory, V. (2007) Real estate auctions gain popularity in cooling market. *The Bakersfield Californian*, July 17.

Guyette, C. (2015a) Detroit's water tug-of-war. *Metro Times*, June 3. Available at: http://www.metrotimes.com/detroit/detroits-water-tug-of-war/Content?oid=2348110

Guyette, C. (2015b) With Detroit's water payment plan a massive failure, Mayor Duggan plans changes. *Democracy Watch*, April 19. Available at: http://www.d-rem.org/curt-guyette-with-detroits-water-payment-plan-a-massive-failure-mayor-duggan-plans-changes/

Haase, A., Rink, D., Grossmann, K., Bernt, M., and Mykhnenko, V. (2014) Conceptualizing urban shrinkage. *Environment and Planning, A*, 46(7): 1519–34.

Hackworth, J. (2007) *The Neoliberal City: Governance, Ideology, and Development in American Urbanism*, Ithaca, NY: Cornell University Press.

Hackworth, J. (2014a) The limits to market-based strategies for addressing land abandonment in shrinking American cities. *Progress in Planning*, 90(2014): 1–37.

Hackworth, J. (2014b) Paradigm, harbinger, extreme or exception? Some thoughts on the role of Detroit in contemporary urban theory. Paper presented at the "Learning from Detroit: Turbulent Urbanism" symposium, Ann Arbor, MI.

Hackworth, J. (2015) Demolition as urban policy in the American Rust Belt. Working paper.

Hall, P. (1988) *Cities of Tomorrow*, Oxford: Blackwell.

Halperin, A. (2015) How Motor City came back from the brink … and left most Detroiters behind. *Mother Jones*.

Handelsblatt (2015) Das neue Detroit im Ruhrgebiet. Available at: http://www.handelsblatt.com/unternehmen/industrie/opel-werk-bochum-wird-abgerissen-das-neue-detroit-im-ruhrgebiet/11870640.html (accessed January 15, 2016).

Hanhörster, H. (2011) Soziales und ethnisches Mosaik. In C. Reicher (ed) *Schichten einer Region: Kartenstücke zur räumlichen Struktur des Ruhrgebiets*, Berlin: Jovis , pp 108–31.

Hanlon, J. (2011) Unsightly urban menaces and the rescaling of residential segregation in the United States. *Journal of Urban History*, 37(5): 732–56.

Harvey, D. (1989a) *The Urban Experience*, Oxford: Blackwell.

Harvey, D. (1989b) From managerialism to entrepreneurialism: The transformation in urban governance in late capitalism. *Geografiska Annaler Series B: Human Geography*, 71(1): 3–17.

Harvey, D (1990) *The Condition of Postmodernity: An Enquiry into the Origins of Cultural Change*, Malden, MA: Blackwell.

Harvey, D. (2005) *A brief History of Neoliberalism*, Oxford: Oxford University Press.

Harvey, D. (2008) The right to the city. *New Left Review*, 53: 23–40.

Harvey, M. (2009) Slums of Detroit: a look at the heart of America's 2nd most deserted city. Available at: http://exiledonline.com/slums-of-detroit-a-look-at-the-heart-of-americas-2nd-most-deserted-city/ (accessed September 18, 2015).

Haus, M. and Heinelt, H. (2004) Politikwissenschaftliche Perspektiven auf den Stand der Planungstheorie. In U. Altrock, S. Günter, S. Hunning, and D. Peters (eds) *Perspektiven der Planungstheorie, edition stadt und region, Bd. 9*, Berlin: Leue.

Häußermann, H. and Siebel, W. (2013) *Festivalisierung der Stadtpolitik: Stadtentwicklung durch Große Projekte*, Berlin: VS Verlag für Sozialwissenschaften.

Häußermann, H. and Walter, S. (1988) Die schrumpfende Stadt und die Stadtsoziologie. In J. Friedrichs (ed) *Soziologische Stadtforschung, Sonderheft 29 der Kölner Zeitschrift für Soziologie und Sozialpsychologie*, Wiesbaden: Springer - VS Springer Fachmedien, pp 78–94.

Heezen, H., Van Zonnenberg, N., and Van Gestel, T. (2009) Beyond Leidsche Rijn. Available at: http://www.beyondutrecht.nl/index2.php

Helms, M. and Guillen, J. (2013) Kevin Orr: city to get out of lighting, transfer service to DTE. *Detroit Free Press*, June 27. Available at: www.freep.com

Hennen, A. (2012) Recovery Park to bring urban agriculture, fish farms, equestrian stables to Detroit's Eastside, *Detroit: Unspun*, July 5. Available at: http://blog.thedetroithub.com/2012/07/05/recovery-park-to-bring-urban-agriculture-fish-farms-equestrian-stables-to-detroits-eastside/

Herbert, S. (2005) The trapdoor of community. *Annals of the Association of American Geographers*, 95(4): 850–65.

Herscher, A. (2012) *The Unreal Estate Guide to Detroit*, Ann Arbor, MI: The University of Michigan Press.

Heßler, M. and Riederer, G. (2014) *Autostädte im 20. Jahrhundert. Wachstums- und Schrumpfungsprozesse in globaler Perspektive, Beiträge zur Stadtgeschichte und Urbanisierungsforschung 16*, Stuttgart: Franz Steiner Verlag.

Hill, A. (2014) Detroit: black problems, white solutions. Available at: http://alexbhill.org/2014/10/16/detroit-black-problems-white-solutions/ (accessed August 18, 2015).

Hollmann, L. (2011) *Kulturhauptstadt Europas – Ein Instrument zur Revitalisierung von Altindustrieregionen. Evaluierung der Kulturhauptstädte, 'Glasgow 1990, Cultural Capital of Europe' und 'RUHR 2010, Essen für das Ruhrgebiet'*, Arbeitspapiere zur Regionalentwicklung. Available at: http://www.uni-kl.de/rur/fileadmin/Medien/Publikationen/E-Paper/AzR_E-Paper_Band11_Hollmann.pdf

Holloway, L. (2014) Rights groups condemn Detroit water shutoffs. *The Root*, July 19. Available at: http://www.theroot.com/articles/culture/2014/07/detroit_civil_rights_groups_condemn_water_shut_off_to_poor.html

Holmes, B. (2010) Report back: the US Social Forum Detroit 2010. Another city for another world. *And/or Evacuate. Occupy Everything*, July 7. Available at: http://occupyeverything.org/2010/us-social-forum-detroit-2010/

Holton, C. (2013) The dead zone: Detroit becomes urban wasteland. Available at: http://www.cbn.com/cbnnews/us/2013/April/The-Dead-Zone-Detroit-Becomes-Urban-Wasteland/ (accessed September 20, 2015).

Hoover, E. and Vernon, R. (1962) *Anatomy of a Metropolis: The Changing Distribution of People and Jobs within the New York Metropolitan Region*, Cambridge, MA: Harvard University Press.

Hospers, G.J. (2004) Restructuring Europe's rustbelt. The case of the German Ruhrgebiet. *Intereconomics*, May/June: 147–56.

Howell, S. (2015) Thinking for ourselves: gathering waters. *We the People of Detroit*, June 1. Available at: http://wethepeopleofdetroit.com/2015/06/01/thinking-for-ourselves-gathering-waters/

Hoyt, A. (2003) *Chicago: City of the Century*, dvd, Boston: WGBH Educational Foundation.

HUD (US Department of Housing and Urban Development) (2014) Vacant and abandoned properties: turning liabilities into assets. *Evidence Matters*, Winter, US Department of Housing and Urban Development, https://www.huduser.gov/portal/periodicals/em/winter14/highlight1.html

Hyde, C. (1980) *Detroit: An Industrial History Guide*, Detroit: Detroit Historical Society.

Immergluck, D. (2009) Core of the crisis: deregulation, the global savings glut, and financial innovation in the subprime debacle. *City & Community*, 8: 341–5.

Immergluck, D. (2011) The local wreckage of global capital: the subprime crisis, federal policy and high-foreclosure neighborhoods in the US. *International Journal of Urban and Regional Research*, 35: 130–46.

Inequality Briefing (2014) Briefing 43. The poorest regions in the UK are the poorest in Northern Europe. August 22. Available at: http://inequalitybriefing.org/brief/briefing-43-the-poorest-regions-of-the-uk-are-the-poorest-in-northern-

Institut der deutschen Wirtschaft Köln (2013) Detroit ist pleite—das Ruhrgebiet bald auch? Available at: http://www.iwkoeln.de/infodienste/iw-nachrichten/beitrag/finanzsituation-der-kommunen-detroit-ist-pleite-das-ruhrgebiet-bald-auch-119835 (accessed January 15, 2016).

Interface Studio (2010) *Mapping of Detroit's industrial land and structures for Detroit Future City*. Available at: http://interface-studio.com/projects/detroit-future-city

Interview (2011a) Developer/business owner. Interview by author.

Interview (2011b) Former Michigan legislator. Interview by author.

Interview (2011c) Former planning official. Interview by author.

Interview (2011d) Mayor's Executive Committee member. Interview by author.

Interview (2011e) Planning official. Interview by author.

Jackson, K. (1985) *Crabgrass Frontier: The Suburbanization of the United States*, New York, NY: Oxford University Press.

Jamiel, D. (2013) Detroit's Dan Gilbert: Henry Ford or Henry Potter? *Truthout*, available at: http://truthout.org/opinion/item/20604-detroits-dan-gilbert-henry-ford-or-henry-potter

Jenkins, B.S. (1991) Sojourner truth housing riots. In W. Wood Henrickson (ed) *Detroit Perspectives: Crossroads and Turning Points*, Detroit: Wayne State University Press.

Karoub, J. (2013) Wall that once divided races in Detroit remains, teaches. *USA Today*, May 1. Available at: http://www.usatoday.com/story/news/nation/2013/05/01/detroit-race-wall/2127165/

Kate, P. (2014) Both sides of eight mile road: unrepentant racist (and Oakland County Executive) L. Brooks Patterson. *The Daily Kos*, January 21. Available at: http://www.dailykos.com/story/2014/1/21/1271388/-Both-Sides-of-Eight-Mile-Road-Unrepentant-Racist-and-Oakland-County-Executive-L-Brooks-Patterson

Katz, B. and Bradley, J. (2013) *The Metropolitan Revolution*, Washington, DC: The Brookings Institution.

Katzman, D.M. (1975) *Before the Ghetto: Black Detroit in the Nineteenth Century*, Urbana, IL: University of Illinois Press.

Kellogg, A. (2010) The do-it-yourself city. *Wall Street Journal*, July 6. Available at: www.wsj.com

Kelley, R. (2015) 'Thinking Dialectically: What Grace Lee Boggs Taught Me', *Praxis Center*. October 13. Available at: http://www.kzoo.edu/praxis/thinking-dialectically/

Kennedy, R. (2014) "Grand bargain" saves the Detroit Institute of Arts. *New York Times*, November 7. Available at: www.nytimes.com

Keteyian, A. and Sarokin, J. (2002) *A City on Fire: The '68 Detroit Tigers*. Film, Black Canyon Productions.

Kinder, K. (2014) Guerrilla-style defensive architecture in Detroit: a self-provisioned security strategy in a neoliberal space of disinvestment. *International Journal of Urban and Regional Research*, 38(5): 1767–84.

Kinder, K. (2015) *DIY Detroit: Making Do in a City Without Services*, Minneapolis, MN: University of Minnesota Press.

Kinkead, D. and Lynch, E. (2012) Opportunity sites for industrial site reutilization. German Marshall Fund for the United States and Detroit Future City, December 18.

Kishore, J. (2014) The Detroit water cutoffs and the social counterrevolution in America. Available at: https://www.wsws.org/en/articles/2014/03/29/pers-m29.html (accessed August 10, 2015).

Klein, R. (2013) How state help to bankrupt Detroit. *Detroit Free Press*, August 4, p 17A.

Kleyman, P. (2015) Detroit gentrification means "forced relocation" of black seniors. Available at: http://newamericamedia.org/2015/06/detroit-gentrification-causing-forced-relocation-of-black-seniors.php (accessed August 20, 2015).

Kohlstadt, M. (2013) Armutsforscher—Das Ruhrgebiet wird abgehängt. Available at: http://www.derwesten.de/staedte/dortmund/armutsforscher-das-ruhrgebiet-wird-abgehaengt-id7824991.html (accessed January 15, 2016).

Koremans, S. (2013) Homes still selling for $1 in Detroit. Available at: http://www.couriermail.com.au/realestate/homes-for-1/story-fnczc1bg-1226559204461 (accessed September 10, 2015).

Kotval, Z. and Mullin, J. (2011) IBA Emscher Park. An American perspective. In C. Reicher, L. Niemann, and A. Uttke (eds) *Internationale Bauausstellung Emscher Park: Impulse. Lokal, regional, national, international*, Essen: Klartext, pp 200–9.

Kruth, J. (2016) Land contracts trip up would be homeowners. *Detroit News*, February 29.

Kühn, M. (2005) Strategien der Regenerierung schrumpfender Städte—ein planungswissenschaftlicher Ansatz. In H.-J. Bürkner, T. Kuder, and M. Kühn (eds) *Regenerierung schrumpfender Städte. Theoretische Zugänge und Forschungsperspektiven*, IRS working paper, Erkner: Leibniz-Institut für Regionalentwicklung und Strukturplanung.

Kurth, J. and MacDonald, C. (2015) Detroit braces for a flood of tax foreclosures, *The Detroit News*, July 1.

Kunzmann, K.R. (2011) Die internationale Wirkung der IBA Emscher Park. In C. Reicher, L. Niemann, and A. Uttke (eds) *Internationale Bauausstellung Emscher Park: Impulse. Lokal, regional, national, international*, Essen: Klartext, pp 168–83.

Kwasniewski, N. (2013) Gärtner in Detroit: Ackerbau in der Pleitestadt. Available at: http://www.spiegel.de/wirtschaft/gartenbewegung-gegen-agrarkonzern-detroit-veraendert-sich-a-916535.html (accessed January 15, 2016).

Laitner, B. (2012) Many Detroiters take safety into their own hands with neighborhood patrols. *Detroit Free Press*, October 21. Available at: www.freep.com

Lampen, A. and Owzar, A. (2008) *Schrumpfende Städte. Ein Phänomen zwischen Antike und Moderne*, Köln, Weimar, Wien: Böhlau Verlag.

Leary, J.P. (2011) Detroitism. *Guernica*, January 15. Available at: https://www.guernicamag.com/features/leary_1_15_11/

Leary, J.P. (2015) Ruin porn: what's behind our fascination with decay? In Link, J. (ed) *Blueprint for Living*, Sydney: ABC Radio.

Lee, M.S. (2015) Think about urban farming to boost jobs, repurpose land in Detroit. *Crains*, April 1. Available at: http://www.crainsdetroit.com/article/20150401/BLOG106/150409982/think-about-urban-farming-to-boost-jobs-repurpose-land-in-detroit

Lees, L., Slater, T., and Wyly, E. (2007) *Gentrification*, New York, NY: Routledge.

Levy, K. (2015) *Detroit Minds Dying*. Video. Available at: http://www.detroitmindsdying.org

Link, J. (2015) Motor City field guide. *Landscape Architecture Magazine*, 105(2): 18–20.

Loveland Technologies (2015) Homepage. Available at: https://makeloveland.com

MacDonald, C. (2011) Private landowners complicate reshaping of Detroit, *The Detroit News*. Available at: http://lottievdada.tumblr.com/post/36904076682/hantzlandia-landgrab-hantzoff-detroitfuture

Macdonald, C. and Kurth, J. (2015a) Foreclosurers fuel Detroit blight, cost city $500 million, *The Detroit News*, June 25.

Macdonald, C. and Kurth, J. (2015b) Gilbert, Quicken Loans entrwined in Detroit blight, *The Detroit News*, June 30.

Madway, D.M. and Pearlman, D.D. (1974) Mortgage foreclosure primer: part III—proposals for change, A. *Clearinghouse Review*, 8: 473.

Mallach, A. (ed) (2012) *Rebuilding America's Legacy Cities: New Directions for the Industrial Heartland*. New York, NY: The American Assembly, Columbia University.

Mallien, J. (2013) Oberhausen ist das deutsche Detroit. Available at: http://www.handelsblatt.com/politik/deutschland/bertelsmann-studie-oberhausen-ist-das-deutsche-detroit/8663254.html (accessed January 15, 2016).

Marchant, Y. and Meffre, R. (2010) *The Ruins of Detroit*, Göttingen: Steidl.

Martelle, S. (2014) *Detroit: A Biography*, Chicago, IL: Chicago Review Press.

Martinez-Fernandez, C. and Wu, T. (2007) Stadtenwicklung in einer differenten Wirklichkeit. Schrumpfende Städte in Australien [Urban development in a different reality: shrinking cities in Australia]. *Berliner Debatte Initial*, 1: 45–60.

Martinez-Fernandez, C., Audirac, I., Fol, S., and Cunnig-Sabot, E. (2012) Shrinking cities—urban challenges of globalization. *International Journal of Urban and Regional Research*, 36(2).

Massey, D. (1995 [1984]) *Spatial Divisions of Labour: Social Structures and the Geography of Production* (2nd edn), New York, NY: Routledge.

Massey, D. and Denton, N. (1993) *American Apartheid: Segregation and the Making of the Underclass*, Cambridge, MA: Harvard University Press.

McArdle, M, (2014) Is New York the next Detroit? *Bloomberg View*, August 5. Available at: http://www.bloombergview.com/articles/2014-08-05/is-new-york-the-next-detroit

McDonald, J. (2014) What happened to and in Detroit? *Urban Studies*, 51(16): 3309–29.

MDOT (Michigan Department of Transport) (2015) National firsts. Available at: http://www.michigan.gov/mdot/0,4616,7-151-9623_11154-129682--,00.html

Meighan, C. (2011) Michigan Left. Film. Available at: http://www.chrismeighan.com/work/michigan-left/

Mele, C. (2000) *Selling the Lower East Side: Culture, Real Estate, and Resistance in New York City*, Minneapolis, MN: University of Minnesota Press.

Metzger, J.T. (2000) Planned abandonment: the neighborhood life-cycle theory and national urban policy. *Housing Policy Debate*, 11: 7–40.

Millhiser, I. (2014) Justice Ginsberg: America has a "real racial problem." *Think Progress*, August 22. Available at: http://thinkprogress.org/justice/2014/08/22/3474542/justice-ginsburg-america-has-a-real-racial-problem/

Millington, N. (2013) Post-industrial imaginaries: nature, representation and ruin in Detroit, Michigan. *International Journal of Urban and Regional Research*, 31(1): 279–96.

Moore, A. (2010) *Detroit Disassembled*, Akron: Akron Art Museum.

Motor City Mapping (2014) Available at: https://www.motorcitymapping.org/#t=overview&s=detroit&f=all (accessed January 20, 2015).

Mukhija, V. and Loukaitou-Sideris, A. (eds) (2014) *The Informal American City: Beyond Taco Tricks and Day Labor*, Cambridge, MA: MIT Press.

NAACP (National Association for the Advancement of Colored People) (2014a) Bankruptcy judge denies motion to suspend Detroit water shutoffs. NAACP webpage update, September 29. Available at: www.naacpldf.org

NAACP (2014b) Legal Defense Fund and American Civil Liberties Union of Michigan press release: ask for immediate moratorium on Detroit's water shut-offs. July 18. Available at: http://www.naacpldf.org/press-release/ldf-and-aclu-michigan-ask-immediate-moratorium-detroits-water-shut-offs

Neill, W. (1995) Promoting the city: image, reality and racism in Detroit. In W. Neill, D. Fitzsimons, and Murtagh, B. (eds) *Reimagining the Pariah City: Urban Development in Belfast and Detroit*, Aldershot: Avebury, pp 113–61.

Nichols, D. (2014) Detroit announces first phase of privatized garbage pickup. *Detroit News*, May 1. Available at: www.detroitnews.com

Öchsner, T. (2013) Das Ruhrgebiet ist Deutschlands neues Armenhaus. *Süddeutsche Zeitung*. 21 December. http://www.sueddeutsche.de/politik/armutsbericht-das-ruhrgebiet-ist-deutschlands-neues-armenhaus-1.1241353 (accessed January 15, 2016).

Olberholtzer, M. (2015) Preview: 2015 Detroit tax foreclosure auction. August 19. Available at: http://www.huffingtonpost.com/michele-oberholtzer/preview-2015-detroit-tax-_b_8000462.html (accessed January 14, 2016).

Oosting, J. (2014) How Michigan's revenue sharing "raid" cost communities billions for local services. *MLIVE*, March 30. Available at: www.mlive.com

Orfield, M. and Luce, T. (2011) Promoting fiscal equity and efficient development practices as the metropolitan scale. In C. Montgomery (ed) *Regional Planning for Sustainable America*, New Brunswick, NJ: Rutgers University Press.

Orr, M. and Stoker, G. (1994) Urban regimes and leadership in Detroit. *Urban Affairs Review*, 30: 48–73.

Osborne, T. and Rose, N. (1999) Governing cities: notes on the spatialisation of virtue. *Environment and Planning D*, 17(6): 737–60.

Owens, C. (2015) Philly City Council helps with water shutoffs and blight prevention. *Next City*, June 25. Available at: http://nextcity.org/daily/entry/philadelphia-water-bills-low-income-payment-plans

Paland, R. (2005) *Chancen und Risiken postforditischer Stadtentwicklungspolitik*, Kassel: Kassel University Press.

Pastier, J., Heatley, M., and Sandalow, M. (2007) *Ballparks: Yesterday and Today*, Chartwell Books.

PBL (Planbureau voor de Leefomgeving) (2006) Krimp and Ruimte. Available at: http://www.pbl.nl/sites/default/files/cms/publicaties/Krimp_en_ruimte.pdf

PBS (Public Broadcasting Systems) (2013) *Henry Ford*. American Experience, Interview: Ford's anti-Semitism, directed by S. Colt. Available at: http://www.pbs.org/wgbh/americanexperience/features/interview/henryford-antisemitism/

Peck, J. (2014) Pushing austerity: state failure, municipal bankruptcy and the crises of fiscal federalism in the USA. *Cambridge Journal of Regions, Economy and Society*, 7(1): 17–44.

Peck, J. (2015) Austerity urbanism. The neoliberal crisis of American cities. In S. Ehmsen and A. Scharenberg (eds) *Series, #1*, Rosa Luxemburg Stiftung, New York Office.

Peck, W.H. (1991) *Detroit Institute of Arts: A Brief History*, Detroit: Wayne State University Press.

Pedroni, T.C. (2011) Urban shrinkage as a performance of whiteness: neoliberal urban restructuring, education, and racial containment in the post-industrial, global niche city. *Discourse: Studies in the Cultural Politics of Education*, 32: 203–15.

Perazzo, J. (2014) The new shame of cities. The David Horowitz Freedom Center.

Pidd, H. (2014) The North-East: not the new Detroit. But poorly served by the national media. *The Guardian*, May 12. Available at: http://www.theguardian.com/uk-news/the-northerner/2014/may/12/the-north-east-not-the-new-detroit-but-poorly-served-by-the-national-media

Pleite-Ruhrstädte (2012) Pleite-Ruhrstädte sparen radikal und erhöhen Steuern. Available at: http://www.welt.de/regionales/duesseldorf/article107272764/Pleite-Ruhrstaedte-sparen-radikal-und-erhoehen-Steuern.html (accessed January 15, 2016).

Power, A., Plöger, J., and Winkler, A. (2010) *Phoenix Cities: The Fall and Rise of Great Industrial Cities*, Bristol: The Policy Press.

PPS (Project for Public Spaces) (2014) Detroit leads the way on place-centered revitalization. March 25. Available at: http://www.pps.org/projects/detroit-leads-the-way-on-place-centered-revitalization/

Pritchett, W.E. (2003) The "public menace" of blight: urban renewal and the private uses of eminent domain. *Yale Law & Policy Review*, 1–52.

Purcell, M. (2002) Excavating Lefebvre: the right to the city and its urban politics of the inhabitant. *GeoJournal*, 58: 99–108.

Quicken Loans (2015) Pressroom. Available at: http://www.quickenloans.com/press-room/leader/dan-gilbert/ (accessed August 18, 2015).

Rajagopal, A. (2016) Game Changers 2016: Ponyride, *Metropolis*, January. Available at: http://www.metropolismag.com/January-2016/Game-Changers-2016-Ponyride/

Raleigh, E. and Galster, G. (2014) Neighborhood disinvestment, abandonment and crime dynamics. Paper presented at the 44th Urban Affairs Association conference, San Antonio, TX.

Reicher, C. (ed) (2011) *Schichten einer Region: Kartenstücke zur räumlichen Struktur des Ruhrgebiets*, Berlin: Jovis.

Reicher, C., Niemann, L., and Uttke, A. (2011) Introduction. IBA Emscher Park: impulses. Local, regional, national, international. In C. Reicher, L. Niemann, and A. Uttke (eds) *Internationale Bauausstellung Emscher Park: Impulse. Lokal, regional, national, international*, Essen: Klartext, pp 16–22.

Relman, J.P., Schlactus, G. and Crook, J.L.(2013) Amici Curiae: Wells Fargo Bank v. City of Richmond, California, in Project, N.H.L. (ed) *CV-13-3663*, CRB.

Rich, W. (1989) *Coleman Young and Detroit Politics*, Detroit: Wayne State University Press.

Richardson, H. and Nam, C.W. (eds) (2014) *Shrinking Cities: A Global Perspective*, London and New York, NY: Routledge.

Roberts, P. and Sykes, H. (2000) *Urban Regeneration: A Handbook*, London: Sage.

Rohe, W. and Galster, G. (2014) The community development block grant turns 40: proposals for expansion and reform. *Housing Policy Debate*, 24(1): 3–13.

Romero, C.L. (2015) Treasury should do much more to increase the effectiveness of the TARP Hardest Hit Fund Blight Elimination Program. Special Inspector General for the Troubled Asset Relief Program.

Ross, A. (2003) *No Collar: The Hidden Cost of the Humane Workplace*, New York, NY: Basic Books.

Rowland-Jou, P. (2014) 100 reasons why it's great up north: how you responded to the Guardian's ill-informed rant. *The Journal*, May 19. Available at: http://www.thejournal.co.uk/news/north-east-news/100-reasons-its-great-up-7106821

Ruggles, S., Genadek, K.; Goeken, R., Grover, J. and Sobek, M. (2015) *Integrated Public Use Microdata Series: Version 6.0* [Machine-readable database]. Minneapolis: University of Minnesota.

Russell, J. (2015) Seattle is the next Detroit. *Pacific Standard*, December 14. Available at: http://www.psmag.com/business-economics/seattle-is-the-next-detroit

Russell, K. (2015) Detroit water assistance funds are running out of money. *WXYZ Detroit*, August 20. Available at: www.wxyz.com

Ryan, B.D. (2012) *Design after Decline: How America Rebuilds Shrinking Cities*, Philadelphia, PA: University of Pennsylvania Press.

Ryan, B.D. and Campo, D. (2013) Autopia's end. The decline and fall of Detroit's automotive manufacturing landscape. *Journal of Planning History*, 2(2): 95–132.

Sabree, E.R. (2012) Interview: Wayne County Deputy Treasurer—Land Management.

Saegert, S., Fields, D., and Libman, K. (2011) Mortgage foreclosure and health disparities: serial displacement as asset extraction in African American populations. *Journal of Urban Health*, 88: 390–402.

Salazar, C. (2014) The assassination of Detroit. Available at: https://www.jacobinmag.com/2014/10/the-assassination-of-detroit/ (accessed September 15, 2015).

Sassen, S. (2000) *Cities in a World Economy*, Thousand Oaks, CA: Sage.

Sassen, S. (2001) *The Global City: New York, London, Tokyo*, Princeton, NJ: Princeton University Press.

Savitch, H., Kantor, P., and Vicari, S. (2002) *Cities in the International Marketplace: The Political Economy of Urban Development in North America and Western Europe*, Princeton, NJ: Princeton University Press.

Schaefer, J. (2013) Kwame Kilpatrick Public Corruption Trial Evidence Revealed, *Detroit Free Press*, March 12.

Schafroth, F. (2014) Why cities can't go bankrupt in Canada or Germany, *Governing*, May 2014. Available at: http://www.governing.com/columns/public-money/gov-municipal-debt-traps-nein.html (accessed December 20, 2016).

Schindler, S. (2014) Detroit after bankruptcy: a case of degrowth machine politics. *Urban Studies Journal Limited*, pp 1–19.

Schlüter, R. (2010) Der wilde Westen. *Art*, 22(2): 18–27.

Schwartz, R. (2015) What happens when Detroit puts down over 150 miles of new bike lanes? Cycling skyrockets. *Good. A Magazine for the Global Citizen*, November 3. Available at: https://www.good.is/articles/detroit-bike-lanes

Self, R.O. (2003) *American Babylon: Race and the Struggle for Postwar Oakland*, Princeton, NJ: Princeton University Press.

SEMCOG (Southeast Michigan Council of Governments) (2011) 2010 census data for city of Detroit neighborhoods, Southeast Michigan Council of Governments report, April 5. Available at: www.CensusDataDetroitQuickFacts.pdf

SEMCOG (2013) Great Lakes Shoreline Cities Green Infrastructure Grant: City of Detroit Water and Sewerage Department: Near Eastside Green Infrastructure Project, narrative statement: work plan. September 11, Detroit.

Semenza, J.C. and March, T.L. (2008) An urban community-based intervention to advance social interactions. *Environment and Behavior*, 41(1): 22–42.

Sheehan, P. (2015) Revitalization by gentrification—Detroit is evicting tens of thousands from their homes this year, even as it trumpets an urban revival. Available at: https://www.jacobinmag.com/2015/05/detroit-foreclosure-redlining-evictions/ (accessed August 28, 2015).

Sibley, D. (1995) *Geographies of Exclusion: Society and Difference in the West*, London and New York, NY: Routledge.

Siegal, N. (2013) Dutch arts scene is under siege. *The New York Times*, January 30. Available at: http://www.nytimes.com/2013/01/30/arts/30iht-dutch30.html

Silver, B. (2003) *Forces of Labor: Workers' Movements and Globalization since 1870*, New York, NY, and Cambridge: Cambridge University Press.

Simone, A. (2004) People as infrastructure: intersecting fragments in Johannesburg. *Public Culture*, 16(3): 407–29.

Slater, T. (2014) There is nothing natural about gentrification. *The New Left Project*, November 24. Available at: http://www.newleftproject. org/index.php/site/article_comments/there_is_nothing_natural_ about_gentrification

Smith, N. (1996) *The New Urban Frontier: Gentrification and the Revanchist City*, London: Routledge.

Smith, N. (2002) New globalism, new urbanism: gentrification as global urban strategy. *Antipode*, 34(3): 427–50.

Snell, R. (2014) Kilpatrick frat brother Beasley convicted of conspiracy. *Detroit News*, December 9.

Snover, A.K., Whitely Binder, J., Lopez, E., Willmott, E., Kay, J., Howell, D., and Simmonds, J. (2007) *Preparing for Climate Change: A Guidebook for Local, Regional and State Governments*, Oakland, CA: ICLEI—Local Governments for Sustainability. Available at: http:// cses.washington.edu/db/pdf/snoveretalgb574.pdf

Soja, E. (1992) *Inside Exopolis: Scenes from Orange County, Variations on a Theme Park: The new American city and the end of public space* (ed M. Sorkin), New York: The Noonday Press.

Solnit, D. (2004) The new radicalism: uprooting the system and building a better world. In D. Solnit (ed) *Globalize Liberation*, San Francisco, CA: City Lights Books.

Solnit, R. (2007) Detroit arcadia: exploring the post-American landscape. *Harpers*, June/July, pp 65–73.

Stanton, T. (2001) *The Final Season*, New York, NY: Thomas Dunne/ St. Martin's Press.

Stevens, Q. (2011) The German "city beach" as a new approach to waterfront development. In G. Desfor, J. Laidley, Q. Stevens, and D. Schubert (eds) *Transforming Urban Waterfronts: Fixity and Flow*, New York, NY: Routledge, pp 235–56.

Stokel-Walker, C (2014) The Guardian Has Really Annoyed A Lot Of People In The North East, *Buzzfeed*. 12 May. https://www. buzzfeed.com/chrisstokelwalker/no-the-guardian-the-north-east- is-not-teetering-88k0?utm_term=.vgY44mjPPk#.cqKggVBRRd

Subcomandante Marcos (2003) The slaves of money—and our rebellion. *The Guardian*, September 10. Available at: http://www. theguardian.com/world/2003/sep/11/globalisation.wto

Sugrue, T. (1996) *The Origins of the Urban Crisis: Race and Inequality in Postwar Detroit*, Princeton, NJ: Princeton University Press.

Sugrue, T. (2005) From Motor City to Motor Metropolis: How the automobile industry reshaped urban America, *Automobile in American Life and Society*, Dearborn: Henry Ford Museum and University of Michigan. Available at: http://www.autolife.umd.umich.edu

Sugrue, T. (2013) Notown. Good news: a few hipsters are discovering Detroit. Bad news: everything else. *Democracy Journal*, 28(Spring). Available at: http://democracyjournal.org/magazine/28/notown/

Sumner, G. (2015) *Detroit in World War II*, Charleston, SC: The History Press.

Swyngedouw, E. (2005) Governance innovation and the citizen: the janus face of governance-beyond-the-state. *Urban Studies*, 42(11): 1991–2006.

Taubman, J. (2011) *Detroit: 138 Square Miles*, Detroit: Museum of Contemporary Art.

The Journal (2014) More criticism for "patronising and misleading" Guardian article labelling North East as UK's Detroit. May 12. Available at: http://www.thejournal.co.uk/news/north-east-news/more-criticism-patronising-misleading-guardian-7109502

Thomas, J.M. (1997) *Redevelopment and Race: Planning a Finer City in Postwar Detroit*, Baltimore, MD: The Johns Hopkins University Press.

Thomas, J.M. and Blake, R. (1996) Faith-based community development and African American neighborhoods. In D. Keating, N. Krumholz, and P. Star (eds) *Revitalizing Urban Neighborhoods*, Lawrence, KS: University Press of Kansas, pp 131–43.

Todd, S. (2016) Making poverty history didn't happen. We should have been tackling the rich. *The Guardian*, April 29.

Tomlinson, M. (2015) A millennial paradise: how once-bankrupt Detroit is making a comeback. *Elide Daily*, August 3. Available at: http://elitedaily.com/life/detroit-next-american-success/1145067/

Turbeville, W. (2013) The Detroit bankruptcy. *Demos* public policy report. Available at: http://www.demos.org/sites/default/files/publications/Detroit_Bankruptcy-Demos.pdf

Turok, I. and Mykhnenko, V. (2006) *Resurgent European Cities?* CPPR Working Paper 2, Glasgow: University of Glasgow.

UMTRI (University of Michigan Transportation Research Institute) (2014) Hitchin' a ride: fewer Americans have their own vehicle. Press release, January 23. Available at: http://www.umtri.umich.edu/what-were-doing/news/hitchin-ride-fewer-americans-have-their-own-vehicle

Unitarian Universalist Service Committee (2015) Human rights experts convene for water affordability and housing summit. Press release, May 29. Available at: http://www.uusc.org/human-rights-experts-convene-for-water-affordability-and-housing-summit

United States American Community Survey 1-yr Estimates. Social Economic Characteristics, 2009, 2012, American Community Survey, Detroit, Michigan.

United States Bureau of Labor Statistics (2015). Available at: http://data.bls.gov/pdq/SurveyOutputServlet

United States Census Bureau (1990) Table 23. Michigan—race and Hispanic origin for selected large cities and other places: earliest census to 1990. Available at: http://www.census.gov/population/www/documentation/twps0076/MItab.pdf (accessed January 17, 2015).

United States Census Bureau (2010) *Profile of General Demographic Characteristics: 2010*, Accessed March 14, 2015. Available at https://factfinder.census.gov/faces/tableservices/jsf/pages/productview.xhtml?pid=DEC_10_DP_DPDP1&src=pt

United States Census Bureau (2015) The American Community Survey. Available at: http://www.census.gov/acs

USEPA (United States Environmental Protection Agency) (2015) Great Lakes basic information: geography & hydrology. Available at: http://www.epa.gov/greatlakes/basicinfo.html?_ga=1.61732076.17 92469235.1426428078 (accessed March 15, 2015).

Valverde, M. (2011) Seeing like a city: the dialectic of modern and premodern ways of seeing in urban governance. *Law & Society Review*, 45(2): 277–312.

Van Buren, D. (2015) The beltline solar district. Briefing memorandum.

Van den Berg, L., Drewett, R., Klaassen, L.H., Rossi, A., and Vijverberg, C.H.T. (1982) *Urban Europe: A Study of Growth and Decline, vol. 1 of Urban Europe*, Oxford: Pergamon Press.

Wacquant, L. (2012) Three steps to a historical anthropology of actually existing neoliberalism. *Social Anthropology*, 20(1): 66–79.

Walker, M.L. (1971) *Urban Blight and Slums*, Harvard: Harvard University Press.

Wallin, B.A. (1998) *From Revenue Sharing to Deficit Sharing*, Washington, DC: Georgetown University Press.

Weber, R. (2002) Extracting value from the city: neoliberalism and urban redevelopment. *Antipode*, 34: 519–40.

Weidner, S. (2004) *Stadtentwicklung unter Schrumpfungsbedingungen: Leitfaden zur Erfassung dieses veränderten Entwicklungsmodus von Stadt und zum Umgang damit in der Stadtentwicklungsplanung*, Norderstedt: Books on Demand GmbH.

Weiss, M. (1987) *The Rise of the Community Builders*, New York, NY: Columbia University Press.

White, E. (2010) Monica Conyers, wife to John Conyers, sentenced to 3 years in prison for Detroit bribes. *The Huffington Post*, May 25.

Wiersum, F. (2010) 21st century ill digital toys. Available at: http://www.lucyindelucht.nl/geweest/in-het-archief-van-2010/living-or-leaving-in-detroit

Williams, P. (2014) 'Drop dead Detroit! The suburban kingpin who is thriving off the city's decline', *New Yorker*, January 27.

Wilgoren, J. (2002) Detroit urban renewal without the renewal. *New York Times*, July 7. Available at: www.nytimes.com

Williams, C. (2013) For some Detroit services, call the D.I.Y. Dept. *ABC News*, May 9. Available at: www.abcnews.go.com

Wilson, W.J. (1996) *When Work Disappears: The World of the New Urban Poor*, New York, NY: Vintage Books.

Wojtowicz, R.J. (2011) Tax reverted auction property. Unpublished raw data, Wayne County Treasurer's Office, Detroit, MI.

Wyly, E., Ponder, C., Nettling, P., Ho, B., Fung, S.E., Liebowitz, Z., and Hammel, D. (2012) New racial meanings of housing in America. *American Quarterly*, 64: 571–604.

Wyputta, A. (2014) Die leise Beerdigung. Available at: http://www.taz.de/!5026971/ (accessed January 15, 2016).

Yearout, J. (2014) Schuttee announces bribery convictions against two corrupt City of Detroit inspectors, Available at: http://www.michigan.gov/ag/0,4534,7-164-58056-322677--,00.html

Zielin, L. (2011) The Depression, deportation and Detroit. *LSA Magazine*, Spring. Available at: http://www.elmuseodelnorte.org/uploads/3/6/1/0/3610241/um_lsa_article_2011.pdf

Index

Note: page numbers in *italic* type refer to Figures; those in **bold** type refer to Tables.

Index